GANGS

Mario L. Hesse | Christopher J. Przemieniecki

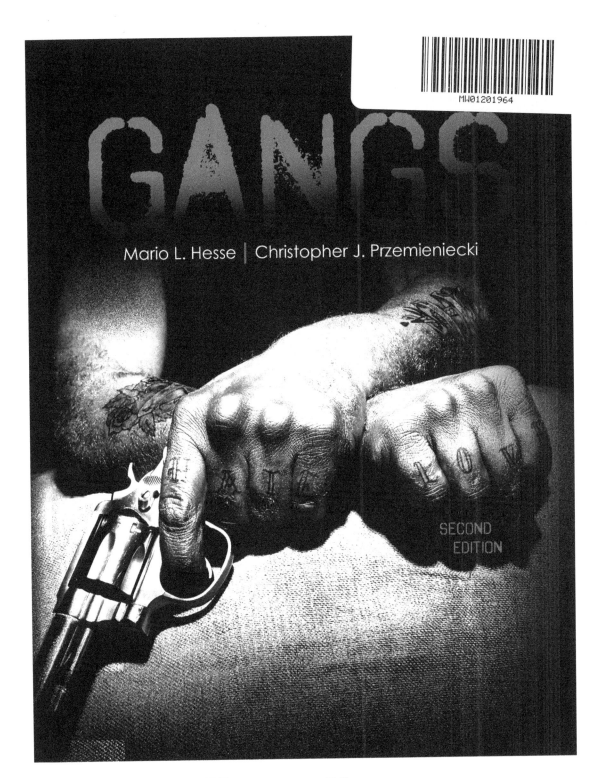

SECOND EDITION

Kendall Hunt
publishing company

Cover image © Shutterstock.com

Kendall Hunt
publishing company

www.kendallhunt.com
Send all inquiries to:
4050 Westmark Drive
Dubuque, IA 52004-1840

Copyright © 2021, 2016 by Kendall Hunt Publishing Company

ISBN 978-1-5249-7686-6

Published in the United States of America

DEDICATION

Mario L. Hesse dedicates this textbook to his mother and father, Gene and Ruby Wortham, the smartest 10-year-old that the knows, Vaughn, and the men and women employed throughout the fields of criminal justice wishing to understand the complexities and intrigue of gangs and gang research.

Christopher J. Przemieniecki dedicates this textbook to Dr. Jeanne Ballantine (Wright State University), Dr. Thomas Ellsworth (Illinois State University) and Dr. Michael Meyer (University of North Dakota) for guiding me on my academic/professional pursuit in criminal justice. This book is also dedicated to the men and women in law enforcement who confront gangs on a daily basis--BE SAFE!

BRIEF CONTENTS

CONTENTS

PREFACE

This textbook is divided into 13 chapters and has been updated and significantly expanded from the First Edition. Each chapter is devoted to exploring the gang phenomenon by providing information about gangs, gang membership and gang crimes. These chapters also give the criminal justice practitioner the necessary tools to better understand and address the gang problem. Additionally, there are chapters within this book that focus on gang-related issues that are typically not found in other criminal justice/gang-related textbooks such as gang members joining the military, mental health concerns among gang members, female gang involvement, theories of gangs and why they join, the Native American gang problem, the financial and entrepreneurial side of operating gangs, the exploration of gangs and gang member in the world of sports, and gangs using the Internet/social media sites to promote and operate the gang. At the end of each chapter, there are discussion questions to challenge the reader and web links to further explore the chapter topic.

Chapter one covers a brief history of the emergence of gangs in the United States from New York City, Chicago, and Los Angeles, including a very brief review of gangs from the South. This chapter also explores the new gang trends and current data on the nature and extent of the number of gangs and gang members in the United States.

Chapter two, a new addition to the 2nd edition of this textbook, explores the various theories that criminologists/sociologists have expressed over the decades when trying to determine why kids join gangs and why gangs flourish in neighborhoods. These theories explore the gang phenomenon from the macro- and micro-level perspectives.

Chapter three, new to the 2nd edition is authored by Jerrod Brown, a mental health expert. Brown provides a serious examination into the mental health issues surrounding the gang lifestyle and how the social, cultural, familial, economic and psychological influences of gangs impact the development of an individual. This chapter also examines the impact of traumatic brain injuries as the result of violence associated with the gang or other types of trauma. Brown offers strategies in dealing with gang members with regards to mental illnesses.

Chapter four, new to the 2nd edition, is about female involvement in gangs. This chapter explores the differences between males and females, and why females fall victim to the gang life. In addition to exploring the past and current research on females and gangs, examples of all-female gangs are discussed.

Chapter five, new to the 2nd edition is authored by Native American gang expert Christopher Grant. Grant provides an examination of the gang problem in Indian Country and offers an explanation into why gangs are so prevalent on Reservations. Grant also explores the cultural differences between native and non-native gangs and the challenges of dealing with gangs in Indian Country.

Chapter six explores the relationship between the police and gangs. From the formation of early police gang units to today's elite gang task forces, this chapter examines how the police have responded to the growing gang problem at the local, state and federal levels. An examination into the use of policing strategies is explored including the necessary tools to combat gangs such as gang databases and education programs aimed at training gang officers to be more informed and effective in combating gangs in their neighborhood.

Chapter seven examines the legal perspective of understanding gangs. An analysis into the complexity of defining gangs is examined and other gang definitions are explored. Another effective tool in combating the gang problem is using gang injunctions, anti-gang laws, and legislative acts. The history and legal parameters of these legal tools are examined, including examples of utilizing juvenile gang courts to address the gang problem.

Chapter eight focuses on gangs and prisons. A brief overview of gangs in prisons is explained and how the term prison gangs evolved into Security Threat Groups. Prison violence, misconduct, and classification is discussed with a list of the most notorious prison gangs in U.S.

Chapter nine, new to the 2nd edition is authored by Phyllis Belak, a finance and fraud expert, provides a look into how gangs make money. While gangs typically make money from drug trafficking and other illegal ventures, Belak's overview into the financial side of how gangs operate is unique to the gang literature.

Chapter ten provides an overview rarely found in gang textbooks – the relationship between gangs and the military. The First Edition of *Gangs* was the first textbook to address this problem and Carter F. Smith, a former Army CID officer and military gang expert, returns with some updates to address this unique problem. This chapter provides many examples of military soldiers who have ties to street gangs, motorcycle gangs and domestic extremists groups. This chapter also provides a look into increases in military-trained gang members over the last 10 years and what can be done about it.

Chapter eleven, a new topic to the 2nd edition, focuses on the connection between gangs and sports. The influence of gangs is not just found on the street but it also extends into the world of sports. This chapter provides a historical account of gang members who also excelled as athletes, which sports are most prone to gang involvement, and how sports can be used to curtail the gang problem in communities.

Chapter twelve, gangs and the mass media, the authors were the first to explore this phenomena and it has been updated and expanded for the 2nd edition. When discussing the portrayal of gangs in the media, it is often mentioned in passing as a point of reference or to provide the reader with a popular culture reference but Hesse and Przemieniecki continue to examine gangs and the media. This chapter is provides a historical review of gangs featured in popular culture but also examines the influence of those portrayals and the power of online gang activity and its potential consequences. As technology advances so do the gangs that use social media platforms and the Internet to share the gang culture with others.

The final chapter, gang prevention and intervention gives readers and criminal justice practitioners an overview of what has worked, and not worked, with regards to prevention and intervention programs that target gangs and gang members. This chapter also notes the need for gang suppression methods and the importance of collaborating between law enforcement, the community, and other interest groups to combat the gang problem.

ACKNOWLEDGEMENTS

The authors wish to thank Carter F. Smith, Christopher Grant, Jerrod Brown and Phyllis Belak for their contribution to this textbook. Their work and areas of expertise with respect to gangs offered a new perspective that is often not discussed in other gang textbooks. The authors would also like to thank Samantha Leonard, a former probation officer and graduate student from West Chester University (PA). Samantha made some major contributions to the chapter on female gangs. The authors would also like to thank Kendall Hunt Publishing, more specifically Paul B. Carty and Angela Willenbring for their patience and giving us the opportunity to expand our material into a second edition. Most importantly, we want to give special thanks to Anita Przemieniecki-Harper for her detailed editorial work and comments to the final manuscript. Finally, we wish to thank those who have purchased this work. We hope you enjoy the new additions to this text. This book represents ongoing research for both of us and we would appreciate any insight you have regarding the topics we chose for this updated edition. Please feel free to contact us if you have questions, clarifications, or insight so that that we can use it to improve on this work.

ABOUT THE AUTHORS

Mario L. Hesse, PhD is a full, tenured professor at the St. Cloud State University (MN) in the Criminal Justice Studies Department. He earned his PhD in sociology from the South Dakota State University. Mario has extensive experience working in the corrections field with adult community-based programs, in juvenile detention centers, and in the juvenile probation office in Minnesota. Mario has published articles in *ACJS Today, Corrections Today, Criminal Justice Review*, and the *Journal of Gang Research*. Currently, Mario is a peer-review editor for the *Journal of Gang Research* and an associate editor for Forensics Scholars Today. He is also the coauthor of a juvenile justice text book titled *Juvenile Justice: The Essentials*. Mario is a frequent presenter at the National Gang Crime Research Center (NGCRC) annual conference held in Chicago, IL and a recipient of the Frederic M. Thrasher Award for 'Superior Research' from the NGCRC.

Christopher J. Przemieniecki, PhD is an Associate Professor at the West Chester University (PA) in the Department of Criminal Justice. He earned his PhD in Criminal Justice from the University of North Dakota. Christopher has published articles about street gangs and other criminal-justice-related issues in *ACJS Today, Deviant Behavior, Journal of Gang Research, FBI-Insighter* and *The Amplifier Magazine, Society of Media Psychology and Technology*, and has authored chapters in criminal-justice-related books and Encyclopedias. Christopher is also a periodic presenter at the National Gang Crime Research Center (NGCRC) annual conference and speaks at other gang conferences/gang training seminars for law enforcement and probation/parole officers around the country. Christopher is a peer-review editor for the *Journal of Gang Research* and a two-time recipient of the Frederic M. Thrasher Award for 'Superior Research' from the NGCRC.

Contributing Authors

We would like to thank the following authors for their contributions to this book:

Carter F. Smith, JD, PhD, (contributed Chapter 10: Gangs in the Military), is a Senior Instructor and Director of Graduate Criminal Justice Studies at Middle Tennessee State University. Dr. Smith was in the Army Criminal Investigation Division (CID) for over 22-years, with 15 of those years at Fort Campbell, KY, where he identified the growing gang problem in the early 1990s and later started the Army's first Gang & Extremist Investigations Team. He investigates and researches topics like spontaneous gang formation, military-trained gang members, gangs and their use of technology, and gang members in colleges and universities. He has been interviewed about gangs by several news sources, and has appeared twice in the History Channel's Gangland series. He was a founding board member of the Tennessee Gang Investigators Association and is a three-time recipient of the Frederic Milton Thrasher Award of the National Gang Crime Research Center. Recent books he has authored or co-authored include *Gangs (2016), Military: Gangsters, Bikers, and Terrorists with Military Training (2019), Gangs and Organized Crime (2018)), and *Private Security Today* (2017).

Jerrod Brown, PhD., (contributed Chapter 3: Gangs and Mental Illness), has multiple years of experience teaching courses at the college level. Jerrod has also been employed in the field of mental health for the past 17 years. In addition to the experience mentioned above, Jerrod has provided consultation services to a number of caregivers, professionals, and organizations on topics related to the field of forensic mental health and has presented multiple presentations to professional and student audiences. Jerrod has completed four separate master's degree programs and holds graduate certificates in Autism Spectrum Disorder (ASD), Other Health Disabilities (OHD), and Traumatic-Brain Injuries (TBI).

Phyllis A. Belak, MBA, MS, CPA, CFE (contributed Chapter 9: Entrepreneurship, Finances and Gangs), is an accounting professor at West Chester University of Pennsylvania. She previously worked in industry as a senior financial analyst. Phyllis earned her MBA from Drexel University and recently earned a MS Criminal Justice from West Chester University. She is a Certified Public Accountant and Certified Fraud Examiner. Professor Belak has published in the Pennsylvania CPA Journal, Accounting Instructor's Report, and the Journal of Business Case Studies. Professor Belak's work has been presented at the Northeastern Association of Business, Economics, and Technology Conference and the Effective Learning Strategies Session for the AAA Mid-Atlantic Region Meeting.

Capt. Christopher Grant (ret), MA (contributed Chapter 5: Gangs and Native Americans), is a 40-year law enforcement veteran and the former commander of the Rapid City SD Police Department's Gang Task Force. Mr. Grant is a graduate of the 181st Session of the FBI National Academy and the current Vice-President of the Midwest Gang Investigators Association Dakotas Chapter. He is a nationally recognized authority on Native American street and prison gang trends and he has worked with law enforcement, educators and tribal leaders on over 70 reservations across Indian Country.

Chapter 1
The Emergence of Gangs in the United States— Then and Now

CHAPTER OBJECTIVES

- Examine the emergence of gangs in the United States.

- Explore gangs from New York, Chicago, and Los Angeles as they first emerged.

- Identify the differences and similarities between each region's growth of gangs.

- Examine the emergence of Black and Hispanic/Latino gangs.

- Describe the newest gang trends throughout the United States.

"The Cat's Alleys, the Degraw Street Gang, the Sackett Street gang, The Harrisons, the Bush Street Gang, and 21 other boys' gangs were the subjects of a report of the New York State Crime Commission, which told, last week, of its findings in the Red Hook section of Brooklyn.

The boys who comprise the gangs have to undergo rigorous initiations before being qualified for membership. In one of the more exclusive gang initiates, usually aged about nine, have to drink twelve glasses of dago-red wine and have a revolver pressed into their temples while they take the pledge.

Source: "Gangs" (1927). Time, 9(13), 11.

Introduction

The above excerpt comes from a 1927 article in *Time* magazine that identifies local gangs in New York City and their activities. However, gangs existed long before any established city in the United States. British crime chronicler, Luke Pike (1873), reported that the first set of active gangs were in Europe. During those times, they were better known as highway robbers. According to Pike, these robbers may have existed as early as the 12th century in Europe, but these types of gangs have very little in common with today's modern-day (street) gangs.

In the United States, it is believed that gangs emerged on the East Coast around 1783 (Sante, 1991). But, it is unlikely that the "street gangs" of the late 1700s have any resemblance to how the gangs of today are defined. Sante notes that the best available evidence suggests that the more serious gangs of the early 19th century are more comparable to the gangs of today. The growth of these gangs, for the most part, was a result of immigration.

Gangs in the 1800s were largely composed of Irish, Jewish, Polish, and other ethnic populations that immigrated to the United States. For example, there were more than three million immigrants that entered the United States from Ireland between 1840 and 1890, and by the turn of the century, an estimated five million Irish settled in the United States. Additionally, 18 million new immigrants arrived between 1890 and 1920 (primarily from Eastern and Southeastern Europe; Barrett & Roediger, 2005).

However, Europeans were not the only ones making their way to the United States, specifically New York City. Within the United States, the African-American population from the South migrated to the North and West, and the Hispanic/Latino population migrated their way to New York City, Chicago, and Los Angeles. Table 1.1 shows a brief historical timeline on the emergence of street gangs in the United States.

Table 1.1: Timeline of the U.S. Street Gang History

EARLY STREET GANGS IN THE NORTHEAST
1780s to 1870s:
• Immigrants from England and Ireland began the formation of gangs in the northeastern part of the United States. Most notable were the Forty Thieves, Dead Rabbits, Plug Uglies, and Whyos. By the mid-1800s, gangs began to get involved in violent crimes.
GANG RE-EMERGENCE AND GROWTH
1880s to 1940s:
• Gangs continued to grow in the Northeast and Midwest. Gangs were primarily established based on ethnicity. Irish gangs such as the Dukies and the Shielders and the arrival of German, Jewish, and Polish immigrants battled for turf. Blacks migrated from the south to Chicago and Italian immigrants established the American Mafia. Gangs were popular in New York City and Chicago.

(Continued)

GANG GROWTH AND CHANGE
1950s to 1990s:
• Major Black street gangs formed in the late 1950s. By the end of the 1960s, the majority of gangs were Black or Hispanic. Migration and immigration contributed to gang membership. Large gang groups were formed, such as the Bloods, Crips, and Latin Kings. In the 1960s and early 1970s, African-American "supergangs" emerged in Chicago such as the Gangster Disciples and the Vice Lords.
GANGS TODAY
2000s to Present:
• During the 2000s, the most active gangs were the Crips, the Latin Kings, MS-13, and the Bloods, and gang membership exceeds over 500,000. Gangs are known for marking their territory (graffiti) and committing a variety of property and violent crimes such as murder, drug, weapon, sex trafficking, prostitution, and thefts. Today, gangs have also established their presence on the Internet and social media.

The Northeast

Early New York City Street Gangs

Understanding the development of the street gang phenomenon on the East Coast is best explained in three distinct phases: (1) post-American Revolution, where unorganized youth were fighting over local turf, (2) the explosion of immigration from the early to late 1800s; and (3) when minority populations, primarily Latino and Black, began to arrive in large numbers in the 1930s and 1940s (Howell, 2012; Pincus & Ehrlich, 1999). As numerous groups of people from different countries crammed into New York City, conflict was imminent. As a result, street gangs grew rapidly.

Initially, early street gangs were viewed as troubled or wayward youth engaging in minor delinquent acts. While these early street gangs were not well organized and lacked sophisticated leadership, the desire to exercise power and control became evident among the gangs. As Howell and Moore (2010) pointed out, these gangs were nothing more than youth fighting over local turf and protecting their neighborhoods.

New York City was the most prominent location in the Northeast for the growth of street gangs. Immigration, poverty, racial/ethnic tensions, and lack of employment opportunities contributed to this growth and significantly impacted the crime rates in New York City (Howell, 2012; Howell & Moore, 2010; Pizarroa & McGloin, 2006). In addition, green-grocery speakeasies and politics also played a significant part in the development of gangs in New York City.

Green-grocery speakeasies established the first defined *turfs* in the streets of New York City. These speakeasies were an Irish invention that used the pub culture, and the men that frequented them, to assist the Irish in becoming politically dominant. The first speakeasy was a grungy bar located on Centre Street in Five Points run by Rosanna Peers. This Five Points store was actually a "fence" where Ms. Peters would buy and resell goods stolen by gangs (Edwards, 2013). Although these stores primarily sold vegetables, it was nothing more than a facade for the true purpose behind these establishments—the sale of liquor.

In the 1820s, the first documented street gang with recognized leadership, was the Forty Thieves (Allender, 2001). The Forty Thieves, comprised Irish immigrants, formed in the Five Points District of New York City. The Five Points District was an area comprising almost 90% foreign-born residents. The Forty Thieves operated along the waterfront and engaged in acts of murder, robbery, and assault and other violent acts (Allender, 2001; Anbinder, 2002). Other notable street gangs in New York City were the Dead Rabbits (allegedly named after someone threw a dead rabbit on the floor during a gang meeting), the Plug Uglies (named after the type of worn hat), the Kerryonians (named after an Irish county), and the Whyos (named after the sound made by a bird or owl calling, "Why-oh"; Allender, 2001; Asbury, 1927; Howell, 2012; Sullivan & Silverstein, 1995). Ironically, the colors blue and red, also adopted by the Bloods and Crips from Los Angeles, was originally worn by Irish gangs in the 1920s. The Roach Guards wore blue, and the Dead Rabbits wore red (Decker & Van Winkle, 1996).

By 1910, roughly 13 million people of approximately 100 million living in the United States were foreign-born and roughly three million of those were living in New York City (Gibson & Jung, 2006). New immigrants were faced with many challenges such as unsanitary living conditions and the lack of adequate housing. The various ethnic groups that resided within the city—the Jews, the Bohemians (Czechs and Slovaks), and the Chinese along with immigrants from Poland, Italy, and Austria—only contributed to the deteriorating conditions because of the economic conditions and quest for the "American Dream" of upward mobility (Sante, 1991). The fact was, New York City could not sustain this influx. Jabob Riis (1890/1997) documented the horrific living conditions in New York City with photos in his classic work *How the Other Half Lives: Studies Among the Tenements of New York*. Riis advocated for city reform and eventually New York City made improvements based on his work. However, within these poor living conditions, the shadowy world of street gangs flourished.

Other immigrants flooding New York City included African-Americans and Puerto Ricans. Torres (1995) pointed out that African-Americans were better positioned than Puerto Ricans to "withstand the ravages of economic and political changes that characterized New York" (p. 63). Essentially, as one family would better themselves and move out of the inner city for better living conditions, new immigrants would fill the void and occupy the residences. As a result, there were more gangs in New York City in the mid-1900s than in any other city in the United States (Asbury, 1927).

By 1916, the police commenced their first war on gangs and arrested, beat, and imprisoned more than 200 gang leaders (Haskins, 1974). The police actions, however, only pushed the gangs to move to outlying areas of New York City and migrate to cities such as Philadelphia and Boston (Chin, 1990).

Politics and Street Gangs

In addition to the flood of immigrants entering the United States, politics played a significant role in contributing to the growth of street gangs in New York City. At the center of most of the gang corruption during late 18th and early 19th century was New York City's Tammany Hall that later became known as the Democratic Party. A forerunner to modern street gangs were the "voting gangs" of the 1800s (Monkkonen, 2001). Shrewd wards and district leaders employed "voting gangs" to ensure victory at the polls in New York City (Haskins, 1974). Gangs were paid and encouraged by politicians to assist in elections. Rival political opponents were often assaulted and intimidated. These types of gangs would harass the new immigrants, primarily the Irish as they arrived in the United States, and get them to vote for the appropriate candidate to obtain the necessary votes for the preferred politician to win elections.

Tammany Hall controlled much of New York City and New York State politics. The organization helped immigrants, primarily the Irish, ascend in American politics from the 1790s up to the 1960s (see Haskins, 1974; Howell, 2012; *Sachems & Sinners: An Informal History of Tammany Hall*, 1955). It was estimated that 30,000 government and political figures owed allegiance to various gang leaders in New York City (Haskins, 1974). Unfortunately, law enforcement officials were powerless to arrest gang members and even when the local police attempted to guard polling stations against illegal voters, the "voting gangs" would beat them.

The Emergence of Black and Hispanic/Latino Street Gangs

The 1930s and 1940s brought about the most intense gang activity in New York City, partly because of the influence from organized crime groups such as the five mafia families: the Bonanno, the Colombo, the Genovese, the Lucchese, and the Gambino Families. The 1930s and 1940s also witnessed the arrival of Hispanics/Latinos from Central America, South America, and the Caribbean. These groups settled in East Harlem, the South Bronx, and Brooklyn (Howell, 2012). As the Hispanic/Latino youth made their presence known in Harlem and the Bronx, gang activity increased in these areas (Howell, 2012).

African-Americans also began to migrate from the rural South to the North in what historians and scholars call the "Great Migration of Blacks" (Tolnay, 2003). Between 1910 and 1930, 14% of New York's population was Black (Bourgois, 2003) and Harlem was one of the first Black ghettos. According to Haskins (1974), "the area could not have been riper for sprouting of street gangs" (p. 80).

The 1940s also witnessed race riots among Italian Americans, Puerto Ricans, and African-Americans (Bourgois, 2003). Bourgois (2003) noted that Puerto Rican immigrants "generated the most antipathy by mainstream society because of their poorer economic status, malnutrition, and disease" (p. 61). Meanwhile, East Harlem experienced juvenile gang fights between Italians and Puerto Ricans. One noticeable trend concerning gangs was gang members were getting younger, more ethnically diverse, more organized, dealing with drugs, and armed with weapons (Haskins, 1974).

Today's New York City Street Gangs

While gangs are not as prevalent today in New York City as they once were, the FBI's 2011 National Gang Threat Assessment reports that since 2009, "gang membership increased most significantly in the Northeast" (National Gang Intelligence Center, 2009, p. 8). There are as many as 22,000 gang members in New York City, the majority coming from the Bronx and close to 50,000 gang members located throughout the state (NGIC, 2009).

Today, turf battles between immigrant populations based on urban renewal efforts and ethnic migrations are a thing of the past. Instead, gang violence in the New York City is increasingly dominated by small, neighborhood-based factions, but the "super-gangs" like the Bloods and Crips still exist (Ferranti, 2015). Presently, officials point to anti-gang offensives such as "Operation Crew Cut" that has deterred street violence and other violent gang-related activities. According to Destefano (2013), "Operation Crew Cut is believed by police to have accounted for as much as a one-third drop in [New York City] homicides, as well as fewer shootings, which this year [2013] are down 26.4% compared to 2012" (para. 5). While the gang violence statistics in New York City are nowhere near the levels of violence that was reached in the 1980s and 1990s, gang-related crimes in 2019 have led to an increase in murders (3% increase from 2018) and shootings (5% increase from 2018) (Chapman & Honan, 2019). However, according to New York State gang expert Rob "Cook" Barrett:

"the biggest trend in New York State has been the influence of hybrid gangs—these groups are known and represent in their cities only... They represent local housing projects, parks, city blocks, and streets.... Buffalo, Syracuse, Albany, Newburgh, Poughkeepsie, and obviously the boroughs of New York all have a heavy presence of local territorial hybrid gangs with nontraditional names like Wave Gang, 4 Block, YGz....Brooklyn, Queens, the Bronx, Mount Vernon, Washington Heights, you name it... they all are seeing a rise in hybrid gangs that are not connected to the traditional "super-gangs" (Bloods, Crips, Kings, etc.)" (cited in Ferranti, 2015).

The Midwest

Early Chicago Street Gangs

When people discuss gangs from the Midwest, an immediate connection is made to the city of Chicago. This is most likely for two reasons. First, Al Capone and the Chicago Mafia, the *Out-fit*, was a dominant fixture in the city of Chicago. Secondly, Frederic Milton Thrasher (1927/2000) conducted his famous study on the 1313 gangs in Chicago and is considered by many as the father of "gangology."

Thrasher (1927/2000) reported that street gangs from Chicago developed out of the White immigrant populations, primarily along ethnic lines. According to Thrasher's research, 37.37% of the gangs examined were Polish, 25% were Italian, 18.94% were Irish, and 5.05 were Jewish (p. 131).

By the mid- to late 1860s, ill-behaved groups, such as those breaking fences and stealing cabbages evolved into ominous gangs. These early Chicago-based youth gangs comprised mainly German and Irish immigrants that would eventually succumb to Polish gangs (Thrasher, 1927/2000). By the late 1800s, Irish gangs (the Dukies and the Shielders) exerted a powerful influence over other groups in the neighborhood (Howell, 2012). Initially, the Irish gangs fought among themselves but they eventually united as the "Mickies" to battle Black gangs (who arrived in the 1920s) as well as German, Jewish, and Polish gangs (Barrett & Roediger, 2005; Howell & Moore, 2010; Perkins, 1987).

Politics and Street Gangs

Just like the gang political connections that were historically present in New York City, Chicago gangs also became entrenched in the patronage networks of the political machines (Adamson, 2000; Lessoff & Connolly, 2013; Thrasher, 1927/2000). Similar to Tammany Hall, Chicago's social athletic clubs (SACs) were crucial components of urban political life (Hagedorn, 2006). SACs were believed to be options for young, adolescents to get off the streets and find a better life. However, SACs were no different than "voting gangs." Despite SACs providing a means to obtain jobs as policemen, firemen, or other legitimate places of employment, the focus of the SACs was getting their Democratic Party officials elected. Thrasher (1927/2000) noted that "the tendency of the gangs to become athletic clubs has been greatly stimulated by the politicians of the city" (p. 456). Even sociologist Edwin Sutherland (1924) commented on the political influence and need for young boys to feverishly support the political machine.

> At the present time a good many gangs are flourishing under the leadership and protection of the politicians. These are frequently called athletic clubs and are fostered even among young boys, evidently with the expectation that political support will be gained in the future. In return for present support and expected future support the politicians extend protection to the boys in their depredation. (p. 156)

Cooley (2011) also reported that gangs "often became acutely engaged with city politics" (p. 911). Just like that in New York City, Chicago gangs were hired to break picket lines, stuff ballot boxes, intimidate voters, and protect establishments from harassment by other gangs (Diamond, 2005; Moore & Williams, 2011; O'Kane, 1992/2009).

The Emergence of Black and Hispanic/Latino Street Gangs

In the 1920s, there were only 63 reported Black gangs and no Mexican-American gangs in Chicago (Thrasher, 1927/2000). However, by the 1940s, the migration of Blacks and Mexicans from the South made their way to Chicago and into the world of gangs. Almost immediately, Mexican and Black youth gangs were engaged in turf battles with Irish gangs. The Irish gangs felt these youth groups encroached on Irish controlled areas (Arredondo, 2004). Additionally, Mexican Americans experienced a great deal of racial discrimination at the hands of European immigrants (Fernández, 2005).

While Mexican Americans already had a small presence in Chicago, the first major migration of Mexican Americans to Chicago occurred in 1919 and continued until 1939 (Arredondo, 2004). Spergel and Grossman (1997) suggested that as Hispanic/Latino gangs grew, they eventually joined the ranks of Chicago's most violent gangs (e.g., Latin Kings).

Similar to New York City's ethnic and racial gang developments, Black gangs also formed because of poverty, racial tensions, and violence. The need for protection and to defend their neighborhoods (i.e., turf), particularly against other White gangs such as the Irish, was a focal concern for Black gangs (Howell, 2012). As racial tension heated up in Chicago, the death of an African-American teenager by a group of white youths sparked the Chicago race riots of 1919. As reported by a *Chicago Tribune* staff reporter,

> They were separated by a line unseen and a law unwritten: The 29th Street beach was for Whites, the 25th Street beach for Blacks. An invisible boundary stretched from the sand into Lake Michigan, parting the races like Moses' staff parted the Red Sea. On this stifling hot summer Sunday, Eugene Williams, a Black teenager, drifted south of that line while swimming with friends. Whites picked up rocks and let fly. (Armstrong, 1919)

It was the Irish gangs that used violence and terror as a means to enforce their own Mason-Dixon Line and contained African-Americans in their overcrowded areas, while racial antagonism flowed prior to the riot. Ultimately, the riot resulted in the deaths of 15 Whites, 23 Blacks, more than 500 people injured, and over 1,000 Black families had their homes destroyed by fire (History.com Staff, 2009).

The Chicago Riots of 1919 is also credited for a type of crime that is typically associated with gangs, drive-by shootings. White gang members would drive through black neighborhoods searching for black residents, firing at them, and then driving swiftly away. Similar to present day drive-by shootings, some residents who were shot and sometimes killed were not always the intended victims (Hagedorn, 2006). This was the only race riot that occurred between the Irish and any other ethnic/racial group. The Irish did not riot with the Italians, Poles, or Jews.

From 1910 to 1930, approximately 200,000 Blacks migrated from the south to Chicago (Tolnay, 2003). Thus, Chicago had the second largest urban Black population in the United States (Miller, 2008). In 1930, 9 out of 10 African-Americans lived in areas that were at least 80% Black and no other ethnic/racial group experienced poverty levels similar to this (Hagedorn, 2006). From the 1940s to the 1950s, the Black population in Chicago increased to around 500,000 (Miller, 2008). Many African-Americans in Chicago moved to an area known as the *Black Belt*. This was a geographic area along State Street on Chicago's South Side. It was estimated that about 375,000 Blacks were living in the *Black Belt* during the 1940s. Unfortunately, this area was only suitable for about 110,000 people (Miller, 2008), and crowded living conditions were a common way of life. Out of poor economic conditions and racial conflicts with White gangs, three major Black street gangs formed in the latter part of the 1950s and early 1960s: the Devil's Disciples, Black P-Stones, and the Vice Lords (Cureton, 2009). The Vice Lords and the Black P-Stone Nation/Black Stone Rangers were formed in the Illinois State Reformatory School in 1958 and 1959, respectively (Knox & Papachristos, 2002). Eventually, the Devil's Disciples split into three factions between 1960 and 1973: the Black Disciples led by David Barksdale, the Black Gangster Disciples led by Larry Hoover, and the Supreme Gangsters better known later as the Gangster Disciples (Cureton, 2009). Violence between these factions were severe and resulted in many unintended consequences:

> By the early sixties, Chicago's Black street gangs had grown to such proportions that they not only posed a threat to themselves but to the Black community as well...were being perceived as predators who preyed on whomever they felt infringed on their lust for power [and] they turned to more criminal activities' and the control of turf became their number one priority . . . . by controlling turf, gangs were able to exercise their muscles to extort monies from businesses and intimate the Black community. (Perkins, 1987, p. 32)

In the 1960s and early 1970s, the African-American "supergangs" emerged in Chicago (Cooley, 2011). The Black Stone Rangers (formed in 1959 from a nine-member street gang then called the Black Stone Raiders) and East Side Disciples inhabited the South Side and the Vice Lords claimed territory on the West Side (Cooley, 2011; McPherson, 1966; Sale, 1971). These gangs grew from small sets to large "nations" with leadership cadres and dues-paying members (Cooley, 2011). Some observers (e.g., Perkins, 1987) blamed these "supergangs" for the rising crime rates and civil disorders in the Chicago areas. Meanwhile, despite efforts to instill Black pride in young people with the Civil Rights Movement and the rise of the Black Panthers, those efforts had little impact on Black gang members (Howell, 2012).

Interestingly, these gangs began to form along loose alliances that established two larger groups called the People Nation and the Folk Nation. The People and Folk Nations are not gangs per se but rather ideological alliances to which gangs belong (e.g., Latin Kings are a People Nation set; the Gangster Disciples are a Folk Nation set). According to the Illinois State Police (1992), Larry Hoover, leader of the Gangster Disciples, formed the Folk Nation in November of 1978, while he was incarcerated in an Illinois prison. Hoover envisioned a single gang and wanted to unite many of the gangs in Chicago. He created the idea of an alliance and persuaded many leaders of large Black, White, and Latino gangs from Chicago to join forces if there was ever a need. Shortly after the Folk Nation was formed, rival gangs (Vice Lords and Latin Kings) formed the People Nation.

Today's Chicago Street Gangs

Today, the gangs in Chicago have changed dramatically when comparing to the past. The old hierarchical super-gangs such as the Gangster Disciples, Latin Kings, and Vice Lords, fighting throughout the city over control of drug trafficking, are largely gone. African-American gangs have fractured into smaller sets, cliques, and neighborhood peer groups. The gangs of today are more affiliated with rappers than with the old gang "chieftains" (Hagedorn, Aspholm, Córdova, Papachristos, & Williams, 2019). While some violence is still drug related, much of it is interpersonal, setting off cycles of retaliation between neighborhood sets. Most of law enforcement and other practitioners working with gangs and addressing the gang problem agree that Chicago-based street gangs still align themselves with the Folk or People Nations, but these alliances do not account for much (Cureton, 2009; Maxson, 1998; Perkins, 1987). Despite the alliances, the gangs within each Nation still fight with one another. In fact, it is not uncommon to find some of the more popular Folk and People gangs like the Gangster Disciples and Latin Kings in other parts of the country.

However, Chicago in the past five years has built a reputation for being the new "gang capital of the United States," a title that had long belonged to the city of Los Angeles. In the past few years, Chicago has seen a significant rise in gang-related activities. The murder rate of Chicago in 2012 was nearly four times higher than that of New York City and more than 2.5 times higher than that of Los Angeles. But, Chicago's population is three times smaller than that of New York City and nearly half of Los Angeles' population. In fact, Chicago had the highest number of homicides among cities with populations of more than one million in 2011. The record jumped to 532 murders in 2012 and recorded 413 in 2013. A significant portion of all those homicides were committed by gang members. Gang members in Chicago were responsible for 58.7% of all homicides in 2010 and 61% of all homicides in 2011. According to the Chicago Police Department (2011), 80% of all shootings and homicides in Chicago have been gang related.

According to the Chicago Crime Commissioni (2018), there are over 100,000 gang members in Chicago and approximately 12,000 police officers within the Chicago PD, which has a gang task force of about 200 officers. The city of Chicago also witnessed a 25% increase in gang activity from 2009 to 2012 (ABCNews, 2012). Gang experts claim that the reason for these staggering numbers showing an increase in gang-related activities are directly related to municipalities having to cut police department's budgets; there are less police officers patrolling the streets, and "the historical hierarchy of Chicago-based street gangs has seemingly come undone, with various factions of former larger gangs all claiming territory, and clearly willing to shoot first at anyone unfamiliar who may be encroaching on said territory" (The Richest.com, 2014).

The West

The Emergence of Los Angeles Street Gangs

The city of Los Angeles was founded by the Spanish in 1781, and California became U.S. territory in 1848 and finally in 1850 became the 31st state. Railroad connections to the East Coast in the 1880s led to a rapid increase in the dominant White population. Soon, English-speaking Whites established control in California and the West, and as a result, many Mexicans lost their land holdings and were ultimately regulated to low-paying jobs (Allen & Turner, 2013). It was the cultural and geographical changes that contributed to gangs growing out of the preexisting Mexican culture in the West. Mexicans and other Hispanic/Latino groups who had traveled up from Mexico to populated areas such as El Paso, Texas, Albuquerque, New Mexico, Los Angeles, and California were seeking a better life (Howell, 2012). In the early 20th century, Los Angeles experienced major industrial and economic booms (e.g., railroad and agriculture) that demanded thousands of workers (Garcia, 1981), and Mexicans filled that need as the primary workforce (Sánchez, 1995).

Although research indicates that immigrating Mexican populations date back as far as the 16th century (Howell, 2012), it is difficult to determine the exact number of Mexicans entering the United States between the late 1800s and the early 1900s. It was not until the 1930 census that Mexicans were included in an immigration report. Officially, the Mexican population grew from approximately 367,000 in the early 1900s to about 700,000 by 1920 (Garcia, 1981). This population explosion was largely due to the Mexican Revolution (1910–1920), which accelerated Mexican immigration into the United States (Howell, 2012).

Prior to World War II, gangs were also not as prevalent as they later became in Southern California (Shelden, Tracy, & Brown, 1997). Some of the research on gang-like groups indicates that these early gangs may have first appeared in the West as early as the 1890s (Rubel, 1965). Additionally, other research asserts that the Treaty of Guadalupe Hidalgo in 1848 was an event that led to the presence of Mexican street gangs in Los Angeles and in other western regions of the United States (see also Vigil, 1998).

Vigil (1983) indicated that these earlier versions of street gangs in the West were what Rubel (1965) described as the tradition of *palomilla*. According to Rubel (1965), this was a coming-of-age cohort among young men:

> The association to which I have reference is called a *palomilla*. *Palomillas* are curiously devoid of formal, let alone corporate, attributes; nevertheless, they represent a remarkably important aspect of the social organization of Mexiquito. Generically, *palomilla* refers to an ego-centric association of young males who interact with some frequency. The word itself is derived from the Spanish *paloma* (dove); thus, a *palomilla* has reference to a covey of doves and, by extension, a company of young men. (pp. 92–93)

Politics and Racial Tensions

Cultural differences were often confused with political dissent following World War II, particularly in southern California. For example, Japanese Americans were detained for suspected criminality while race riots raged on from New York to Los Angeles that ultimately reinforced racial barriers and segregation (Pagán, 2003). However, two critical events in southern California that further set the stage for the emergence of Los Angeles street gangs were fueled by racial tensions in the community. The first event was the Sleepy Lagoon murder of 1942. The Sleepy Lagoon murder surrounded events that occurred on August 1 and 2, 1942, between two gangs, the Downy Boys (a Caucasian gang) and the 38th Street gang (a Mexican-American gang) (Ramirez, 2009). The Sleepy Lagoon incident ended with the death of Jose Diaz and a trial in Los Angeles that concluded with the conviction of five young Mexican-American men, alleged members of the 38th Street gang (Pagán, 2003). Just five months later, the Zoot Suit Riot erupted.

The second event was the Zoot Suit Riots of 1943. The word "Zoot" which means something worn or performed in an extravagant style was a product of the Jazz era and the streets of Harlem, New York in the mid-1930s (Alford, 2004). The long-standing tensions between military men and civilian youths played a role in the outbreak of the Zoot Suit Riots (Mazón, 1984; Pagán, 2003). For those Hispanic/Latinos, wearing zoot suits became a powerful symbol of pride, but it also represented deviance among the public's perceptions and stripping off zoot suites was an act of humiliation toward those rebellious minority youth (e.g., Peiss, 2011). The riot lasted five days.

The Emergence of Hispanic/Latino (Chicano) Street Gangs

In the 1920s, Mexicans (Chicanos) lived near the downtown area of Los Angeles. These settlement areas were called *cholo courts*. *Cholo courts* were "rundown shacks hastily and meagerly put together by immigrants" (Vigil, 1990, p. 116). This impoverished area is where some of the poorest people lived and this was where some of East Los Angeles' most notorious Mexican (Chicano) gangs and later other Hispanic/Latino gangs thrived (Vigil, 1990, 1998). For those gang members living in *cholo courts*, they were identified as *cholos* because of their style of dress, speech, gestures, tattoos, and graffiti. Researchers have noted that adolescent gang members who struggled to form an identity turned to the Mexican culture as a means of establishing an identity and embracing it (Lopez & O'Donnell-Brummett, 2003). This pride and uniqueness to one's own heritage/ethnic group helped shape the Chicano gang lifestyle (Belitz & Valdez, 1994). Today, these *cholo* courts are referred to as *barrios*.

While some of these early Chicano street gangs were referred to as "boy gangs" (Bogardus, 1943), these "boy gangs" were the forerunners to the modern Chicano gangs of East Los Angeles (Shelden et al., 1997). Howell (2012) reported that the earliest and most firmly established gangs were established in *barrios*. These Chicano gangs only became visible after police and school officials reported conflicts between the barrio youths (Vigil & Long, 1990).

While immigration and the regeneration of a street gang subculture continues today, Southern California gangs were also fueled by the Vietnam War, the War on Poverty, and the Chicano movement (also called the Chicano Civil Rights Movement) of the 1960s and 1970s (Howell, 2012). As the Vietnam War depleted the *barrios* of generations of role models, the War on Poverty eliminated jobs, and the Chicano movement brought attention to the suffering *barrio* populations, gangs grew rapidly. According to Vigil (1990), "gang violence mushroomed in the aftermath of these events, for *choloization* did return to replace the War on Poverty, and street models began to reclaim their turf from activists and lead new generations of barrio youth" (p. 126).

The Emergence of Black Street Gangs

Like the Mexicans, Blacks from the South were also seeking a better life in the West, only to be confronted with racial tensions and segregation. As reported by Cureton (2009),

> the West was considered the land of prosperity because of employment opportunities in factories. In addition, the West appeared to offer an escape from Southern oppression, but the reality was that it turned out to be fertile territory for traditional White supremacist ideology, institutional inequality (in housing, education, and employment), and restrictions relative to where Blacks could socialize. (p. 355)

Cureton (2009) contended that this segregation, as well as racial tensions and violence, fueled the growth of Black street gangs in Los Angeles and the *gangsterism* perspective. The presumption is that predatory Black male groups evolved from a variety of community transitional stages. From 1929 up through the 2000s, Blacks made their way to Los Angeles, and as they moved near Whites in urban areas, sparks of interracial conflict were inevitable. As communities became more isolated and socially disorganized, "street gangs became entrenched in the social fabric of the urban underclass. Marginalized male residents did not accept exclusion from mainstream society's opportunities, so hustling drugs, guns, and stolen goods, prostituting women, and gambling became suitable alternatives for inclusion in a capitalistic, material-driven culture" (p. 352).

Eventually, "neighborhoods became ganglands" and respect was the "social currency that governed street interaction and length of survival" (p. 352). *Gangsterism* is reflected in the "street protocol, dealing with enemies, the value of gang alliances, seizing control of turf, drug and gun distribution, and recreation" (p. 352). Essentially, the emergent *gangsterism* perspective hypothesizes that the community evolves into "hood" enclaves. Thus, the street gang was the most important social network organization for urban youth and the number one organization that male youth turned to negotiate manhood (Cureton, 2009).

Other researchers documented Black gang formation in Los Angeles differently. For example, Alonso (2004) reported that the late 1940s (residential segregation, police brutality, and racially motivated violence) and early 1970s (aftermath of the 1960s civil rights movements and assassinations of Los Angeles activists) were two periods of gang formation in South Los Angeles. Additionally, Bell and Jenkins (1991) reported that inner-city children were impacted by the exposure to chronic violence in the neighborhood. According to these authors, children who were exposed to violence are associated with later perpetration of violence (e.g., protection against victimization or retaliation for some prior incident). In the late 1940s, there were three racial riots that occurred: Manual Arts High in 1946, Canoga Park High in 1947, and John Adams High in 1949 (Vigil, 2002). Historically, these schools were primarily turf battle grounds for gangs:

> Black gangs, until the 1970s tended to be predominantly defined by school-based turfs rather than by the microscopically drawn neighborhood territorialities of Chicano gangs. Furthermore, early South Central gangs such as the Businessmen, Slausons, Gladiators, Farmers, Parks, Outlaws, Watts, Boot Hill, Rebel Rousers, Roman Twenties served also as the architects of social space in new and usually hostile settings. As tens of thousands of 1940s and 1950s Black immigrants crammed into the overcrowded, absentee-landlord-dominated neighborhoods of the ghetto's Eastside, low-rider gangs offered cool worlds of urban socialization for poor young newcomers from rural Texas, Louisiana and Mississippi. (Davis, 1992, p. 311)

Unlike the Mexican gangs, Black gangs were not geographically located in restricted areas (e.g., barrios). Black gangs encompassed wider areas, and because of this lack of geographic restriction, Black gangs appear to have evolved out of Black–White racial conflicts (Howell, 2012). In addition, antagonism from White youth groups (e.g., Spook Hunters) manifested into racial hate crimes. Essentially, Black males had learned that sticking together proved a successful coping strategy. Therefore, brotherhoods such as the Slausons, Farmers, Businessmen, Gladiators, Watts Gang, and Devil Hunters were formed to defend Black legitimacy (Cureton, 2009). These Black defense groups, which were initially liberators or pioneers, defended their home turf as well as expanded their territory by traveling to battle White youth groups. However, "the African American community suffered from poor schools, housing, and unemployment which was three times the national average" (National Geographic Channel [NatGeo],

2009) and, like the Chicago race riots of 1919, the 1965 Watts riot gave birth to a variety of new Black street gangs. The two most famous and widely known are the Crips and the Bloods.

The origins of the Crips are heavily disputed. Historians reported that after the Watts riot, Raymond Washington started a local gang with 10 of his friends and called themselves "the Cribs" (NatGeo, 2009). It was suggested that the name was eventually changed to Crips because gang members began carrying around canes to display their "pimp" status. Also, in a *Los Angeles Sentinel* article, February 1972, referred to some members as "Crips" (for cripples). Other reports suggest that Bunchy Carter, a former Black Panther president, and Raymond Washington were the primary founders of the Crips (Cureton, 2009). Meanwhile, the movie *Tales of the Crypt* became the inspiration for the name "Crip" because the gang members "wanted to convey that just as dead people were placed in crypts, anyone messed with them— the Crips—would end up in one also" (Greenan, Britz, Rush, & Barker, 2000, p. 124). Lastly, it is suggested that high-school students, Raymond Washington and Stanley "Tookie" Williams started the Crips as a means of protecting themselves and their friends from other gangs in the area who were committing crimes (Dunn, 1999). Regardless of how the Crips originated, what is not disputed is that the Bloods street gang was formed as a reaction to the Crips.

The Crips and Bloods have loosely structured and unstructured "sets" that are mostly from specific neighborhoods in South Central Los Angeles. Typically, gang members dress in a distinctive fashion, display colors (blue associated with Crips and red with Bloods), and have unique symbols (e.g., graffiti, hand signs) that identify who they are. Alonso (2004) reported that "Crip identity took over the streets of South Los Angeles and swept Southside schools in an epidemic of gang shootings and street fights by 1972 when there were 18 Black gangs in Los Angeles County" (p. 669). However, Robert Walker, a former Special Agent for the DEA and gang expert, indicated that "by the end of 1972, every area of South Central Los Angeles, including Compton, East Compton, Florence, Firestone, Athens, Willowbrook, and Carson had been divided up and was totally saturated with a street gang presence" (Walker, n.d.). Walker also noted that *Crip* street gangs were in place by late 1971. By 1978, the gangs had multiplied to 60, and by the 1990s, there were more than 270 gangs in the Los Angeles County area (Howell, 2012).

Today's Los Angeles Street Gangs

California, primarily Los Angeles, and the surrounding communities have produced some of America's most notorious gangs: the Bloods and Crips; prison gangs (STGs) such as Mexican Mafia (La Eme), La Nuestra Familia, and the Aryan Brotherhood (AB); 18th Street gang and Mara Salvatrucha (MS-13) gang; and the Tiny Rascals (Asian gang). In fact, the city of Los Angeles was considered the "gang capital of the world" for decades.

The most significant and recognizable Black gangs in the West are the Bloods and Crips. The Bloods membership is estimated between 5,000 and 20,000 gang members while the Crips membership is significantly larger estimated between 30,000 and 35,000 gang members (U.S. Department of Justice, 2015). Crips and Bloods subscribe to territorial ownership, material acquisition, money, power, social status, and respect. In the early 1980s, lethal violence became the preferred method to seize control of territory, drugs (primarily cocaine), and guns (Cureto, 2009).

The most significant Mexican-American- and Hispanic/Latino-based street gangs in the West are Mara Salvatrucha (MS-13), 18th Street gang, and Florencia 13. MS-13 and the 18th Street gang have garnered the most public fear, prompting the FBI to create a special task force to deal with these two gangs. Other Hispanic/Latino/Chicano gangs include the Norteños (Norte14) and Sureños (Sur13) who have also significantly grown in Northern and Southern California, respectively (FBI, 2011). Additionally, as reported in the FBI's 2011 National Gang Threat Assessment report, Asian gangs are also involved in a host of criminal activities that include violent crime, drug and human trafficking, and white-collar crime.

From 1988-1998, gang crimes and gang-related homicides were at an all-time high and this time period became known as the "decade of death" (Rodriguez & Martinez, 2017; Brenhoff, 2017), but since the 2000s, the gang crime rate has fluctuated. As Brenhoff (2017) points out, gang crime rates were declining from 2012-2014 and the reasons were attributed to smarter policing, the Racketeer Influenced and Corrupt Organizations Act (RICO) effect, rising home prices, decline of the "corner boy" because of gang injunctions, fewer young kids joining gangs due to fear of Mexican Mafia, and intervention over suppression. Unfortunately, the Los Angeles Police Department reported that violent, gang-related crime actually increased by 63% from 2014-2015 (Gazar, 2017). In 2019, the Los Angeles Police Department estimated there are over 450 active gangs with a combined membership of more than 45,000 gang members (LAPD, 2020).

The South

Unlike the emergent gang problems of the Northeast, Midwest, and West, the South has a much broader scope for gang phenomenon with no one city serving as the focal point like New York, Chicago, or Los Angeles. While the South lacked a central large city that would have provided a springboard for gang growth, opinions differ over what role big city gangs have in the emergence of youth gangs in smaller cities. Zevitz and Takata (1992) reported that little empirical evidence exists to support or refute the big city gang connection and concluded that gang development is the result of the outgrowth of underlying social and economic conditions in a community, not the product of big city street gang diffusion. Regardless of the big city versus small city gang influence debate, prior to the 1970s, gangs were not perceived as a threat in the South. Most cities in Texas, Florida, Georgia, and Louisiana did report delinquent and criminal activities but described these activities as disruptive local groups rather than gangs

(Howell, 2012). However, in Walter Miller's (1975) first multi-city gang study, Miami, Florida and San Antonio, Texas were identified as cities with a serious gang problem. By the mid-to-late 1990s, southern states recorded an increase in the number of new gangs where approximately 200 cities with populations of 100,000 or more reported youth gang problems (Miller, 2001). Florida (23%), South Carolina (15%), Alabama (12%), and Texas (8%) saw an increase in the number of gangs in their states (Howell & Griffiths, 2016).

Today, Houston, Texas and Miami, Florida have emerged as a major gang center for the South region with New Orleans and Atlanta not far behind (Howell & Griffiths, 2016). As gang homicide increase in the South and drug trafficking continues to be a major problem for law enforcement, many of these gangs, particularly in Texas, have some connection to Texas prison gangs/STGs (e.g., the Texas Syndicate, the Mexican Mafia, and Tango Blast; Morgan & Shelley, 2014). One prison gang, the Tango Blast, similar to the Mexican Mafia in the California penal system, has close ties to Houston and is well established inside the Texas prison system. According to a *Houston Chronicle* article,

> Houston has about 21,000 gang members, police said, with about one-quarter to one-third affiliated with a group called "Tango Blast Houstone." That loose affiliation of Hispanic ex-prison inmates is part of a larger statewide gang and identified as a "top threat." (Glenn, 2014, para. 3)

The Latin Disciples, Hoover Crips, Bounty Hunters, Southwest *Cholos*, Bloods, and MS-13 are among the other major gangs in the Houston area. While some have unique ties to Houston, others have either borrowed the symbols, colors, and names from Chicago- and Los Angeles-based street gangs or gang members themselves who arrived from Chicago and Los Angeles in Houston and established a "set" in the area and expanded the gangs' illegal activities.

Other Gangs and Gang Trends

Hybrid Gangs

By the late 1980s and 1990s, law enforcement was faced with new types of gangs, hybrid gangs, Asian gangs, and Native American gangs. Hybrid gangs are essentially a mixture of racial and ethnic groups that often "cut and paste" bits of gang imagery and big city gang lore into their local versions of gangs, while other gangs are home grown (Howell, 2007). According to Starbuck, Howell, and Lindquist (2001),

> Hybrid gang culture is characterized by members of different racial/ethnic groups participating in a single gang, individuals participating in multiple gangs, unclear rules or codes of conduct, symbolic associations with more than one well-established gang (e.g., use of colors and graffiti

from different gangs), cooperation of rival gangs in criminal activity, and frequent mergers of small gangs. (p. 1)

Additionally, hybrid gangs tend to have the following nontraditional features: (1) they may or may not have an allegiance to a traditional gang color; (2) local gangs may adopt the symbols of large gangs in more than one city; (3) gang members may change their affiliation from one gang to another; or (4) it is not uncommon for a gang member to claim multiple affiliations, sometimes involving rival gangs (Starbuck et al., 2001). Early American gangs were homogeneous with respect to race/ethnicity, but immigration, the mobility of gangs, and the diffusion of gang culture have contributed to the emergence of hybrid (cosmopolitan) gangs (Howell, 2012).

Asian Gangs

Asian gangs are typically located in the West, but there are pockets of Asian gangs in the Midwest (Minneapolis) and the East Coast (New York) and are composed of several independent identities that are mostly Chinese, Japanese, Filipino, Hmong, Laotian, Cambodian, or Vietnamese. The origin of Asian youth gangs is not very different from that of other gangs. Toy (1992) indicated that it is not the cultural conflict and social factors that influenced deviant behavior or the collapse of traditional family, but in fact, the victimization committed by other ethnic groups that led to gang membership among Asians. Vigil (2002) stated that Asian gangs, primarily Vietnamese, draw the most attention because they are different when compared to Black and Hispanic/Latino gangs. Asian gangs have a more fluid structure and are not concerned so much with territory as traditional Black and Hispanic/Latino street gangs. This difference is elaborated by the FBI:

> Although often considered street gangs, Asian gangs operate similar to Asian Criminal enterprises with a more structured organization and hierarchy. They are not turf-oriented like most African-American and Hispanic street gangs and typically maintain a low profile to avoid law enforcement scrutiny. Asian gang members are known to prey on their own race and often develop a relationship with their victims before victimizing them. (NGIC, 2011, p. 18)

However, the gang structure is changing as some law enforcement agencies attribute recent Asian gang membership to the recruitment of non-Asian members to compete more effectively with other street gangs for territory and dominance of illicit markets. In fact, Asian gang members in California are reported to maintain marijuana cultivation houses and pay members of the Asian community to reside in them (NGIC, 2011).

Native American Gangs

Native American gangs are another type of gang that provide a unique challenge for law enforcement and those interested in examining the extent of the problem on Indian reservations. First, tribal police are relatively small when compared to the geographic size of their jurisdiction. For example, there are currently over 200 Navajo Nation police officers responsible for patrolling over 27,000 square miles. Second, Native Americans are typically not open to outside researchers to conduct studies on Indian Reservations. Lastly, national-level gangs such as the Bloods, Crips, Norteños, Sureños, and many Mexican drug cartels are using Indian Reservation as a base to move drugs because of the lack of police presence and the vastness of the land (FBI, 2011).

The documentation of Native American gangs is sparse, as most studies did not emerge until the 1990s, and focused on individual tribes on Indian Reservations (see Hailer & Hart, 1999; Henderson, Kunitz, & Levy, 1999; Nielsen, Zion, & Hailer, 1998). It was not until 2000 that the first comprehensive study focusing on gangs in Indian Country was initiated by the National Youth Gang Center (currently known as the National Gang Center; see Major & Egley, 2002). Major and Egley (2002) reported that 74% of law enforcement serving tribal areas had not experienced gang problems until after 1990. Today, estimates on the number of Native American gangs are sketchy or outdated as gathering data has proven to be difficult for researchers and law-enforcement officials. Although there had been substantial anecdotal evidence of increasing gang activity among American Indian populations, no recent national studies provided reliable data about the levels of participation (Clarke, 2002). However, what law enforcement and gang experts have noted is the Native American gang population has increased on Indian Reservations and in the U.S. prison system (Grant, 2013; NGIC, 2011).

Typically, Native American gang members emulate national-level gangs such as the Bloods, Crips, Norteños, and Sureños. They also borrow many of the common identifiers such as colors, signs, symbols, and names. However, some native gangs are formed specific to their culture and heritage such as the Native Mob and Native Pride, which both primarily operate in the Upper Midwest (North Dakota, Minnesota, South Dakota, and Wisconsin). The Native Mob and Native Pride were also originally formed in the U.S. prison system and then expanded onto reservations. Although most gangs in Indian Country are disorganized and lack significant structure, Native American gangs have provided national-level gangs and drug cartels a haven for drug trafficking because the police are understaffed and underfunded and large geographic areas of reservations make it difficult to patrol. National Native American Gang Specialist Christopher Grant, the former Chief of Detectives and Area Gang Task Force Commander for the Rapid City Police Department in South Dakota, provides a detailed perspective to the National American gang problem in Chapter 9.

Current Gang Trends

According to media and police reports, there are an estimated 850,000 to 1.4 million gang members in the United States and over 30,000 identified gangs. However, according to the National Gang Center (2015), which surveys law enforcement agencies annually regarding the number of active gang members in their jurisdictions, reported an 8.6% increase from 2013 to 2014. Unfortunately, the National Gang Center has not produced any recent reports data regarding gangs so much of the information is speculative. In the past decade, annual estimates of the number of gang members have averaged around 770,000 nationally. While the National Gang Center attempts to identify the number of gang members in the United States, other researchers suggest that there are an estimated 1,059,000 juvenile gang members alone, representing 2.0% (about 1 of every 50 juveniles) of persons between the ages of 5 and 17 years in the U.S. population (Pyrooz & Sweeten, 2015). Figure 1.1 shows the estimated number of gangs since 1996.

Figure 1.1:   Estimate of gang members in the U.S. National Gang Center.

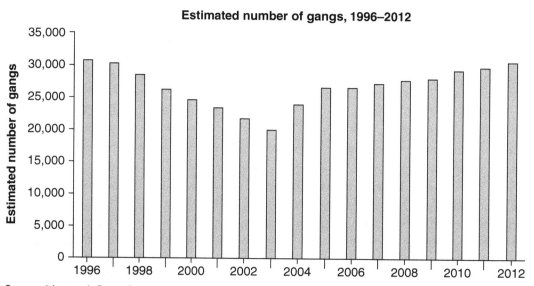

Source: National Gang Center (2015).

Concluding Thoughts

Gangs have been emerging and evolving in U.S. cities since the early 1800s. As gangs first emerged in New York City around the 1820s, the cities of Chicago and Los Angeles were not far behind. Immigration was the impetus to help create local gangs but eventually racial and ethnic differences, social conditions, and violence contributed to the formation of larger and more sophisticated gangs. Since New York City, Chicago, and Los Angeles are most noted for their gang activities and the birth of some famous street gangs like the Forty Thieves, Dead Rabbits, Pug Uglies, the Bloods, the Crips, Gangster Disciples, Vice Lords, and Latin Kings, it was not until the late 1970s and early 1980s that the South would begin to experience a significant presence of gangs. New waves of immigration also gave birth to hybrid and other types of gangs, and researchers and law enforcement officials began to take notice of Asian and Native American gangs. Socioeconomic conditions, racial tension, immigration, migration, cultural clashes, industry, and peer relationships all have played a part in the emergence of gang life in the United States.

Most gangs tend to be organized by geography and many are formed around racial or ethnic origin and heritage. One very distinct feature about gangs is that they are predominately male. According to Campbell (1990), males make up the vast majority of gang membership, but female participation in gangs is increasing. Gangs tend to concentrate in communities where there is low-income, public-housing projects and in the urban section of the city. It is no secret that these areas provide peer associations that take on great importance for adolescents. Today, the formation of gangs is an extension of those early immigrants who formed gangs because they needed to support one another and also to ensure that the right politicians would win elections, always for a price. Early immigrants faced many obstacles adjusting to life in America and politics was one way to get ahead in life. Today, adolescent peer groups join gangs for the need of peer acceptance, belonging, safety, power, and the excitement (Spergel et al., 1994). Gangs are also more widespread and diverse and are now found in urban, suburban, and rural settings.

As distinct as each gang region is in the United States from one another, the culture of the gang is similar. The world of gangs is engulfed by drugs, weapons, violence, and money. Each day, law enforcement combats the growing gang problem in large and small communities alike. Nonetheless, each region's gang culture is continually impacted by waves of immigrants and U.S. border policy politics, primarily in the West and Southern states that border Mexico. These regional differences clearly show that one should not assume that the gang dynamics are the same across each region. In fact, as gang scholar and expert James Howell (2012) has sternly expressed, "sweeping generalizations are ill-advised" (p. 25).

Discussion Points and Questions

1. What role did the racial/ethnic conflict play in New York, Chicago, Los Angeles, and the South in the development of street gangs?

2. How and why is immigration important for the emergence of gangs in any particular area?

3. Why is gang emergence in the South different from the cities discussed?

4. What impact did sociodemographics have on the emergence of gangs?

5. What impact did politics have on the emergence of gangs?

Web Links

Federal Bureau of Investigation—Gangs:
http://www.fbi.gov/about-us/investigate/vc_majorthefts/gangs

National Gang Center (formerly the National Youth Gang Center):
http://www.nationalgangcenter.gov/

National Gang Crime Research Center:
http://www.ngcrc.com/

Office of Juvenile Justice and Delinquency Prevention:
http://www.ojjdp.gov/

REFERENCES

ABCNews. (2012). Hidden America: Don't shoot I want grow up: Statistics surrounding gang violence in Chicago. Retrieved from https://abcnews.go.com/Nightline/fullpage/chicago-gang-violence-numbers-17509042.

Adamson, C. (2000). Defensive localism in white and black: A comparative history of European-American and African-American youth gangs. *Ethnic and Racial Studies, 23*(2), 272–298.

Alford, H. (2004). The Zoot Suit: Its history and influence. *Fashion Theory: The Journal of Dress, Body & Culture, 8*(2), 225–236.

Allen, J. P., & Turner, E. (2013). Ethnic change and enclaves in Los Angeles. *Association of American Geographers.* Retrieved from http://www.aag.org/cs/news_detail?pressrelease.id=2058

Allender, D. M. (2001). Gangs in Middle America. Are they a threat? *FBI Law Enforcement Bulletin, 70*(12), 1–35. Retrieved from https://www.hsdl.org/?view&did=456866.

Alonso, A. A. (2004). Racialized identities and the formation of Black gangs in Los Angeles. *Urban Geography, 25*(7), 658–674.

Anbinder, T. (2002). *Five points: The nineteenth-century New York City neighborhood that invented tap dance, stole elections and became the world's most notorious slum.* New York, NY: Free Press.

Armstrong, K. (1919, July 27). The 1919 race riots. Thirty-eight people are killed after an invisible line is crossed. *Chicago Tribune Company, LLC.* Retrieved from http://www.chicagotribune.com/news/politics/chi-chicagodays-raceriots-story,0,1206660.story

Arredondo, G. F. (2004). Navigating: Ethno-racial currents, Mexicans in Chicago 1919-1939. *Journal of Urban History, 30,* 399–427.

Asbury, H. (1927). *The gangs of New York: An informal history of the New York underworld.* London, England: Arrow Books.

Barrett, J. R., & Roediger, D. R. (2005). The Irish and the "Americanization" of the "new immigrants" in the streets and in the churches of the urban United States, 1900–1930. *Journal of American Ethnic History, 24*(4), 3–33.

Belitz, J., & Valdez, D. (1994). Clinical issues in the treatment of Chicano male gang youth. *Hispanic Journal of Behavioral Sciences, 16*(1), 57–74.

Bell, C. C., & Jenkins, E. J. (1991). Traumatic stress and children. *Journal of Health Care for the Poor and Underserved, 2*(1), 175–185.

Brenhoff, A. (2017, December 6). Behind LA's dramatic decline in gang violence. Huffington Post. Retrieved from https://www.huffpost.com/entry/gang-violence-decline_n_6656840

Bogardus, E. (1943). Gangs of Mexican-American youth. *Sociology and Social Research, 28,* 55–56.

Bourgois, P. (2003). *In search of respect: Selling crack in El Barrio* (2nd ed.). New York, NY: Cambridge University Press.

Campbell, A. (1990). Female participation in gangs. In C. R. Huff (Ed.), *Gangs in America* (pp. 163–182). Newbury Park, CA: SAGE.

Chapman, B. & Honan, K. (2019, November 6). Gang-related crimes drive up murders, shootings in New York City; but crime levels remain at historically low levels in the city. Wall Street Journal (online), New York, N.Y.

Chicago Police Department. (2011). *2011 Chicago Murder Analysis.* Retrieved from http://home.chicagopolice.org/wp-content/uploads/2014/12/2011-Murder-Report.pdf

Chin, K. (1990). Gang violence in Chinatown. In C. R. Huff (Ed.), *Gangs in America* (pp. 129–145). Newbury Park, CA: SAGE.

Clarke, A. S. (2002). Social and emotional distress among American Indian and Alaska Native students: Research findings. *ERIC Digest*, 1–8. Retrieved from http://files.eric.ed.gov/fulltext/ED459988.pdf

Cooley, W. (2011). Stones run it: Taking back control of organized crime in Chicago, 1940–1975. *Journal of Urban History, 37*(6), 911–932.

Cureton, S. R. (2009). Something wicked this way comes: A historical account of black gangsterism offers wisdom and warning for African American leadership. *Journal of Black Studies, 40*(2), 347–361.

Davis, M. (1992). *City of quartz: Excavating the future in Los Angeles.* London, England: Vintage.

Decker, S. H., & Van Winkle, B. (1996). Life in the gang: Family, friends, and violence. In A. Egley, C. L. Maxson, J. Miller, & M. W. Klein (Eds.), *The modern gang reader* (3rd ed., pp. 14–19). Los Angeles, CA: Roxbury.

Destefano, A. M. (2013). New York City murder rate in 2013 falling to historic low, says NYPD. *Newsday.* Retrieved from http://www.huffingtonpost.com/2013/07/03/new-york-city-murder-rate-2013-low-nypd_n_3537832.html

Diamond, A. J. (2005). Gangs. In the "Encyclopedia of Chicago." Chicago, IL: Chicago Historical Society. Retrieved from http://www.encyclopedia.chicagohistory.org/pages/497.html

Dunn, J. (1999). *Los Angeles Crips and Bloods: Past and Present.* Ethics of Development in a global Environment (EDGE). Poverty & Prejudice: Gangs of All Colors. Retrieved from https://web.stanford.edu/class/e297c/poverty_prejudice/gangcolor/lacrips.htm

Edwards, W. (2013). *The real gangs of New York. New York, NY:* Absolute Crime Books.

Federal Bureau of Investigation [FBI]. (2011). *National gang threat assessment, emerging trends.* Washington, DC: U.S. Department of Justice, Federal Bureau of Investigation, National Gang Intelligence Center. Retrieved from http://www.fbi.gov/stats-services/publications/2011-national-gang-threat-assessment/2011-national-gang-threat-assessment-emerging-trends

Fernández, L. (2005). From the near west side to 18th Street: Mexican community formation and activism in mid-twentieth century Chicago. *Journal of the Illinois State Historical Society, 98*, 162–183.

Ferranti, S. (2015, August 18). How New York gang culture is changing. *Vice.* Retrieved from https://www.vice.com/en_us/article/5gj9kb/how-new-york-citys-gang-culture-is-changing-818

Gangs. (1927). *Time, 9*(13), 11.

Garcia, M. T. (1981). *Desert immigrants: The Mexicans of El Paso, 1880–1920.* New Haven, CT: Yale University Press.

Gazzar, B. (2017, March 21). LAPD says gang-related crime in West San Fernando Valley has spiked since 2014. *Los Angeles Daily News.* Retrieved from https://www.dailynews.com/2017/03/21/lapd-says-gang-related-crime-in-west-san-fernando-valley-has-spiked-since-2014/

Gibson, C., & Jung, K. (2006). *Historical census statistics on the foreign-born population of the United States: 1850 to 2000* (Population Division Working Paper No. 81). Washington, DC: U.S. Bureau of the Census. Retrieved from http://www.census.gov/population/www/documentation/twps0081/twps0081.pdf

Glenn, M. (2014, April 17). Gang members soar past 100,000 in Texas. *Houston Chronicle.* Retrieved from http://www.houstonchronicle.com/news/houston-texas/houston/article/Gang-members-soar-past-100-000-in-Texas-5411969.php

Grant, C. (2013). *Native American involvement in the gang subculture: Current trends & dynamics.* Washington, DC: Community Corrections Institute, Bureau of Justice Assistance, Office of Justice Programs, U.S. Department of Justice.

Greenan, S., Britz, M. T., Rush, J., & Barker, T. (2000). *Gangs: An international approach.* Upper Saddle River, NJ: Prentice Hall.

Hagedorn, J. M. (2006). Race not space: A revisionist history of gangs in Chicago. *Journal of African American History, 91*(2), 194–208.

Hagedorn, J. M., Aspholm, R., Córdova, T., Papachristos, A. V., & Williams, L. (2019, April 16). Chicago's gangs have changed. Our violence intervention strategies should too. *Chicago Reporter.* Retrieved from https://www.chicagoreporter.com/chicagos-gangs-have-changed-our-violence-intervention-strategies-should-too/

Hailer, J. A., & Hart, C. B. (1999). A new breed of warrior: The emergence of American Indian youth gangs. *Journal of Gang Research, 7*(1), 23–33.

Haskins, J. (1974). *Street gangs: Yesterday and today.* Wayne, PA: Hastings Books.

Henderson, E., Kunitz, S. J., & Levy, J. E. (1999). The origins of Navajo youth gangs. *American Indian Culture and Research Journal, 23*(3), 243–264.

History.com Staff. (2009). *The Chicago race riots of 1919.* Retrieved from http://www.history.com/topics/black-history/chicago-race-riot-of-1919

Howell, J. C. (2007). Menacing or mimicking? Realities of youth gangs. *Juvenile and Family Court Journal, 58*(2), 39–50.

Howell, J. C. (2012). *Gangs in America's communities.* Thousand Oaks, CA: SAGE.

Howell, J. C., & Griffiths, E. (2016). *Gangs in America's communities* (2nd ed.). Los Angeles, CA: SAGE.

Howell, J. C., & Moore, J. P. (2010). History of street gangs in the United States. *Institute for Intergovernmental Research, National Gang Center Bulletin, 4,* 1–25. Retrieved from http://www.nationalgangcenter.gov/Content/Documents/History-of-Street-Gangs.pdf

Illinois State Police. (1992, April). Illinois gangs. *Criminal Intelligence Bulletin, 49.* Springfield, IL: Author.

Knox, G. W., & Papachristos, A. V. (2002). *The vice lords: A gang profile analysis.* Peotone, IL: New Chicago School Press.

LAPD. (2020), Gangs. *Official Site of the Los Angeles Police Department.* Retrieved from http://www.lapdonline.org/get_informed/content_basic_view/1396

Lessoff, A., & Connolly, J. J. (2013). From political insult to political theory: The boss, the machine, and the pluralist city. *Journal of Policy History, 25*(2), 139–172.

Lopez, D. A., & O'Donnell-Brummett, P. (2003). Gang membership and acculturation: ARS-MA-II and choloization. *Crime & Delinquency, 49*(4), 627–642.

Major, A. K., & Egley, A. (2002). *2000 survey of youth gangs in Indian country.* Washington, DC: U.S. Department of Justice, Office of Justice Programs, Office of Juvenile Justice & Delinquency Prevention, National Youth Gang Center Fact Sheet.

Maxson, C. L. (1998). *Gang members on the move.* Juvenile Justice Bulletin. Youth Gang Series. Washington, DC: Office of Juvenile Justice and Delinquency Prevention.

Mazón, M. (1984). *The zoot-suit riots: The psychology of symbolic annihilation.* Austin: University of Texas Press.

McPherson, J. A. (1966). Blackstone Rangers. *Atlantic, 223*(5), 74–83.

Miller, B. J. (2008). The struggle over redevelopment at Cabrini-Green, 1989–2004. *Journal of Urban History, 34*(6), 944–960.

Miller, W. B. (1975). *Violence by youth gangs and youth groups as a crime problem in major American cities.* Washington, DC: U.S. Department of Justice, Office of Justice Programs, Office of Juvenile Justice and Delinquency Prevention.

Miller, W. B. (2001). *The growth of youth gang problems in the United States: 1970–1998.* Washington, DC: Office of Juvenile Justice and Delinquency Prevention. Retrieved from https://www.ncjrs.gov/pdffiles1/ojjdp/181868-1.pdf and https://www.ncjrs.gov/pdffiles1/ojjdp/181868-2.pdf

Monkkonen, E. H. (2001). *Murder in New York City.* Los Angeles: University of California Press.

Moore, N. Y., & Williams, L (2011). *The Almighty Black P-Stone Nation: The rise, fall, and resurgence of an American gang.* Chicago, IL: Chicago Review Press.

Morgan, K. A., & Shelley, W. W. (2014). *Juvenile street gangs. The Encyclopedia of Criminology and Criminal Justice.* Malden, MA: Wiley-Blackwell.

National Gang Center. (2015). *National youth gang survey analysis: Measuring the extent of gang problems.* Retrieved from http://www.nationalgangcenter.gov/Survey-Analysis/Measuring-the-Extent-of-Gang-Problems#estimatednumbergangs

National Gang Intelligence Center. (2009). *National gang threat assessment: 2009.* Washington, DC: U.S. Department of Justice, Federal Bureau of Investigation.

National Gang Intelligence Center. (2011). *National gang threat assessment—Emerging trends.* Washington, DC: U.S. Department of Justice, Federal Bureau of Investigation.

National Geographic Channel (NatGeo). (2009). *Bloods and Crips LA Gangs—History of the Crips.* Retrieved from http://channel.nationalgeographic.com/videos/history-of-the-crips/

Nielsen, M. O., Zion, J. W., & Hailer, J. A. (1998). Navajo Nation gang formation and intervention initiatives. In K. Hazlehurst & C. Hazlehurst (Eds.), *Gangs and youth subcultures: International explorations* (pp. 141–163). New Brunswick, NJ: Transaction Publishers.

O'Kane, J. M. (2009). *The crooked ladder: Gangsters, ethnicity, and the American dream.* New Brunswick, NJ: Transaction Publishers. (*Original work published* 1992)

Pagán, E. O. (2003). *Murder at the sleepy lagoon: Zoot suits, race, riot in Wartime L.A.* Chapel Hill: The University of North Carolina Press.

Peiss, K. (2011). *Zoot suit: The enigmatic career of an extreme style.* Philadelphia: University of Pennsylvania Press.

Perkins, U. E. (1987). *Explosion of Chicago's black street gangs: 1900 to the present.* Chicago, IL: Third World Press.

Pike, L. O. (1873). *A history of crime in England: Illustrating the changes of the laws in the progress of civilisation: Written from the public records and other contemporary evidence* (pp. 274–277). London, England: Smith, Elder.

Pincus, F. L., & Ehrlich, H. J. (1999). Immigration. In F. L. Pincus & H. J. Ehrlich (Eds.), *Race and ethnic conflict* (pp. 223–228). Boulder, CO: Westview Press.

Pizarroa, J. M., & McGloin, J. M. (2006). Explaining gang homicides in Newark, New Jersey collective behavior or social disorganization? *Journal of Criminal Justice, 34*(2), 195–207.

Pyrooz, D. C., & Sweeten, G. (2015). Gang membership between ages 5 and 17 years in the United States. *Journal of Adolescent Health, 56*(4), 414–419.

Ramirez, C. S. (2009). *The woman in the zoot suit: Gender, nationalism, and the cultural politics of memory.* Durham, NC: Duke University Press.

Riis, J. A. (1997). *How the other half lives: Studies among the tenements of New York.* New York, NY: Penguin. (Original work published 1890)

Rodríguez, J & Martínez, R. (2017, March 18). The gangs of L.A.: What ever happened to the gangbanger? *New York Times.* Retrieved from https://www.nytimes.com/2017/03/18/opinion/sunday/the-gangs-of-la.html?auth=login-email&login=email

Rubel, A. J. (1965). The Mexican-American palomilla. *Anthropological Linguistics, 7*(4), 92–97.

Sachems & Sinners: An informal history of Tammany Hall. (1955). *Time, 66*(8), 16–18. Retrieved from *http://content.time.com/time/magazine/article/0,9171,807536,00.html*

Sale, R. T. (1971). *The Blackstone Rangers.* New York, NY: Popular Library.

Sánchez, G. J. (1995). *Becoming Mexican American: Ethnicity, culture, and identity in Chicano Los Angeles, 1900–1945.* New York, NY: Oxford University Press.

Sante, L. (1991). *Low life: Lures and snares of old New York.* New York, NY: Vintage Books.

Shelden, R. G., Tracy, S. K., & Brown, W. B. (1997). *Youth gangs in American society.* Belmont, CA: Wadsworth.

Spergel, I., Chance, R., Ehrensaft, K., Regulus, T., Kane, C., Laseter, R., . . . Oh, S. (1994). *Gang suppression and intervention: Community models.* Washington, DC: U.S. Department of Justice, Office of Juvenile Justice and Delinquency Prevention.

Spergel, I. A., & Grossman, S. F. (1997). The little village project: A community approach to the gang problem. *Social Work, 42*(5), 456–470.

Starbuck, D., Howell, J. C., & Lindquist, D. J. (2001). *Hybrid and other modern gangs.* U.S. Department of Justice, Office of Justice Programs, Office of Juvenile Justice and Delinquency Prevention. Retrieved from https://www.nationalgangcenter.gov/Content/Documents/Hybrid-and-Other-Modern-Gangs.pdf

Sullivan, J. P., & Silverstein, M. E. (1995). Disaster within us: Urban conflict and street gang violence in Los Angeles. *Journal of Gang Research, 2*(4), 11–30.

Sutherland, E. H. (1924). *Criminology.* Philadelphia, PA: J. B. Lippincott.

The Richest.com. (2014, July 26). *The 6 most gang infested cities in America.* Retrieved from https://www.therichest.com/most-shocking/the-most-gang-infested-cities-in-america/

Thrasher, F. M. (2000). *The gang: A study of 1,313 gangs in Chicago.* Chicago, IL: University of Chicago Press, New Chicago School Press. (Original work published 1927)

Tolnay, S. E. (2003). The African American "great migration" and beyond. *Annual Review of Sociology, 29,* 209–232. doi:10.1146/annurev.soc.29.010202.1

Torres, A. (1995). *Between melting pot and mosaic: African Americans and Puerto Ricans in the New York political economy.* Philadelphia, PA: Temple University Press.

Toy, C. (1992). Coming out to play: Reasons to join and participate in Asian gangs. *The Gang Journal, 1*(1), 13–29.

U.S. Department of Justice. (2015). *Criminal street gangs.* Retrieved from http://www.justice.gov/criminal-ocgs/gallery/criminal-street-gangs

Vigil, J. D. (1983). Chicano gangs: One response to Mexican urban adaptation in the Los Angeles area. *Urban Anthropology, 12*(1), 45–75.

Vigil, J. D. (1990). Cholos and gangs: Culture change and street youth in Los Angeles. In C. R. Huff (Ed.), *Gangs in America* (pp. 116–128). Newbury Park, CA: SAGE.

Vigil, J. D. (1998). *From Indians to Chicanos: The dynamics of Mexican-American culture.* Prospect Heights, IL: Waveland Press.

Vigil, D. (2002). *Rainbow of gangs: Street cultures in the mega-city.* Austin: University of Texas Press.

Vigil, J. D., & Long, J. M. (1990). Emic and etic perspectives on gang culture: The Chicano case. In C. R. Huff (Ed.), *Gangs in America* (pp. 55–68). Newbury Park, CA: SAGE.

Walker, R. (n.d.). *Crips and bloods history. A firsthand account of their real history and the myths surrounding the origin and founders of the gangs.* Retrieved from http://www.gangsorus.com/crips_bloods_history.htm

Zevitz, R. G., & Takata, S. R. (1992). Metropolitan gang influence and the emergence of group delinquency in a regional community. *Journal of Criminal Justice, 20*(2), 93–106.

Chapter 2

Theories of Gangs and Gang Membership

Introduction

A question often asked is 'why do kids join gangs?' and the answer is never simple. Understanding and explaining juvenile or adult gang behavior can be addressed in many forms. These explanatory schemes or models, or theories can come from the biological, psychological, sociological, political, economic, anthropologic, and environmental perspectives. In the world of street gangs, these are all potential reasons as to why juveniles join and commit crimes while in a gang. Each of the theories discussed in this chapter fall within the field of criminology. Furthermore, it is essential that practitioners in the field of criminal justice understand the theoretical aspects of crime to ensure a better understanding of the relationship between crime, gangs, and theory.

So what theories explain the gang phenomena? The answer is there are many possibilities. The reasons for gangs and gang members committing crimes are numerous. Since most gang activity is related to juvenile delinquency, one could argue that gang-involvement is correlated with single-parent households or where the youth lives. Other reasons for engaging in gang activity is youth peer relationships, drugs and alcohol, lack of education, or the influences of the media. Regardless of the explanation, the theories listed in this chapter offer an attempt to explain the gang phenomenon. In order to answer the original question of 'why do kids join gangs?' – the answer is "well, it depends". It depends on many factors that are worth exploring in order to gain a better understanding of the gang problem in the United States.

Since Thrasher's (1927) study of gangs, criminal justice officials have continued to address such gang issues as: (1) why are gangs formed, (2) why do individuals stay in gangs, and (3) what is to be done legislatively to ensure public safety from gangs? The Office of Juvenile Justice and Delinquency (OJJDP) has addressed these questions over several annual publications. The gang problem in the United States is neither new, nor unusual, as outlined in Chapter 1; and each theoretical approach to explaining gangs is unique to the academic discipline from which it comes. In dealing with gang-related issues, having a better understanding of the the-oretical explanations offered by the academic disciples within criminology provides students, law enforcement officials, lawyers, and criminal justice practitioners with more ammunition to deal with gangs and gang members.

Gangs and Delinquency: An Overview

Most delinquent acts committed by youth are not gang members; and gang membership is not necessarily synonymous with delinquent behavior. That being said, the gang problem has existed for over a century impacting communities, schools and families alike, and law enforcement and the court system is inundated with cases of gang violence. The problem with identifying gangs is that gangs are not always committing crime. Gang members are not in a constant cycle of violence as often perpetuated by movies, television shows, and the news. In fact, gangs do much less. Prominent gang researcher Malcolm Klein (1997) stated this about gangs and gang members:

> For the most part, gang members do very little—sleep, get up late, hang around, brag a lot, eat again, drink, hang around some more. It's a boring life; the only thing that is equally boring is being a researcher watching gang members (p. 11).

As Huff (1989) observed, gang members spend more time in deviant adolescent behavior (skipping school, disobeying parents), and only the more delinquent gangs and gang members engage in serious criminal behavior. Fagan (1990) surveyed samples of students and dropouts in Chicago, Los Angeles, and San Diego and observed involvement of both gang and non-gang youths in delinquency and drug use. However, higher percent of the gang members in his sample were involved in delinquency and substance abuse than non-gang members. In a National Institute of Justice survey, city police departments reported far more gang members than gang-related incidents (Curry et al, 1994). Thornberry, Krohn, Lizzotte, and Chard-Wi-erschem (1993) conducted a longitudinal study to compare youths' crime patterns prior to, during, and after gang involvement. They found that gang members did not have higher rates of delinquency or drug use before entering the gang, but once they became members, their rates increased substantially; and the rates of delinquency decreased when gang members left the gang. Esbensen and his associates had similar conclusions from their studies of youths in high-risk urban neighborhoods. Gang members are already delinquent before joining the gang, but gang membership does slightly increase their delinquent activity (Esbensen & Huizinga, 1993). Gang members were found to be similar to youths who were self-reported serious offenders but were not members of a gang (Esbensen, Huizinga, & Weiher, 1995).

Nonetheless, when gangs are not doing what Klein has observed and others have noted, gangs and gang members are creating havoc in communities and schools with acts of violence and terror. According to the National Gang Center (2014), about half of all homicides in Chicago are gang-related. In New York City, the NYPD has reported that while the overall crime rate continues to drop, gang-related crimes have led to an increase in murders and shootings in New York City in 2019 (Chapman & Honan, 2019). Finally, James Howell, a senior research associate at the National Gang Center attributes the rise of gangs and gang-related violence in the U.S. to larger gangs breaking up into warring factions. According to Howell, there has been an "8 percent increase in number of gangs, an 11 percent increase in members and a 23 percent increase in gang-related homicides" (Axelrod, 2015).

Why Youth Join Gangs

Why join a gang? The formation of juvenile gangs, or any gang for that matter, is an extension of adolescent peer groups. Youth join gangs for a variety of reasons: the need for affiliation (i.e., peer acceptance, belonging, and recognition); lack of positive role models; status and power; safety and security, the thrill, excitement and power; boredom; family history of gang involvement; low socioeconomic status; the community norm – 'everyone does it' mentality; a limited view of the world; cultural barriers and prejudices; lack of employment possibilities and education; media glorification of gangs; and access to drugs, money and girls. Even hip-hop/rapper Snoop Dogg, a constant promoter of the Los Angeles Crip gang culture, is quoted in an interview with DJ Lantern on Invasion Radio saying:

> *"What people don't understand is joining a gang ain't bad, it's cool, it's fine. When you in the hood, joining a gang it's cool because all your friends are in the gang, all your family's in the gang. We're not just killing people every night, we're just hanging out, having a good time."* (For full interview see, https://www.youtube.com/watch?v=U0OgLyb8Y_Y or https://www.brainyquote.com/quotes/snoop_dogg_436685)

The formation of gangs are more widespread and diverse than the stereotypical group of lower-class minority youth from inner-city urban areas. Gangs are now found in smaller cities, suburban areas, and even youth in small town and rural communities are emulating gang behavior. It is still true that the majority of gangs are located in larger cities, primarily in the lower socioeconomic urban areas. Though, because most youth from those areas do *not* join gangs, additional factors are required to explain why youth join gangs. Researchers have identified a number of *characteristics or risk factors* that are associated with *gang membership* (Esbensen, 2000). The first are *individual and family demographics.* Gang members are primarily male, though females may account for up to one-third of youth gang members (Esbensen & Winfree, 1998), and join gangs and participate for reasons that differ from male members (Curry, 1998). Gangs in urban areas are believed to be primarily African American or Hispanic, but Whites accounted for 30% of gang members in small cities and rural counties (Esbensen, 2000). Some gang youth do come from two-parent families, but gangs are made up primarily of minority youth residing in single-parent households. The second characteristics are *personal attributes.* Gang members have more antisocial beliefs (Hill, Howell, Hawkins, & Battin-Pearson, 1999) and more delinquent self-concepts. Gang members tend to be more impulsive, engage in more risk-seeking behavior, were less committed to school, and have less communication and attachment with their parents (Esbensen, 2000). The third characteristics are *peer group, school, and community factors.* The strongest predictor of gang membership is a high level of interaction with and influence of antisocial peers (Battin-Peterson, Thornberry, Hawkins, & Kroh, 1998). Gang youth are less committed to school than non-gang youth (Hill et al., 1999). Community factors predominate gang research, and studies indicate that poverty, unemployment, the absence of meaningful jobs, and social disorganization contribute to the presence of gangs (Fagan, 1990; Huff, 1990). Gangs are clearly more prevalent in urban areas and are more likely to emerge in neighborhoods characterized by economic distress and social disorganization (Esbensen, 2000).

Crime Theory: A Brief

Street gang literature serves as one of the best illustrations for researchers to lean toward or adopt when addressing gang dynamic paradigms (Short, 1985). Katz and Jackson-Jacobs (2004) stated that the study of gangs may be the most frustrating of all challenges in crime research. Perhaps the reason is that the range of gang theories extend from macro-level sociological factors (e.g., social disorganization, poverty), to micro-level explanations focused on social interactions and processes (e.g., differential association), to individual-level variables (e.g., self-control and social control (McGloin & Decker, 2010). As an example, during Short and Strodtbeck's (1965) Chicago field research, they recognized the importance of considering all levels of crime explanation with gang dynamics. Relying on data sources which included observations, Short and Strodtbeck initially planned to investigate individual and macro-level explanatory factors (e.g., social control and differential association, respectively). However, it became clear to the authors that group processes were at minimum as accountable, if not more accountable, for generating a majority of the delinquent conduct. As an example, Short and Strodtbeck learned that aggression between gangs was often initiated by gang leaders who believed that their status was vulnerable. Short and Strodtbeck's findings emphasized the need for incorporation among levels of explanation as a means to comprehend gang behavior.

Historically, the early schools of thought in the criminological practice were those of the Classical, Positivist, and Chicago schools of thought. The Classical School, most associated with the works of Beccaria and Bentham, involved the issues of *free will* and *human rights*. Bentham, concerned with the premise of *utilitarianism*, surmised that individuals weigh the *pains against the pleasures* with regard to committing a crime. In other words, Bentham felt that individuals were human calculators and weighed the pain of committing an illegal act versus the pleasure on the rewards of such an act. Furthermore, Bentham felt that the punishment should be greater than the pleasure obtained by the individual (see, for example, Bentham, 1879; Brunius, 1958; Mitchell, 1968). Positivists, associated with Lombroso, unlike the classical reformers, sought to explain the world around them. Positivist criminologists sought to explain behavior through observations. Delinquent behaviors were determined by biological, psychological, and social traits. Positivists' collected data to explain individual types and social phenomena. Finally, the Chicago school (social structural theories) focused upon human behavior, which is a result of the physical environment in which an individual resides (see, for example, Shaw & McKay, 1931, 1936, 1942). To categorize the wide range of criminological explanations is beyond the scope of this chapter. However, the basic principal theories regarding gang activity and criminality are presented below.

Gang Crime Theory: Social Structure

Social structure theorists claim that forces such as social disorganization, status frustration, and cultural deviance lead lower-class youths to become involved in delinquent behavior. Social structural theories of crime and delinquency are varied, but center on the main themes of social structure and institutions to maintain that social structure. Social structure refers to the order of society (i.e., the relationships between individuals, groups, organizations, etc.) and how that order influences one's daily activities. The institutions that help maintain the social structure include the family, religion, school, government, and the media. Social structural theories address crime and delinquency as an effect on individuals. These theories are less concerned with why youth become delinquent than with why certain ecological areas, that is, the distribution of crime and delinquency within a geographical area experience high delinquency rates. Therefore, we can easily apply these social structure explanations of delinquency to gang dynamics. Again, these explanations focus on the social and cultural environment in which adolescents grow up and on the subcultural groups with which they become involved (i.e., gangs). Social structure theorists, relying on official statistics as the primary measure of crime, claim that such forces as cultural deviance, social disorganization, and status frustration lead lower-class youths to become involved in delinquent behavior. Three categories of social structure explanations are (1) *social disorganization theory*, (2) *strain theory*, and (3) *subculture theory*.

Social Disorganization Theory (SDT)

SDT emerged as a result of environmental and social conditions that materialized at the turn of the 20th century in Chicago which included high rates of juvenile delinquency and various social problems within the city. Early sociologists, including Thomas and Znaniecki (1918) and Park and Burgess (1924), set out to account for the high levels of deviant and criminal behavior. Their conclusion was that juvenile delinquency and crime is caused by the nature of the environment in which people live (e.g., immigration levels, poverty, etc.), which leads to higher crime and delinquency rates.

Thrasher's 1927 work is thought as the origination of SDT as applied to youth gangs. Thrasher believed that gangs originated through the effort of boys to create a society for themselves. This society satisfied their needs that were otherwise not being met through their communities, schools, and families and emerged largely from environmental and social conditions. As a result, high rates of juvenile delinquency and various social problems within Chicago occurred. SDT would then consider gang involvement as an alternative possibility for youth who otherwise lack social connectedness with personal and community institutions. This lack of connection can originate from a number of entities: immigration, migration, political, economic or social changes, rapid industrialization or urbanization, radical shifts in the labor market, community division, family disruption, or the failure of schools to meet the needs of a changing population (Jones, Roper, Stys, Wilson, & Correctional Service Canada, Research Branch, 2004).

Shaw and McKay (1942) used official police statistics and topographic maps to explain that delinquency and gang formation occur in an area around the city center, which was an area generally in a state of social instability (i.e., disorganization). They found that regardless of the individuals who lived in this area, the crime rates remained constant over time, illustrating that it was the social disorganization, which they defined as urbanization, residential mobility, poverty, and ethnic and racial heterogeneity were considered the key contributing factors to gang formation and maintenance (Shaw & McKay, 1931, 1936, 1942). This theory directs attention *not to* individual responsibility for crime, but rather to the need for adequate housing, quality public schools, and equal employment opportunities. Therefore, SDT would stress that gang formation is not abnormal, but a normal response by normal individuals to abnormal social situations.

Strain Theory

Strain theory is the second type of social structure theory. This theory explains deviant behavior as an unavoidable outcome of the strain individuals experience when society does not provide adequate and approved means to achieve culturally valued goals. Strain and social disorganization are similar because they emphasize the relationship between social variables such as poverty, economic opportunity, and available goods and services to crime and delinquency. Merton's (1957) anomie theory acknowledged the strain that lower-class youth felt in attempting to achieve middle-class aspirations. Merton noted that the deviant response to strain was innovation and defined it as the use of illegitimate or unconventional means of obtaining the culturally valued goal.[1] As an example, when a society places cultural value on financial success (e.g., wealth), but only provides legally sanctioned means to achieve these goals; those excluded may turn to criminal means to attain. Strain theory would identify gang membership as a consequence of the discrepancy between financial success and a lack of means by which to achieve. Additionally, strain theory assumes that all youth subscribe to similar financial goals. However, many youth do not possess legitimate resources with which to attain these goals, and in order for youth to compensate for a lack of means, these youth must resort to illegal activity. Research has depicted gang members as working class youth who experience strain resulting in status frustration, which may be resolved by the youth associating with similar likeminded youth, which organically leads to the formation of a delinquent subculture (i.e., a youth gang) where instant gratification, fighting, and destructive behavior become the new values (Bordua, 1961; Cohen, 1955; Cohen & Short, 1958; Goldstein, 1994).

Differential opportunity theory is yet another variation of strain theory. The *opportunity-structure theories* (Cloward & Ohlin, 1960) prompted government-funded policies such as "Head Start" and jobs programs for lower-class youth as a way to enhance educational and employment opportunities and reduce delinquency. Cloward and Ohlin (1960) proposed that gang affiliation was the result of lower-class boys lacking access to socially-defined goals. However, they argued that the type of gang that developed would depend on the type of area in which they developed, as even illegitimate means were unevenly distributed. The authors theorized that *criminal gangs* would evolve in stable neighborhoods and focus on crimes that reap large financial rewards, *conflict gangs* would develop in more transient neighborhoods and aim to achieve status through threat, and *retreatist gangs* develop in both types of neighborhoods and are composed of those individuals who did not qualify for the other two types of gangs (Cloward & Ohlin, 1960).

---

1. The four other responses are: conformity is the acceptance of both the culturally valued goals and the legitimate ways of pursuing and attaining them; ritualism is for those who pursue the legitimate means of attaining goals, but who set more humble and achievable goals for themselves; retreatism applies to people who reject the culturally valued goals of a society and reject the legitimate means of attaining them; and, rebellion applies to people that reject the culturally valued goals of a society and the legitimate means of attaining them, but instead of retreating, they attempt replacing both with different goals and means.

Robert Agnew (1992) extended Merton's theory of strain and anomie to better explain varieties of delinquent behavior through a *General Strain Theory*. Agnew identified three sources of strain: (1) *failure to achieve positively valued goals*, basically the same as Merton's (1938) theory of anomie, (2) strain caused by the *removal of positively valued stimuli* from the individual. Examples include the loss of a girl- or boyfriend, death of a loved one, divorce or separation of parents, or leaving friends and moving to a new neighborhood or school, and (3) strain as the *presentation of negative stimuli*, such as child abuse and neglect, physical punishment, family and peer conflict, stressful life conditions, school failure, and criminal victimization (Agnew, 1992, p. 57). Agnew's General Strain Theory has made an important contribution to explaining delinquency. The theory helps to explain how stressful incidents and sources of strain in the life course influence patterns of offending. There is ample research support for the general strain theory. Youth who report being "hassled" by peers, have bad peer relationships, experience victimization or similar "negative life events" are also the persons most likely to engage in delinquency (Agnew, Brezina, Wright, & Cullen, 2002; Agnew & White, 1992). Research shows that indicators of strain such as family breakup, unemployment, moving, feelings of dissatisfaction with friends and school, and other life stressors are positively related to delinquency (Aseltine, Gore & Gordon, 2000; Paternoster & Mazerolle, 1994).

Subculture Theory

The subculture theory, also referred to as cultural strain theory, of delinquency and gang development grew out of the strain theory and is based on the assumption that all youth share similar goals and economic aspirations. However, it differs in postulating that instead of striving to attain the same goals as middle-class youth, lower-class youth create their own, new, subculture in which to attain status. This subculture consists of norms and criteria that are suitable to a criminal lifestyle (e.g., hostility, achieving recognition through crime and hedonism). Honesty and hard work make little sense to youth growing up in a neighborhood where poverty, unemployment, and crime are part of life. Drug dealing and prostitution are viewed by many lower-class youth as a way to overcome unemployment and poverty. Youth learn to value being tough and "street smart." Using threats and physical attacks are preferred over verbal negotiation for resolving conflicts in some subcultures (Lawrence & Hesse, 2009). Walter Miller (1958) hypothesized that a far different set of values permeated lower-class structure and that these values naturally lead to increased levels of delinquent and gang involvement. He proposed six "focal concerns" that defined life for lower-class boys: fate, autonomy, smartness, toughness, excitement, and trouble. It is the commitment to these values and not to those of the dominant culture that contributed to problematic behavior. Miller's "focal concerns" accurately describe the attitudes and behaviors of many lower-class and even middle-class youth today. Getting into trouble is common among many youth, and a reason given for much delinquent activity is excitement ("because we were bored"). Poor school performance among lower-class students may be explained by the value placed on "street smarts" over being smart in the classroom; and one's life success being ruled by fate more than personal goals and achievements. Many youth carry guns to protect themselves, thus displaying their toughness and autonomy. The primary reason for weapons in schools is because youth who feel threatened and fearful believe they cannot depend on school officials for protection and must take matters into their own hands. Street-smart youth take care of themselves and do not depend on police for protection.

Coward and Ohlin (1960) suggested that delinquents are socialized within cohesive delinquent groups to hold values and attitudes that permit illegal behavior. The most frequently stressed variables in subculture formulations are delinquent associates and peer approval for delinquency (Segrave & Hastad, 1985). Albert Cohen (1955) proposed that working-class and lower-class boys develop frustrations about achieving middle-class standards that they are not equipped to meet. To resolve these status concerns, they turn to the group affiliation of the gang to set up their own value system that provides status for negative-based behaviors. Cohen asserts that this value system is transmitted throughout generations, fostering on ongoing gang subculture.

Gang Crime Theory: Social Process

Social process theories are a grouping of criminological theories that support explanations of why people engage in criminal behavior. It should be noted that social process explanations of delinquency focus *not on societal structures* but on social interactions between individuals and environmental influences that may contribute to delinquent behavior. The social process theories that will be presented include (1) *differential association* and (2) *social control theory*. Each of these theories has a specific explanation for why individuals engage in criminal acts, but they all hold that socialization is the key to understanding crime. Differential association theory holds that delinquency is a learned behavior as youth interact closely with other deviant youth. Control theory asserts that delinquency is more likely among youth who lack social bonds and positive social interactions among parents and peers.

Differential Association Theory

Proposed by Edwin Sutherland (1934) differential association theory hypothesizes that criminal behavior is learned through the interactions with other youth, expressly within intimate social groups. Not only are techniques taught, but so are the specific motives, drives, rationalizations, and attitudes behind the criminal activities. Thus, it is theorized that youth will lean toward or away from crime according to the norms and beliefs of their associates. The theory is founded on a number of propositions: (1) criminal behavior is learned, (2) criminal behavior is learned in interaction with other persons during the process of communication, (3) the principle part of the learning of criminal behavior occurs within intimate personal groups, (4) when criminal behavior is learned, the learning includes (a) techniques of committing the crime; and (b) the specific direction of motives, drives, rationalizations, and attitudes, (5) the specific direction of the motives and drives is learned from definitions of the legal codes as favorable or unfavorable, (6) a person becomes delinquent because of an excess of definitions favorable to violation of law over definitions unfavorable to violation of law, which is the principle of differential association, (7) differential association may vary in frequency, duration, priority, and intensity, (8) the process of learning criminal behavior by association with criminal and anti-criminal patterns involves all of the mechanisms that are involved in any other learning, and (9) while criminal behavior is an expression of general needs and values, it is not explained by those general needs and values since non-criminal behavior is an expression of the same needs and values (Sutherland & Cressey, 1970, pp. 75–77). Differential association has been substantiated with research indicating that criminal attitudes and associates are two of the most significant correlates of criminal conduct (see, for example, Andrews et al., 2012).

Sutherland's Differential Association theory remains an important explanation for juvenile delinquency and juvenile gang crime. It is difficult to argue against a principle that maintains crime is learned like any other behavior. On a positive note, this explanation also holds that youth are changeable and can be taught prosocial behavior. Delinquency prevention efforts may be effective when they are directed at reducing the criminal influence among groups of youth gangs. Sutherland's differential association theory has stimulated considerable research on explaining delinquent behavior. Burgess and Akers (1966) reformulated the differential association theory, and Akers's (1985) theory developed an explanation of deviant behavior according to a social learning approach. This is a "general social-psychological theory that offers an explanation of the full range of criminal and deviant behavior (onset, persistence, desistence, and change) and embraces social, nonsocial, and cultural factors operating to both motivate and control criminal behavior and to both promote and undermine conformity" (McGloin & Decker, 2010, p. 87; see also Akers, 1998).

Control Theory

Social control theory assumes that deviance is a natural part of the human experience and that everyone has the propensity to become involved in criminal behavior. Therefore, control theories begin with the premise that the way to understand delinquency is to know the characteristics of persons who conform, and *do not* engage in delinquency. The focal question therefore is *not* "Why do youth become delinquent?" but rather "Why do most youth not engage in repetitive, serious delinquency?" It attempts to explain why it is that some people conform to the moral order (the rules and regulations of society) while others deviate from it. In general, control theory postulates that those who do not become involved in gang activity possess a stronger bond with the moral order than those that do become involved.

Gresham Sykes and David Matza (1957) theorized that individuals used a variety of techniques to suspend their bond with societal values and become involved in criminality. They denied responsibility for the actions, denied that the crime caused any injury, denied that the crime had a true victim, and blamed the authority figures who were condemning them, or professed to serve loyalties more important than the rules of society (i.e., friendship). Walter Reckless (1961) held that internal factors such as self-control and external factors such as parental supervision, discipline, and social institutions help to "insulate" or "contain" persons from crime. Reckless and his associates emphasized that inner containment, or self-concept, was a major variable in steering youth away from delinquency (Reckless, Dinitz, & Kay, 1957). There are problems in developing operational definitions for a valid and reliable measure of self-concept, but studies have confirmed that the greater the self-esteem, the less likely a youth is to become involved in delinquent behavior (see, for example, Brezina & Topalli, 2012; Jensen, 1973; Ludwig & Pittman, 1999).

Travis Hirschi (1969) developed the most prominent social control theory based on self-report results of a large sample of youth. Hirschi explained the presence or absence of delinquent involvement based on four elements of the social bond: attachment, commitment, involvement, and belief. *Attachment* refers to the ties of affection and respect that youth have for family, friends, role models, employment, school, clubs, and will help youth avoid the temptation to commit delinquent acts. *Commitment* to socially acceptable activities and values, such as educational and employment goals, helps youth avoid delinquency by increasing the cost and risks involved. *Involvement* in conventional activities keeps youth occupied and reduces their opportunities to commit deviant acts. *Belief* refers to respect for the law and societal norms, and derives from close relations with other positive role models, especially parents. The theory has generated a considerable amount of research.

The nature of peer relationships has an intervening effect on parental attachment, school experiences, and delinquency. Attachment to peers does not necessarily mean less attachment to parents. It appears to depend on to whom one is attached, and the nature of one's peer attachments. Linden and Hackler (1973) found that self-reported delinquency was inversely related to ties to parents and conventional peers, but positively related to ties to deviant peers. Others suggest that parental attachment affects delinquency, which affects school performance, which in turn affects parental attachment (Liska & Reed, 1985, pp. 556, 557). Parents, not school, are the major institutional sources of delinquency control, for lower class more than middle class youth (Liska & Reed, 1985, pp. 557, 558). According to Hirschi's control theory, delinquents are less dependent on peers than are non-delinquents, a finding which has been supported by other research. In a study comparing non-delinquent high school students with a group of court-adjudicated students on supervision and also attending school, the delinquents scored higher on the *self-sufficient* scale while non-delinquents scored higher on *group dependence* (Lawrence, 1985). Youth with more friends who admitted to some delinquency reported a higher number of delinquent acts themselves, and this held true even for students with higher school attachment. Those with more delinquent friends and lower school attachment reported the highest self-reported delinquency rate. The findings indicate that peer relationships are more important than school attachment in explaining delinquent behavior (see, for example, Crosnoe, 2002; Haynie, 2002).

School involvement tends to reduce involvement in delinquency. Boys in Hirschi's sample who felt they had nothing to do were more likely to become involved in delinquent acts. He theorized that lack of involvement and commitment to school releases youth from a major source of time-structuring (Hirschi, 1969, pp. 187–196). Hirschi's claim for the positive benefit of involvement has been supported by other studies. Laub and Sampson (1993) found that weak school attachment and poor school performance have the strongest effects on delinquency. Gottfredson and Hirschi (1990) explained that the relationship stems from the school system's rewards and discipline that also increases young peoples' level of self-control. Schools require students to be in a certain place on time, to be orderly and attentive; and schools reward good behavior and performance. They also note the important role of parents in support of education. The discipline, structure, rewards, and greater self-control provided by schools can only happen when students have parental support and regularly attend school. Parents and schools share an interdependent relationship as the two most important factors that enable most youth avoid serious involvement in delinquency.

Gang Crime Theory: Social Reaction

Social reaction theories focus more on how society, social institutions, and government officials react to crime and delinquency, than on why offenders commit crime. The theories we have discussed so far explain juvenile delinquency as a function of individual choices or characteristics, social structure, or social processes that influence delinquent involvement. However, the social reaction theories are different in that they explain crime as the result of how laws are written and enforced, and how social institutions and justice agencies react to crime and criminals.

Social reaction theorists also point to the stigmatizing effect of the judicial and correctional processes, so offenders tend to be labeled and restricted from reintegration back into society even after serving their sentence. Despite not being as popular or having as much research support as many other theories, *labeling* and *conflict* theories do offer interesting insights on societal reactions to crime, and how changes in laws and policies could help in crime reduction.

Labeling Theory

Labeling theory argues that no behavior in and of itself is necessarily deviant; it is the labeling of a behavior as deviant that makes it so. As a result, individuals are not criminals until society has labeled them as such. In addition, labeling theory asserts that labeling an individual a "gang member" results in these labels becoming the individuals' *master status*, or primary identity. Once this identity is internalized, the individual considers himself or herself as a gang member and nothing else, and acts according to the stereotypical role of a gang member. Labeling theory focuses more on why some youth continue to repeat delinquent acts and often escalate to more serious delinquency. The primary assumption of the labeling perspective is that repeated delinquent behavior is caused by society's reaction to minor deviant behavior. Frank Tannenbaum's *Crime and the Community* (1938) first suggested that the very process of identifying and segregating deviant persons as criminals increased the likelihood that the behavior would continue. Major proponents of labeling theory are Lemert (1951) and Becker (1963). Lemert differentiated between "primary deviance," referring to behavior of the individual; and "secondary deviance," resulting from society's response to that behavior which resulted in a status, role, or individual identity. Becker's *Outsiders* proposed that those in society who make and enforce the rules "create" deviants by labeling persons, who in turn tend to act out the deviant behaviors consistent with their new identity.

Labeling theory provides an explanation for why youths who become involved in minor deviant acts often will continue offending and escalate to more serious deliquent acts following initial contact with police and juvenile authorities. The theory emphasizes the important role of rule-making, power, and reactions of society and justice system authorities. As part of the symbolic interactionist perspective, labeling theory points out that some persons do tend to take on the roles and self-concepts expected of them. However, Labeling Theory lacks clear cut definitions and testable hypotheses. (Gibbs, 1966) For example, it does not explain why youth initially commit deviant or delinquent acts, and tends to minimize the importance of delinquency. The theory appears to excuse the behavior of the delinquent and make society the culprit. The reasons or motives for why youth engage in delinquency are not explained. Overall, labeling theory has been widely criticized by criminologists and has little empirical support.

Conflict Theory

Conflict or "critical" theory shares a similarity with labeling theory in its focus on social and political institutions as causes of crime, rather than individual characteristics and criminal tendencies of offenders. Conflict theorists or critical criminologists point to the presence of conflict and competition among social classes and groups in society (Quinney, 1974). Examples that come to mind are the differences in values and beliefs between gender, race, ethnicity, political parties, and religious groups. Conflict results when competing groups vie for power and attempt to implement laws and policies that support their views. Nowhere is this conflict more evident than in the criminal justice system, where law enforcement practices, judicial sentencing policies, and correctional trends have changed dramatically over the years. Competing groups try to convince others that their beliefs and policies offer the best answer to solve what they believe to be the most urgent types of crime problems in the nation. Conflict theory offers an explanation for why certain deviant and illegal behaviors are punished more severely than other deviant and illegal behaviors. The theory explains why the number of persons arrested, convicted, and sentenced to prison has increased with criminal law and sentencing changes, despite the fact that criminal and deviant behavior has remained fairly stable over the years. That is, certain laws "criminalize" behavior that is not a crime in other countries; that was not a serious crime in this country in the past; and is considered more of a medical or social deviance problem than a crime. A clear example is the emphasis placed on drug enforcement in America. Certain drugs have been identified as dangerous and addicting, and hence the use, possession, and sale of those drugs result in severe sentences, including jail and prison time. Other drugs, such as tobacco and alcohol, despite causing serious medical, behavioral, and social problems, do not receive the same severe criminal sanctions as marijuana and other drugs. Conflict theorists claim that economic forces, business interests (such as the alcohol and tobacco lobbies), and public sentiment of those in power are responsible for the differential enforcement of drug use. Criminal laws and their enforcement tend to focus more on crimes committed by the lower class, while many "white-collar" crimes are ignored or punished lightly. Critical or conflict theorists contend that laws written by those in power are done so to serve their own interests, and to keep the lower classes in their place. An examination of the crimes committed by the thousands of persons in our growing prison population is evidence that conflict theorists have raised a critical issue in the administration of justice in America (Reiman, 1995). Most prisons and jails in America today house more persons convicted of drug offenses than property or violent offenses.

Critical theorists view juvenile delinquency and juvenile justice in terms of a capitalist, class-structured society. They point to economic and social inequities that increase the probability of lower-class youth turning to crime because so few opportunities are open to them. Critical criminologists contend that the origin of the concept of "delinquency" and juvenile justice in America is based on economic and class differences. Anthony Platt (1977) argued that the role of the *child savers* in creating a separate system of juvenile justice was not so much to save wayward children, but an effort by wealthy upper-class persons to maintain the existing class structure and to control the behavior of lower-class youth. Conflict theorists view schools as social control institutions whose primary purpose is to prepare young people for entry into the work world, and to assure that they conform to the existing capitalist structure. Lower class and minority youth do not enjoy the same social, economic, and educational opportunities as middle- and upper-class White youth in America (Ward, 2012). Most youth and families look to education as the primary means by which they can compete for good jobs, and improve their social standing. Equal quality education is not available to all youth, however, as differences in school funding have resulted in what has been described as savage inequalities in schools throughout the United States (see, for example, Kozol & Perluss, 1992; Mourshed, Farrell, & Barton, 2013; Scherer, 1993). Conflict theorists argue that competition among social classes restricts equal quality education and employment opportunities for some youth.

News media depictions of crime and criminals tend to focus more on blacks as offenders (Bjornstrom, Kaufman, Peterson, & Slater, 2010). Newspapers are more likely to identify race in a crime story when an African American is the suspect (Dixon & Linz, 2000); and minorities are overrepresented as perpetrators of crime (Oliver & Fonash, 2002; Oliver, Jackson, Moses, & Dangerfield, 2004). Despite higher rates of Black victimization, White victims are shown at a much higher rate on television news and in newspaper coverage (see, for example, Dorfman & Schiraldi, 2001). Persons of color are shown primarily for their role as perpetrators of crime, whereas Whites are shown primarily for their role as victims of crime (see, for example, Skogan, 1995). Regarding gang news coverage, Thompson, Young, and Burns (2000) found:

> [t]hat gang news tended to be primarily social disorder and moral disorder news. Social disorder news stories involve phenomena that present a threat to valued institutions, such as the family, and preferred social patterns, such as public safety. Repeatedly, stories about gangs presented readers with fear-provoking images of families torn apart, schools turned into battle grounds, and communities paralyzed with fear. Gang stories also portrayed threats to the moral order by suggesting that gangs reject commonly held standards of decency and morality. (p. 427)

The implication is that crime and violence involving gangs, specifically Black and other minority gangs, considered normal, everyday events in lower-class communities. This supports what critical criminologists claim is a differential response by law enforcement and the judicial system to Blacks and other racial and ethnic minorities. Race has played a prominent role in recent legislative changes in juvenile-gang laws and juvenile-gang court practices (see, for example, Bjerregaard, 2003; Kennedy, 2012). In an analysis of historical events, political developments, and media studies, Feld (2003) argued that recent "get-tough" crime policies have unfairly targeted Blacks so that they are overrepresented at every stage of the justice process, despite federal mandates to examine and reduce the disproportionate confinement of minorities in detention and correctional facilities.

Concluding Thoughts

The best criminological theories of delinquency and gang involvement have been tested repeatedly to determine how well they explain delinquency causation among the greatest number of youth and in a variety of social settings. The theories that are cited the most and tested most frequently using different samples of youth in different geographical regions and social settings are those that are considered the best theories to explain delinquency. Perhaps the most important criterion of a good theory according to gang researchers, practitioners, and policy makers is whether the theory recommends policies, programs, and strategies for crime reduction and delinquency prevention, which are discussed in Chapter 7.

Explanations of delinquency may be fairly judged by seasoned criminologists as well as by students of criminal justice as to whether they make sense, are observable and testable and whether they answer the "so what" question: "So what does the theory recommend to prevent delinquency?" The most effective delinquency and gang prevention policies are those that have a firm theoretical and empirical basis.

Social structural theories of crime and delinquency are varied, but center on the main themes of social structure and institutions to maintain that social structure. Social structure refers to the order of society (i.e., the relationships between individuals, groups, organizations, etc.) and how that order influences one's daily activities. Three categories of social structure explanations are (1) *social disorganization theory*, (2) *strain theory*, and (3) *subculture theory*.

Social process theories are a grouping of criminological theories that support explanations of why people engage in criminal behavior. It should be noted that social process explanations of delinquency focus *not on societal structures* but on social interactions between individuals and environmental influences that may contribute to delinquent behavior. The social process theories that have been presented include (1) *differential association* and (2) *social control theory*.

Social reaction theories focus more on how society, social institutions, and government officials react to crime and delinquency, than on why offenders commit crime. Despite not being as popular or having as much research support as many other theories, *labeling* and *conflict* theories do offer interesting insights on societal reactions to crime, and how changes in laws and policies will help in crime reduction.

Although juveniles and young adults may join gangs for the same general reasons, further research is needed to more clearly explain the causes of gang delinquency. Further research is also needed to examine how the juvenile justice system responds to all types of gang crimes. Gangs and gang members are evident in many American cities, large and small. Nonetheless, the gang problem of this magnitude clearly presents a challenge for law enforcement officials and other criminal justice practitioners who deal with gang members on a daily basis, and calls for a concerted community-wide effort to respond to the problem.

Discussion Points and Questions

1. Think of your personal observations of small towns, suburbs, and large cities or metro areas and describe the reasons for different levels of crime and delinquency and gang membership according to the social structure theories.

2. Give an example of how gang membership can be explained by differential association or social learning.

3. Think of two examples of youth: one who is characterized by the elements of the social strain theory and another for whom social controls are weak or absent. Explain how the absence of social control place those youth at risk for gang membership.

4. Think of an example of how a rule, law, or policy (in school, at work, or in the government) favors some individuals or groups and seems unfairly targeted against other individuals or groups.

5. Pick one of the theories discussed in this chapter that makes most sense to you. Next, suggest a legislative change, policy, or program that may be an effective delinquency prevention strategy based on your favorite theory.

Web Sources

Justice Academy – NIJ-Gangs
https://www.justiceacademy.org/debate/associations-and-institutions/
national-institute-of-justice/nij-gangs/

The National Gang Center:
https://www.nationalgangcenter.gov/

The Office of Juvenile Justice and Delinquency Prevention (OJJDP):
http://www.ojjdp.ncjrs.org/

REFERENCES

Agnew, R. (1992). Foundation for a general strain theory of crime and delinquency. *Criminology, 30*(1), 47–88.

Agnew, R., & White, H. R. (1992). An empirical test of general strain theory. *Criminology, 30*(4), 475–500.

Agnew, R., Brezina, T., Wright, J. P., & Cullen, F. T. (2002). Strain, personality traits, and delinquency: Extending general strain theory. *Criminology, 40*(1), 43–72.

Akers, R. L. (1985). *Deviant behavior: A social learning approach.* Belmont, CA: Wadsworth.

Akers, R. L. (1998). *Social learning and social structure: A general theory of crime and deviance.* Boston, MA: Northeastern University Press.

Andrews, D. A., Guzzo, L., Raynor, P., Rowe, R. C., Rettinger, L. J., Brews, A., & Wormith, J. S. (2012). Are the major risk/need factors predictive of both female and male reoffending? A test with the eight domains of the Level of Service/Case Management Inventory. *International Journal of Offender Therapy and Comparative Criminology, 56*(1), 113–133.

Aseltine, R. H., Jr., Gore, S., & Gordon, J. (2000). Life stress, anger and anxiety, and delinquency: An empirical test of general strain theory. *Journal of Health and Social Behavior, 41*(3), 256–275.

Axelrod, T. (2015, March 6). Gang violence is on the rise, even as overall violence declines. *U.S. News.* Retrieved from https://www.usnews.com/news/articles/2015/03/06/gang-violence-is-on-the-rise-even-as-overall-violence-declines

Battin-Peterson, S. R., Thornberry, T. P., Hawkins, J. D., & Kroh, M. D. (1998). *Gang membership, delinquent peers, and delinquent behavior.* Washington, DC: U.S. Department of Justice, Office of Justice Programs, Office of Juvenile Justice and Delinquency Prevention.

Becker, H. S. (1963). *Outsiders: Studies in the sociology of deviance.* New York, NY: Free Press.

Bentham, J. (1879). *An introduction to the principles of morals and legislation.* Oxford, England: Clarendon Press.

Bjerregaard, B. (2003). Antigang legislation and its potential impact: The promises and the pitfalls. *Criminal Justice Policy Review, 14*(2), 171–192.

Bjerregaard, B., & Smith, C. (1993). Gender differences in gang participation, delinquency, and substance use. *Journal of Quantitative Criminology, 9*(4), 329–355.

Bjornstrom, E. E., Kaufman, R. L., Peterson, R. D., & Slater, M. D. (2010). Race and ethnic representations of lawbreakers and victims in crime news: A national study of television coverage. *Social Problems, 57*(2), 269–293.

Bordua, D. J. (1961). Delinquent subcultures: Sociological interpretations of gang delinquency. *The Annals of the American Academy of Political and Social Science, 338*(1), 119–136.

Brezina, T., & Topalli, V. (2012). Criminal self-efficacy: Exploring the correlates and consequences of a "successful criminal" identity. *Criminal Justice and Behavior, 39*(8), 1042–1062.

Brunius, T. (1958). Jeremy Bentham's moral calculus. *Acta Sociologica, 3*(1), 73–85.

Burgess, R. L., & Akers, R. L. (1966). A differential association-reinforcement theory of criminal behavior. *Social Problems, 14*, 128–147.

Chapman, B. & Honan, K. (2019, November 6). Gang-related crimes drive up murders, shootings in New York City. *The Wall Street Journal.* Retrieved from https://www.wsj.com/articles/gang-related-crimes-drive-up-murders-shootings-in-new-york-city-11573080007

Cloward, R. A., & Ohlin, L. E. (1960). *Delinquency and opportunity: A theory of delinquent gangs.* New York, NY: Free Press.

Cohen, A. (1955). *Delinquent boys.* New York, NY: Free Press.

Cohen, A. K., & Short, J. F. (1958). Research in delinquent subcultures. *Journal of Social Issues, 14*(3), 20–37.

Crosnoe, R. (2002). High school curriculum track and adolescent association with delinquent friends. *Journal of Adolescent Research, 17*(2), 143–167.

Curry, G. D. (1998). Female gang involvement. *Journal of Research in Crime and Delinquency, 35*(1), 100–118.

Curry, G. D., & Spergel, I. A. (1988). Gang homicide, delinquency, and community. *Criminology, 26*(3), 381–406.

Curry, G. D., Ball, R. A., & Fox, R. J. (1994). *Gang crime and law enforcement recordkeeping: National Institute of Justice Research in Brief.* Washington, DC: U.S. Department of Justice.

Decker, S. H., Melde, C., & Pyrooz, D. C. (2013). What do we know about gangs and gang members and where do we go from here? *Justice Quarterly, 30*(3), 369–402.

Dixon, T. L., & Linz, D. (2000). Overrepresentation and underrepresentation of African Americans and Latinos as lawbreakers on television news. *Journal of Communication, 50*(2), 131–154.

Dorfman, L., & Schiraldi, V. (2001). *Off balance: Youth, race & crime in the news.* Washington, DC: Building Blocks for Youth.

Esbensen, F. (2000). Preventing adolescent gang involvement. *OJJDP Juvenile Justice Bulletin.* Washington, DC: U.S. Department of Justice.

Esbensen, F., & Huizinga, D. (1993). Gangs, drugs, and delinquency in a survey of urban youth. *Criminology, 31*(4), 565–589.

Esbensen, F., Huizinga, D., & Weiher, A. W. (1995). Gang and non-gang youth: Differences in explanatory factors. In M. W. Klein, C. L. Maxson, & J. Miller (Eds.), *The modern gang reader* (pp. 192–201). Los Angeles, CA: Roxbury.

Esbensen, F., & Winfree, L. T. (1998). Race and gender differences between gang and non-gang youth: Results from a multisite survey. *Justice Quarterly, 15*(3), 505–526.

Fagan, J. (1990). Social processes of delinquency and drug use among urban gangs. In C. R. Huff (Ed.), *Gangs in America* (pp. 183–219). Newbury Park, CA: SAGE.

Feld, B. C. (2003). The politics of race and juvenile justice: The "due process revolution" and the conservative reaction. *Justice Quarterly, 20*(4), 765–800.

Gibbs, J. P. (1966). Conceptions of deviant behavior: The old and the new. *Pacific Sociological Review, 9*(1), 9–14.

Goldstein, A. P. (1994). Delinquent gangs. In *Aggressive behavior* (pp. 255–273). Boston, MA: Springer.

Gottfredson, D. C. (2001). *Schools and delinquency.* New York, NY: Cambridge University Press.

Gottfredson, M., & Hirschi, T. (1990). *A general theory of crime.* Palo Alto, CA: Stanford University Press.

Haynie, D. L. (2002). Friendship networks and delinquency: The relative nature of peer delinquency. *Journal of Quantitative Criminology, 18*(2), 99–134.

Hill, K. G., Howell, J. C., Hawkins, J. D., & Battin-Pearson, S. R. (1999). Childhood risk factors for adolescent gang membership: Results from the Seattle social development project. *Journal of Research in Crime and Delinquency, 36*(3), 300–322.

Hirschi, T. (1969). *Causes of delinquency.* Berkeley: University of California Press.

Horowitz, R. (1990). Sociological perspectives on gangs: Conflicting definitions and concepts. In C. R. Huff (Ed.), *Gangs in America* (pp. 37–54). Newbury Park, CA: SAGE.

Howell, J. C. (2003). *Preventing and reducing juvenile delinquency: A comprehensive framework.* Thousand Oaks, CA: SAGE.

Huff, C. R. (1989). Youth gangs and public policy. *Crime & Delinquency, 35*(4), 524–537.

Huff, C. R. (1990). Introduction: Two generations of gang research. In C. R. Huff (Ed.), *Gangs in America* (pp. 24–34). Newbury Park, California: SAGE.

Jensen, G. F. (1973). Inner containment and delinquency. *Journal of Criminal Law and Criminology, 64*(4), 464–470.

Jones, D., Roper, V., Stys, Y., Wilson, C., & Correctional Service Canada, Research Branch. (2004). *Street gangs: A review of theory, interventions, and implications for corrections.* Ottawa, Ontario: Research Branch, Correctional Service of Canada.

Katz, J., & Jackson-Jacobs, C. (2004). The criminologists' gang. In *The Blackwell companion to criminology* (pp. 91–124). New York, NY: Wiley.

Kennedy, R. (2012). *Race, crime, and the law.* New York, NY: Vintage.

Kozol, J., & Perluss, D. (1992). Savage inequalities: Children in America's schools. *Clearinghouse Review, 26,* 398.

Laub, J. H., & Sampson, R. J. (1993). Turning points in the life course: Why change matters to the study of crime. *Criminology, 31*(3), 301–325.

Lawrence, R. (1985). School performance, containment theory, and delinquent behavior. *Youth & Society, 17*(1), 69–95.

Lawrence, R., & Hesse, M. (2009). *Juvenile justice: The essentials.* Thousand Oaks, CA: SAGE.

Lemert, E. M. (1951). *Social pathology: A systematic approach to the theory of sociopathic behavior.* New York, NY: McGraw-Hill.

Linden, E., & Hackler, J. C. (1973). Affective ties and delinquency. *Pacific Sociological Review, 16*(1), 27–46.

Liska, A. E., & Reed, M. D. (1985). Ties to conventional institutions and delinquency: Estimating reciprocal effects. *American Sociological Review, 50*(4), 547–560.

Ludwig, K. B., & Pittman, J. F. (1999). Adolescent prosocial values and self-efficacy in relation to delinquency, risky sexual behavior, and drug use. *Youth & Society, 30*(4), 461–482.

McGloin, J. M., & Decker, S. H. (2010). Theories of gang behavior and public policy. In H. D. Barlow & S. H. Decker (Eds.), *Criminology and public policy: Putting theory to work* (pp. 150–165). Philadelphia, PA: Temple University Press.

Merton, R. K. (1938). Social structure and anomie. *American Sociological Review, 3*(5), 672–682.

Merton, R. K. (1957). *Social theory and social structure.* Glencoe, IL: Free Press.

Miller, W. B. (1958). Lower class culture as a generating milieu of gang delinquency. *Journal of Social Issues, 14*(3), 5–19.

Mitchell, W. C. (1968). Bentham's felicific calculus. In A. N. Page (Ed.), pp. 30–48 (Reprinted from *Political Science Quarterly, 33*, 161–183). (Original work published 1918)

Mourshed, M., Farrell, D., & Barton, D. (2013). Education to employment: Designing a system that works. *McKinsey Center for Government.* Retrieved from https://www.mckinsey.com/~/media/McKinsey/Industries/Social%20Sector/Our%20Insights/Education%20to%20employment%20Designing%20a%20system%20that%20works/Education%20to%20employment%20designing%20a%20system%20that%20works.ashx

National Gang Center. (2014). National youth gang survey analysis. Retrieved from http://www.nationalgangcenter.gov/Survey-Analysis

Oliver, M. B., Jackson, R. L., Moses, N. N., & Dangerfield, C. L. (2004). The face of crime: Viewers' memory of race-related facial features of individuals pictured in the news. *Journal of Communication, 54*(1), 88–104.

Oliver, M. B., & Fonash, D. (2002). Race and crime in the news: Whites' identification and misidentification of violent and nonviolent criminal suspects. *Media Psychology, 4*(2), 137–156.

Park, R. E., & Burgess, E. W. (1924). *Introduction to the science of sociology* (Vol. 574). Chicago, IL: University of Chicago Press.

Paternoster, R., & Mazerolle, P. (1994). General strain theory and delinquency: A replication and extension. *Journal of Research in Crime and Delinquency, 31*(3), 235–263.

Platt, A. M. (1977). *The child savers: The invention of delinquency.* Chicago, IL: University of Chicago Press.

Quinney, R. (Ed.). (1974). *Criminal justice in America: A critical understanding.* Boston, MA: Little, Brown.

Reckless, W. C. (1961). A new theory of delinquency and crime. *Federal Probation, 25*, 42–46.

Reckless, W. C., Dinitz, S., & Kay, B. (1957). The self-component in potential delinquency and potential non-delinquency. *American Sociological Review, 22*(5), 566–570.

Reiman, J. (1995). *The rich get richer and the poor get prison: Ideology, crime, and criminal justice.* Boston, MA: Allyn and Bacon.

Scherer, M. (1993). On savage inequalities: A conversation with Jonathan Kozol. *Educational Leadership, 50*(4), 4–9.

Segrave, J. O., & Hastad, D. N. (1985). Evaluating three models of delinquency causation for males and females: Strain theory, subculture theory, and control theory. *Sociological Focus, 18*(1), 1–17.

Shaw, C. R., & McKay, H. D. (1931). Social factors in juvenile delinquency, Vol. II of Report on the Causes of Crime (National Commission on Law Observance and Enforcement, Report No. 13). Washington, DC: U.S. Government Printing Office.

Shaw, C. R., & McKay, H. D. (1936). *Are broken homes a causative factor in juvenile delinquency?* (No. 187). Chicago, IL: The Institute for Juvenile Research and Behavior Research Fund.

Shaw, C. R., & McKay, H. D. (1942). *Juvenile delinquency in urban areas.* Chicago, IL: University of Chicago Press.

Short, J. F. (1985). The level of explanation of problem. In R. Meier (Ed.), *Theoretical methods in criminology* (pp. 51–72). Beverly Hills, CA: SAGE.

Short, J. F., & Strodtbeck, F. L. (1965). *Group process and gang delinquency.* Chicago, IL: University of Chicago Press.

Skogan, W. G. (1995). Crime and the racial fears of white Americans. *The Annals of the American Academy of Political and Social Science, 539*(1), 59–71.

Spergel, I., Curry, D., Chance, R., Kane, C., Ross, R., Alexander, A., . . . Oh, S. (1994). *Gang suppression and intervention: Problem and response: Research summary.* Washington, DC: Office of Juvenile Justice and Delinquency Prevention.

Sutherland, E. H. (1934). *Principles of criminology* (2nd ed.). Philadelphia, PA: J. B. Lippincott.

Sutherland, E. H., & Cressey, D. (1970). Differential association. In *Crime and delinquency: A reader* (pp. 252–270). London, England: Macmillan.

Sykes, G. M., & Matza, D. (1957). Techniques of neutralization: A theory of delinquency. *American Sociological Review, 22*(6), 664–670.

Tannenbaum, F. (1938). *Crime and the community.* Boston, MA: Ginn.

Thomas, W. I., & Znaniecki, F. (1918). *The Polish peasant in Europe and America: Monograph of an immigrant group* (Vol. 2). Chicago, IL: University of Chicago Press.

Thompson, C. Y., Young, R. L., & Burns, R. (2000). Representing gangs in the news: Media constructions of criminal gangs. *Sociological Spectrum, 20*(4), 409–432.

Thornberry, T. P., Krohn, M. D., Lizzotte, A., & Chard-Wierschem, D. (1993). The role of juvenile gangs in facilitating delinquent behavior. *Journal of Research in Crime and Delinquency, 30*(1): 55–87. doi:10.1177/0022427893030001005

Thrasher, F. M. (1927). *The gang: A study of 1313 gangs in Chicago.* Chicago, IL: University of Chicago Press.

Ward, G. K. (2012). *The black child-savers: Racial democracy and juvenile justice.* Chicago, IL: University of Chicago Press.

Chapter 3

Gangs and Mental Illness

CHAPTER OBJECTIVES

- Analyze key research findings, statistics, and concepts associated with gang involvement and mental illness, trauma, and brain-based injuries

- Consider screening and assessment options to identify gang members impacted by mental illness, trauma, and traumatic brain injury

- Review intervention and treatment approaches appropriate for gang members impacted by mental illness, trauma, and traumatic brain injury

---

Introduction

A diverse range of pernicious and negative life experiences place adolescents at risk for gang involvement. For instance, youth gang members entering the juvenile justice system are more likely than the general population to present with mood disorders (e.g., depression and bipolar disorder), anxiety disorders, substance abuse, behavioral disinhibition (e.g., impulsivity), self-harming behaviors, victimization, and trauma. Exposure to trauma can come from a diverse range of experiences including neglect and abuse in one's household or subjection to violence dating back to early childhood. Not only do these troubling experiences place youth at risk for post-traumatic stress disorder (PTSD), but also traumatic brain injuries (TBI). Common symptoms of traumatic brain injuries are social (e.g., vulnerability to manipulation) and adaptive functioning (e.g., poor decision-making and judgment) deficits, which are characteristic of individuals who become entangled in the criminal justice system.

Moving beyond the risk of involvement, gang membership itself exacerbates many of the troubling life experiences (e.g., trauma and traumatic brain injuries) that contributed to the initial involvement. For example, initiation rituals may involve submitting one's self to a serious beating and even committing extremely violent acts. Similarly, the day-to-day activities of gang life may require participation in or exposure to violent crimes. These examples illustrate how gang life can have devastating consequences (e.g., increased psychiatric distress and substance use) in an already troubled individual. As such, trauma and traumatic brain injuries can exacerbate the long-term emotional, physical, social, and economic consequences of gang membership when unidentified and untreated.

To help limit the continuance of criminal justice involvement, criminal justice, forensic mental health, and human service professionals that work with adolescent gang members should practice trauma-informed care and brain-injury informed approaches. This approach to management, intervention, and treatment is characterized by a sensitivity to the ubiquity of trauma and traumatic brain injuries and their diverse effects on survivors. Such care considers how trauma and traumatic brain injuries impact an individual's capacity to navigate and receive treatment and other services. Improved screening and assessment of traumatic brain injuries along with the implementation of trauma-informed care approaches and policies that maintain safety and security for the individual and the community are both necessary steps. Further, professionals who encounter and work with gang members would benefit from learning about trauma, childhood adversity, PTSD, and traumatic brain injuries in general.

NEWS CLIP 3-1:

GANG MEMBERS "EXPERIENCE PTSD EQUAL TO TROOPS AT WAR"

Gang members in the capital are experiencing levels of PTSD equal to troops in a war zone, experts have said. Research by criminologists in London suggests living with violence, abuse at home, and drug use all lead to high levels of paranoia, anxiety, and depression.

Source: BBC News. Gang members 'experience PTSD equal to troops in war'. Retrieved from https://www.bbc.com/news/av/uk-england-london-44396463/gang-members-experience-ptsd-equal-to-troops-in-war

Mental Illness: An Overview

The decision to join a gang can be driven by a number of individual, social, familial, community, and experiential risk factors (Herrenkohl et al., 2000; Hill, Howell, Hawkins, & Battin-Pearson, 1999; Howell & Egley, 2005; Klein & Maxson, 2006). Individual risk factors include neuropsychological deficits like disinhibition, impulsivity, and risk-seeking (Esbensen & Weerman, 2005), low self-esteem (Donnellan, Trzesniewski, Robins, Moffitt, & Caspi, 2005; Dukes, Martinez, & Stein, 1997), behavioral disorders (e.g., oppositional defiance disorder and attention-deficit/hyperactivity disorder) and developmental level. In terms of development, people typically join gangs between the ages of 12 and 18 (Rizzo, 2003; Spergel, 1995). Social causes of gang membership may include peer pressure, an attempt to fit in, or the need for protection in their school or community (Hill et al., 1999; Hill, Lui, & Hawkins, 2001; Sirpal, 1997). Familial risk factors include limited parental attachment, poor supervision or monitoring of the youth (Sharp, Aldridge, & Medina, 2006; Thornberry, Krohn, Lizotte, Smith, & Tobin, 2003), and exposure to family members involved in crime and/or gangs (Eitle, Gunkel, & Van Gundy, 2004; Sharp et al., 2006; Spergel, 1995). Community risk factors include low socioeconomic status (Rizzo, 2003; Spergel, 1995), neighborhood disadvantage (Hagedorn, 2005; Lane, 2002; Thrasher, 1927), environmental deterioration and social disorganization (Dupéré, Lacourse, Willms, Vitaro, & Tremblay, 2007; Tita, Cohen, & Engberg, 2005), and the high prevalence of gang membership (Spergel, 1995). Beyond these risk factors, personal exposure to violence and other forms of abuse along with victimization also increase the risk of gang membership.

Foremost among the consequences of gang membership is an increased predisposition to criminal and violent behavior (Lenzi et al., 2015; Spergel, 1995; Thornberry, 1998). For example, Coid and colleagues (2013) found that gang members, relative to non-members, are more likely to experience thoughts of violence and report positive attitudes toward the use of violence. Further, research has found that gang members are more likely than non-members to engage in serious criminal behavior, possess a firearm, or sell drugs (Bjerregaard & Lizotte, 1995; Esbensen & Huizinga, 1993). Similarly, members of gangs are at an extremely elevated risk of participating in assaultive behavior or committing a drive-by shooting (Wood & Dennard, 2017). Other work has found that members of gangs are an estimated 100 times more likely to commit a homicide than non-members (Melde & Esbensen, 2012). This increased risk for criminal behavior including violence is particularly true of adolescents who join gangs (Battin-Pearson, Thornberry, Hawkins, & Krohn, 1998; Fagan, 1989; Huff, 1998; Thornberry & Burch, 1997). Unsurprisingly, this uptick in criminal behaviors confers a higher likelihood of arrest, conviction, and incarceration (Gatti, Tremblay, Vitaro, & McDuff, 2005; Lacourse, Nagin, Tremblay, Vitaro, & Claes, 2003; Thornberry et al., 2003), and exposure to various forms of trauma and an elevated risk of sustaining a traumatic brain injury.

Beyond crime and punishment, gang membership can have diverse consequences that stretch across the lifespan (Gebo, 2016). In fact, joining a gang during adolescence can alter the trajectory of an individual's life in a number of realms (Gilman, Hill, & Hawkins, 2014). For example, one relatively proximal consequence is that gang membership decreases the likelihood of graduating from high school (Gebo, 2016; Gilman et al., 2014; Thornberry et al., 2003). This contributes to distal consequences including under-employment or unemployment, unreliable income, and unstable living conditions (Gilman et al., 2014). Other consequences include disrupted relationships with family members, limited social growth and functioning, and exposure to violence and victimization (Decker & Van Winkle, 1996; Peterson, Taylor, & Esbensen, 2004).

The trauma of exposure to violence and victimization may have particularly deleterious effects on mental health. In general, members of gangs are more likely to need and utilize mental health treatment services relative to non-members (Coid et al., 2013). This treatment is often for anxiety, mood (e.g., major depression and bipolar), psychotic (e.g., schizophrenia), behavioral (e.g., ADHD and conduct disorder), personality (e.g., antisocial and borderline), substance use, and traumatic (e.g., PTSD and traumatic brain injuries) disorders (Coid et al., 2013; Melde & Esbensen, 2014; Wood & Dennard, 2017). Even if some of these problems pre-existed, gang membership (Neville, Goodall, Gavine, Williams, & Donnelly, 2015) and the participation in gang activities, including violent behavior likely exacerbate the symptoms. For example, the experience of psychological trauma through participation in or victimization of violent behavior contributes to the use of substances and the deterioration of mental health. The resulting vicious cycle can be hard to escape and lead to ongoing involvement in gang activity and criminal justice involvement. As this cycle continues, youth gang members may be at an elevated risk of sustaining one or more traumatic brain injuries.

In light of the pervasive mental health concerns in gang-involved adolescents, traditional law enforcement strategies cannot adequately address this societal issue (Ross, Arsenault, & Lopez, 2016). Instead, criminal justice, forensic mental health, and human service professionals that work with this population must become equipped with the knowledge and skills to provide both trauma- and brain-injury informed services. This includes a better understanding of how individuals with trauma and brain injuries present with symptoms, cope with challenges, and access and experience services. Similarly, professionals should become familiar with ways of improving screening, assessment, and treatment of trauma and brain-related issues. Beyond this, there is a great need for systematic research on the mental health needs and treatment of adolescent gang members, as there is minimal published research in this area (Coid et al., 2013; Fisher, Gardner, & Montgomery, 2008). Such advancements in the field and research have the potential to limit the short- and long-term consequences of trauma and traumatic brain injury among gang-involved adolescents.

NEWS CLIP 3-2:

TRAUMATIC BRAIN INJURY SHOULD BE A FACTOR WHEN JUDGING INDIVIDUALS ACCUSED OF CRIMES

Can a traumatic brain injury increase the odds that an individual will commit a crime? And if the answer is yes, should such an injury factor into how we judge people accused of crimes?

Source: Bozelko, C. Traumatic brain injury should be a factor when judging individuals accused of crimes. Retrieved from https://www.statnews.com/2017/12/07/traumatic-brain-injury-crime/

Trauma

Trauma can be caused via several different experiences. This includes neglect, abuse (e.g., emotional, physical, and sexual), exposure to violence in the community and at home, witnessing or experiencing a serious accident (e.g., car crash), the death of a loved one, or other deeply affecting events (Buka, Stichick, Birdthistle, & Earls, 2001; Javanbakht, Rosenberg, Haddad, & Arfken, 2018; Osofsky, 1995; The National Child Traumatic Stress Network, n.d.; Tull, Berghoff, Wheeless, Cohen, & Gratz, 2018). The experience of such events is particularly common among children and adolescents. In fact, an estimated 25% of American youth go through a "high magnitude event" of trauma prior to turning 16 years old (Costello, Erkanli, Fairbank, & Angold, 2002).

When occurring during childhood, such events may be referred to as adverse childhood experiences (ACEs; Chatterjee et al., 2018; Folger et al., 2018). These can have long-term consequences on the young adult's development. For example, Steinberg (2009) reported that psychological trauma during childhood can precipitate a negative cascade in cognition where the youth becomes preoccupied with self-protection and the detection of threats (Pine, 2007). Over an extended period of time, the neurological stress of "survival mode" (Ford, 2009; Ford, Kerig, Desai, & Feierman, 2016; Ford & Courtois, 2013; Ford & Hawke, 2012) can have a detrimental effect on the individual's affective and social development and contribute to psychological and physical ailments (Ford & Blaustein, 2013). These consequences are consistent with what Cook and colleagues (2005) described as the repercussions of a complex trauma.

Wilcox, Storr, and Breslau (2009) surmise that somewhere between 15% and 24% of youth exposed to violence go on to develop PTSD. In these instances, the experience of the trauma overwhelms the youth's capacity to cope. The individual can suffer from a range of affective and behavioral symptoms when exposure to such events results in trauma (Rheingold et al., 2004). Five common sets of symptoms include (a) nervousness or jumpiness, (b) re-experiencing the traumatic event, (c) difficulty sleeping including nightmares, (d) withdrawal from or avoidance of situations that may trigger memories of the trauma, and (e) attentional deficits (e.g., distractibility; The National Child Traumatic Stress Network, n.d.).

The response to traumatic events can vary widely depending on the individual. Symptoms often gradually decrease with time but can persist or even worsen for some individuals in the absence of treatment. These divergent trajectories may be accounted for by a range of individual- (e.g., genetic disposition, temperament, personality, and coping style) and environmental-level (e.g., support system, community, and previous experiences) factors (The National Child Traumatic Stress Network, n.d.). These factors may be protective against the consequences of trauma or predispose the individual to consequences like PTSD.

Post-traumatic stress disorder (PTSD) is commonly comorbid with other psychiatric symptoms along with school and work issues (Ford, Hartman, Hawke, & Chapman, 2008). Frequently co-occurring forms of psychopathology may include psychosis (Braakman, Kortmann,

& Van den Brink, 2009; David, Kutcher, Jackson, & Mellman, 1999), mood disorders (e.g., depression and bipolar disorder; Kilpatrick et al., 2003), anxiety, affective disturbances, for example, callousness and emotional numbing (Bennett, Kerig, Chaplo, McGee, & Baucom, 2014; Bennett & Kerig, 2014; Bennett, Modrowski, Kerig, & Chaplo, 2015), and self-harm, including suicidality (Chapman & Ford, 2008). A common coping mechanism that individuals with PTSD often rely on is the use of alcohol and other substances (Lane et al., 2017), which can exacerbate many of the aforementioned psychiatric symptomatology. Consequences of these problems include poor performance in academic and work settings, resulting in low education attainment or unemployment (Ford & Hawke, 2012).

Beyond school and work, trauma also contributes to behavioral problems like delinquency and gang involvement (Bennett et al., 2014). For instance, children with a history of physical abuse go on to exhibit higher rates of delinquency during adolescence than children without a history of physical abuse (Malinkosky-Rummell & Hansen, 1993). Similarly, the Rochester Youth Development Study found that children with a history of maltreatment exhibit higher rates of both self-report and official records of violent and antisocial behavior later during adolescence. Not only does other longitudinal research substantiate this link between trauma and subsequent delinquency (Kerig & Becker, 2010, 2015), but some research has even found that the association between trauma and delinquency is explained in part by PTSD symptoms including avoidance, hyper-arousal, and disassociation (Allwood, Bell, & Horan, 2011; Kerig, Vanderzee, Becker, & Ward, 2012). These PTSD symptoms increase the likelihood of disinhibition, aggression, and oppositional defiance, all of which are established risk factors for antisocial behavior (Kerig & Becker, 2010).

In fact, a history of maltreatment (e.g., physical abuse, exposure to violence, and environmental deprivation) is a common risk factor for joining a gang (Thornberry et al., 2003). This connection may be explained, at least in part, by the detrimental effects of trauma on emotion regulation, coping skills, perceptions of safety (Paton, Crouch, & Camic, 2009). Alternatively, the youth's decision to join a gang may be driven by an effort to seek out basic needs (e.g., money and food), a sense of belonging, and safety (The National Child Traumatic Stress Network, n.d.).

Regardless of the reason for delinquency and gang involvement, participation in these acts, in turn, drastically increases the risk of experiencing trauma in a reciprocal nature. This exposure to trauma may occur as a result of participating in a criminal act against another individual or being the victim of a crime (Kerig, Wainryb, Twali, & Chaplo, 2013). On one hand, the perpetration of crime and violence can result in gruesome injuries and even death, which can have a profound psychological effect (Boyle, 2011). Such violence can be commonplace among gangs and a requirement of membership, in some cases (Crimmins, Cleary, Brownstein, Spunt, & Warley, 2000). On the other hand, the likelihood of victimization also increases as a function of adolescence (Wood, Foy, Layne, Pynoos, & James, 2002) and gang membership. Relative to adults, adolescents are approximately three times as likely to be victimized by violence (Sickmund, Snyder, & Poe-Yamagata, 1997). Further, a comparison of self-reported victimization ratings before joining gangs versus after leaving gangs revealed that the likelihood of violent victimization was greatest during gang membership (Taylor, Freng, Esbensen, & Peterson, 2008). This growing body of research investigating the impact of victimization among gang members is essential because it shines a light on a group in need of treatment that has been traditionally neglected (Taylor, 2008).

NEWS CLIP 3-3:

YOUNG GANG MEMBERS ALSO AT RISK OF DEVELOPING PTSD

Until recently, researchers have associated PTSD with being a victim of trauma. Now, new findings from the U.S. suggest that the act of killing or perpetrating violence could be even more traumatic than being a victim.

Source: Robinson, G. Young gang members also at risk of developing post-traumatic stress disorder. http:// theconversation.com/young-gang-members-also-at-risk-of-developing-post-traumatic-stress-disorder-90068

The combination of trauma experienced both before and during gang membership is a heavy weight upon current and former gang members (Taylor, 2008). This is supported by findings that incarcerated adolescent gang members are typically exposed to neglect, physical and sexual abuse, and violence at higher rates than those not in gangs (The National Child Traumatic Stress Network, n.d.). This includes a substantially higher risk of nonviolent and violent crime including being shot at (Sickmund et al., 1997; Wood et al., 2002). As such, it should come as no surprise that PTSD is one of the largest mental health concerns for adolescent gang members involved in the criminal justice system (Dierkhising et al., 2013; Wood et al., 2002). Other common mental disorders in this population include psychosis, depression, anxiety, behavioral disorders (e.g., conduct disorder), and self-harm (Coid et al., 2013; Fazel, Doll, & Långström, 2008; Madan, Mrug, & Windle, 2011).

Complicating matters, adolescent gang members are likely to receive care and support that is less than adequate if at all (Bonevski et al., 2014). A first-step toward rectifying this state is the routine assessment of gang membership (Coid et al., 2013). This assessment may make sense upon contact with the criminal justice system or upon hospital admission, both strong opportunities for intervention (Rahtz, Bhui, Smuk, Hutchison, & Korszun, 2017). When appropriate, trauma-informed interventions are essential for youth with a history of gang membership and trauma. Nonetheless, there is a strong need for the development of interventions and policies to help address this public health quandary (Bailey, Smith, Huey, McDaniel, & Babeva, 2014).

Traumatic Brain Injuries

Another type of trauma of concern in children and adolescents is traumatic brain injury (TBI), which may be common among youth gang members. TBI can be defined as a disruption in cognitive functioning caused by an external force's influence on the head, for example, a blow to or a puncture wound of the skull (Williams, McAuliffe, Cohen, Parsonage, & Ramsbotham, 2015). TBIs are typically caused by falls, vehicular accidents, interpersonal violence, or being struck by an object (Faul, Xu, Wald, & Coronado, 2010; Langlois, Rutland-Brown, & Thomas, 2006; Williams, McAuliffe, et al., 2015). Those most at risk for suffering from TBIs are children less than 5 years old and adolescents between the ages of 15 and 19 (Langlois et al., 2006; Vaughn, Salas-Wright, DeLisi, & Perron, 2014). These injuries can have short- to long-term consequences that range from minor to severe and may be lethal in some cases (Hayman-Abello, Rourke, & Fuerst, 2003).

TBIs can have deleterious neurocognitive and developmental consequences when sustained during childhood and adolescence (Emery et al., 2016; Keightley et al., 2014; McKinlay, Corrigan, Horwood, & Fergusson, 2014; Schachar, Park, & Dennis, 2015; Thurman, 2016; Weil, Karelina, Gaier, Corrigan, & Corrigan, 2016). This includes cognitive (e.g., information processing and memory), affective (e.g., emotion regulation), mental health (e.g., ADHD), behavioral (e.g., impulse control), and social impairments (e.g., communication skills and empathy; Anderson, Godfrey, Rosenfeld, & Catroppa, 2012; Janusz, Kirkwood, Yeates, & Taylor, 2002; Tonks et al., 2009; Williams, Cordan, Mewse, Tonks, & Burgess, 2010). When not adequately addressed by treatment, symptoms of TBI can contribute to a variety of short- and long-term outcomes including troubles at school and work. For instance, youth with TBI may display poor academic performance (Ewing-Cobbs et al., 2004) and struggle to maintain positive relationships with peers (Rosema, Crowe, & Anderson, 2012; Yeates et al., 2007).

TBIs may also place youth at risk for later delinquency and criminal behaviors (Morgan & Lilienfeld, 2000; Ogilvie, Stewart, Chan, & Shum, 2011) that could persist across their life spans (Loeber & Farrington, 2000). Research has found elevated rates of TBIs and neuropsychological dysfunction among samples of adolescents and adults involved in the criminal justice system relative to the general population (McKinlay et al., 2014; Morgan & Lilienfeld, 2000). In a study of 186 offenders under 20 years of age, Williams, Cordan, Mewse, Tonks, & Burgess, 2010) reported that 46% of participants had suffered at least one TBI. Similarly, Hux and colleagues found that approximately 50% of adolescents with delinquency issues suffered from a TBI. In a third of those with a TBI, the parents of the youth believed that the TBI had a harmful impact on behavior and cognition for an extended period of time (Hux, Bond, Skinner, Belau, & Sanger, 1998). These TBIs were typically the result of falls, vehicular accidents, or altercations (Hux et al., 1998; found in Perron & Howard, 2008).

NEWS CLIP 3-4:

TRAUMATIC BRAIN INJURY AND INCARCERATION: ENDING A VICIOUS CYCLE

Denver—At age 14, Matthew Espinoza was shot seven times, including one bullet to the head. After waking up from a 3½-month coma, he knew something was wrong. "I wasn't like I used to be," Espinoza, now 38, says, adding that he started to experience hallucinations, migraines, dizziness, and memory loss.

Source: Leins, C. Denver-based study exposes the strong connection between traumatic brain injury and incarceration. Retrieved from https://www.usnews.com/news/best-states/articles/2018-08-22/denver-based-project-exposes-link-between-brain-injury-and-incarceration

Other research indicates that adolescent offenders often have experienced multiple TBIs (Williams, Chitsabesan, Lennox, Tariq, & Shaw, 2015). In fact, the presence of multiple TBIs may exacerbate the antisocial behaviors of adolescent offenders. For example, one study reported that a history of multiple TBIs was related to a higher number of previous convictions and the presence of three of more TBIs predicted a history of violence (Williams et al., 2010). Moving beyond the number of TBIs, the severity of any given TBI could also confer a greater risk of offending and violence (Williams, Chitsabesan, et al., 2015).

Despite the wealth of evidence on the prevalence of TBIs among criminal justice-involved individuals, questions remain about the causal relationship between TBI and antisocial behavior (Williams, McAuliffe, et al., 2015). This is in part due to the complex roles of genetic and environmental factors in establishing a causal link. For instance, youths could commit antisocial behaviors for many reasons including personality, peers, mental illness, substance use, victimization, and social disadvantage (Williams, McAuliffe, et al., 2015). In fact, many of these risk factors for antisocial behavior are also risk factors for TBI (McKinlay et al., 2014; Turkstra, Jones, & Toler, 2003; Yates et al., 2006). These entangled relationships are exemplified by the fact that youth who use illicit substances are more likely to suffer TBIs and commit antisocial behavior (Winqvist, Jokelainen, Luukinen, & Hillbom, 2006). As such, youth who suffered from a TBI and went on to commit delinquent and criminal acts very well may have done so in the absence of a TBI (Williams, McAuliffe, et al., 2015).

This trouble discerning the causal impact of TBIs on antisocial behaviors emphasizes the importance of longitudinal research. Fortunately, there is a burgeoning body of longitudinal research on this topic. In a population-based study of over 12,000 people in Finland, Timonen et al. (2002) reported that TBIs in childhood or adolescence quadrupled the risk of both mental illness and offending during adulthood. A strong need for additional research in this area remains. In particular, it is essential that research (a) explores the impact of TBIs incurred during childhood on later antisocial behavior during adolescence, (b) examines if these findings translate from adolescent offenders in general to adolescent gang members, and (c) identifies potential treatment options that help reduce future offending (Williams, Cordan, et al., 2010).

Prevention and Intervention

Professionals working in human service, mental health, and criminal justice settings have an opportunity to reduce and prevent gang-related crime and violence. This can be accomplished by providing adolescent gang members with interventions designed to encourage desistance from gang activities and improve mental health. Familiarity with evidence-based practices in the assessment, treatment, and case management of these youth is necessary (Bowers, 2008; Sanders, Schneiderman, Loken, Lankenau, & Bloom, 2009). This section summarizes common risk factors, intervention options, and case-management goals for adolescent gang members.

Any allocation of interventions or services requires the recognition and identification of the individual's risk factors for delinquency and gang involvement. In children 5 years old or younger, noted risk factors include cognitive deficits, attachment issues with their primary caregiver, acts of aggression, and hypervigilance of potential threats. Among children between the ages of 6 and 12, common risk factors are victimization, a lack of parental supervision, poor relationships with peers, deficits in social information processing, weak academic performance, and antisocial behavior (Guerra, Dierkhising, & Payne, 2014). Regardless of age, social and economic disadvantage and deprivation contribute to a host of negative outcomes, including both delinquency and gang involvement alike (Guerra et al., 2014).

Another prominent risk factor among criminal justice- and gang-involved youth, particularly girls, is the presence of trauma (e.g., Harris et al., 2012; Kerig, Chaplo, Bennett, & Modrowski, 2016). This can take the form of a traumatic brain injury or exposure to violence and victimization. In both types, a thorough screening and assessment of the cause and its consequences on the youth's functioning is imperative. An ideal time to conduct such screening and assessment is at the point of entry into the criminal justice system. Information gleamed in these assessments can be instrumental in informing placement and sentencing decisions. In some instances, criminal justice-involved youth are able to adequately self-report information about the traumatic experience (Abram et al., 2004; Ford et al., 2008). Nonetheless, more work is needed to develop and refine such screening and assessment instruments.

Upon proper assessment, psychosocial interventions that address trauma among justice-involved youth are essential services in criminal justice settings (Ford, Chapman, Connor, & Cruise, 2012; Kerig et al., 2012) and settings where youth are at risk for criminal justice-involvement (Danielson, Begle, Ayer, & Hanson, 2012; Ford, Chapman, Mack, & Pearson, 2006; Ford, Kerig, & Olafson, 2014). Such treatment should endeavor to help youth process any traumatic memories, whether old or recent (Ford & Cloitre, 2009). Further, the treatment approach may include working with former gang members who can serve as role models and can assist with the development of prosocial trajectories of re-entry (Arroyo, 2001). Other strategies to incorporate include creating a calm and safe environment, maintaining flexibility, allowing the youth to provide input on the treatment strategy, identifying clear boundaries and consequences, and teaching techniques and skills to overcome stress and anxiety (e.g., emotional regulation and breathing exercises).

Last but not least, professionals should work with criminal justice- and gang-involved youth to develop protective factors against persistent antisocial behavior and other forms of maladjustment (Guerra et al., 2014). First, this should include the development of strong and secure relationships with primary caregivers, family members, and mentors. Second, the establishment of prosocial relationships with peers and minimization of contact with antisocial peers are essential. Third, professionals should help ensure continued pursuit of academic achievement. Fourth, professionals must assist clients develop skills relevant to employment and identify employment opportunities. Together, these protective factors have the potential to maximize a young adult's support system and opportunities for the successful reintegration into society.

Concluding Thoughts

As highlighted in this chapter, both trauma in and involvement with gangs can have deleterious consequences on youth, including increased risk of sustaining a traumatic brain injury. Not only does trauma increase the risk of delinquency and gang membership, but involvement with gangs only leads to additional trauma and possible traumatic brain injury. This vicious cycle of trauma and antisocial behavior increases the likelihood of long-term involvement in the criminal justice system. As such, trauma and gang membership serve as important intervention opportunities. Professionals working in criminal justice, forensic mental health, and human service settings have the potential to assist young adults in overcoming trauma and gang entanglements. Interventions should be trauma and brain injury-informed and tailored to individualized risks and needs. Such care has the potential to improve long-term outcomes and public safety.

Discussion Points and Questions

1.   How and why can gang involvement lead to the development of post-traumatic stress disorder (PTSD)?
2.   What impact does gang involvement have on an individual's mental health?
3.   How and why can gang involvement lead to the development of head injury?
4.   What prevention and intervention strategies are most appropriate for gang members who have been diagnosed with PTSD and traumatic brain injury (TBI)?

Web Sources

Brain Injury Association of America:

https://www.biausa.org/

Traumatic Brain Injury-Mayo Clinic:

https://www.mayoclinic.org/diseases-conditions/traumatic-brain-injury/symptoms-causes/syc-20378557

Traumatic Brain Injury-CDC:

https://www.cdc.gov/traumaticbraininjury/index.html

PTSD Alliance:

http://www.ptsdalliance.org/

National Institute of Mental Health:

https://www.nimh.nih.gov/health/topics/post-traumatic-stress-disorder-ptsd/index.shtml

REFERENCES

Abram, K., Teplin, L., Charles, D., Longworth, S., McLelland, G., & Dulcan, M. (2004). Posttraumatic stress disorder and trauma in youth in juvenile detention. *Archives of General Psychiatry, 61*, 403–410.

Allwood, M. A., Bell, D. J., & Horan, J. (2011). Posttrauma numbing of fear, detachment, and arousal predict delinquent behaviors in early adolescence. *Journal of Clinical Child & Adolescent Psychology, 40*(5), 659–667.

Anderson, V., Godfrey, C., Rosenfeld, J. V., & Catroppa, C. (2012). Predictors of cognitive function and recovery 10 years after traumatic brain injury in young children. *Pediatrics, 129*(2), e254–e261. doi:10.1542/peds.2011-0311

Arroyo, W. (2001). PTSD in children and adolescents in the juvenile justice system. *PTSD in Children and Adolescents, 20*, 59–86.

Bailey, C. E., Smith, C., Huey, S. R., McDaniel, D. D., & Babeva, K. (2014). Unrecognized posttraumatic stress disorder as a treatment barrier for a gang-involved juvenile offender. *Journal of Aggression, Maltreatment & Trauma, 23*, 199–214.

Battin-Pearson, S. R., Thornberry, T. P., Hawkins, J. D., & Krohn, M. D. (1998). Gang membership, delinquent peers, and delinquent behavior. *Juvenile Justice Bulletin, 36*(1), 93–115.

Bennett, D. C., & Kerig, P. K. (2014). Investigating the construct of trauma-related acquired callousness among delinquent youth: Differences in emotion processing. *Journal of Traumatic Stress, 27*(4), 415–422.

Bennett, D. C., Kerig, P. K., Chaplo, S. D., McGee, A. B., & Baucom, B. R. (2014). Validation of the five-factor model of PTSD symptom structure among delinquent youth. *Psychological Trauma: Theory, Research, Practice, and Policy, 6*(4), 438.

Bennett, D. C., Modrowski, C. A., Kerig, P. K., & Chaplo, S. D. (2015). Investigating the dissociative subtype of posttraumatic stress disorder in a sample of traumatized detained youth. *Psychological Trauma: Theory, Research, Practice, and Policy, 7*(5), 465.

Bishop, A. S., Hill, K. G., Gilman, A. B., Howell, J. C., Catalano, R. F., & Hawkins, J. D. (2017). Developmental pathways of youth gang membership: A structural test of the social development model. *Journal of Crime and Justice, 40*(3), 275–296.

Bjerregaard, B., & Lizotte, A. J. (1995). Gun ownership and gang membership. *Journal of Criminal Law and Criminology, 86*, 37.

Bonevski, B., Randell, M., Paul, C., Chapman, K., Twyman, L., Bryant, J., . . . Hughes, C. (2014). Reaching the hard-to-reach: A systematic review of strategies for improving health and medical research with socially disadvantaged groups. *BMC Medical Research Methodology, 14*(1), 42.

Bowers, L. G. (2008). Does your hospital have a procedure for recognizing and responding to gang behavior? *Journal of Healthcare Protection Management: Publication of the International Association for Hospital Security, 24*(2), 80–83.

Boyle, G. (2011). *Tattoos on the heart: The power of boundless compassion.* New York, NY: Free Press.

Braakman, M. H., Kortmann, F. A. M., & Van den Brink, W. (2009). Validity of "posttraumatic stress disorder with secondary psychotic features": A review of the evidence. *Acta Psychiatrica Scandinavica, 119*(1), 15–24.

Buka, S. L., Stichick, T. L., Birdthistle, I., & Earls, F. J. (2001). Youth exposure to violence: Prevalence, risks, and consequences. *American Journal of Orthopsychiatry, 71*(3), 298–310.

Chapman, J. F., & Ford, J. D. (2008). Relationships between suicide risk, traumatic experiences, and substance use among juvenile detainees screened with the MAYSI–2 and Suicide Ideation Questionnaire. *Archives of Suicide Research, 12*(1), 50–61.

Chatterjee, D., McMorris, B., Gower, A. L., Forster, M., Borowsky, I. W., & Eisenberg, M. E. (2018). Adverse childhood experiences and early initiation of marijuana and alcohol use: The potential moderating effects of internal assets. *Substance Use & Misuse*, 1–9.

Coid, J. W., Ullrich, S., Keers, R., Bebbington, P., Destavola, B. L., Kallis, C., . . . Donnelly, P. (2013). Gang membership, violence and psychiatric co-morbidity. *American Journal of Psychiatry, 170*(9), 985–993.

Cook, A., Spinazzola, J., Ford, J., Lanktree, C., Blaustein, M., Cloitre, M., . . . Van der Kolk, B. (2005). Complex trauma in children and adolescents. *Psychiatric Analysis, 35*(5), 390–398.

Costello, E. J., Erkanli, A., Fairbank, J. A., & Angold, A. (2002). The prevalence of potentially traumatic events in childhood and adolescence. *Journal of Traumatic Stress: Official Publication of the International Society for Traumatic Stress Studies, 15*(2), 99–112.

Crimmins, S. M., Cleary, S. D., Brownstein, H. H., Spunt, B. J., & Warley, R. M. (2000). Trauma, drugs
and violence among juvenile offenders. *Journal of Psychoactive Drugs, 32*(1), 43–54.

Danielson, C. K., Begle, A. M., Ayer, L., & Hanson, R. F. (2012). Psychosocial treatment of traumatized juveniles. In *Handbook of juvenile forensic psychology and psychiatry* (pp. 467–483). Boston, MA: Springer.

David, D., Kutcher, G. S., Jackson, E. I., & Mellman, T. A. (1999). Psychotic symptoms in combat-related posttraumatic stress disorder. *Journal of Clinical Psychiatry, 60*, 29–32.

Decker, S. H., & Van Winkle, B. (1996). *Life in the gang: Family, friends, and violence.* Cambridge, England: Cambridge University Press.

Dierkhising, C. B., Ko, S. J., Woods-Jaeger, B., Briggs, E. C., Lee, R., & Pynoos, R. S. (2013). Trauma histories among justice-involved youth: Findings from the National Child Traumatic Stress Network. *European Journal of Psychotraumatology, 4*(1), 20274.

Dmitrieva, J., Gibson, L., Steinberg, L., Piquero, A., & Fagan, J. (2014). Predictors and consequences of gang membership: Comparing gang members, gang leaders, and non-gang-affiliated adjudicated youth. *Journal of Research on Adolescence, 24*(2), 220–234.

Donnellan, M. B., Trzesniewski, K. H., Robins, R. W., Moffitt, T. E., & Caspi, A. (2005). Low self-esteem is related to aggression, antisocial behavior, and delinquency. *Psychological science, 16*(4), 328–335.

Dukes, R. L., Martinez, R. O., & Stein, J. A. (1997). Precursors and consequences of membership in youth gangs. *Youth & Society, 29*(2), 139–165.

Dupéré, V., Lacourse, É., Willms, J. D., Vitaro, F., & Tremblay, R. E. (2007). Affiliation to youth gangs during adolescence: The interaction between childhood psychopathic tendencies and neighborhood disadvantage. *Journal of Abnormal Child Psychology, 35*(6), 1035–1045.

Egley, A., Jr., Howell, J. C., & Harris, M. (2014). *Highlights of the 2012 National Youth Gang Survey. Juvenile Justice Fact Sheet.* Washington, DC: Office of Juvenile Justice and Delinquency Prevention.

Eitle, D., Gunkel, S., & Van Gundy, K. (2004). Cumulative exposure to stressful life events and male gang membership. *Journal of Criminal Justice, 32*(2), 95–111.

Emery, C. A., Barlow, K. M., Brooks, B. L., Max, J. E., Villavicencio-Requis, A., Gnanakumar, V., . . . Yeates, K. O. (2016). A systematic review of psychiatric, psychological, and behavioural outcomes following mild traumatic brain injury in children and adolescents. *Canadian Journal of Psychiatry, 61*(5), 259–269.

Esbensen, F. A., & Huizinga, D. (1993). Gangs, drugs, and delinquency in a survey of urban youth. *Criminology, 31*(4), 565–589.

Esbensen, F. A., & Weerman, F. M. (2005). Youth gangs and troublesome youth groups in the United States and the Netherlands: A cross-national comparison. *European Journal of Criminology, 2*(1), 5–37.

Ewing-Cobbs, L., Barnes, M., Fletcher, J. M., Levin, H. S., Swank, P. R., & Song, J. (2004). Modeling of longitudinal academic achievement scores after pediatric traumatic brain injury. *Developmental Neuropsychology, 25*(1–2), 107–133.

Fagan, J. A. (1989). The social organization of drug dealing among urban gangs. *Criminology, 27*, 633–669.

Faul, M., Xu, L., Wald, M. M., & Coronado, V. G. (2010). *Traumatic brain injury in the United States. Emergency department visits, hospitalizations, and deaths.* Atlanta, GA: Centers for Disease Control and Prevention, National Center for Injury Prevention and Control.

Fazel, S., Doll, H., & Långström, N. (2008). Mental disorders among adolescents in juvenile detention and correctional facilities: A systematic review and metaregression analysis of 25 surveys. *Journal of the American Academy of Child & Adolescent Psychiatry, 47*(9), 1010–1019.

Fisher, H., Gardner, F. E., & Montgomery, P. (2008). Cognitive-behavioural interventions for preventing youth gang involvement for children and young people (7–16). *The Cochrane Database of Systematic Reviews, 2*, CD007008–CD007008.

Folger, A. T., Eismann, E. A., Stephenson, N. B., Shapiro, R. A., Macaluso, M., Brownrigg, M. E., & Gillespie, R. J. (2018). Parental adverse childhood experiences and offspring development at 2 years of age. *Pediatrics*, e20172826.

Ford, J. D., & Blaustein, M. E. (2013). Systemic self-regulation: A framework for trauma informed services in residential juvenile justice programs. *Journal of Family Violence, 28*(7), 665–677.

Ford, J. D. (2009). Neurobiological and developmental research: Clinical implications. In C. A. Courtois & J. D. Ford (Eds.), *Treating complex traumatic stress disorders: An evidence-based guide* (pp. 31–58). New York: Guilford Press.

Ford, J. D., & Cloitre, M. (2009). Best practices in psychotherapy for children and adolescents. In C. A. Courtois & J. D. Ford (Eds.), *Treating complex traumatic stress disorders: An evidence-based guide* (pp. 59–81). New York, NY: Guilford.

Ford, J. D., & Courtois, C. A. (2013). *Treating complex traumatic stress disorders in children and adolescents.* New York, NY: Guilford.

Ford, J. D., & Hawke, J. (2012). Trauma affect regulation psychoeducation group and milieu intervention outcomes in juvenile detention facilities. *Journal of Aggression, Maltreatment & Trauma, 21*(4), 365–384. doi:10.1080/10926771.2012.673538

Ford, J. D., Kerig, P. K., & Olafson, E. (2014). Evidence-informed interventions for posttraumatic stress problems with youth involved in the juvenile justice system. Los Angeles, CA: *National Child Traumatic Stress Network.* Retrieved from https://www.nctsn.org/sites/default/files/resources//trauma_focused_interventions_for_youth_in_jj.pdf

Ford, J. D., Chapman, J., Connor, D. F., & Cruise, K. R. (2012). Complex trauma and aggression in secure juvenile justice settings. Criminal Justice and Behavior, 39(6), 694–724.

Ford, J. D., Chapman, J., Mack, J. M., & Pearson, G. (2006). Pathways from traumatic child victimization to delinquency: Implications for juvenile and permanency court proceedings and decisions. Juvenile and Family Court Journal, 57(1), 13–26.

Ford, J. D., Hartman, J. K., Hawke, J., & Chapman, J. F. (2008). Traumatic victimization, posttraumatic stress disorder, suicidal ideation, and substance abuse risk among juvenile justice-involved youth. Journal of Child & Adolescent Trauma, 1(1), 75–92.

Ford, J. D., Kerig, P. K., Desai, N., & Feierman, J. (2016). Psychosocial Interventions for Traumatized Youth in the Juvenile Justice System: Research, Evidence Base, and Clinical/Legal Challenges. *Journal of Juvenile Justice, 5*(1), 31-49.

Gatti, U., Tremblay, R. E., Vitaro, F., & McDuff, P. (2005). Youth gangs, delinquency and drug use: A test of the selection, facilitation, and enhancement hypotheses. *Journal of Child Psychology and Psychiatry, 46*(11), 1178–1190.

Gebo, E. (2016). An integrated public health and criminal justice approach to gangs: What can research tell us? *Preventive Medicine Reports, 4,* 376–380.

Gilman, A. B., Hill, K. G., & Hawkins, J. D. (2014). Long-term consequences of adolescent gang membership for adult functioning. *American Journal of Public Health, 104*(5), 938–945.

Guerra, N. G., Dierkhising, C. B., & Payne, P. R. (2014). How should we identify and intervene with youth at risk of joining gangs? Retrieved from https://www.ncjrs.gov/pdffiles1/nij/239234.pdf#page=66

Hagedorn, J. M. (2005). The global impact of gangs. *Journal of Contemporary Criminal Justice, 21,* 153–169.

Harris, T. B., Elkins, S., Butler, A., Shelton, M., Robles, B., Kwok, S., . . . Sargent, A. J. (2012). Youth gang members: Psychiatric disorders and substance use. *Laws, 2,* 392–400.

Hayman-Abello, S. E., Rourke, B. P., & Fuerst, D. R. (2003). Psychosocial status after pediatric traumatic brain injury: A subtype analysis using the Child Behavior Checklist. *Journal of the International Neuropsychological Society, 9*(6), 887–898.

Herrenkohl, T. I., Maguin, E., Hill, K. G., Hawkins, J. D., Abbott, R. D., & Catalano, R. F. (2000). Developmental risk factors for youth violence. *Journal of Adolescent Health, 26*(3), 176–186.

Hill, K. G., Howell, J. C., Hawkins, J. D., & Battin-Pearson, S. R. (1999). Childhood risk factors for adolescent gang membership: Results from the Seattle Social Development Project. *Journal of Research in Crime and Delinquency, 36*(3), 300–322.

Hill, K. G., Lui, C., & Hawkins, J. D. (2001). *Early precursors of gang membership: A study of Seattle youth.* Washington, DC: US Department of Justice, Office of Justice Programs, Office of Juvenile Justice and Delinquency Prevention.

Howell, J. C., & Egley, A., Jr. (2005). Moving risk factors into developmental theories of gang membership. *Youth Violence and Juvenile Justice, 3*(4), 334–354.

Howell, J. C., & Moore, J. P. (2010). *History of street gangs in the United States.* Washington, DC: US Department of Justice, Bureau of Justice Assistance, and Office of Juvenile Justice and Delinquency Prevention.

Huff, C. R. (1998). *Comparing the criminal behavior of youth gangs and at-risk youths* (National Institute of Justice Research in Brief). Washington, DC: U.S. Department of Justice, Office of Justice Programs.

Hux, K., Bond, V., Skinner, S., Belau, D., & Sanger, D. (1998). Parental report of occurrences and consequences of traumatic brain injury among delinquent and non-delinquent youth. *Brain Injury, 12*(8), 667-681.

Janusz, J. A., Kirkwood, M. W., Yeates, K. O., & Taylor, H. G. (2002). Social problem-solving skills in children with traumatic brain injury: Long-term outcomes and prediction of social competence. *Child Neuropsychology, 8*(3), 179–194.

Javanbakht, A., Rosenberg, D., Haddad, L., & Arfken, C. L. (2018). Mental health in Syrian refugee children resettling in the United States: War trauma, migration, and the role of parental stress. *Journal of the American Academy of Child & Adolescent Psychiatry, 57*(3), 209–211.

Keightley, M., Sinopoli, K., Davis, K., Green, R., Mikulis, D., Wennberg, R., . . . Tator, C. (2014). Is there evidence for neurodegenerative change following traumatic brain injury in children and youth? A scoping review. *Frontiers in Human Neuroscience, 8,* 139.

Kerig, P. K., & Becker, S. P. (2010). From internalizing to externalizing: Theoretical models of the processes linking PTSD to juvenile delinquency. In S. J. Egan (Ed.), *Posttraumatic stress disorder (PTSD): Causes, symptoms and treatment* (pp. 1–46). Hauppauge, NY: Nova Science.

Kerig, P. K., & Becker, S. P. (2015). Early abuse and neglect as predictors of antisocial outcomes in adolescence and adulthood. In J. Morizot & L. Kazemian (Eds.), *The development of criminal and antisocial behavior: Theoretical foundations and practical applications* (pp. 181–199). New York, NY: Springer.

Kerig, P. K., Chaplo, S. D., Bennett, D. C., & Modrowski, C. A. (2016). "Harm as harm" gang membership, perpetration trauma, and posttraumatic stress symptoms among youth in the juvenile justice system. *Criminal Justice and Behavior, 43*(5), 635–652.

Kerig, P. K., Vanderzee, K. L., Becker, S. P., & Ward, R. M. (2012). Deconstructing PTSD: Traumatic experiences, posttraumatic symptom clusters, and mental health problems among delinquent youth. *Journal of Child & Adolescent Trauma, 5*(2), 129–144.

Kerig, P. K., Wainryb, C., Twali, M. S., & Chaplo, S. D. (2013). America's child soldiers: Toward a research agenda for studying gang-involved youth in the United States. *Journal of Aggression, Maltreatment & Trauma, 22*(7), 773–795.

Kilpatrick, D. G., Ruggiero, K. J., Acierno, R., Saunders, B. E., Resnick, H. S., & Best, C. L. (2003). Violence and risk of PTSD, major depression, substance abuse/dependence, and comorbidity: results from the National Survey of Adolescents. Journal of consulting and clinical psychology, 71(4), 692-700.

Klein, M. W., & Maxson, C. L. (2006). *Street gang patterns and policies*. New York, NY: Oxford University Press.

Lacourse, E., Nagin, D., Tremblay, R. E., Vitaro, F., & Claes, M. (2003). Developmental trajectories of boys' delinquent group membership and facilitation of violent behaviors during adolescence. *Development and Psychopathology, 15*(1), 183–197.

Lane, J. (2002). Fear of gang crime: A qualitative examination of the four perspectives. *Journal of Research in Crime and Delinquency, 39*(4), 437–471.

Lane, S. D., Rubinstein, R. A., Bergen-Cico, D., Jennings-Bey, T., Fish, L. S., Larsen, D. A., . . . Robinson, J. A. (2017). Neighborhood trauma due to violence: A multilevel analysis. *Journal of Health Care for the Poor and Underserved, 28*(1), 446–462.

Langlois, J., Rutland-Brown, W., & Thomas, K. (2006). *Traumatic brain injury in the United States: Emergency department visits, hospitalizations, and deaths*. Atlanta, GA: Centers for Disease Control and Prevention, National Center for Injury Prevention.

Lenzi, M., Sharkey, J., Vieno, A., Mayworm, A., Dougherty, D., & Nylund-Gibson, K. (2015). Adolescent gang involvement: The role of individual, family, peer, and school factors in a multilevel perspective. *Aggressive Behavior, 41*(4), 386–397.

Loeber, R., & Farrington, D. P. (2000). Young children who commit crime: Epidemiology, developmental origins, risk factors, early interventions, and policy implications. *Development and Psychopathology, 12*(4), 737–762.

Madan, A., Mrug, S., & Windle, M. (2011). Brief report: Do delinquency and community violence exposure explain internalizing problems in early adolescent gang members? *Journal of Adolescence, 34*(5), 1093–1096.

Malinkosky-Rummell, R., & Hansen, D. (1993). Long-term consequences of childhood physical abuse. *Psychological Bulletin, 114*, 68–79.

McKinlay, A., Corrigan, J., Horwood, L. J., & Fergusson, D. M. (2014). Substance abuse and criminal activities following traumatic brain injury in childhood, adolescence, and early adulthood. *Journal of Head Trauma Rehabilitation, 29*(6), 498–506.

Melde, C., & Esbensen, F. A. (2012). The onset of (Euro) gang membership as a turning point in the life course. In *Youth gangs in international perspective* (pp. 169–187). New York, NY: Springer.

Melde, C., & Esbensen, F. A. (2014). The relative impact of gang status transitions: Identifying the mechanisms of change in delinquency. *Journal of Research in Crime and Delinquency, 51*(3), 349–376.

Moore, J. W. (1998). Understanding youth street gangs: Economic restructuring and the urban underclass. In M. W. Watts (Ed.), *Cross-cultural perspectives on youth and violence* (pp. 65–78). Stamford, CT: JAI.

Morgan, A. B., & Lilienfeld, S. O. (2000). A meta-analytic review of the relation between antisocial behavior and neuropsychological measures of executive function. *Clinical Psychology Review, 20*(1), 113–136.

National Child Traumatic Stress Network. (n.d.). *Your child and gangs: What you need to know about trauma: Tips for parents.* Retrieved from https://www.nctsn.org/resources/your-child-and-gangs-what-you-need-know-about-trauma-tips-parents

National Youth Gang Center. (2013). National Youth Gang Survey analysis. Retrieved from https://www.nationalgangcenter.gov/survey-analysis

Neville, F. G., Goodall, C. A., Gavine, A. J., Williams, D. J., & Donnelly, P. D. (2015). Public health, youth violence, and perpetrator well-being. *Peace and Conflict: Journal of Peace Psychology, 21*(3), 322–333.

Ogilvie, J. M., Stewart, A. L., Chan, R. C., & Shum, D. H. (2011). Neuropsychological measures of executive function and antisocial behavior: A meta-analysis. *Criminology, 49*(4), 1063–1107.

Osofsky, J. D. (1995). The effect of exposure to violence on young children. *American Psychologist, 50*(9), 782–788.

Paton, J., Crouch, W., & Camic, P. (2009). Young offenders' experiences of traumatic life events. *Clinical Child Psychology and Psychiatry, 14*, 43–62.

Perron, B. E., & Howard, M. O. (2008). Prevalence and correlates of traumatic brain injury among delinquent youths. *Criminal Behaviour and Mental Health, 18*, 243–255.

Peterson, D., Taylor, T. J., & Esbensen, F. A. (2004). Gang membership and violent victimization. *Justice Quarterly, 21*(4), 793–815.

Pine, D. S. (2007). Research review: A neuroscience framework for pediatric anxiety disorders. *Journal of Child Psychology and Psychiatry, 48*, 631–648.

Pyrooz, D. C. (2014). "From your first cigarette to your last dyin'day": The patterning of gang membership in the life-course. *Journal of Quantitative Criminology, 30*(2), 349–372.

Pyrooz, D. C., & Densley, J. A. (2016). Selection into street gangs: Signaling theory, gang membership, and criminal offending. *Journal of Research in Crime and Delinquency, 53*(4), 447–481.

Pyrooz, D. C., & Sweeten, G. (2015). Gang membership between ages 5 and 17 years in the United States. *Journal of Adolescent Health, 56*(4), 414–419.

Rahtz, E., Bhui, K., Smuk, M., Hutchison, I., & Korszun, A. (2017). Violent injury predicts poor psychological outcomes after traumatic injury in a hard-to-reach population: An observational cohort study. *BMJ Open, 7*(5), e014712.

Rheingold, A. A., Smith, D. W., Ruggiero, K. J., Saunders, B. E., Kilpatrick, D. G., & Resnick, H. S. (2004). Loss, trauma exposure, and mental health in a representative sample of 12- to 17-year-old youth: Data from the national survey of adolescents. *Journal of Loss and Trauma, 9*(1), 1–19.

Rizzo, M. (2003). Why do children join gangs? *Journal of Gang Research, 11*(1), 65–75.

Rosema, S., Crowe, L., & Anderson, V. (2012). Social function in children and adolescents after traumatic brain injury: A systematic review 1989–2011. *Journal of Neurotrauma, 29*(7), 1277–1291.

Ross, L., Arsenault, S., & Lopez, S. M. (2016). *Problem analysis in community violence assessments: Revealing early childhood trauma as a driver of youth and gang violence.* Mosakowski Institute for Public Enterprise. Retrieved from http://commons.clarku.edu/mosakowskiinstitute/69

Sanders, B., Schneiderman, J. U., Loken, A., Lankenau, S. E., & Bloom, J. J. (2009). Gang youth as a vulnerable population for nursing intervention. *Public Health Nursing, 26*(4), 346–352.

Schachar, R. J., Park, L. S., & Dennis, M. (2015). Mental health implications of traumatic brain injury (TBI) in children and youth. *Journal of the Canadian Academy of Child and Adolescent Psychiatry, 24*(2), 100–108.

Sharp, C., Aldridge, J., & Medina, J. (2006). *Delinquent youth groups and offending behavior: Findings from the 2004 Offending, Crime and Justice Survey* (Home Office Online Report 14/06). London, England: Home Office.

Sickmund, M., Snyder, H., & Poe-Yamagata, E. (1997). *Juvenile offenders and victims: 1997 update on violence.* Washington, DC: Office of Juvenile Justice and Delinquency Prevention.

Sirpal, S. K. (1997). Causes of gang participation and strategies for prevention in gang members' own words. *Journal of Gang Research, 4*(2), 13–22.

Spergel, I. A. (1995). *The youth gang problem: A community approach.* New York, NY: Oxford University Press.

Steinberg, L. (2009). Adolescent development and juvenile justice. *Annual Review of Clinical Psychology, 5*, 459–485.

Taylor, T. J., Freng, A., Esbensen, F. A., & Peterson, D. (2008). Youth gang membership and serious violent victimization: The importance of lifestyles and routine activities. *Journal of Interpersonal Violence, 23*(10), 1441–1464.

Thornberry, T. P. (1998). Membership in youth gangs and involvement in serious and violent offending. In R. Loeber & D. P. Farrington (Eds.), *Serious and violent offenders: Risk factors and successful interventions* (pp. 147–166). Thousand Oaks, CA: SAGE.

Thornberry, T. P., & Burch, I. I. J. H. (1997). Gang members and delinquent behavior. *Bulletin. Office of Justice Programs. Office of Juvenile Justice and Delinquency Prevention.* Washington, DC: U.S. Department of Justice.

Thornberry, T. P., Krohn, M. D., Lizotte, A. J., Smith, C., & Tobin, K. (2003). *Gangs and delinquency in developmental perspective.* Cambridge, England: Cambridge University Press.

Thurman, D. J. (2016). The epidemiology of traumatic brain injury in children and youths: A review of research since 1990. *Journal of Child Neurology, 31*(1), 20–27.

Timonen, M., Miettunen, J., Hakko, H., Zitting, P., Veijola, J., von Wendt, L., & Räsänen, P. (2002). The association of preceding traumatic brain injury with mental disorders, alcoholism and criminality: The Northern Finland 1966 Birth Cohort Study. *Psychiatry Research, 113*(3), 217–226.

Tita, G. E., Cohen, J., & Engberg, J. (2005). An ecological study of the location of gang "set space." *Social Problems, 52,* 272–299.

Tonks, J., Slater, A., Frampton, I., Wall, S. E., Yates, P., & Williams, W. H. (2009). The development of emotion and empathy skills after childhood brain injury. *Developmental Medicine & Child Neurology, 51*(1), 8–16.

Trasher, F. M. (1927). *The gang: A study of 1,313 gangs in Chicago.* Chicago, IL: University of Chicago Press.

Tull, M. T., Berghoff, C. R., Wheeless, L. E., Cohen, R. T., & Gratz, K. L. (2018). PTSD symptom severity and emotion regulation strategy use during trauma cue exposure among patients with substance use disorders: Associations with negative affect, craving, and cortisol reactivity. *Behavior Therapy, 49*(1), 57–70.

Turkstra, L., Jones, D., & Toler, H. L. (2003). Brain injury and violent crime. *Brain Injury, 17*(1), 39–47.

Vaughn, M. G., Salas-Wright, C. P., DeLisi, M., & Perron, B. (2014). Correlates of traumatic brain injury among juvenile offenders: A multi-site study. *Criminal Behaviour and Mental Health, 24*(3), 188–203.

Weil, Z. M., Karelina, K., Gaier, K. R., Corrigan, T. E., & Corrigan, J. D. (2016). Juvenile traumatic brain injury increases alcohol consumption and reward in female mice. *Journal of Neurotrauma, 33*(9), 895–903.

Wilcox, H. C., Storr, C. L., & Breslau, N. (2009). Posttraumatic stress disorder and suicide attempts in a community sample of urban American young adults. *Archives of General Psychiatry, 66*(3), 305–311.

Williams, H., Chitsabesan, P., Lennox, C., Tariq, O., & Shaw, J. (2015). Traumatic brain injury in juvenile offenders: Findings from the comprehensive health assessment tool study and the development of a specialist linkworker service. *Journal of Head Trauma Rehabilitation, 30*(2), 106–115.

Williams, W. H., Cordan, G., Mewse, A. J., Tonks, J., & Burgess, C. N. (2010). Self-reported traumatic brain injury in male young offenders: A risk factor for re-offending, poor mental health and violence? *Neuropsychological Rehabilitation, 20*(6), 801–812.

Williams, W. H., McAuliffe, K. A., Cohen, M. H., Parsonage, M., & Ramsbotham, J. (2015). Traumatic brain injury and juvenile offending: Complex causal links offer multiple targets to reduce crime. *Journal of Head Trauma Rehabilitation, 30*(2), 69–74.

Williams, W. H., Mewse, A. J., Tonks, J., Mills, S., Burgess, C. N., & Cordan, G. (2010). Traumatic brain injury in a prison population: Prevalence and risk for re-offending. *Brain Injury, 24*(10), 1184–1188.

Winqvist, S., Jokelainen, J., Luukinen, H., & Hillbom, M. (2006). Adolescents' drinking habits predict later occurrence of traumatic brain injury: 35-year follow-up of the northern Finland 1966 birth cohort. *Journal of Adolescent Health, 39*(2), 275–e1.

Wood, J., & Dennard, S. (2017). Gang membership: Links to violence exposure, paranoia, PTSD, anxiety, and forced control of behavior in prison. *Psychiatry, 80*(1), 30–41.

Wood, J., Foy, D. W., Layne, C., Pynoos, R., & James, C. B. (2002). An examination of the relationships between violence exposure, posttraumatic stress symptomatology, and delinquent activity: An "ecopathological" model of delinquent behavior among incarcerated adolescents. *Journal of Aggression, Maltreatment & Trauma, 6*(1), 127–147.

Yates, P. J., Williams, W. H., Harris, A., Round, A., & Jenkins, R. (2006). An epidemiological study of head injuries in a UK population attending an emergency department. *Journal of Neurology, Neurosurgery, and Psychiatry, 77*, 699-701.

Yeates, K. O., Bigler, E. D., Dennis, M., Gerhardt, C. A., Rubin, K. H., Stancin, T., . . . Vannatta, K. (2007). Social outcomes in childhood brain disorder: A heuristic integration of social neuroscience and developmental psychology. *Psychological Bulletin, 133*(3), 535.

Chapter 4

Girls and Gangs

CHAPTER OBJECTIVES

- Explore the past and current research on female gangs.

- Examine why females choose to join gangs and different types of gang initiations.

- Discuss the different types of all-female gangs.

- Examine the most recent data on female gang membership.

- Explore how law enforcement is dealing with female gangs and the challenges they face.

"GIRL GANG" ACCUSED OF "TERRORIZING THE COMMUNITY" IN D.C.

WASHINGTON, D.C. – An Advisory Neighborhood Commissioner had recently accused an all-girl gang of attacking people in D.C. and putting their exploits on social media. ANC Commissioner Robbie Woodland explained that the all-girl gang, comprising teenagers, has been terrorizing much of Southeast D.C.

The ANC Commissioner provided examples of a mother and her three children beaten by approximately 30 gang members at the Anacostia Metro Station. She also shared a video of a women being dragged out of her bed and beaten. The Commissioner is working with the Metro PD gang task force in trying to identify the gang members.

Source: Ford, S. (2019, June 28). 'Girl gang' accused of 'terrorizing the community' in D.C., putting it on social media. WJLA/ABC 7. Retrieved from https://wjla.com/news/local/girl-gang-terrorizing-dc-social-media

Introduction

While most street gangs and violence associated with the gang members involve males, some gangs are actually comprised of females. Similar to male gangs, the data suggests that a typical female gang member is a minority, between the ages of 14 and 25, and from an urban setting. Even though female gang involvement is not as prevalent as males' participation, females can still play a critical role in the formation and vitality of street gangs, and present unique challenges for law enforcement officials.

Although the exact numbers for female gang membership varies, the National Gang Center (n.d.) estimates that females account for roughly 10% of all gang members. The same report indicates that law enforcement agencies overwhelmingly report a greater percentage of male gang members versus female gang members. This is typical of most finding from law enforcement data, but one that is challenged by other research methodologies.

With regards to delinquent acts, female gang members have greater delinquency rates than female and male non-members (see, Bjerregaard & Smith, 1993; Miller, 2002). Noted gang researcher and anthropologist Walter Miller theorized that female gang members can function in one of three capacities: (1) independently functioning units, (2) coed gangs, and (3) female auxiliaries to male gangs. As defined by Miller, independently functioning all-female gang units operate under their own gang colors and name, without the oversight from existing male gangs. Coed gangs, the second possible unit, possess both male and female members while most of the leadership positions are held by males. However, Taylor (1993) reported that positions and power held by female gang members tends to vary from gang to gang. Those positions and power often rely on the gang's structure. Female auxiliary gangs also adopt the symbols of and adapt the name of an existing male gang, but operate semi-autonomously. This is to say that the female gang acts in the interests of the male gang while the female gang independently controls member initiation and internal business of the group.

Prior Research on Female Gangs and Gang Membership

Historically, the research on females involved with street gangs is relatively scarce when compared to the extent of research on male gangs. However, there are some seminal studies that have explored female gang involvement. The earliest mention of females taking part in gang activity was in the late 19th century, when the street gangs in New York City were still evolving (Howell, 2016). Accounts from this time period tell stories of girls acting as lookouts for street fights with rival gangs, evading police, running errands, or acting as decoys for their male counterparts. The earliest female gang members were often thought of as "tomboys," or girls that were trying too hard to fit in with the boys (Campbell, 1984; Howell, 2016; Thrasher, 1927; Thomas, 1923). These girls were often viewed as "little sisters" to the older male gang members, which according to Howell (2016), is still similar to the roles that many females play in gangs today.

Most research prior to the 1980s did not regard female gang membership as significant or worth reporting to officials; nonetheless, there are reports of females gang members in some of the early work on street gangs. Prominent gang researcher Frederick M. Thrasher (1927) included female gang members in his seminal work on street gangs from Chicago in the 1920s. It was one of the first studies to recognize that females played a role in street gangs. Most of Thrasher's discussion on females in gangs involved their sexual capacity. According to Thrasher, while sex was considered a secondary activity in early adolescence, once the boys reached their late teens, sex received much more attention. However, it was not all about sex and the gang. Thrasher concluded that there were "hardcore" female gang members but there were other females who served as an auxiliary member of the gang such as a look-out or girlfriend to a gang member. Thrasher observed that the total number of gangs in Chicago, only six gangs had female members, and only two of them were female-only gangs. Thrasher further documented that the females in the gangs were often used by the male members and took part in less-serious crimes. Both these attributes apply to females involved in gangs today.

Herbert Asbury (1927) also wrote about female gang members in his book, *Gangs of New York* (late made into a Hollywood film of the same name) and how some were skilled fighters such as the famous Hell-Cat Maggie and Battle Annie. Female gangsters in New York City also had ties to the Five Points gangs as they served as lookouts, decoys, ran errands, and spied in brothels.

Another interesting book that was published in 1949 called *Jailbait: The Story of Juvenile Delinquency* was written under the pseudonym William Bernard and it presented information about female gangs. Bernard's (1949) research is a descriptive qualitative analysis of females engaged in sex, lust, rapes, and street gang wars. Bernard explored how some girls used sex as a weapon to commit crimes by seducing men and robbing them, and used sex to further the tension between rival gangs. As the post-war concern for juvenile delinquency rates were rising, more youths were committing crimes and involved with gangs, and the implications that females were contributing to this rise was unfathomable. Bernard noted that "more girls are engaged in gangsterism; and they are committing more severe crimes" (cited in Chesney-Lind & Hagedorn, 1999, p. 45). For Bernard, the rise of female delinquents and those involved with gangs was viewed as a significant problem but much of his conclusions relied on anecdotal evidence, self-reporting activities, and sensational reporting that was not verified. Nonetheless, female delinquents and gangs members were a genuine concern for law enforcement. According to Bernard, law enforcement officials viewed female gang members as not only sex objects but as "auxiliary" members of the gang who carried the males' weapons, drugs, created alibis for the gang members, and spied on other gangs.

Seminal Research on Female Gangs and Gang Members

There have been previous mentions of female gangs in newspaper reports, magazines, journal articles, and books but most authors neglected to mention the role of females in a gang, except for their sexual role. Journalists, gang researchers, and social workers have covered female gangs. For example, Black female gangs from New York City were featured in *The New Yorker* (see Rice, 1963) and the National Center for Juvenile Justice observed Black female gangs in Philadelphia (see Brown, 1977). In Southern California, the Los Angeles Human Relations Bureau examined Latino-based female gangs to get a better understanding (see Quicker, 1983), whereas in Washington DC, African American female gang members are exposed to same ghetto-specific lifestyle as male gang members (Hannerz, 1969). In the Boston area, gang expert Walter Miller (1973) examined White female gangs and their involvement in the gang lifestyle.

However, it was not until Anne Campbell (1984) conducted her ground-breaking study called *The Girls in the Gang* on female gangs in New York City that changed the approach to researching gangs. Campbell's study did not just explore the kinds of crimes female delinquents committed and their affiliation to gangs, but explored the needs, desires, and challenges of female gang participants. As mentioned earlier, female gang members were mostly ignored in much of early research. Female gangs were only mentioned as a passing observation, what the gang members did or how their sexuality helped the male counterpart; but not why they joined. Campbell explained that a void existed because gang studies involving females typically focused on family disruption or the sex-role stereotypes when females were involved with gangs. Most of the earlier studies were intent on solving the gang problem and how law enforcement dealt with gangs instead of addressing the impact gangs have on females. In other words, previous studies were male-oriented narratives, written by males, from a male perspective, offering a male-oriented solution. Campbell and those researchers that followed her (see Chesney-Lind & Hagedorn, 1999; Miller, 2001, 2008; Sanchez & Rodriguez, 2008; Sikes, 1998) represented the other perspective, a much needed one by observing the female gangs and interacting with them to understand things from the female gang members' perspective.

Campbell (1984) successfully joined three female gangs that represented the racial and geographic diversity of current gang life in New York City and focused on an individual girl from each gang for almost 2 years, giving them a voice on what life was like in the world of street gangs. The first was the leader of the Sandman Ladies, a Puerto-Rican motorcycle gang from Manhattan's Upper West Side. The second was a Hispanic/African American in a gang called the Sex Girls, named after Essex Street in Brooklyn. The third was a member of the Five Percent Nation, an African American group based in Brooklyn. While Campbell explored their lives in the world of street gangs, a common theme between each girls' life was poverty, teen pregnancy, drug abuse, and violence.

Since Campbell's study, other key studies followed exploring females and their involvement in the gang world. Feminist criminologist/sociologist Jodi Miller (2001) examined the causes, nature, and meaning of female gang involvement including how and why girls join gangs, the initiation rituals, the gang rules, inter-gang rivalries, and criminal activities. Miller (2008) followed up later with another analysis into the lives of African-American females involved in the gang world and the harsh realities of sexual harassment, sexual assault, dating violence, and even gang rape. Moore (1991) and Harris (1988) explored Latino-based female gangs from Southern California and Taylor (1993) explored how young women and girls from Detroit, Michigan got involved with the drug trade and an urban gang lifestyle. Lastly, veteran journalist Gina Sikes (1998) spent a year in the ghettos following the lives of several key gang members in South Central Los Angeles, San Antonio, and Milwaukee. Sikes discovered that while the police typically dismissed the females for their involvement in gangs, these girls are just as dangerous as their male counterparts, carrying guns, knives, defending their turf, terrorizing the neighborhood, and engaging in violent gang activities.

Why Do Females Join Gangs?

Females, like males, join gangs for many of the same reasons. Females are looking for a surrogate family, a sense of belonging, protection, and relief from economic hardships. Many female youths live in impoverished communities that are prone to gang violence, and have friends and family members involved with gangs. For some females, it is easier to give in and join a gang, rather than attempt to shy away from them entirely. Other females have family influences that drive them into gang life, as well as other societal factors, such as the lack of job opportunities or educational attainment.

Females that are typically surrounded by crime and violence also feel pressured to join a gang. Many of these women were born into communities with an already established gang problem, and the opportunities to leave are minimal. These types of communities are often impoverished, drug-ridden, and house some of the most broken families. Many young females may already have family members, such as brothers or uncles that are involved with gangs, and therefore, they may feel that they need to follow in the footsteps of the family.

Females also join gangs for the other benefits that they offer—protection. Some gangs are formed to protect the youth, their families, and the neighborhood. Since the family system plays an important role in a female's decision to join a gang, girls that come from "underclass" families, abusive families, or run away from home are more likely to join a gang than those that are not (Huff, 2002). Girls are also more likely to have alcoholic or drug-addicted parents than the males based on this study (Huff, 2002).

The societal and familial roles mentioned above certainly have an impact on a female's decision to join a gang. However, it should be noted that there are some females that join gangs simply because they wish to get involved in gang life. For example, members of one female gang in Miller's (1973) study from the Molls, who align themselves with the Hoods in

Boston, were "corner gang girls that talked tough, showed off and looked menacing but they were young teenagers wise before their time" (p. 32). This gang included females from the ages of 13 to 16 who were mostly white, Irish-German Catholics. The Moll gang was engaged in criminal behavior, theft, drinking, vandalism, sexual offenses, truancy, and assaults. The Molls wanted to participate in the same type of criminal activities as the male gangs and imitated their behavior. They were known in the area as the "bad girls."

If the "bad girls" were problematic for law enforcement officials in the 1960s and 1970s, then the "Bad Barbies" is a modern example of how dangerous and violent a female gang is. The all-female gang, also called the One Seven Hoes, is associated with the Trinitarios, a violent Dominican-American street gang from New York City. The Bad Barbie's mode of operandi was to coax rival gang members into a trap, by the promise of sex or the obtainment of drugs, and there the Trinitarios would exact violence against that individual often resulting in serious bodily harm, or even death. Law enforcement officials and gang cops in New York City call is the "the Venus fly trap." While the Bad Barbies are a female gang, they are still considered the property of the male gang Trinitarios, who regularly rape or pimp out the girls. The females also act as decoys and mules, often carrying weapons and drugs, typically in baby strollers, for the gang (see News Clip 4.1).

Gang Member Initiation

The gang initiation process for females is very similar to the requirements for a male to join a street gang. The most common type of gang initiation for a female gang hopeful is to commit a serious crime or get "jumped-in" or "beat-in." Getting "jumped-in/beat-in" requires the female to fight with a number of males, and possibly other female gang members, for a specific amount of time (e.g., 10-15 seconds). However, there is another initiation process that only applies to females, and it is degrading and brutal. When a female tries to join a predominantly male gang, she can also be "sexed-in" or "diced-in." This type of initiation requires a female to have sex with one or multiple male gang members at once. The expression "diced-in" refers to the rolling a die or dice, and the number of dots on the die determines the total number of gang members that female has to have sex with in order to join the gang. This initiation is humiliating and is tantamount to rape. Unfortunately, when a female chooses this option she does not gain the respect of her fellow gang members. During Miller's (2001) study, many interviewees reported knowing someone that had been sexed-in, but they themselves choose to be jumped-in and avoid the stigma. An example of how dangerous being "sexed-in" is occurred in Texas where two female gang hopefuls had sex with an HIV positive gang member (Knox, 2000). Also, females who choose to be "sexed-in" are more likely to be victims of continuous abuse by the gang members because they now view that female as less important despite joining the gang.

NEWS CLIP 4-1:

INSIDE THE GIRL GANG THAT LURES MALE ENEMIES TO THEIR DEATHS

NEW YORK CITY – The Trinitarios' all-girl gang, the Bad Barbies, with their membership at one time reaching more than 100, are a violent group of women who are known to hide drugs in weapons in baby strollers are close associates to the Trinitarios.

The leader of the Bad Barbies, Maria Mejia, and a femme fatale was arrested for luring men from rival gangs to the Trinitarios where the rival gang member would face a brutal attack or a violent death by a gun, knife, or machete. The trick in convincing the unsuspecting men into a trap was called the "Venus fly trap." Her actions have led to the death of several rival gang members by the Trinitarios.

Traditionally, the Trinitarios are a Dominican street gang originally from the Caribbean Islands now based out of New York City, and the Bad Barbies are just as violent as their male counterparts. In fact, female Trinitarios' members have been known to hide drugs and weapons in baby strollers when the police arrive because they know that the police will not search the stroller. The women also help the Trinitarios gang members by providing safe houses to store drugs and hide from law enforcement. Often male gang members will seek refuge in homes in New Jersey and the Bronx that are maintained by female members.

Unlike the Latin Kings and Queens that put male and female gang members on equal footing, the Trinitarios are misogynist and have a patriarchal rule of the women. Despite Mejia, the female gang leader of the Trinitarios, the male gang members are still in control.

Source: Vincent, I. (2018, June 30). Inside the girl gang that lures male enemies to their deaths. New York Post. Retrieved from https://nypost.com/2018/06/30/inside-the-girl-gang-that-lures-male-enemies-to-their-deaths/.

Past and Current Trends: Female Gang Data

The first official nationwide survey conducted by Walter Miller (1975) of gang membership, estimated that less than 10% of all gang members were female. Meanwhile, criminologist and gang researcher David Curry (2014) noted that female gang membership in the United States is between 6% and 13% and like their male counterparts, they come from urban areas (see Figure 4.1).

Figure 4.1: Percentage of female gang members by type of jurisdiction in the year 2000.

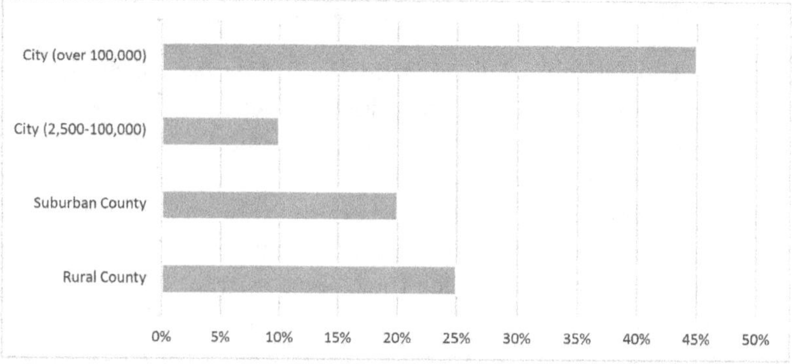

Adapted from: Curry, D. G. (2014). Confronting Gangs. New York: Oxford University Press.

The early reports from the National Gang Youth Survey concluded that some cities did not report females as gang members, but rather reported them as "associates" of gang members. It found that at least 32% of police departments that reported gang activity did not keep records or statistics on females involved with gangs (see Moore & Hagedorn, 2001). In a more recent study, according to the National Council on Crime and Delinquency:

> "About two thirds (67%) of participants identified as an "associate," and about one quarter (28%) as a "gang member." A small percentage (5%) did not identify as a gang member or an associate; however, they were involved with gang activity or knew gang members in their neighborhood and were thus considered "at risk" for gang involvement" (see Wolf, Bogie, Castro, Glesmann, & Yusuf, 2017).

The FBI has also suggested that there is a rise in female gang membership (FBI, 2011), but there is no empirical data to support this claim. Previous studies mentioned above have shown that since the 1970s, the female gang membership rate has been steady somewhere between 5% and 30%. Young females tend to commit "a wider range of delinquent behavior that is stereotypically recognized, but most of this behavior and the subsequent offenses all fall under the category of "hanging out" or "partying" (Huff, 2002). A breakdown of types of offenses committed by males vs. female gang members can be seen in Figure 4.2.

Figure 4.2: Proportion of gang offenses by type and by gender in 2000.

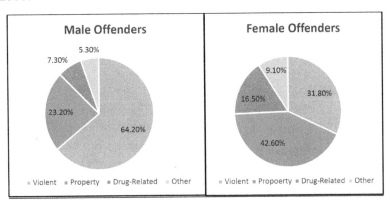

Adapted from: Curry, D. G. (2014). Confronting Gangs. New York: Oxford University Press.

Female-Only Gangs

There are many male-only street gangs in the United States. Then there are street gangs that comprising both males and females, known as hybrid gangs. Lastly, there are female-only gangs, but they are rare. As mentioned earlier, most active female gang members are viewed as "auxiliary members" or seen as a subgroup or supporter of the male gang. Miller's (1975) study suggested that about half of all male gangs have some type of a "female auxiliary" group involved with their gang. Although this type of role does not necessarily downplay their involvement in a gang, it is important to note that a female's position in this setting can be just as important as the males, despite not being in top leadership positions (Knox, 2000).

Miller's (1975) nationwide study of gangs, found that female-only gangs are rare, and constitute less than 10% of the total number of gangs. Miller also concluded that "the rarest of gangs involving females were independent, autonomous female gangs" (cited in Curry, 2014, p. 204). Curry's (1994) study of female gang membership revealed that females make up an "extremely small proportion" of the total number of people in a gang, Meanwhile, Peterson, Miller and Esbensen's (2001) study concluded that less than 13% of female gang members reported as a female-only gang. This confirms Miller's (1975) and Curry's (1994) earlier conclusions of how small the percentage is of female gangs in the United States.

Two of the more popular male street gangs, the Chicago's Vice Lords and the Latin Kings each have an all-female equivalent to the gang—the Vice Queens (see Fisherman, 1995) and the Latin Queens (see Brotherton & Barrios, 2004). In fact, the Almighty Latin King and Queen Nation is a highly organized criminal enterprise that puts male and female members on an equal footing. Unlike other male-dominated street gangs, if a Latin Queen has a higher rank within the gang hierarchy, male gang members are required to take orders from her.

Other prominent all-female gangs were the Dagger Debs, a Puerto Rican gang in New York City (see Hanson, 1964), the Molls from Boston, as previously mentioned (see Miller, 1973), and some more recent gang names such as the Harlem Hiltons, Hood Barbies, Billion Dolla Beauties, Gun Clappin Divas, and 2 Gurl Gunnas all from New York City (see Hamilton, 2011). While most of these female gangs operate independently of other gangs, they are still closely tied to their male-counterparts and serve as an "auxiliary" gang.

As the gang violence has risen in the United States, violence committed by females is minimal, but there are exceptions. One example of a girl gang from Texas that conducted serious acts of violence by robbing convenient stores at gunpoint in the summer of 1999. The gang of girls were labeled by the media as the "Queens of Armed Robbery" before finally being caught (Wood, 2000). Another more recent all-female gang called the Felony Lane Gang (not to be confused with another gang of the same name that consisted of men committing the same crime) was caught in Indiana after a string of heists in Florida and Georgia where the women targeted gyms, parks, and day care centers, breaking into cars and stealing purses (Hunter, 2019).

Challenges to Law Enforcement

So what makes female-only gangs different from other types of gangs? While there are some major differences, such as the overall lower level of violence and types of crimes that are committed, some of the details remain the same. One benefit that female gangs have over their male counterpart is that citizens are more likely to call the police if they see a group of males hanging out late at night as opposed to a group of females (Huff, 2002). This allows females to potentially get away with crimes, as they generally seem less suspicious.

Females also have different duties to the gang than male gang members such as concealing and/or carrying weapons for the male gang members, providing sexual favors, and sometimes fighting against rival girls from a rival gang (Huff, 2002). The role that women play is critical to the males in the gang because a female is less likely to be searched, apprehended, or arrested. Because of this, females are more likely to carry weapons and hold drugs for their male counterparts (Knox, 2000). Females are also used as drug runners and/or the pick-up person for drug deals.

Since Jody Miller (2001) found that the overall level of criminal activity committed by females is "less serious" than that of men, law enforcement officials do not take females as seriously as they should. Now, for those gang officers in areas with a concentrated gang problem, male or female gang members get noticed. However, for those law enforcement officers in less persuasive areas of female gang involvement, those officers tend to overlook the impact that a female gang member has on the gang.

Conclusion

Overall, the impact of females involved in gangs in the United States is far less significant than that of male gang members. With the number of females involved in gangs still hovering around 10%, male gang members continue to be the focus for communities and law enforcement officials. Despite recognizing that females are less violent than males, these female gang members can still pose a threat to a community. It is important to remember that not all gangs and gang members operate in the same manner, and therefore, the participants can still be potentially dangerous. There have been plenty of examples where female gang members have committed serious crimes and engaged in serious offenses.

Over the decades, all these studies have revealed that females join street gangs for many of the same reasons as their male counterparts but unfortunately they are subjected to a harsh initiation process. Despite the desire to be equal, women still play a lesser role within gangs than that of men. Females are used to perform simple tasks, take part in less serious criminal activity, and are victimized sexually. Females are sexually abused at the hands of their male counterparts, and may face many other types of abuse within the gang. The risk of these types of victimization is much higher for women who come from broken homes, with high rates of drug and alcohol abuse in the home and physical abuse.

Female gang members definitely offer a unique challenge for community residents and law enforcement. By understanding the female gang member, a more effective focus can be placed on females in gangs to address strategies on how to prevent their involvement and how to cope with living in a gang culture. With so much emphasis on tackling the gang problem, it is often thought of as a male-problem so all the approaches in dealing with gangs often ignore the female gang member. With less attention on female gang members from a police perspective and limited focus on prevention strategies, it is more likely that the female gang activities will go unnoticed, and in what some have predicted, female gang membership and female gang violence will rise. Time will tell.

Discussion Points and Questions

1. Why was gang research so slow to notice the involvement of girls in gangs?
2. Explain the more serious criminal activity of modern-day female gangs.
3. Why does a mixture of males and females in gangs elevate the criminal involvement of the group as a whole?
4. What challenges do law enforcement face when dealing with female gang members?

Websites

National Public Radio - One Woman Shares How She Was Drawn Into A Gang At An Early Age

https://www.npr.org/2017/09/21/552708125/

Gangland – From Girl to Gangster, Season 2, Episode 12

https://www.youtube.com/watch?v=uKm-D5vGNeU

National Crime Council on Crime & Delinquency - Girls and Gangs

https://www.nccdglobal.org/sites/default/files/Girls%20and%20Gangs%20Executive%20Summary.pdf

REFERENCES

Asbury, H. (1927). *Gangs of New York: An informal history of the underworld.* New York, NY: Thunder Mouth Press.

Bernard, W. (1949). *Jailbait: The story of juvenile delinquency.* Garden City, NY: Garden City Books.

Bjerregaard, B., & Smith, C. (1993). Gender differences in gang participation, delinquency, and substance use. *Journal of Quantitative Criminology, 9*(4), 329–355.

Brotherton, D. C. & Barrios, L. (2004). *The Almighty Latin King and Queen Nation: Street politics and the transformation of a New York City gang.* New York: Columbia University Press.

Brown, W. K. (1977). Black female gangs in Philadelphia. *International Journal of Offender Therapy and Comparative Criminology, 21*(3), 221-228. doi: 10.1177/0306624X7702100303

Campbell, A. (1984). *The girls in the gang.* New York: Basil Blackwell.

Chesney-Lind, M. & Hagedorn, J. M. (1999). Girls, gangs, and violence: Reinventing the liberated female crook. In M. Chesney-Lind & J. M. Hagedorn (Eds.) *Female gangs in America: Essays on girls, gangs and gender* (pp. 295-310). Chicago, IL: Lake View Press.

Curry, G. D. (1994). Gang-related violence. *Clearinghouse Review: National Clearinghouse for Legal Services, 28,* 443–451.

Curry, D. G. (2014). *Confronting gangs.* New York, NY: Oxford University Press.

Federal Bureau of Investigation [FBI]. (2011). 2011 national gang threat assessment – emerging trends. *National Gang Intelligence Center.* Retrieved from https://www.fbi.gov/file-repository/stats-services-publications-2011-national-gang-threat-assessment-2011%20national%20gang%20threat%20assessment%20%20emerging%20trends.pdf/view

Fisherman, L. T. (1995). Vice Queens: An ethnographic study of Black female gang behavior. In M. W. Klein, C. L. Maxson, & J. Miller (Eds.). *Modern Gang Reader* (pp. 83-92). Roxbury Publishing Company.

Hamilton, B. (2011, December 4). Rise of the girl gangs. *New York Post*. Retrieved from https://nypost.com/2011/12/04/rise-of-the-girl-gangs/

Hannerz, U. (1969). *Soulside: Inquiries into ghetto culture and community*. New York: Columbia University Press.

Harris, M. C. (1988). Cholas: Latino girls and gangs. New York, NY: AMS Press.

Howell, J. C. (2016). *Gangs in America's communities*. Los Angeles, CA: SAGE.

Huff, C. R. (2002). *Gangs in America*. New York, NY: SAGE.

Hunter, B. (2019, February 27). All-female gang taunted cops to "do ya job." *Toronto Sun*. Retrieved from https://torontosun.com/news/world/all-female-gang-taunted-cops-to-do-ya-job

Knox, G. W. (2000). *An introduction to gangs*. Ann Arbor, MI: New Chicago School Press.

Miller, J. (2001). One of the guys: Girls, gangs, and gender. *Critical Criminology, 10*(3), 243-245.

Miller, J. (2002). Young women in street gangs: Risk factors, delinquency, and victimization risk. In W. Reed & S. Decker (Eds.), *Responding to gangs: Evaluation and research*, (pp. 67-–105). Washington, DC: National Institute of Justice.

Miller, J. (2008). Violence against urban African American girls: Challenges for feminist advocacy. *Journal of Contemporary Criminal Justice, 24*(2), 148-162.

Miller, W. (1973). Race, sex and gangs. *Society, 11*(1), 32–35.

Moore, J. W. 1991. *Going down to the Barrio*. Philadelphia, PA: Temple University Press

Moore, J. W. & Hagedorn, J. (2001, March). Female gangs: A focus on research. *OJJDP Juvenile Justice Bulletin*. Washington, DC. Retrieved from https://www.ncjrs.gov/pdffiles1/ojjdp/186159.pdf

National Institute of Justice. (2011, October 28). What is a gang? Definitions. Retrieved from National Institute of Justice: https://www.nij.gov/topics/crime/gangs/pages/definitions.aspx

Peterson, D., Miller, J.,& Esbensen, A. (2001).The impact of sex composition on gangs and gang member delinquency, Criminology, 38(2), 411-440.

Quicker, J. (1983). *Homegirls: Characterizing Chicana gangs*. San Pedro, CA: International Universities Press.

Rice, R. (1963, October 12). The Persian Queens. *The New Yorker*. Retrieved from https://www.newyorker.com/magazine/1963/10/19/the-persian-queens

Sanchez, R. & Rodriguez, S. (2008). Lady Q: *The rise and fall of a Latin Queen*. Chicago, IL: Chicago Review Press.

Sikes, G. (1998). *8 Ball Chicks: A year in the violent world of girl gangs*. Anchor Books.

Taylor, C. S. (1993). *Girls, gangs, women, and drugs*. East Lansing, MI: Michigan State University Press.

Thomas, W. I. (1923). *The unadjusted girl*. Boston, MA: Little, Brown.

Thrasher, F. M. (1927). The gang: A study of 1,313 gangs in Chicago. Chicago, IL: The University of Chicago Press.

Wolf, A.M., Bogie, A, Castro, E., Glesmann, C, & Yusuf, A. (2017). Girls and gangs: Improving our understanding and ability to respond, Executive Summary. *National Council on Crime & Delinquency.* Retrieved from http://www.nccdglobal.org/sites/default/files/Girls%20 and%20Gangs%20Executive%20Summary.pdf

Wood, S. (2000, October 11). Robbery queens: Where are they now? *Houston Chronicle.* Retrieved from https://www.chron.com/neighborhood/article/Robbery-Queens-Where-are-they-now-9916283.php

Chapter 5

Gangs and Native Americans

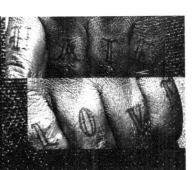

```
┌─────────────────────────────────────────────────────────────────────┐
```

CHAPTER OBJECTIVES

- Provides an overview of Native American Gang Subculture

- Explores the history, past, and current trends and dynamics of Native American gangs

- Examines current trends of Native American street/prison gangs

- Discusses factors that influence the gang problem in Indian Country

FEDS PROSECUTE MAJOR AMERICAN INDIAN GANG

MINNEAPOLIS, MN—Two members of the American Indian gang, the Native Mob were sentenced to 24 years and 43 years in prison, respectively. The Native Mob had terrorized reservations and urban communities in Minnesota and other states. This is the 27th Native Mob gang member to be sentenced to prison since September 2014.

The Native American gang, with approximately 200 members is one of the largest and most violent Native American gangs in the country. The gang was charged with racketeering, conspiracy, murder, attempted murder, distribution of drugs and other crimes. Prosecutors and law enforcement claimed that the gang leader Wakinyan Wakun McArthur had wielded extraordinary authority and control over Native Mob members. According to officials, McArthur ran gang council meetings where crimes were planned, sought to resolve disputes within his own gang, and concentrated his efforts on "rival gang members, rival drug dealers, informants, police officers and cooperating witnesses."

Source: Furst, R. (2014, September 30). Feds wind up major prosecution of American Indian gang. StarTribune.com. Retrieved from http://www.startribune.com/native-mob-case-wraps-up-with-gang-leader-getting-43-years/277590771/?page=all&refresh=true

Understanding the Gang Problem in Indian Country

As the present-day gang issue across America expands, one area that has remained relatively untouched by the growing problem of criminal street gang activity in the United State is Indian Country. Tribal communities, many of which are rural and far removed from the larger cities where gang activity typically flourishes, simply do not experience gang activity or behaviors commonly associated with individuals claiming gang affiliation. However, the late 1980s and early 1990s witnessed a steady and consistent increase in gang behavior in Indian Country. This primarily occurred only in a handful of reservations typically found in the Southwest, Northwest, and Midwest regions of the United States. While there are still reservations across the country today that have not felt the impact of the gang subculture, many tribal communities are experiencing gang activity ranging from low-level criminal acts to significant levels of violence, drug distribution, and other forms of criminal behavior.

There is very limited research conducted into the extent of gang activity occurring across Indian Country. Most of the information on gangs is derived primarily from law enforcement data, informal interviews of gang members, and other anecdotal information. In fact, the first comprehensive study focused on Indian Country gang activity did not occur until 2000, when the Office of Juvenile Justice and Delinquency Prevention, in conjunction with the National Youth Gang Center (currently known as the National Gang Center) conducted the largest and most comprehensive survey of Native American gangs. The study was an attempt to determine the type, extent, and impact of gang activity occurring in tribal communities across the United States (Major & Egley, 2002).

To facilitate the study, the National Youth Gang Center (NYGC) designed a survey instrument that was sent to each federally recognized tribe at the time (as of 2019, there are 573). While only 52% of the tribal communities responded to the survey, 23% of those tribes reported having active street gangs in their communities, while 70% indicated they had no gang activity occurring at all and the remaining 7% indicated they were unable to make a determination one way or the other (Major, Egley, Howell, Mendenhall, & Armstrong, 2004).

In one study conducted by the University of Minnesota, researchers found 14,000 youth in 50 tribes located in 12 states, where 15% of American Indian youth on reservations reported some level of gang activity (Joseph & Taylor, 2003). It was also reported that younger teens participate in gang activity at higher levels than older teens.

In 1997, Navajo Nation estimated that approximately 60 youth gangs existed in Navajo country (Henderson, Kunitz, & Levy, 1999). According to Henderson et al. there was a wide variability among youth who identified themselves as gang members. The authors did note that some gangs were simply street corner groups while others had hardened members. As with other ethnic groups, sociodemographic conditions were the contributing factors in creating an environment for gang formation. Additionally, Henderson et al. concluded that "gang prevention is not simply, or even fundamentally, a law enforcement issue, it is a public health issue in the broadest sense" (p. 258). However, this study was primarily based on individual accounts, interviews, and law enforcement data (Freng, 2013).

As of 2000, 23% of law enforcement agencies reported active gangs, which comprised primarily juvenile males, 40% of communities responded that their community had active gangs, and most communities had one to five gangs. Finally, based on 1997 data, it was estimated that there were 4,500 gang members and roughly 400 gangs on or near tribal lands (Freng, 2013).

In 2010, the now defunct National Drug Intelligence Center (NDIC) conducted a similar study using a different methodological approach. Rather than mailing survey instruments to tribal communities, the NDIC used its cadre of intelligence analysts and field representatives to physically visit tribal communities and conduct face-to-face interviews with individuals who were known or believed to have knowledge about gang activity occurring on the reservations. The NDIC (2011) did not seek to reach every tribal community in Indian Country; but instead identified at least one of the following criteria to assess the extent of the gang problem:

A. Reservations that have an identified gang presence as determined through previous intelligence assessments, federal investigations, congressional testimony, or open-source research; or,

B. Reservations bordering major metropolitan areas that have a gang presence, or reservations within 100 miles of a major U.S. interstate (NDIC, 2011).

A total of 132 tribal communities in the Great Lakes Region, Pacific Region, Southwest Region, and West Central Region of the United States met the criteria for the study. Notably, 81% of the tribal communities identified for the study reported that gang activity was occurring (NDIC, 2011).

While the findings of these two studies illustrate that gangs do exists in Indian Country no matter how small, it clearly demonstrates that gang activity is growing and needs to be addressed. As tribal officials come to terms with this problem and law enforcement anti-gang task forces look to combat this problem, the FBI calls the gang problem in Indian Country—a "silent crisis" (Kennecke, 2019).

Native American Street Gangs: Current Trends

The prevalence and extent of the Native American gang problem is typically confined to three areas in the United States: the Northwest, Southwest, and Midwest states. Some of the most problematic Indian Reservations known for gang activity are Pine Ridge Reservation located in South Dakota and Nebraska, Fort Berthold Reservation located in North Dakota, Tohono O'odham Nation, and the Navajo Nation Reservations located in Arizona, Pawnee Nation Reservation in Oklahoma, and Puyallup Reservation in Washington. While not all Indian Reservations are influenced by urban street gangs, most Native gangs from the Minnesota, Wisconsin, and Dakota areas are influenced by Chicago-based street gangs and those Native gangs in New Mexico and Arizona are being influenced by Los Angeles-based street gangs. The impact of big city gang culture is changing the youth dynamics in Indian Country. In addition, the U.S.–Mexico border, and Seattle's close proximity to Canadian-based gangs also influence the gang trends on reservations.

Despite the documented growth of gangs in Indian Country in the 1990s, the structure of Native American gangs do not reflect those gangs established in an urban setting. According to the 2011 National Gang Intelligence Center report "most gangs in Indian Country are disorganized, lack significant structure and ties to national-level gangs, and are incapable of attaining control over large geographic areas or populations" (p. 33). While some Native American gangs in Indian Country are involved in serious crimes and violent activities, Indian Reservations are now being used to facilitate and expand drug operations for drug-trafficking organizations and other urban-based national-level street gangs (FBI, 2011).

Gang Formation and Identity

One of the most significant contributing factor to the growth of gangs on Indian Reservations and their how they acquire their identity are the influences of the urban (inner-city) street gang subculture. When gangs form within tribal communities, it is not unusual for those individuals to identify the group by a unique, localized name (e.g., Odd Squad, The Boyz, and Red Nation Klique). However, the usual trend in most tribal communities is for the group to identify with and adopt names and symbols of major urban-street gangs such as Bloods, Crips, Gangster Disciples, Vice Lords, and Latin Kings. The Native gang names are now called Native Gangster Bloods, Native Gangster Crips, Native Gangster Disciples, Native Latin Kings, and the Red Skin Kingz. Because of this, the type and style of most gangs and gang activity in Indian Country are best described as fitting the "hybrid" form of gang behavior/membership.

Hybrid gangs mainly comprise local individuals who claim affiliation with a national gang (e.g., Bloods, Crips), primarily for the purpose of capitalizing on the notoriety that the national gang has already established. Within the hybrid gang form, local members may use and/or mix the national gang's signs, symbols and representing styles (i.e., clothes), and switch gang membership or allegiance (Starbuck, Howell, & Lindquist, 2001).

Regardless of how the gang is formed, the primary purpose is to mirror the behavior of a major gang because there is instant name recognition and the notoriety associated with claiming affiliation with a nationally recognized street gang. Also by identifying with major urban street gangs, tribal gang members seek to gain power through intimidation and violence or the threat of violence. The Native gang is also creating a climate of fear among other gangs on the reservation or with individuals within the community. While much of this behavior is localized to tribal communities, gang influences transplanted to tribal communities from urban areas is a problem.

The migration of Native Americans from Indian County to urban areas in the hope for a better life is another way gangs are formed. Some families move to improve their employment and housing situations, others leave for a greater sense of safety and security. However, some leave expressly for the purpose of avoiding their children from being exposed to drug and alcohol abuse, gang activity, and other forms of violence on the reservation. This changing population demographic, the aspect of urban-based Native American gang involvement must be considered when discussing gang activity occurring in tribal communities.

For Native Americans who were born and raised in a non-tribal community, but within an urban environment, social adjustment to the gang culture is less challenging than it is for Native Americans who migrate to an urban environment from the reservation. While most Native Americans who move to an urban area make the adjustment, it is typically the youth who struggle the most. Those individuals are often homeless, unemployed and/or marginalized and have the greatest potential for gravitating to an urban street gang lifestyle. Their motive for doing so is often based on the need or desire for protection, profit, or power. Julia Hailer (2008), an American Indian scholar and Native gang expert addressed the American Indian youth involvement with regard to urban street gangs and observed that:

> Like other minority groups moving into the cities, American Indians have had to overcome socioeconomic obstacles, cultural adjustments, and psychological struggles. These factors would indicate that the urban environment is ripe for American Indian youth to turn to gangs as other minority youth have done—that the structural factors are in place which lead to a breakdown in traditional social controls (family, school, and law enforcement) that impact an individual's decision-making skills about turning to a gang to fulfill those economic, social, and psychological needs. (Hailer, 2008, p. 71)

For Native American gang members who relocate from urban areas to tribal communities do so to escape or disconnect from the pressures of the urban gang or drug lifestyle. Others relocate for the purpose of re-connecting with their family, for work, or for cultural or spiritual reasons. Regardless, these individuals typically do not pose a threat to the community or to law enforcement as their reasons are legitimate and appropriate. However, then there are those individuals who relocate to the tribal community for the purpose of engaging in gang recruitment, establishing drug distribution networks, or other nefarious motives. One example of this occurred at Lac Courte Oreilles Reservation in Wisconsin in 2005. A tribal member who was a member of the Latin Kings in Milwaukee transplanted his gang influence, and his cocaine distribution activity, to the reservation for the primary purpose of establishing a drug market for the Latin Kings on the reservation (Zielinski, 2005). The violence and criminal activity associated with this movement resulted in a federal indictment of multiple tribal and non-tribal gang members, many of whom still remain incarcerated today (see *United States v. Acosta*, 2008).

Another example of a tribal gang member moving to a tribal community to "set up shop" was in Navajo Nation by a street gang known as Insane Cobraz Nation, or simply "Cobraz". This gang was started by a tribal member who lived in Chicago, IL, in the 1990s, and while living there, he became a member of the Spanish Cobras street gang. Upon returning to Navajo Country a few years later, the individual initiated the Insane Cobraz Nation street gang, using the same signs and symbols of the Chicago gang (citation). Today, the Cobraz are one of the largest Native American street gangs in Southwest Indian Country.

When the urban-based gang-involved Native Americans return to their tribal communities, they often find what Hailer (2008) refers to as a receptive peer group comprising young Native Americans who are bored and alienated from their traditional lifestyle, seeking to absorb a popular youth culture marked by a gang lifestyle. To some degree, the urban-based tribal member coming back to the reservation is seen as a "big fish in a little pond," in that he or she is seen as someone who has street credibility based on their urban experience. It is these individuals who are at least partially responsible for the formation of many gangs that are currently active in Indian Country.

It is also important to consider the fact that a tribal member does not have to actually live in an urban area to be associated with urban gangs. Tribal members attending off-reservation schools, or occasionally associating with urban gang members through friendships, relationships, or social media pose the same risk as if they were exposed to that lifestyle on a daily basis. There also exists the element of non-tribal members moving to reservations to cohabitate with or marry tribal members. While the majority of these relationships are legitimate, some occur for the purpose of providing an individual with access to the tribal community for motives that are less than honorable, such as gang recruitment or drug distribution.

Gang influence is not isolated to urban Native American gang members impacting tribal communities. The gang influence is also between tribal communities. Gang involvement is also influenced by changing schools, meeting friends, family relationships and, in some instances, through the cultural events that involve large gatherings of Native American people such as a Pow Wow or other cultural tradition.

Lastly, while claiming affiliation with a national-level gang, a trend has emerged in what appears to be an effort for many Native gang members in Indian Country to more fully self-identify as a Native American street gang. In other words, rather than claiming affiliation with African-American gangs (i.e., Bloods and Crips) or Hispanic gangs (i.e., Sureños and Norteños), some gang-involved Native Americans appear intent on identifying as separate and unique Native American gang structure.

The most famous example of a local Native gang establishing themselves as a legitimate force is the Wild Boyz, a gang that originated on the Pine Ridge Reservation in South Dakota. In 2010, the History Channel's "Gangland" series profiled the Wild Boyz and interviewed a number of members of this gang. In the broadcast segment, one of the Wild Boyz members states "Us guys didn't wanna be no Black gang, no Mexican gang…didn't wanna copy off nothin'…this is from Pine Ridge…west side Wild Boyz from the Rez."

Whether a real sentiment or merely bravado, this statement reflects a trend that is occurring in other parts of Indian Country. Native American street gangs such as Sovereign Natural Warriors in Wisconsin and Native Mob in Minnesota were formerly aligned with major gang structures (Gangster Disciples and Vice Lords), but are self-identified as Native American gangs. These gangs no longer claim national gang affiliation, but instead embrace a unique identity that often involves allowing only Native American membership, as well as the use of traditional symbolism and language within the gang behavior.

Gang Organization and Structure

Similar to many street gangs across the country, the majority of Native American street gangs are fragmented, unorganized, and lack a leader. If leadership in any form exists within such gangs, it usually takes the form of "shot callers", or individuals within the gang who have the ability to influence others, have access to money, alcohol, or drugs, or who have a reputation for criminal or violent behavior. Still, most of the activity of the gang is unplanned and spontaneous. The extent of the gang activity depends on what is happening in the community, neighborhood, school, or home. The lack of predictability makes identifying or predicting patterns of gang behavior difficult to observe among Native American gangs. However, there are exceptions.

In the early to mid-1990s, several Native American males began associating with the Vice Lords criminal street gang in south Minneapolis, Minnesota, primarily for the purpose of drug distribution. Eventually, due to various issues between Vice Lords members and their Native American counterparts, a split occurred between the two groups, resulting in the formation of the street and prison gang known today as the Native Mob, or the Native Mob Family.

The Native Mob is one of the few Native American-based street gangs with an organizational hierarchy. The gang uses the terms "chief" and "co-chief," similar to Ojibwe words "*ogema*" or "*co-ogema*" to represent their highest levels of leadership in the group. These individuals are responsible for determining the types of criminal activity the gang engages in and assuring that such acts are planned and carried out. Other ranks within Native Mob include "treasurer," the person responsible for the distribution of money or other items of value to members of the gang. "war chief" is the person responsible for responding to threats from rival gangs or problematic individuals, and the "chief enforcer" is the person responsible for maintaining discipline within the gang and punishing violators of the gang's by-laws. The gang's by-laws usually consist of several pages of rules and regulations members are expected to follow. While this degree of organizational structure is not seen among most Native American gangs, the Native Mob is indicative of the potential every Native American gang holds in terms of establishing an organizational hierarchy.

Gang Membership, Alignment, and Opposition

The size and number of active gangs on reservations across Indian Country varies. It is not unusual for a gang to form, only to fade out of existence after a short period of time, or be absorbed by a larger gang in the community. Many smaller reservations tend to have only a few active gangs, and membership within such gangs tends to be low, often involving anywhere from 5 to 25 individuals at any given time.

However, many of Indian Country's larger reservations are experiencing issues involving multiple gangs and a greater number of participants. For example, on the Navajo Nation Reservation, over 225 active gangs have been identified, with approximately 1,500 to 2,500 individuals claiming some level of gang affiliation (Grant, 2013; Patterson, 2009).

In South Dakota, the Pine Ridge Reservation has approximately 30 to 40 active gangs with several hundred individuals involved in gang activity of one degree or another (Eckholm, 2009). While this level of gang activity is not reflective of the majority of reservations across Indian Country, both are examples of how significant the gang issue can become in tribal communities.

When multiple gangs are present within the tribal community, there tends to be a degree of both alignment and opposition that occurs. For many Native American gangs, it is not unusual for relatives within an extended family to not only claim similar gang affiliation, but also potentially with rival gang affiliation as well. The reasons for this vary from one tribal community to another and are often dependent on individual family dynamics. Be that as it may, multiple gangs within a tribal community will often result in some gangs aligning with each other, and some opposing each other.

Gang alignment in tribal communities is more about co-existence than cooperation. In other words, individuals claiming different gang sets essentially adopt a "leave each other alone" attitude, or they may align because certain members of each gang are related or because each gang claims the same major gang affiliation (i.e., West Side Bloods, East Side Bloods). Despite this, there is always the potential for violence to occur between these groups because of the presence of the gangster mentality within their membership.

The dynamics of gang opposition vary as well. Rival gangs within a tribal community may limit their animosity to disrespect, threats, and intimidation, or may express their dislike for each other through violence, as well as alcohol or drug consumption. Indian Country has experienced its share of gang violence over the years, in terms of homicides and felony assaults, and is no more immune from gang violence than any other community in the United States.

Another dynamic among Indian Country gangs is gang allegiance. While gang allegiance does not frequently occur, it is not unusual for a gang member to "flip" to another gang within the tribal community, and completely change their affiliation. Based on interviews with tribal gang members conducted by native gang specialist and former RC, SD Police Area Gage Commander Christopher Grant, two of the most important aspects of gang involvement in the tribal community are gaining power and protection. A young Native American who feels unsafe or insecure in their neighborhood, housing area, school or community, will most likely gravitate toward the gang lifestyle. A young Native will often choose to participate in the gang that is seen as more influential and provides the greatest degree of protection in the community. However, the power base of any gang always has the potential to change at any moment. Gang members are incarcerated, move away, or age out of their gang lifestyle. In addition, a gang that has power in the community for a period of time may be replaced by another, resulting in some individuals to change their gang allegiance.

Native American Prison Gangs: Current Trends

As street gang activity has increased in tribal communities, so too has Native American gang activity in the correctional system. While not every local, state, or federal prison facility has a Native American gang presence, there are correctional facilities across the country that deal with Native American gangs every day. According to Prison Policy Institute (2014), over 15,000 natives are incarcerated and some of the highest incarceration rates for Native Americans are in Alaska (38%), North Dakota (29%), South Dakota (29%), Montana (22%), New Mexico (11%), and Arizona (10%). While some Native Americans remain free of gang involvement during incarceration, others bring their street gang affiliation into prison with them, or they become active gang members once in a prison environment.

Some of the more popular and noteworthy Native American prison gangs are the Warrior Society, Dine' Pride, Indian Brotherhood, and Native Nation. To join these prison gangs, one has to be Native American. Native American prison gangs will also typically disassociate from prison gangs of other races and ethnicities. While alignments between Native American prison gangs and other groups do exist, typically with Hispanic prison gangs, it is increasingly common for incarcerated Native Americans to form their unique gang structures and self-identify as a Native gang.

Like other racial and ethnic groups, a prison gang, or Security Threat Group (STG), is usually dependent on the number of individuals from that group within the correctional setting. In correctional facilities with low Native American inmate populations, the majority of Native Americans who become gang-involved usually do so for the primary purpose of protection against other inmates. In such cases it is not unusual for Native American inmates to align with an existing prison gang, typically a Hispanic gang.

In prisons that have a significant Native American population, it is not uncommon to have a "stand-alone" Native American prison gang. Often these types of gangs are merely extensions of the street gang activity an inmate was involved in prior to being incarcerated. A well-known Native American prison gang that is also active on the street is the Native Mob, a gang from Minnesota.

Unlike most Native American street gangs, Native American prison gangs are generally more organized and disciplined. It is not unusual for a Native American prison gang to have rules and regulations, as well as a rank structure and leadership hierarchy. For example, the Indian Brotherhood prison gang in Oklahoma expects their members to adhere to a strictly designed set of by-laws and organizational hierarchy (cite). In Arizona, the Warrior Society and Dine' Pride prison gangs are very prominent. Both gangs have membership rules, qualification requirements for admission, and specific signs and symbols that are culturally based (Arizona Department of Corrections, 2019a, 2019b).

Most Native American prison gangs are also closed and secretive, and their members typically deny they are a gang. Members often assert they are in a "brotherhood," a cultural group or a "warrior society." The primary purpose of the prison gang is to protect their brethren and honor their cultural traditions.

Finally, while most inmates released from prison/jail cease their gang involvement, others often take their prison gang affiliation back to their tribal and non-tribal communities. Examples of such prison gangs operating on the street, besides Native Mob include Indian Brotherhood in Oklahoma, Indian Pride Organization in Oregon, East River Skins in South Dakota, and Native Nation in North Dakota.

Factors Contributing to the Influence of Gangs in Indian Country

There has been a significant amount of research conducted regarding the social, environmental, and psychological factors that contribute to gang involvement. While the list of potential contributing factors is extensive and isolating a specific set of factors within any community to determine why gangs exist is challenging, Indian Country is not immune to those factors. Even though tribal communities are distinct and diverse in terms of their history, culture, language, and traditions, as well as their socio-economic and infrastructural status, many tribal communities share similar social challenges, several of which are known to be contributing factors to the influence of gang activity. While the following factors are not reflective on the entirety of Indian Country, each currently impacts the growth of gangs across the United States, tribal community or not.

Poverty and Unemployment

One of the most prevalent contributing factors to gang involvement in any community is low socio-economic status, manifested in the form of poverty and unemployment. This is an issue that impacts many tribal communities. According to the U.S. Bureau of Labor Statistics (2019), Native Americans and Alaskan Natives have the highest poverty and unemployment rates in the United States. Furthermore, more than one in four Native Americans and Alaska Natives who reside off reservations live in poverty and more than one in three Native Americans who reside on reservations are impoverished (Krogstad, 2014). In some states, such as South Dakota, the poverty level among Native Americans is well above the national average. In fact, Pine Ridge Reservation (South Dakota) has the lowest level life expectancy and some of the poorest communities in the United States (Re-Member.org, 2019).

Since poverty and unemployment are powerful incentives for young Native Americans to turn to gang involvement, some youth gang members in Indian Country acquire income through activities such as drug distribution, theft, and other forms of criminal behavior. In addition, young people in Indian Country also see images of success projected by the media, and do not see the means to achieve success due to their social conditions. As wealth, power and prestige are flaunted in the media, the reality is poverty and unemployment exist and this translates into feelings of frustration and anger that can manifest into behaviors that are reflective of gang behavior.

Education

While there are ample opportunities for young Native Americans to receive a quality education, both within and outside Indian Country, a long-standing issue that remains both problematic and unresolved is the drop-out rate among urban Native Americans and those living on Reservations. Despite best efforts of those attempting to address the issue, Native American youth continue to track behind non-Native Americans in education achievement.

According to the most recent graduation data, only 65% of Native American public education students graduated from high school, a drop-out rate of 35%, the highest of all races and ethnicities (Education World, n.d.). Meanwhile, the data for Native American youth attending tribal schools or Bureau of Indian Education (BIE) schools reveal similar graduation rates of 53% in tribal communities (Bureau of Indian Education, 2019).

For Indian youth, the lack of education is another factor known to contribute to gang involvement. The youth who are uneducated, or under-educated, lack the qualifications and opportunities to obtain employment, tend to gravitate toward behaviors that are self-destructive, and pose the greatest risk for falling into the gang lifestyle.

Substance Abuse

One of the most thoroughly documented issues that plague many tribal communities and their families in Indian Country is alcohol abuse and dependency. Although Native Americans only make up 1.7% of the U.S. population, Native Americans experience substance abuse and addiction at much higher rates than other ethnic groups (American Addiction Centers, 2020) Multiple studies conducted over the years reveal that Native Americans residing on reservations consistently experience higher rates of alcohol use than any other ethnic group in America, resulting in multiple risk factors for physical and mental health issues, accidents, violent crime, and suicide (Laramine, 1988; Szlemko, Wood, & Thurman, 2006; American Addiction Centers, 2020; Sunrise House, 2020).

Alcohol and drug consumption is commonplace among Indian Country gang members, and much of the violence in tribal communities, whether gang-involved or not, has a connection to substance abuse (Kaliszewski, 2020). However, some tribal gang members are involved in gang behavior primarily because it provides greater access to drugs and alcohol, both of which are often obtained through criminal means.

Illicit drug use and dependency in Indian Country is also a major issue. In 2008, the National Drug Intelligence Center (NDIC) conducted a study of illicit drug use on 80 reservations across Indian Country and subsequently reported that Native American substance-abuse levels are higher than those for any other demographic group (NDIC, 2008). As early as 2006, the Department of Justice (2006) reported that Indian Country was targeted by Mexican Drug Cartels and it is now estimated that over 70% of meth in the United States is being imported from Mexico. In addition, the FBI's National Gang Threat Assessment (FBI, 2013) report found that both national and local street gangs were increasingly distributing retail-level quantities of illicit drugs on reservations, as well as engaging in gang-related criminal activities in tribal communities to facilitate their drug distribution operations, including intimidation, assaults, and burglary.

More recently, reports of Mexican Drug Cartels are utilizing Reservations to traffic their drugs (see News Clip 5.1). The vastness of the land, the close proximity to the US–Mexican border and the lack of a sufficient law enforcement presence leaves Indian Country vulnerable for cartels to move their drugs across the Reservation and to other parts of the United States. For example, the Bureau of Indian Affairs (BIA) Drug Agents and the Native American Targeted Investigations of Violent Enterprises (NATIVE) Task Force Task Force, along with Department of Security Investigations Special Response Team and Arizona Department of Public Safety conducted an undercover operation that successfully purchased approximately 30,000 fentanyl pills (opioids) from a drug organization (Gibson, 2019, 2017).

NEWS CLIP 5-1:

DRUG TRAFFICKERS FIND HAVEN IN SHADOWS OF INDIAN COUNTRY

ST. REGIS MOHAWK RESERVATION, NY—Native American Reservations have become a critical link for the drug underworld. Because of their geography, tribal sovereignty, and an undermanned law enforcement presence, traffickers are able to transport high-potency marijuana and Ecstasy from eastern Canada into cities on the East Coast, and have facilitated the passage of cocaine and methamphetamine from Mexico to cities in the West and Midwest. To complicate matters, drug traffickers are marrying Indian women to establish themselves on the Reservations. In fact, at Lac Courte Oreilles Reservations in Wisconsin, several Latin King gang members married Indian women and built a $3 million crack cocaine ring in the upper Midwest.

Another element of Reservations that complicate the detection of illegal funds moving in and out of an area is the surge of casinos on Reservations. Casinos on Reservations are operated by tribal communities and when those tribal members have ties to drug rings the money can flow more freely without detection.

Unfortunately, the drugs on Reservations impact the tribal members as they get addicted to drugs and resort to violence. For example in Blackfeet Nation in Montana, unemployment reached 85% and drug-related violence and addiction were rampant.

At the Wind River Reservation in Wyoming, a tribal court judge was arrested for his involvement in a drug ring. "It's destroying our culture, our way of life, killing our people," said tribal member Darrel Rides, a drug and alcohol counselor.

Source: Kershaw, S. (2006, February 19). Drug traffickers find haven in shadows of Indian Country. New York Times. Retrieved from https://www.nytimes.com/2006/02/19/us/drug-traffickers-find-haven-in-shadows-of-indian-country.html

Family-Based Gang Involvement

Traditional Native American culture has always placed significant emphasis on the importance of both the nuclear and extended family as a source of nurturing, support, and protection for tribal youth. Today, most tribal families across Indian Country are healthy and well-grounded, providing their children with the love, respect, and attention they need. Because of this, and despite the social challenges many Native American youth face every day, most tribal youth stay uninvolved in gang activity, as they understand that such behavior is not only destructive, but is also in opposition to their traditional culture. Unfortunately, this is not always the case, because within some tribal communities, the core of the gang problem can often be found within individual family dynamics. Christopher Grant, a former Rapid City Police Detective and leading Native American gang expert, explains that, "There's nothing within Native American culture that connects to being a gang member. Part of the reason some of these young people in Indian Country move and embrace the gang subculture is because they're disconnected from their own traditional culture" (Kennecke, 2019).

A significant degree of the gang activity occurring in Indian Country has a family nexus, in that certain tribal gangs are merely an extension or manifestation of long-standing problems between tribal familial groups. In some circumstances, what may have started years ago as animosity between two or more tribal families, has now evolved into opposing family-based gang factions. Once this occurs, the involved families typically expect their immediate members, as well as other relatives, to align with or claim allegiance to their family-based gang. In such circumstances it is not at all unusual to observe multiple members of a Native American gang related to each other on some level, and in opposition to another group (gang) that shares common familial relationships. As well, family-based gang activity has become multi-generational on many reservations, resulting in gang involvement at increasingly younger ages, due to the influence exerted by gang-involved parents, siblings or extended family members. The family-based dynamic makes the gang issue even more problematic to address, since most tribal communities are close-knit and community members are often related to each other on some level.

Tribal youth gang involvement sometimes stems from having parents or guardians who are absent, uncommitted, or disinterested in what their children are involved with or who they associate with. Additionally, some tribal youth experience consistent patterns of physical, sexual, or emotional abuse at home. Lastly, some young people in Indian Country have parents who are incarcerated or consumed by substance abuse or mental health issues, leaving their children to fend for themselves or to be raised by grandparents or other relatives, many of whom are unaware of or unfamiliar with the gang lifestyle and its manifestations. It is these family elements that result in a young person being more likely to associate with gang activity as a replacement for their biological family, since the gang offers the perception of refuge, often purporting to provide the protection, support, attention, and belonging young people seek. *Indian Country Today* best explained this disconnect between parents/grandparents from those youth who are displaying gang-like behaviors:

> Instead of learning how to be truthful and strong from their parents, our children are learning how to be gangsters and drug users…Instead of learning the wisdom of the ages and respect from their grandparents, these children are learning to respect basketball players, football players and rock musicians…Instead of learning their Native songs from the reservations, they are learning rap songs from the ghettos. (cited in Grant & Feimer, 2007)

Scott Davis, the executive director of the North Dakota Indian Affairs Commission and a member of the Standing Rock Sioux Tribe, also expressed his opinion about the role of males in Native American societies today by stating:

> "Today we are witnessing many young Native Americans joining gangs. These gangs exist in urban cities and also within our tribal nations. Research, studies and data show there are many reasons as to why they join gangs…I see one of the reasons our young warriors join gangs to be connected to the lack of fatherhood. While there are many positive male role models in Indian Country, there is also an absence of father figures in too many tribal families. This void leaves tribal youth, especially males, in the position of having to determine their own path, resulting in some turning to gang and drug-involved peers for guidance. This is not consistent with our traditional ways, and the impact on both tribal families and tribal communities can be devastating." (cited in Grant, 2013)

Cultural Disconnection

To more fully appreciate many of the social challenges Native Americans face today, one must look back 150 years to find the roots of what is appropriately referred to as "historical trauma." The Native American Center for Excellence, a component of the Substance Abuse and Mental Health Services Administration (SAMHSA), describes historical trauma (also known as multi-generational trauma) as being based upon "shared experiences by American Indian and Alaska Native people of historic traumatic events like displacement, forced assimilation, language and cultural suppression, and boarding schools, and it is passed down through generations. There is a sense of powerlessness and hopelessness associated with historical trauma that contributes to high rates of alcoholism, substance abuse, suicide and other health issues" (NACE-SAMHSA, 2019).

According to Grant, who has interviewed many tribal leaders over the years, cultural disconnection is an important contributing factor to young Native Americans gravitating to the gang lifestyle. Unfortunately, despite the fact that most tribal communities offer cultural opportunities to tribal members, such opportunities are often not taken advantage of to the degree they should be, not only by young people, but often by their parents, guardians, or elders as well.

Grant and Feimer (2007) studied native gang members and their understanding of traditional Native American culture. Included in the study were current gang members, former gang members, and persons with no gang affiliation from the Sioux Tribes (Lakota, Nakota, and Dakota). The majority of the respondents (76%) characterized their knowledge of their culture as being strong or moderate, although 24% indicated that they knew nothing about their culture. However, a critical question to the survey was "How important do you think knowledge of the Native American culture and heritage is to preventing gang activity among

Native American youth?" Approximately, 96% of those interviewed indicated that such knowledge was either very important or somewhat important to preventing gang activity. While these findings suggest that cultural connectivity is not an absolute barrier to gang involvement among tribal youth, it can be a preventative factor to gang involvement. Sadly, many of these Native American gang members readily acknowledge they possess limited knowledge of their own history, language, culture, and traditions.

Interviews conducted by Grant (2013) reveal the cultural disconnect between tribal lifestyle and traditions and the gang lifestyle. For example, a tribal gang member from the Lake Traverse Reservation in South Dakota was asked "Why did you choose the gang life instead of embracing your traditional Native American culture?" His response:

> "The reason I chose the gang life and culture is because it was fun and not as boring as sitting in class learning about your heritage, where Native Americans came from and how we became Sisseton Wahpeton Oyate (The People). I never did want to learn all that when I could be on the street learning street values and everything having to do with the street, you know, gang life, gang language, colors, the way they dress, the way they act. It's more fun because you get to move around, be outside, party, hang-out with friends. Back when I was a kid they were teaching it (heritage) in school. I didn't want to sit in school and listen to them. To me it was nonsense. It would come in one ear and out the other." (Grant, 2013)

In another interview conducted by Grant, a former member of the Native Gangster Bloods from the Puyallup Reservation in Washington, was asked whether being culturally disconnected would be a contributing factor to gang involvement among Native American youth. The Native Gangster Blood responded:

> "Yes, I believe it's huge. Most urban and rural Natives don't have that cultural presence and by the time they get it, it's usually too late. You're also dealing with the competition of today's society and the environment of the community. You've got these guys who are the role models of what's cool, with the cars, the money, the girls, and without knowing your culture, you're more apt to hang on with that gang lifestyle. I would encourage young people, parents, uncles and aunties to get involved with their culture. Hang on to it. Practice it. It worked for me to get back into my (cultural) lifestyle to learn what a true warrior is." (cited in Grant, 2013)

While the lack of cultural connectivity is one of the many contributing factors to gang involvement in Indian Country, ongoing efforts to revitalize traditional culture have resulted in positive outcomes. For example, while statistics suggests that the majority of Native Americans today speak only English, numerous efforts have been made to preserve Native American languages through various programs and initiatives (Koyfman, 2017). Instilling pride in culture strengthens not only tribal communities, but the young people who reside in them as well, thus providing a barrier to the gang lifestyle.

Criminal Justice Resource Challenges

While most non-tribal communities experiencing gang activities in their neighborhoods usually have basic criminal justice resources to combat these behaviors, such is not always the case in Indian Country. In fact, many tribal law enforcement agencies across Indian Country remain seriously understaffed, due to not only budgeting issues, but also the lack of qualified candidates, lack of available housing for law enforcement personnel, lack of adequate compensation compared to non-tribal agencies, and other issues (Wakeling, Jorgensen, Michaelson, & Begay, 2001). The Department of Justice also reports that turnover among Indian Country law enforcement officers remains high, resulting in the constant need to recruit and train replacement officers, thereby affecting the ability to create an effective community policing atmosphere (Wakeling et al., 2001).

Each day, many tribal law enforcement agencies struggle with the lack of adequate resources to effectively provide for public safety in their communities, where crime rates are often greater than those in non-tribal communities. This lack of resources often results in extended response times to calls for service, since officers typically have to drive many miles to respond to the scene, often with no backup or assistance. This fact is not lost on those involved in gang activity in tribal communities, who often believe they can engage in criminal behavior with impunity due to the decreased likelihood that they will be apprehended.

One example of this is found within the Tohono O'odham Nation in south central Arizona, the third largest Native American reservation in the United States, and home to one of the busiest smuggling and drug trafficking corridors in North America (Harris, Epstein, Frey, Simon, & Madden, 2019). The Tohono O'odham Nation is a reservation that encompasses 4,400 square miles of remote desert and mountain terrain. With limited number of sworn police officers not only to protect the interior boundaries of the reservation, but also to patrol the 75 miles of shared international border with Mexico, this is a daunting task complicated by the growing gang problem. In 2002, it was reported by *Indianz.com* that there are 34 gangs on the Tohono O'odham Nation in Arizona and the police have identified approximately 400 members involved in gangs on the reservation (*Indianz.com*, 2018). More recently, Stern (2018) reported the slaying of a woman by gang members in Tohono O'odham Nation, which, in addition to the drug cartel influence on the reservation, is proof that the Crips and Bloods culture from Los Angeles is alive and well on the reservation.

The same situation can be found on the Fort Berthold Reservation in North Dakota, an area encompassing 1,500 square miles where the three affiliated tribes are Mandan, Hidatsa, and Arikara, known as MHA Nation. Fort Berthold Reservation first became famous for their oil boom on and near the reservation but soon tribal officials were inundated with gang influences from Mexican drug-trafficking organizations and Mara Salvatrucha (aka, MS-13). The problem increased to the point that officials from the Three Tribe Nation brought in

Guatemalan gang experts in 2013 to teach local law enforcement officials how to detect members of MS-13 (Carcamo, 2015).

The same issues extend into the area of tribal jails and tribal courts, both of which struggle with limited resources as well. While not every reservation necessarily requires an adult jail or juvenile detention facility, many large tribal communities that need one or both of these resources do not have them, due to budget constraints that prevent the construction or staffing of such facilities. Rather, many tribes contract with city or county entities to house tribal offenders. While this process is workable, it is often expensive and unwieldy, in that such facilities are typically located many miles from the tribal community.

One example of this is found on the Wind River Reservation in Wyoming, which encompasses approximately 3,400 square miles and has a population of approximately 23,000 people. Wind River, which is the seventh largest reservation by land area in the United States, is policed by approximately 20 Bureau of Indian Affairs police officers who regularly deal with significant gang, drug, and violent crime issues. A federal detention facility on the reservation allows for the incarceration of adult criminal offenders, and until recently, juvenile offenders were placed in a detention facility in Lander, Wyoming, which is a non-tribal community bordering the reservation. In 2012, the detention facility in Lander closed, requiring BIA law enforcement to find other options for provision of this service. Currently, the BIA is utilizing the services of a detention facility in Busby, Montana, resulting in officers having to drive approximately 300 miles, one way, to reach this facility. Doing so takes an officer out of service for at least ten hours, considering the time it takes to drive to this location, book the juvenile offender, and drive back to the reservation. The problem is exacerbated by the need for an officer to make a return trip to the facility to transport the juvenile back to the reservation for tribal court.

This fact results in tribal officers having to be extremely selective about which juvenile offenders are incarcerated, leading to the frequency of either not arresting juveniles or releasing them to parents or guardians, even in the event of serious offenses. And on reservations without an adult correctional facility, many criminal offenders are released on their own recognizance, often in situations where they would be incarcerated for their criminal offenses in non-native communities. The result, once again, is the perpetuation of attitudes of disrespect for the rule of law, creating the impression among criminal offenders, including gang members, that they are unlikely to be held accountable for the crimes they commit.

Responding to Gangs in Indian Country

Despite the insurmountable odds of dealing with the gang problem in Indian Country, tribal communities have taken a strong stance to address the gang issue. Through efforts such as hosting community gang awareness workshops for adults, providing gang prevention education for youth, forming community action teams that address social infrastructural issues, and enhancing cultural opportunities for youth, some tribal communities are successfully impacting their gang issues.

There are also tribal law enforcement agencies in Indian Country that are successfully addressing gang behavior from a collaborative suppression standpoint. For example, the Native American Drug and Gang Initiative (NADGI) Task Force, which was created in 2007 as a collaborative alliance between the Wisconsin Division of Criminal Investigation and the nine tribal communities in Wisconsin, provide their own law enforcement services. NADGI is primarily designed to provide resources, specialized funding and training opportunities to these nine tribal agencies, as well as working in conjunction with other statewide local, county, state, and federal law enforcement agencies to conduct tactical and strategic investigations and gather and disseminate information pertaining to gangs, drugs, and firearms in Wisconsin tribal communities. In 2016, the Task Force received the Honoring Nations Award from the Harvard Project on American Indian Economic Development (HPAIED; NBC15, 2016).

Another example of positive collaboration between tribal and non-tribal law enforcement officials is the FBI's Safe Trails Task Force (STTF) concept (FBI, 2019). Currently, there are 16 active STTF teams across Indian Country. Initiated in 1994, the purpose of the program was to: Unite the FBI with other federal, state, local, and tribal law enforcement agencies in a collaborative effort to combat the growth of crime in Indian Country. STTFs allow participating agencies to combine limited resources and increase investigative coordination in Indian Country to target violent crime, drugs, gangs, and gaming violations.

Concluding Thoughts

Tolerance and ambivalence toward gangs by tribal community residents gave rise to the opportunity for gangs to survive and flourish (Conly, 1993). While many individuals in tribal communities recognized and understood the potential impact of gang activity, others embraced attitudes of minimization, denial, and apathy about such behavior. One reason for this is the mistaken impression that activity by young tribal members is somehow not the same as those behaviors occurring off the Reservation. Some members of a tribal community deny and minimize the behavior, choosing to "sweep it under the rug" than to actually address the problem. There is also the belief that Native youth do not engage in such destructive behaviors. This attitude by tribal community elders and others are partially responsible for the growth of gangs in Indian Country.

Sadly, once gang activity becomes entrenched in the tribal community, it is difficult to change the dynamic, especially when multiple gangs have formed. As a result of gang-related behaviors, attitudes of denial are often replaced by fear of retaliation, fear of ostracism, or fear of reprisal. Some tribal members tend to consider the gang problem just another social problem that is part of the tribal community's fabric, others choose to live with what is occurring, instead of combating the problem, and some feel a sense of helplessness.

While the Native American gang issue presents unique challenges on many levels, Indian Country remains strong and resilient through the years of experience dealing with adversity. By utilizing focused leadership, tenacity, and collaboration, the growth of the gang problem can be mitigated, and in many instances reversed, as long as tribal communities recognize that gang activity is not only unacceptable, but is also not a part of the traditional culture.

Obviously, the characteristics of Native American gangs are dependent on the dynamics of the tribal community, the behavior of the gang members, and potential outside influences. While smaller and more geographically isolated reservations tend to have fewer gangs and gang members, large reservations have a more extensive problem. In the smaller communities, criminal activity primarily involves lower-level offenses such as criminal destruction of property (graffiti, vandalism, slashed tires, broken windows), drug usage, weapon offenses, threats, intimidation, and occasional assaults. On larger reservations, with greater populations and land mass, criminal activity includes not only the low-level offenses but also drug distribution, burglary, robbery, felony assaults, and murder.

Regardless of the geographic size of the reservation or its population, the impact of gang activity is relative. Gangs and gang members engage in an inordinate amount of criminal activity in Indian Country and these gang-related issues drain tribal law enforcement, the court resources, and jails/detention centers.

Discussion Points and Questions

1. Why are Native American so susceptible to the gang world?
2. What factors contribute to the gang problem on Native American reservations?
3. What makes reservations so attractive for drug cartels?
4. What can a tribal community do to reduce the likelihood of a young person from joining a gang?

Websites

Division of Drug Enforcement, Bureau of Indian Affairs –Office of Justice Services
https://www.bia.gov/sites/bia.gov/files/assets/bia/ojs/ojs/pdf/DOI_BIA_OJS_
DDE_2018_Annual_Report_Sec508.pdf

Bureau of Indian Education

https://www.bie.edu/index.htm

Gangland: Wild Boyz – Into the Badland (Season 7, Episode 4)

https://www.youtube.com/watch?v=3KQICOZlCHc

REFERENCES

American Addiction Centers. (2020). Risks of alcoholism among Native Americans. Retrieved from https://americanaddictioncenters.org/alcoholism-treatment/native-americans

Arizona Department of Corrections. (2019a). *Dine pride.* Retrieved from https://corrections.az.gov/dine-pride-0

Arizona Department of Corrections. (2019b). *Warrior society.* Retrieved from https://corrections.az.gov/warrior-society-0

Bureau of Indian Education (2019). *Reports.* Retrieved from https://www.bie.edu/HowAreWeDoing/index.htm

Carcamo, C. (2015, February 22). Drug explosion follows oil boom on North Dakota Indian reservation. *Los Angeles Times.* Retrieved from https://www.latimes.com/nation/la-na-ff-north-dakota-meth-20150222-story.html

Conly, C. (1993). *Street gangs: Current knowledge and strategies.* U.S. Department of Justice, Office of Justice Programs, National Institute of Justice.

Department of Justice. (2006, November). Methamphetamine in Indian Country: An American problem uniquely affecting Indian Country. *The National Congress of American Indians.* Retrieved from https://www.justice.gov/archive/tribal/docs/fv_tjs/session_1/session1_presentations/Meth_Overview.pdf

Eckholm, E. (2009). Gang Violence Grows on an Indian Reservation. The New York Times, December, 13, 2009. Retrieved 25, May 2019, from https://www.nytimes.com/2009/12/14/us/14gangs.html

Education World. (n.d.). *Native Americans struggle, build pride.* Retrieved from https://www.educationworld.com/a_issues/schools/schools012.shtml

Federal Bureau of Investigation [FBI]. (2011). *2011 National Gang Threat Assessment Report.* Retrieved from https://www.fbi.gov/stats-services/publications/2011-national-gang-threat-assessment

Federal Bureau of Investigation [FBI]. (2011). *2013 National Gang Threat Assessment Report.* Retrieved from https://www.fbi.gov/file-repository/stats-services-publications-national-gang-report-2013/view

Federal Bureau of Investigation [FBI]. (2019). *Indian Country crime: Safe Trail Task Forces.* Retrieved from https://www.fbi.gov/investigate/violent-crime/indian-country-crime

Freng, A. (2013). American Indian gangs. In J. I. Ross (Ed.), *American Indians at risk* (pp. 11–23). Santa Barbara, CA: ABC-CLIO, LLC.

Gibson, D. (2017, March 23). Indian Reservations have become highways for drug cartels. *Inquizitr.com.* Retrieved from https://www.inquisitr.com/opinion/4079999/indian-reservations-have-become-highways-for-drug-cartels/

Gibson, D. (2019, March). Mexican drug cartels use Indian Reservation to smuggle fentanyl into U.S. *Illegal Alien Crime Report.* Retrieved from https://www.illegalaliencrimereport.com/mexican-drug-cartels-use-indian-reservation-to-smuggle-fentanyl-into-u-s/

Grant, C. M. (2013). Native American Involvement in the Gang Subculture: Current Trends & Dynamics. Community Corrections Institute Bureau of Justice Assistance, Office of Justice Programs, U.S. Department of Justice. Retrieved 25, May 2019 from http://www.communitycorrections.org/images/publications/NAInvolveinGangs-Trends.pdf

Grant, C. & Feimer, S. (2007). Street gangs in Indian Country: A clash of cultures. *Journal of Gang Research, 14*(4), 27–66.

Hailer, J. (2008). *American Indian youth involvement in urban street gangs: Invisible no more?* (Unpublished doctoral dissertation). University of Arizona, American Indian Studies, Tucson.

Harris, D, Epstein, B, Frey, J. C., Simon, E., & Madden, P. (2019). On tribal land along US-Mexico border, drug and human smuggling corrupts an ancient culture. *ABCNEWS.* Retrieved from https://abcnews.go.com/US/tribal-land-us-mexico-border-drug-human-smuggling/story?id=63064992

Henderson, E., Kunitz, S. J., & Levy, J. J. (1999) The origins of Navajo youth gangs. *American Indian Culture and Research Journal,23*(3), 243-264.

Indianz.com. (2018, November 25). Gangs hit Tohono O'odham Nation hard. *Indianz.com.* Retrieved from https://www.indianz.com/News/show.asp?ID=2002/11/25/tohono

Joseph, J., & Taylor, D. (2003). Native American youth gangs. *Journal of Gang Research, 10*(2), 45-54.

Kaliszewski, M. (2020, February 19). Alcohol and drug abuse among Native Americans. *American Addiction Centers.* Retrieved from https://americanaddictioncenters.org/rehab-guide/addiction-statistics/native-americans

Kennecke, A. (2019, August 7). Native America teenagers and gangs. *KELOLAND News.* Retrieved from https://www.keloland.com/news/investigates/native-american-teenagers-and-gangs/

Koyfman, S. (2017, October 4). What was, and what is: Native American languages in the US. *Babbel Magazine.* Retrieved from https://www.babbel.com/en/magazine/native-american-languages-in-the-us/

Krogstad, J. M. (2014, June 13). One-in-four Native Americans and Alaska Natives are living in poverty. *FactTank News in the Numbers: Pew Research Center.* Retrieved from https://www.pewresearch.org/fact-tank/2014/06/13/1-in-4-native-americans-and-alaska-natives-are-living-in-poverty/

Lamarine, R. J. (1988). Alcohol abuse among Native Americans. *Journal of Community Health, 13*, 143-155.

Major, A., & Egley, A. (2002). *2000 survey of youth gangs in Indian Country.* OJJDP, National Youth Center. Retrieved from https://www.nationalgangcenter.gov/Content/Documents/Youth-Gangs-in-Indian-Country-2000.pdf

Major, A., Egley, A., Howell, J., Mendenhall, B., & Armstrong, T. (2004, March). Youth gangs in Indian Country. *OJJDP Juvenile Justice Bulletin.* Washington, DC: U.S. Department of Justice, Office of Justice Programs, Office of Juvenile Justice and Delinquency Prevention.

National Drug Intelligence Center [NDIC]. (2008). *Indian Country drug threat assessment.* Retrieved from https://www.justice.gov/archive/ndic/pubs28/29239/29239p.pdf

National Drug Intelligence Center. (2011). *Gangs in Indian Country threat assessment.* Retrieved from https://www.justice.gov/archive/ndic/pubs44/44849/44849p.pdf

FederalNational Gang Intelligence Center [NGIC]. (2013).

National Urban Indian Family Coalition. (2008). *The status of urban American Indian and Alaska Native children and families today.* Retrieved from https://www.aecf.org/resources/urban-indian-america/

Native American Center for Excellence and the Substance Abuse and Mental Health Services Administration [NACE-SAMHSA]. (2019). *Historical trauma.* Retrieved from https://www.samhsa.gov/

NBC15. (2016, November 15). Wisconsin drug and gang task force recognized nationally. *NBC15.com.* Retrieved from https://www.nbc15.com/content/news/Wisconsin-drug-and-gang-taskforce-recognized-nationally-401292176.html

Patterson, J. M. (2009, August 6). Public safety chief reports 225 gangs on rez. *Navajo Times.* Retrieved from https://navajotimes.com/news/2009/0809/080509gangs.php

Prison Policy Institute. (2014). *Breaking down mass incarceration in the 2010 Census: state-by-state incarceration rates by race/ethnicity.* Retrieved from https://www.prisonpolicy.org/reports/rates.html

Re-Member.org. (2019). Pine Ridge Indian Reservation. Retrieved from https://www.re-member.org/pine-ridge-reservation.aspx

Starbuck, D., Howell, J., & Lindquist, D. (2001, December). Hybrid and other modern gangs. *Juvenile Justice Bulletin.* Washington, DC: Office of Juvenile Justice and Delinquency Prevention. Department of Homeland Security Digital Library. Retrieved from https://www.hsdl.org/?view&did=456755

Stern, R. (2018, March 5). Shotgun slaying of woman spotlights gang problems on Tohono O'odham Nation. *Phoenix New Times.* Retrieved from https://www.phoenixnewtimes.com/news/shotgun-slaying-highlights-gang-problems-on-tohono-oodham-nation-10194697

Sunrise House. (2020). Addiction among Native Americans. Retrieved from https://sunrise-house.com/addiction-demographics/native-americans/

Szlemko, W. J., Wood, J. W., & Thurman, P. J. (2006). Native Americans and alcohol: Past, present, and future. *Journal of General Psychology, 133*(4), 435–451.

Wakeling, S., Jorgensen, M., Michaelson, S., & Begay, M. (2001). *Policing on American Indian Reservations.* Washington, DC: National Institute of Justice. U.S. Department of Justice, Office of Justice Programs. Retrieved from https://www.ncjrs.gov/pdffiles1/nij/188095.pdf

U.S. Bureau of Labor Statistics. (2019, November). *American Indians and Alaska Natives in the U.S. labor force.* Retrieved from https://www.bls.gov/opub/mlr/2019/article/american-indians-and-alaska-natives-in-the-u-s-labor-force.htm

United States v. Acosta, 534 F.3d 574 (7th Cir. 2008)

Zielinski, G. (2005, July 2). Gang plunges tribe into turmoil: Rural reservation struggles to recover from big city crime brought by Latin Kings. *The Milwaukee Sentinel Journal.* Retrieved from https://www.alipac.us/f12/gang-plunges-tribe-into-turmoil-4943/

https://www.bls.gov/opub/mlr/2019/article/american-indians-and-alaska-natives-in-the-u-s-labor-force.htm

Chapter 6

Gangs and the Police

NEWS CLIP 6-1:

FBI ANNOUNCES MAJOR TAKEDOWN OF PITTSBURGH-AREA GANGS

Pittsburgh, PA—Local, state, and federal officials have put a massive dent in a local gang and drug activity after dismantling three violent gangs in the Pittsburgh area: Hustlas Don't Sleep, Sco, and Darkside Smashers 44. Over 100 people have been indicted and 13 gang members have been arrested. Authorities seized over 400 bricks of heroin laced with fentanyl, crack cocaine, and over 100 guns. According to the FBI, "the gangs are responsible for homicides, shootings, robberies, assaults, and other violent behavior that slows neighborhood revitalization in the city of Pittsburgh."

Source: Allen, B. (2019, November 25). *FBI Announces Major Takedown Of Pittsburgh-Area Gangs.* CBS Channel 2 KDKA Pittsburgh. *Retrieved from https://pittsburgh.cbslocal.com/2019/11/25/ fbi-searching-for-man-part-of-drug-traffickers-group/*

The Formation of Police Anti-Gang Units

The arrest of the Grape Street Gang members in Trenton, New Jersey [see above news story], is an example of the collective effort by multiple law enforcement agencies combating street gangs. Law enforcement has been dealing with gangs and gang members and their destructive lifestyle for decades. In fact, communities and law enforcement agencies across the United States have been dealing with various types of gangs that terrorize neighborhoods such as street gangs, outlaw motorcycle gangs, prison gangs, drug cartels, criminal organizations, domestic extremists, and other groups. While most gang members sit around, drink, smoke, and tell stories (Klein, 2009; Vigil, 1988; Yablonsky, 1997), gangs and their behaviors are a legitimate concern for law enforcement officials because gangs have the ability to be organized, sophisticated, and systematic in their illegal activities. Gangs are also very unpredictable and found in urban, suburban, and rural areas. Thus, no community is free from potentially falling victim to gang violence. Gangs are responsible for a multitude of violent and property crimes such as drug and weapon offenses, carjacking and drive-by shootings, robberies and burglaries, and acts of vandalism (i.e., graffiti) and these crimes are often committed on behalf of the gang or for personal gain. The gang lifestyle, while appealing to some on the surface, disrupts families, students, and keeps neighborhoods in a constant fear.

The gang problem is nothing new and has a long history as briefly discussed in Chapter 1. As street gangs grew dramatically across the United States, the need to create a specialized task force to combat gangs was apparent and necessary. Figure 6.1 shows the initial reports identifying cities with gang problems in 1970. The cities identified by the National Youth Gang Survey where New York, Philadelphia, Detroit, Chicago, San Francisco, and Los Angeles. Figure 6.2 shows the significant and alarming growth of gangs throughout the United States by 1992. The gang problem was no longer isolated to the major cities located on the East Coast, in the Midwest, or in the West. In fact, large, medium, and small towns were now plagued with the migration of gang members.

The large growth of gangs from the 1970s to the 1990s precipitated the need for the formation of more specialized police units which are able to confront the gang problem with understanding, urgency, and precision. These specialized police gang units or anti-gang units are designed to "hit" gangs and gang members hard and fast to eradicate these groups from communities (Delaney, 2014). While the data (increase in gang presence) indicated the need for police anti-gang units, other factors that contributed to the formation of these specialized units were public and political pressure, the increase in gang-related crimes, journalistic news accounts of gang activities, and influential community members demanding attention to the gang problem that promotes action.

Figure 6.1: Cities with identifiable gang problems, 1970.

● Problem site ○ No problem

Source: 1975 National Youth Gang Survey conducted by Walter Miller, as cited in Curry and Decker (2003). Confronting gangs: Crime and community. Los Angeles, CA: Roxbury Publishing.

Figure 6.2: Cities experiencing gang member migration through 1992.

Number of cities = 694

Source: Maxson, C. (1998). Gangs members on the move. Office of Juvenile Justice & Delinquency Prevention, Juvenile Justice Bulletin. Washington, DC: U.S. Department of Justice. Retrieved from https://www.ncjrs.gov/pdffiles/171153.pdf

Historically, juvenile bureaus, community-relation departments, and crime prevention teams were the groups responding to gangs (Huff, 1993). Today, a police gang unit is a combination of street knowledge, intelligence gathering, teamwork, and the presence of passionate police officers. Katz and Webb (2006) explained that it takes a unique individual to be a gang cop where self-motivation, prior experience, and the ability to speak a foreign language (preferably Spanish) are key characteristics for a police officer to join an anti-gang unit and be successful.

Similar to narcotics units or vice squads, police gang units specialize in recognizing gang colors, tattoos, codes, and symbols. A police gang unit or anti-gang unit is a "secondary or tertiary functional division within a police organization, with at least one sworn officer whose sole function is to engage in gang control efforts" (Katz & Webb, 2006, p. 10). It is the job of the gang cop to truly understand the gang culture. The police gang unit needs to know their territory, the rules and regulations for each gang in their neighborhood, and who the gang members are. Thus, gathering intelligence is an important function for any gang officer. Taking a proactive approach by maintaining close contact with gang members is critical to the success of combating gangs in the community.

Canadian gang expert Michael Chettleburgh (2007) suggested that police gang units are formed as a continuum. On one end of the continuum, the police take a very reactive approach to combating gang-related crimes. On the other end of the continuum is the proactive approach where there are gang specialists or "gang hunters" (Chettleburgh, 2007) whose only job is to suppress gangs at all costs. For a police gang unit to be successful, understanding the gang problem in the community, getting to know the gang members, and establishing informants are important for gang cops to follow. In the middle of the continuum are the rank-and-file police officers who patrol the streets daily. It is those officers who encounter gang members on a daily basis who can be most successful in suppression and prevention of gang activity (Chettleburgh, 2007).

Prior to the 1970s, it was primarily large cities like Chicago, New York, and Los Angeles which had officers working in specialized units that focused on gangs. According to a Bureau of Justice Statistics Report, there were only seven police gang units between 1970 and 1979 (Langton, 2010). As Figure 6.3 shows, the creation of police gang units has steadily increased since the 1970s. A census of law enforcement gang units found that there were 365 gang units comprised of local police and sheriff's departments that had 100 or more sworn officers, with at least one officer dedicated to gangs. According to the report, most police gang units deal with street gangs (98%), taggers (80%), and outlaw motorcycle gangs (57%). Police gang units spend most of their time gathering intelligence (33%) and investigating gang-related crimes (32%) (Langton, 2010). The largest growth of police gang units occurred from 1986 to 1990 and again from 2004 to 2006. Katz and Webb (2006) argued that this rise and development of police gang units is attributed to factors such as responding to an increase in gang-related

Figure 6.3:   Police gang units, 1975–2007.

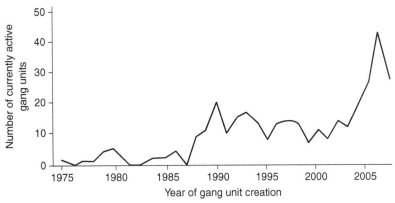

Source: Langston, L. (2010). Gang units in large local law enforcement agencies, 2007. Washington, DC: Bureau of Justice Statistics. U.S. Department of Justice.

crimes, public awareness and political pressures, moral panics, and the organization's ability to secure finances to combat gang violence in their communities. Regardless of the reasons, over 85% of specialized gang units were created in a 10-year time frame, between 1990 and 2000 (Katz, Maguire, & Roneck, 2002). It should come as no surprise, as this was the height of law enforcements response to the gang problem in the United States.

In an extensive look into the formation of police gang units, Katz and Webb (2006) explained that it is only natural for police agencies to respond by creating specialized gang units when gang membership is increasing. Furthermore, the police strategy that is most likely to be implemented, and is also very popular with the public, is gang suppression. Gang suppression typically consists of programs and/or actions led by multiple police gang units (local, county, state, federal) that are designed to eradicate gang behavior and gang membership though supervision, arrest, prosecution, and incarceration. Gang suppression is deemed the most successful police strategy in reducing gang violence in communities (see News Clip 4.1).

Unfortunately, like other specialized task forces within a department, police gang units are often isolated and sometimes do not interact well with the community (Katz & Webb, 2006). One of the most famous examples of a failed gang unit was Los Angeles Police Department's (LAPD) Community Resources Against Street Hoodlums Rampart Division task force, famously known as CRASH (discussed later in this chapter). In fact, ineffective problem-solving activities, a lack of understanding the community needs, and vague organizational and jurisdictional boundaries are a recipe for behavior that is the "antithesis of the principles of effective community policing by isolating themselves from the community, from other agencies, and indeed from their own law enforcement agency" (Decker, 2007, p. 731).

NEWS CLIP 6-2:

13 ARRESTED DURING "OPERATION BLACK RHINO"

SANTA ANA, CA—In a multi-agency operation called 'Operation Black Rhino', thirteen gang members from the Santa Ana-based Townsend Street gang was arrested. This gang was described as one of the most violent and active gangs in Orange County. In addition to the raids on the street, deputies at the Orange County jail searched the cells of inmates associated with the violent gang. Many of the gang members arrested had prior convictions, felony arrests and were on probation. During the arrests the following items were seized – multiple hand guns, assault rifle, bulletproof vest, 3 pounds of drugs, and $16,000 in cash.

Source: Von Quednow, C. & Yost, C. (2019). 13 arrested during "Operation Black Rhino" *targeting Santa Ana Gang. KTLA 5 News, Santa Ana, CA. Retrieved from https://ktla. com/2019/11/07/13-arrested-during-operation-black-rhino-targeting-santa-ana-gang/*

Implementing Police-Based Strategies to Combat Street Gangs

Implementing a strategy to combat gangs takes a collective effort by law enforcement officials, policymakers, and members of the community. A police gang unit is best suited to take a proactive approach by gathering information about gangs, infiltrating the gang, or strategizing ways to curb gang violence. One proactive approach in combating street gangs is utilizing the counter-insurgency method. As Delaney (2014) pointed out, there are increasing numbers of retired combat-experienced military officials becoming police officers and using the counterinsurgency approach to help curb gang violence.

Going after gangs and gang members included strategies such as implementing "sweeps" or targeting "hot spots" where there is a high presence of gangs. While this approach is effective, it is only a temporary solution to a larger problem as the gang presence will most likely be diverted to other areas. Nonetheless, sweeps and raids that result in multiple arrests make great stories for headline news (see News Clip 6.2).

One example of a police-based strategy approach to combat gangs occurred in Boston, Massachusetts. In the 1990s, gang activity and youth violence skyrocketed prompting the Boston Police Department (PD) to join forces with violence intervention and prevention specialists, school administrators, public officials, hospitals, and community activists in an effort to take a community-wide approach to reduce gun and gang violence. This innovative problem-oriented policing approach was called "Operation Ceasefire." The program began

NEWS CLIP 6-3:

OPERATION WAR READY

POTTSTOWN, PA—34 gang members who called themselves 'Straight Cash Money Gang' were arrested as the result of ongoing investigating of gang activity in Pottstown, PA. The Berks County and Montgomery County anti-gang squads and local police officers joined forces for "Operation War Ready" in order to put a stop to the ongoing rivalry between 'Brotha from Anotha' and 'Straight Cash Money Gang". Both gangs used firearms and other methods of intimidation to terrorize local residents.

Source: WPVI-Philadelphia. (2015, May 15). Dozens arrested in Montgomery Co. gang case. ABC 6 Action News. Retrieved from https://6abc.com/news/dozens-arrested-in-montgomery-co-%20gang-case-/722842/

in 1996 and the success of the program was immediate. "Operation Ceasefire" "was associated with a 63% decrease in youth homicides, 32% decrease in monthly number of shots-fired calls, and a 25% decrease in monthly number of gun assaults" (McDevitt, Braga, Nurge, & Buerger, 2003, p. 67). The success of the program was twofold. First, law enforcement officials saturated areas when a gang-related crime occurred. Second, various social services agencies assisted in removing gang members from the gang.

While "Operation Ceasefire" is credited for reducing gangs and gang violence, the gang problem was not completely eliminated. As older gangs were dismantled and dissolved, there was an increase in female gangs and younger gang members aligning themselves with national gangs such as the Bloods, Crips, and the Chicago-based People and Folk nations (Latin Kings and Gangster Disciples). Interestingly, these new gangs had no affiliation to these national gangs but many youth adopted the names of these gangs and mimicked their colors, behaviors, and symbols (Decker, 2003). Regardless, Boston saw a significant decline in the gang violence and continued to maintain its focus on suppressing gangs and working with outreach groups to prevent gang activity.

Another example of a police-based strategy method was established in Los Angeles, California, where the LAPD in 2007 initiated the "Top 10 Most Wanted Gang Members" by offering up to $50,000 for anyone who could provide information about a suspected gang member (McGreevy & Winton, 2007). Despite early criticism of the program claiming it was a publicity stunt, the initiative garnered tremendous success. The LAPD has also recruited former gang members to assist them in curbing gang violence in the area (for a complete list of the LAPD's Top 10 Gang Members list, click http://www.lapdonline.org/top_ten_most_wanted_gang_members).

Just south of Los Angeles, the San Diego PD's anti-gang unit initiated the American Intelligence-Led Policing (ILP) program in 2007. ILP is an "executive implantation of the intelligence cycle to support proactive decision making for resource allocation and crime prevention" (Bureau of Justice Assistance, 2009, p. 4). San Diego's anti-gang unit made several high-profile arrests on gang leaders and significantly reduced the homicide rate and violent gang sets (Howell & Griffiths, 2016).

In St. Louis, Missouri, the St. Louis Metropolitan PD received a grant to participate in the COPS Anti-Gang Initiative, a federally funded program that was first implemented in 1996. Like many other cities across the United States in the mid-1990s, St. Louis' gang problem was growing rapidly and 50% of the gang members were youth under the age of 18 years (Decker, 2003). The St. Louis PD anti-gang program was designed to target two known gang areas with a zero-tolerance enforcement initiative. The strategic approach was to enforce curfews, use consent-to-search tactics to reduce guns on the street, and focus on intelligence gathering by the Gang Intelligence Unit. While the program did not garner the success of reducing gang-related crime rates like Boston's "Operation Ceasefire" program, it was effective in gathering intelligence about local street gangs. Unfortunately, in St. Louis, the lack of integration between law enforcement and outreach groups proved that reducing youth violence must be a collaborative effort, and not just a single agency approach. As Spergel and Curry (1993) concluded, the most successful gang intervention programs are the ones that combine suppression, community organization, and opportunity provisions. In this case, the St. Louis COPS program failed.

Another city that participated in the COPS Anti-Gang Initiative was Detroit, Michigan in 1996. Unlike St. Louis, the Detroit PD took a very aggressive suppression approach—cracking down on juveniles for curfew and truancy violations. The specialized gang unit also cracked down on littering, loitering, public gambling, and public urination (Decker, 2003). Ultimately, the Detroit PD was successful at reducing the number of gang-related problems, gun violence, assaults, robberies, and burglaries. However, Decker (2003) pointed out that the success of reducing gang crimes could be more related to the overly aggressive police suppression tactics than any of the collaborative efforts between law enforcement and community programs.

Federal Approaches to Combating Gangs

COPS Anti-Gang Initiative (CAGI)

Since gangs have been a persistent problem for law enforcement and communities, the Department of Justice (DOJ) initiated a competitive grant program for multi-jurisdictional task forces aimed at addressing the gang problem and advancing public safety in the community. In 2019, the OFFDP (Office of Juvenile Justice and Delinqency Prevention, division of the DOJ) awarded over $7 Million to various. The duration of the grant is for two years (24 months) and must focus on enforcement, prevention/education, and intervention of gang activity. The grant may not be used to fund the prosecution of gang-related activities. CAGI funding must be used to support regional anti-gang task forces focusing on enforcement, prevention/education, and intervention of gang activity. Up to $7 million in funding (subject to availability funding) may be available for CAGI. Each grant is two years (24 months) in duration, and there is no local match. Each grant recipient may receive a maximum of $750,000. For a listing of current grant recipients at the state level see, https://ojjdp.ojp.gov/states.

The Violent Gang Task Force

In order to address the growing violent gang problem in the 1980s and 1990s, the Federal Bureau of Investigation (FBI) created the Safe Streets Violent Crime Initiative in 1992. The purpose of this initiative was to give FBI field offices the ability to address violent street gangs and drug-related crimes through collaborative efforts with local, state, and federal officials. The idea was for these agencies to work together on violent crimes and street gangs. This collaboration became known as the Violent Gang Safe Streets Task Force. For more information, see http://www.fbi.gov/about-us/investigate/vc_majorthefts/gangs/violent-gangs-task-forces.

As of 2020, the FBI's Safe Streets and Gang Unit administer 160 Violent Gang Safe Streets Task Forces nationwide. The program is staffed by over 800 FBI agents, more than 1,500 state and local law enforcement personnel, and nearly 100 other federal law enforcement agents (FBI, 2015a). Working under the U.S. Code, Titles 18 and 21, these task forces pursue violent gangs through constant, proactive, and coordinated investigations, including violations such as racketeering, drug conspiracy, and firearms violations. This collaborative effort between federal, state, and local law enforcement agencies gives the Safe Streets Task Force (SSTF) more resources to combat gangs, better gang intelligence, and avoid duplicating investigative efforts (FBI, 2015a).

According to the FBI, one of the key facets to the SSTF is the implementation of Enterprise Theory of Investigation (ETI). ETI combines street-level enforcement activity with high-level sophisticated techniques such as consensual monitoring, financial analysis, and wire-taps in order to root out and prosecute the entire gang. The purpose is to break the gang's structure. The SSTF works to dismantle low level street gangs up to prosecuting high ranking gang leaders. The ETI approach has shown its effectiveness in federal racketeering, drug conspiracy, and firearms investigations (McFeely, 2001).

National Gang Task Force and Other Federal Programs

As the gang problem in the United States continued to grow, it also got more violent. The need to concentrate on a few specific violent gangs was necessary. Throughout the late 1990s and early 2000s, the growth of Mara Salvatrucha (MS-13) and the 18th Street gang had become a significant problem for law enforcement officials and communities on the East Coast (Maryland and Virginia), West Coast (California), and those southwestern states bordering Mexico (Arizona, New Mexico, and Texas).

In a unified effort to deal with this growing gang problem, several agencies from the Department of Justice joined forces: the Federal Bureau of Investigation (FBI), the Drug Enforcement Administration (DEA), the Alcohol, Tobacco, Firearms and Explosives (ATF), the Federal Bureau of Prisons (BOP), Immigration Customs Enforcement (ICE), the US Marshalls Service (Reference DOJ organization chart, https://www.justice.gov/agencies/chart). These agencies collaborated to create the national Gang Targeting Enforcement Coordinating Center (GangTECC). The focus of GangTECC is to share intelligence and help other agencies with investigations at the federal, state, and local levels (Franco, 2008).

By 2004, MS-13 was identified in 42 states and had a strong presence in Houston, Los Angeles, New York City, and Washington, D.C. As the problem grew, it became apparent that the level of violence displayed by MS-13 needed more attention by the FBI. By December of 2004, the FBI created the National Gang Task Force (NGTF) to specifically focus on combating MS-13, the 18th Street gang, and other transnational gangs. The NGTF would provide support to local, state, and other federal agencies in dealing with MS-13 and other violent street gangs.

Following the creation of the NGTF, the FBI recognized that the Hispanic/Latino-based street gangs were not just a U.S. problem. In fact, these gangs were also flourishing in Central and South America and they were also affecting the United States. Recognizing the need to collaborate with other countries, the FBI instituted a number of program initiatives aimed at combating the transnational gang problem with law enforcement agencies from Central America: Mexico, El Salvador, Honduras, Nicaragua, Guatemala, Costa Rica, Panama, and Belize. One example of this collaboration was the creation of the Central American Fingerprint Exploitation (CAFÉ) database. CAFÉ is a database that is merged with criminal records found in the U.S. Integrated Automated Fingerprint Identification System (IAFIS) database. This merger helps law enforcement on both sides of the border identify key members of MS-13 and other Hispanic/Latino-based gangs that have committed gang-related crimes. Other programs between the U.S. law enforcement agencies and Central American law enforcement agencies include the Central American Law Enforcement Exchange (CALEE) Initiative, the Central American Intelligence Program (CAIP) Initiative, and the Central American Criminal History Information Program (CHIP) Initiative. All these programs provide training opportunities for law enforcement personnel working within anti-gang units. The programs give law enforcement agencies the opportunity to exchange gang intelligence with one another, share reports on successful gang prevention and intervention programs, and provide critical information on the types of gang members being deported to their home country. As MS-13 continued to be an international problem, the FBI partnered with the

Policia Naccional Civil (PNC) in El Salvador where FBI agents work with the National Police and prosecutors in investigating gang-related crimes. This program is called the Transnational Anti-Gang (TAG) initiative (FBI, 2015b; Franco, 2008).

Several other federal agencies besides the FBI within the Department of Justice are also engaged in fighting gangs. For example, since gangs are often involved in drug trafficking, the Drug Enforcement Agency (DEA) also plays a crucial role in combating gangs. Weapons trafficking is another gang activity that law enforcement faces and that responsibility is shared with the Bureau of Alcohol, Tobacco, Firearms, and Explosives (ATF). The ATF typically works with the DOJ Criminal Division on a "gang squad" task force where they investigate both domestic and transnational gangs (Franco, 2008). The ATF is also the lead Department of Justice agency in the Regional Area Gang Enforcement (RAGE) task force, which includes agents and officers from ATF, FBI, ICE, and other state and local law enforcement agencies. In addition, the ATF is the lead agency for 15 Violent Crime Impact Teams (VCITs), 13 of which focus on gang activity tied to homicides (Haynes, 2010). The ATF is also involved in several federal task forces and leads the investigations of violent gang crime through its firearms tracing system and the National Tracing Center (NTC), as well as through the Regional Crime Gun Centers (RCGCs) located in major cities plagued by gang violence. Lastly, the ATF provides national training programs for federal, state, and local law enforcement officers and prosecutors as part of the Project Safe Neighborhoods (PSN) program on street-level gun recoveries, enforcement tactics, and firearms identification and tracking procedures (Haynes, 2010).

In 2005, U.S. Immigration and Customs Enforcement (ICE) initiated "Operation Community Shield" to combat the threats posed by MS-13 gang (U.S. Immigration and Customs Enforcement [ICE], 2015). ICE identified MS-13, the 18th Street gang, and other street gangs as "having a presence across the United States, a significant foreign-born membership and history of violence" (Franco, 2008, p. 15). By 2015, some 10 years after "Operation Community Shield" was launched in 2005, more than 30,000 gang members and associates have been arrested, representing over 350 different gangs, including nearly 5,000 MS-13 gang members arrested (Milford, 2015; see also News Clip 6.3). The US Customs and Border Protection (CBP) agency has also collected gang intelligence on MS-13 since the early 2000s. In 2006, U.S. Customs and Border Protection (CBP) agency was also collecting gang intelligence on MS-13 since the early 2000s. In 2006, CBP arrested 208 MS-13 gang members mostly in the Rio Grande Valley sector in Texas (Kane, 2006).

NEWS CLIP 6-3:

HSI- HOUSTON ARRESTS 23 GANG MEMBERS, TARGETING MS-13

HOUSTON—As gang activity has increased in Houston over the years, HSI Houston and the Texas Anti-Gang (TAG) Center have increased their law enforcement efforts to combat the problem. Special agents with Homeland Security Investigations (HSI) Houston, along with various federal, state, and local law enforcement agencies, arrested 23 gang members and gang associates during a 26-day surge operation targeting MS-13 gang members. Thirteen of those arrested during this operation are confirmed MS-13 gang members or gang associates including three Salvadoran nationals arrested on murder charges. In fiscal year 2018, HSI arrested 959 MS-13 gang members and associates nationwide.

Source: U.S. Immigration and Customs Enforcement. (2019, June 4). ICE Houston arrests 23 gang members, associates during operation targeting MS-13. Washington, DC: Department of Homeland Security. Retrieved from https://www.ice.gov/news/releases/ice-houston-arrests-23-gang-members-associates-during-operation-targeting-ms-13

National Gang Intelligence Center (NGIC)

In 2005, Congress directed the FBI to create the National Gang Intelligence Center (NGIC) to address the growing gang problems in the United States. This multi-agency fusion center comprising the FBI, DEA, ATF, ICE, CBP, BOP, U.S. Marshals Service, and the U.S. Department of Defense (Army, Navy, Air Force) integrates and shares gang intelligence resources. The purpose of the NGIC is to provide law enforcement agencies across the country with information on the growth, migration, and criminal activities of street gangs. NGIC utilizes its resources at the FBI and provides state and local law enforcement agencies with descriptive and analytical information about gangs. NGIC also provides agencies with strategic, operational, and tactical analysis for those agencies requesting help to combat their local gang problem.

The NGIC also partnered with the now-defunct National Drug Intelligence Center (NDIC) to collect data on gangs, gang members, and other gang-related issues, which and produced a biannual FBI *National Gang Threat Assessment Report* for local, state, and federal agencies. (Latest report listed is from 2015, see https://www.fbi.gov/resources/library.) While this report has been extensively utilized by law enforcement agencies to get pertinent information about gangs and identify which groups are defined as gangs versus not gangs, critical for prosecutorial efforts, it is not without its critics.

In 2012, the hip hop/rap group Insane Clown Posse (ICP) (see http://www.insaneclown-posse.com/) from Detroit, Michigan, sued the FBI for labeling the followers of ICP, known as "Juggalos," as a "gang" in the 2011 *National Gang Threat Assessment Report (FBI, 2011)*. By defining "Juggalos" as a gang this label gave law enforcement officials the power to make arrests, stop and frisk individuals, shutdown concerts, and even prevent an individual from joining the U.S. Army because of his ICP tattoo (see Duke, 2014; see also video clip http://www.cnn.com/2014/01/08/showbiz/juggalo-gang-lawsuit/). In July 2014, a federal judge dismissed ICPs lawsuit against the FBI and the Department of Justice stating that the FBIs report of classifying the Juggalos as a "loosely organized hybrid gang in the 2011 FBI report on gangs is "descriptive," and not "prescriptive," thus it does not break any laws (Ohlheiser, 2014). ICP claims that the FBI report was "unwarranted and unlawful," and it only prompted local law enforcement officials to harass fans wearing ICP jewelry and other symbols related to the group (Ohlheiser, 2014). After challenging earlier decisions, in October 2017, ICP presented their case to the 6th Circuit Court of Appeals, but again lost their case to the FBI.

Infamous Anti-Gang Police Unit: The LAPD CRASH Unit

In 1973, the 77th Street Division of the LAPD created a unit called Total Resource Against Street Hoodlums (TRASH) to respond to the growing problem of street gangs in Southern California. The emphasis for the officers assigned to TRASH was to obtain information about street gangs, share gang intelligence between districts, and engage in gang-related crime prevention programs. Shortly after complaints from activists and politicians about the use of the acronym TRASH, the LAPD changed the police gang unit to CRASH.

As the gang problem continued to grow in Los Angeles and in the surrounding communities, the anti-gang unit CRASH was implemented in the LAPD's Divisions, the most notorious was the Rampart Division. Officers assigned to the CRASH unit operated in a carefree and haphazard manner. The CRASH officer had "freedom of movement and activity" and was "gung-ho" in nature (PBS Frontline, 2001). For more than two decades, the LAPD CRASH unit tackled the gang problem and made over 25,000 arrests of suspected gang activities (Barrett & Browne, 2004). In fact, the success of CRASH inspired the making of the Holly-wood film *Colors*, starring Robert Duvall and Sean Penn. Other films inspired by the Rampart CRASH scandal include *Training Day* (2001), *L.A.P.D.: To Protect and to Serve* (2001), *Direct Action* (2004), *Dirty* (2005), *Street Kings* (2008), *Faster* (2010), and *Rampart* (2011). The television series, *The Shield* (2002–2008) also used the Rampart scandal for storylines as it depicted a band of rogue Los Angeles police officers.

CRASH employed tactics that were considered not only successful, but also very controversial. But in the late 1990s, the CRASH unit at the LAPD Rampart Division began to unfold as evidence of corruption, shootings, beatings, framing of suspects, stealing and dealing drugs, intimidation tactics, planting false evidence, and other major cover-ups were discovered. In fact, more than 70 police officers were implicated in the scandal (Young, 2008). The initial downfall of the CRASH unit began in March 1998 when LAPD officials discovered that eight pounds of cocaine went missing from an evidence room with a street value of $80,000. The missing evidence was linked back to CRASH officer Rafael Perez. While there are accounts of earlier cases of LAPD CRASH officers behaving badly, such as Rampart CRASH officer Brian Hewitt, who beat an 18th Street gang member while in police custody, it was Perez's arrest and his cooperation with investigators that led to a much larger scandal. Initially, investigators did not know the extent of the corruption that existed in the Rampart CRASH unit until Perez was arrested for the missing cocaine. Confused when questioned, Perez instead asked police officials, "Is this about the bank robbery?" Despite Perez implicating more than 70 officers, over 100 criminal convictions were overturned and the scandal cost the city more than $125 million in civil law suits.

The LAPD Rampart CRASH officers were brazen and wore a distinctive patch (see http://www.patchgallery.com/main/displayimage.php?pid=29975). The officers were known to wear the ominous insignia that many say symbolized their suspicious brand of policing (Lait & Glovers, 2000). The insignia was also tattooed on some of the CRASH officers. The Rampart CRASH insignia had the image of a grinning skull with demonic red eyes wearing a cowboy hat. On the cowboy hat, there is a police badge and fanned out behind the skull are four playing cards—Aces and Eight's—the so-called "dead man's hand" (Lait & Glovers, 2000). The Rampart CRASH scandal not only involved a police gang unit that went rogue but it is believed that some members of the unit had ties to the Bloods, the notorious criminal street gang from South Central LA. To further complicate the apparent relationship between some members of the Bloods and the LAPD CRASH unit officers, it is believed by some that a few members of the CRASH unit were responsible for the death of Christopher Wallace (also known as the Notorious B.I.G. (aka, Biggie Smalls). The death of Wallace according to Sullivan (2011) is the result of hip hop mogul Suge Knight of Death Row Records, a known Blood affiliate, and LAPD Rampart CRASH officer David Mack responding to the earlier death of Tupac Shakur fueling the rivalry between the East Coast vs. West Coast rap industry. (PBS Frontline, 2001; Sullivan, 2011).

In March 2000, all of LAPD's CRASH units were disbanded and a new anti-gang unit was formed, the LAPD Gang and Narcotics Division. While the extent of the Rampart Scandal will never be known, some believe there are crimes potentially committed by former CRASH officers that will remain unsolved. However, it is important to note that not all CRASH officers were corrupt.

The LAPD CRASH unit was not the only anti-gang police agency in the United States that engaged in corruptive and/or inappropriate behavior. For example, in 2009, the Minneapolis Metro Gang Strike Force was guilty of widespread impropriety such as receiving stolen goods, seizing goods and cash from criminals, falsifying evidence, creating improper documentation, engaging in illegal searches and seizures, assaults, excessive force, destruction of property, false imprisonment, and many other forms of violence and illegal acts. Although no Metro Gang Strike Force officer was arrested for misconduct, the city of paid out $3 million to those who were victimized by the gang unit for their unscrupulous behavior (Luger & Egelhof, 2009; Mannix, 2011; Nelson, 2009). In another example, in March 2018, the Buffalo Police Department disbanded their police gang unit called Strike Force, which targeted gangs, guns, and drug activity, in the face of criticism of what some regarded as its heavy-handed tactics (Porat & Heaney, 2018). The Detroit Police Department's Gang Squad, made famous by the National Geographic Channel airing of *Inside Detroit Gang Squad*, was disbanded in 2013 by the then-mayor David Bing and then-Interim police chief Chester Logan who decided to restructure the department so there would be more beat cops on the streets (Wells, 2013). Although the Detroit Gang Squad was also known for its excessive tactics in combating the street gang problem, there was only one case where three Gang Squad members were sued by a 19-year-old who was beaten during a traffic stop in 2009. The confrontation was caught on a surveillance camera and the lawsuit was settled out of court (Williams, 2013).

Education and Resources for Police Gang Units

Since gangs are constantly evolving, it is important for law enforcement officials to stay abreast of these changes. Each year throughout the country, local, state, and federal agencies send police gang unit officers, juvenile probation officers, educators, policymakers, and prevention/intervention specialists to educational workshops and conferences that specifically address street gangs. These workshops, conferences, and educational training seminars provide individuals an opportunity to share information with one another, learn about the latest trends in gang activities, get the most up-to-date research on gangs, and develop new strategies to combat gang problems in their communities.

In addition to gang education, PDs have special access to a variety of data sharing software programs and analytic tools and investigative resources at their disposal for identifying gangs and gathering gang intelligence. These types of resources provide additional support in combating the gang problem.

Gang Education and Online Sources

One of the earliest recognized gang conferences was held in California known as the *First Youth Gang Conference* in February 1980. Initiated by the California Attorney General, the conference recommended that agencies form groups to help identify the types of gangs in the neighborhood and the extent of the gang violence. It was also important to find programs that would reduce gang activities. After a series of committee hearings, the First Youth Gang Task Force in California was created. The goal of the task force was to address the growing problem of youth gangs, identify gang characteristics, and find ways to divert and prevent gang membership (Aguirra, 2011).

Since that first youth gang conference over four decades ago, local, state, and federal agencies have been sending police, corrections, probation and parole, and juvenile officers to specialized workshops, seminars and conference on the gang phenomenon throughout the country. Almost every state has some type of conference focused on gang-related issues. Today, some of the most popular and well-known training workshops/conferences that address the gang problem are the National Gang Crime Research Center's (NGCRC) annual conference held in Chicago; the Middle Atlantic-Great Lakes Organized Crime Law Enforcement Network (MAGLOCLEN) which supports police gang units from New York, New Jersey, Delaware, Maryland, Pennsylvania, Ohio, Michigan, and Indiana; and the California Gang Investigators Association Conference (CGIA), the oldest and largest gang conference in the nation. CGIA was founded in 1977 but it did not have their first fully sponsored conference until 1991.

Another organization that works with law enforcement agencies to combat gangs is the National Alliance of Gang Investigators Association (NAGIA). NAGIA was formed in 1998 and, as of 2020, services 23 state and regional gang investigator associations. NAGIA "provides for leadership in developing and recommending strategies to prevent and control gang crime, administers professional training as well as assists criminal justice professionals and the public in identifying and tracking gangs, gang members and the gang crime around the world" (see National Alliance of Gang Investigators' Association [NAGIA], 2015, www.nagia.com).

Another information sharing and communication network that supports gang intelligence is called the Regional Information Sharing System (RISS). RISS is a critical analytical and investigative support services that aims to enhance officer safety. RISS also supports efforts against organized crimes, violent crime, gang activity, drug trafficking, terrorism, human trafficking, identity theft, and other regional priorities (see Regional Information Sharing System [RISS], 2015, www.riss.net/).

Two additional online resources that are very helpful to police gang units are the Global Incident Map (www.globalincidentmap.com) and Gang Enforcement Company (www.gangenforcement.com). The Global Incident Map features a global display of terrorism and other suspected gang activities around the United States and the Gang Enforcement Company is an online resource for all seeking expert opinions, investigative insights, documentaries, as well as television and web-series consulting on anti-gang police units.

Gang Databases

Monitoring gang members and identifying which gang they belong to has always been left up to those who know the gangs and gang members the best. Unfortunately, gang members might travel outside a PD's jurisdiction, thus leaving the police with little information about the gang member. However, technology has significantly improved, and this has given law enforcement the ability to share with other agencies information about gangs and the identification of gang members. One tool that is effective in keeping information about gang members are gang databases. Gang databases are computer based programs that give police officers the ability to enter data about a gang member and the gang. Before the technology of gang databases, one of the most effective tool used by the LAPD CRASH officers were "I-cards," also known as "Intelligence cards" or paper cards that contained information about each gang member in the area (Barrett & Browne, 2004). This was how police officers tracked gang members. This early method of tracking gang members eventually led to the CAL-Gang interstate computer gang tracking system used today by California law enforcement officials. The CAL-Gang system is able to collect information about the gang status of an individual, the name of their gang, any tattoos, types of crimes, and who their gang-related peers are (see http://oag.ca.gov/calgang for more information about CAL-Gang database).

Another popular gang database is called GangNET. Similar to CAL-Gang, GangNet collects data on gang members and the information can be shared with agencies locally, regionally, and nationally, if needed. The information is immediate, thus reducing the lag time between entering the data and viewing it (see http://www.sra.com/gangnet/ for more information).

Prior to computer data bases, Field Interview (FI) cards were used by PDs where the officer collects information about the suspected gang member, their association with the gang, their tattoos, location, clothing style, colors, and other biographical information that might prove to be useful at a later date (O'Deane & Murphy, 2010). Regardless of the system being used to track gang members, the majority of gang databases are viewed as a valuable tool for law enforcement officials in order to combat street gangs. At the peak of gang activity in the early to mid-1990s, over 70% of police departments used an automated database to track gang members (Johnson, Webster, Connors & Saenz, 1995); but today, that number is closer to 90% (National Gang Center, 2019).

The use of gang databases is not without criticism. One concern is that not all jurisdictions define gang members in the same way. Entering information about an individual might lead gang cops to misidentify a person as a gang member when they are not. Another fault of gang databases is girls are not typically found or entered into these databases (Curry, Decker & Pyrooz, 2014). In fact, less than 5% of female membership is recorded into gang databases (Klein, 2009). Gang databases are also criticized for being too restrictive and too vague. Most PDs require that a "documented" gang member meet two or three of the following criteria:

- Self-admission
- Identification by a "reliable informant"
- Identification by other informants

- Use of "gang style" clothing
- Gang tattoos
- Frequents gang territories
- Contacts (by officers) in the company of gang members
- Arrests with known gang members (Klein, 2009, p. 718).

The problem with how police departments document gang members is that there is too much subjectivity in recording the information. It is possible to misidentify an individual as a suspected gang member when they are not, and visa-a-versa. Former LAPD Sgt Ronald K Jackson and former LA Sheriff's Department Deputy and current California Gang Investigator's Association Executive Director Wes McBride, argued that "gang files should be re-examined on a regular basis" (Jackson & McBride, 1996, p. 103). Gangs and gang members are fluid and when an identified member has left the gang, provisions should be made to expunge their name from the file. Jackson and McBride (1996) also supported purging the gang file when a member becomes inactive for over 2 years. The integrity of the gang file and the individual rights is paramount. However, purging can lead to valuable information being lost about the gang member, particularly if they return to their gang lifestyle (Jackson & McBride, 1996).

In a report conducted by the Youth Justice Coalition (2012), transparency and accountability in California's gang database gang injunctions are lacking. Furthermore, the requirements for gang officers to determine gang membership are based on very loose and subjective observations. One concern with the CAL-Gang database is that the information collected on potential gang members is secretive, meaning that no one but law enforcement is privy to the information entered into the database. In addition, individuals who are placed in the database have no recourse to remove their names from the database through some type of an appeals process. Once the information is collected about a suspected gang member, then that individual is permanently labeled as an active gang member or an "associate." Typically, most individuals who are added to the database have not been arrested or accused of a crime. But the consequences of being identified as a gang member have lasting effects. Currently, there are approximately over 200,000 people across California are on the CAL-Gang database, and almost 50% of them are Black men from Los Angeles County between ages 21 and 24 years (Muniz, 2014). However, California is not the only place coming under heavy criticism for using gang databases. Recently, the Chicago PD and New York PD have come under scrutiny for their use of gang databases and efforts are underway to either eliminate the databases or revise them. While many departments still utilize gang databases, others have stopped using them. For example, recently in Portland, Oregon, the Portland Police Bureau decided to eliminate their use of their gang databases by "purging" over 300 names (Townes, 2017). Eliminating the gang database does not mean that police officers will stop investigating and arresting those involved in gang-related activities.

Concluding Thoughts

As gangs continue to grow in the United States, the need for a specialized police unit and police-based strategies to combat the gang problem in communities is ever paramount. Anti-gang units utilize many administrative and legal tools to assist them in dealing with gangs. From collecting information and intelligence about gang members and placing their names and other key characteristics about them in a gang database to engaging in suppression techniques, law enforcement officials are on the offensive. However, a gang unit that is given free reins to eradicate gang activities at all costs is wrong, inappropriate, and a recipe for disaster like LAPDs CRASH unit. The CRASH unit is an example of a police gang unit that went rogue. Anti-gang units need to be structured, monitored, and officers need to work within the law, not outside the law, to achieve their goals.

Police-based strategies such as gang suppression programs most often find success when coupled with social opportunities (i.e., community interaction). The example of Boston's "Operation Ceasefire" program was successful because of the collaborative effort between the police, community leaders, and outreach workers. Boston's efforts paid off and gang violence was reduced. The attempt to curb gang violence in St. Louis proved that failing to work together does not decrease gang violence. The lack of changes in the gang-related crime rates indicates that police/community collaboration is the best method in hopes to reduce gang violence. While gang suppression continues to be the preferred approach to reduce gang violence, alternative approaches should continue to be explored. As gang expert and researcher Scott Decker points out, "we must move beyond the hook 'em and book 'em mentality" to combat gangs (cited in Ritter, Simon, & Mahendra, 2013, p. 5). Collaboration must still be emphasized as the primary focus to reduce gang membership.

Collaboration does not just exist with local law enforcement and communities but also between local, state, federal, and international gang task forces. The FBI has created many gang task forces such as the Violent Gang SSTF, the National Gang Task Force, and the National Gang Intelligence Center and has collaborated with many Central American law enforcement agencies on gang identification and training programs to combat the gang problem in the United States and across the borders.

Regardless of the prevention, intervention, or suppression method, gang cops need resources and those resources come in the form of education workshops, seminars, assessment reports, and the sharing of ideas with one another. Organizations such as the NAGIA and the National Gang Crime Research Center (NGCRC) provide excellent resources for gang officers to receive up-to-date information on gang trends, changes in gang activities, and understanding the gang culture.

Police have been dealing with street gangs for many decades and the problem is not about to go away anytime soon. Effective police-based gang strategies, proper training and education, and collaborative efforts between agencies are necessary for an anti-gang unit to be successful in combating the gang problem in their neighborhood.

Discussion Points and Questions

1. What are some of the reasons anti-gang police units are created? How does your local police department handle gangs in the community?
2. Is combating the gang problem more effective as a proactive or reactive approach?
3. Why is gang education so important? Where can gang cops get training about street gangs?
4. What are the benefits and criticisms of using gang databases to keep track of gang members? How else can gang cops track gang members?
5. Can community-based resources be successfully implemented when trying to combat gang-related crimes?

Web Links

Federal Bureau of Investigation, General Information and News about Gangs:
www.fbi.gov/about-us/investigate/vc_majorthefts/gangs/gangs

National Gang Intelligence Center:
www.fbi.gov/about-us/investigate/vc_majorthefts/gangs/ngic

Global Incident Map: A Global Display of Terrorism and Other Suspicious Events:
www.globalincidentmap.com

Gang Enforcement (training and information center):
www.gangenforcement.com

Law Enforcement Education and job Resource Site:
www.lawenforcementedu.net/police-officer/police-gang-unit/

National Gang Crime Research Center
www.ngcrc.com

National Alliance of Gang Investigator's Association:

www.nagia.org

California Gang Investigators Association

www.ccgiaonline.org

REFERENCES

Allen, B. (2019, November 25). FBI Announces Major Takedown Of Pittsburgh-Area Gangs. *CBS Channel 2 KDKA Pittsburgh.* Retrieved from https://pittsburgh.cbslocal.com/2019/11/25/fbi-searching-for-man-part-of-drug-traffickers-group/

Aguirre, A. (2011). *The dynamics and sociology of criminal street gangs: Just a little respect.* Santa Ana, CA: Police & Fire Publishing.

Barrett, B., & Browne, P. W. (2004, September 27). Recipe for failure: Inadequate resources keep LAPD handcuffed. *The Daily Bulletin.* Retrieved from   http://lang.dailybulletin.com/socal/gangs/articles/ALL_p2main.asp

Bureau of Justice Assistance. (2009). *Navigating your agency's path to intelligence-led policing.* Washington, DC: U.S. Department of Justice's Global Justice Information Sharing Initiative, U.S. Department of Justice. Retrieved from https://it.ojp.gov/documents/d/Navigating%20Your%20Agency%27s%20Path%20to%20Intelligence-Led%20Policing.pdf

Chettleburgh, M. (2007). *Young thugs: Inside the dangerous world of Canadian street gangs.* Toronto, Ontario, Canada: HarperCollins.

Curry, G. D., & Decker, S. H. (2003). *Confronting gangs: Crime and community* (2nd ed.). Los Angeles, CA: Roxbury.

Curry, G. D., Decker, S. H., & Pyrooz, D. C. (2014). *Confronting gangs: Crime and community* (3rd ed.). New York, NY: Oxford University Press.

Decker, S. H. (2003). *Policing gangs and youth violence.* Belmont, CA: Thompson Wadsworth.

Decker, S. H. (2007). Expand the use of police gang units. *Criminology & Public Policy, 6*(4), 729–733.

Delaney, T. (2014). *American street gangs* (2nd ed.). Boston, MA: Pearson.

Duke, A. (2014, January 9). *Insane clown posse sues FBI for labeling "Juagglos" as a gang.* Retrieved from https://www.cnn.com/2014/01/08/showbiz/juggalo-gang-lawsuit/index.html

Federal Bureau of Investigation [FBI]. (2011). 2011 national gang threat assessment – emerging trends. *National Gang Intelligence Center.* Retrieved from https://www.fbi.gov/file-repository/stats-services-publications-2011-national-gang-threat-assessment-2011%20national%20gang%20threat%20assessment%20%20emerging%20trends.pdf/view

Federal Bureau of Investigation [FBI]. (2015a). *Gangs: Violent gang task forces.* Retrieved from https://www.fbi.gov/investigate/violent-crime/gangs/violent-gang-task-forces

Federal Bureau of Investigation [FBI}. (2015b). *Going global on gangs: New partnership targets MS-13.* Retrieved from https://www.fbi.gov/news/stories/2007/october/ms13tag_101007

Franco, C. (2008). *The MS-13 and 18th Street gangs: Emerging transnational gang threats?* (CRS Report RL34233). Washington, DC: Congressional Research Service, Library of Congress.

Haynes, S. D. (2010). Proven law enforcement strategies. *United States Attorney's Bulletin, 58*(2), 1–14.

Howell, J. C., & Griffiths, E. (2016). *Gangs in America's communities* (2nd ed.). Los Angeles, CA: SAGE.

Huff, C. R. (1993). Gangs and public policy: Macrolevel interventions. In A. P. Goldstein & C. R. Huff (Eds.), *The gang intervention handbook* (pp. 463–475). Champaign, IL: Research Press.

Jackson, R. K., & McBride, W. D. (1996). *Understanding street gangs.* Incline Village, NV: Copper-house.

Johnson, C. M., Webster, B. A., Connors, E. F., & Saenz, D. J. (1995). Gang enforcement problems and strategies: National survey findings. *Journal of Gang Research, 3,* 1–18.

Kane, L. (2006, October/November). CBP confronts U.S.'s "Most Dangerous Gang." *Customs and Border Protection Today.* Washington, DC: Department of Homeland Security. U.S. Customs and Border Protection. Retrieved from http://sks.sirs.com

Katz, C. M., & Webb, V. J. (2006). *Policing gangs in America.* New York, NY: Cambridge University Press.

Katz, C. M., Maguire, E., & Roneck, D. (2002). The creation of specialized police gang units: Testing contingency, social threat, and resource-dependency explanations. *Policing: An International Journal of Police Strategies and Management, 49*(3), 485–516.

Klein, M. W. (2009). Street gang databases: A view from the gang capitol of the United States. *Criminology & Public Policy, 8*(4), 717–721.

Lait, M., & Glovers, S. (2000, February 8). Insignia of Rampart anti-gang unit raises concerns. *Los Angeles Times.* Retrieved from http://articles.latimes.com/2000/feb/08/local/me-62143

Langton, L. (2010). Gang units in large local law enforcement agencies, 2007. *Bureau of Justice Statistics, Special Report.* Washington, DC: U.S. Department of Justice. Office of Justice Programs.

Luger, A. M., & Egelhof, J. P. (2009, August 20). Report of the Metro Gang Strike Force Review Panel. *Minnesota Department of Public Safety.* Retrieved form https://dps.mn.gov/divisions/co/about/Documents/final_report_mgsf_review_panel.pdf

Mannix, A. (2011, June 21). Metro Gang Strike Force gets off scot free. *CityPages.com.* Retrieved from http://www.citypages.com/news/metro-gang-strike-force-gets-off-scot-free-6537957

Maxson, C. (1998). Gangs members on the move. *Office of Juvenile Justice & Delinquency Prevention, Juvenile Justice Bulletin.* Washington, DC: U.S. Department of Justice. Retrieved from https://www.ncjrs.gov/pdffiles/171153.pdf

McDevitt, J., Braga, A. A., Nurge, D., & Buerger, M. (2003). Boston's youth violence prevention program: A comprehensive community-wide approach. In S. H. Decker (Ed.), *Policing gangs and youth violence* (pp. 53–76). Belmont, CA: Wadsworth/Thompson Learning.

McFeely, R. (2001). Enterprise theory of investigation. *Law Enforcement Bulletin, 70*(5), 19–25.

McGreevy, P., & Winton, R. (2007, March 9). Arrests generate publicity, criticism. *LA Times.* Retrieved from http://articles.latimes.com/2007/mar/09/local/me-topten9

Milford, R. (2015, April 9). *Nearly 5,000 MS-13 gang members arrested by ICE over the past 5 years.* Retrieved from https://www.breitbart.com/border/2015/04/09/nearly-5000-ms-13-gang-members-arrested-by-ice-over-past-5-years/

Muniz, A. (2014). Maintaining racial boundaries: Criminalization, neighborhood context, and the origins of gang injunctions. *Social Problems, 61*(2), 216–236.

National Alliance of Gang Investigators' Association. (2015). Retrieved from http://www.nagia.org/

National Gang Center. (2019). *Gang databases.* Retrieved from https://www.nationalgangcenter.gov/

Nelson, T. (2009, August 5). Behind the scenes with the gang strike force. *MPRNews.com.* Retrieved from https://www.mprnews.org/story/2009/08/05/gangstrikeforce-report

O'Deane, M., & Murphy, W. P. (2010, September 23). *Identifying and documenting gang members.* Retrieved from http://www.policemag.com/channel/gangs/articles/2010/09/identifying-and-documenting-gang-members/page/3.aspx

Ohlheiser, A. (2014, July 8). Insane Clown Posse loses FBI lawsuit; Juggalos a "gang." *The Wire.* Retrieved from http://www.thewire.com/national/2014/07/insane-clown-posse-loses-fbi-lawsuit-juggalos-a-gang/374093/

PBS Frontline. (2001). *The Rampart scandal.* Retrieved from http://www.pbs.org/wgbh/pages/frontline/shows/lapd/scandal/

Porat, D., & Heaney, J. (2018, February 9). Buffalo police disbanding troubled Strike Force. *Investigative Post.* Retrieved from https://www.investigativepost.org/2018/02/09/buffalo-police-disbanding-troubled-strike-force/

Regional Information Sharing System. (2015). Retrieved from https://www.riss.net/

Ritter, N., Simon, T. R., & Mahendra, R. R. (2013). Changing course: Preventing gang membership. *National Institute of Justice Journal, 273*, 16–27. Washington, DC: U.S. Department of Justice. Retrieved from https://www.ncjrs.gov/pdffiles1/nij/244144.pdf

Spergel, I. A., & Curry, G. D. (1993). The National Youth Gang Survey: A research and development process. In A. P. Goldstein & C. R. Huff (Eds.), *The gang intervention handbook* (pp. 359–400). Champaign, IL: Research Press.

Sullivan, R. (2011, January 7). The unsolved mystery of the Notorious B.I.G. *Rolling Stone Magazine.* Retrieved from http://www.rollingstone.com/music/news/the-unsolved-mystery-of-the-notorious-b-i-g-20110107

U.S. Immigration and Customs Enforcement [ICE]. (2015). *National gang unit: Operation community shield overview.* Washington, DC: Department of Homeland Security. Retrieved from http://www.ice.gov/national-gang-unit

U.S. Immigration and Customs Enforcement. (2019, June 4). *ICE Houston arrests 23 gang members, associates during operation targeting MS-13. Washington, DC:* Department of Homeland Security. Retrieved from https://www.ice.gov/news/releases/ice-houston-arrests-23-gang-members-associates-during-operation-targeting-ms-13

Vigil, J. D. (1988). *Barrio gangs: Street life and identity in Southern California.* Austin: University of Texas Press.

Von Quednow, C. & Yost, C. (2019). 13 arrested during 'Operation Black Rhino' targeting Santa Ana Gang. *KTLA.* Retrieved from https://ktla.com/news/local-news/13-arrested-during-operation-black-rhino-targeting-santa-ana-gang/

Wells, K. (2013, March 5). Why Detroit is breaking up its Gang Squad. *MichiganRadio.org.* Retrieved from https://www.michiganradio.org/post/why-detroit-breaking-its-gang-squad

Williams, C. (2013, January 23). Detroit to redeploy officers, disband Gang Squad. *MacombDaily.com.* Retrieved from https://www.macombdaily.com/news/nation-world-news/detroit-to-redeploy-officers-disband-gang-squad/article_c6bfdd81-fca0-5675-96be-4bce13d9e2fb.html

Yablonsky, L. (1997). *Gangsters: Fifty years of madness, drugs, and death on the street of America.* New York: New York University Press.

Young, R. (2008, July). *The outcome of the Rampart scandal investigations.* Retrieved from http://www.pbs.org/wgbh/pages/frontline/shows/lapd/later/outcome.html

Youth Justice Coalition. (2012). *Tracked and trapped: Youth of color, gang databases and gang injunctions.* Retrieved from http://www.youth4justice.org/wp-content/uploads/2012/12/TrackedandTrapped.pdf

Chapter 7
The Courts and Gangs: Laws, Legislation, and Injunctions

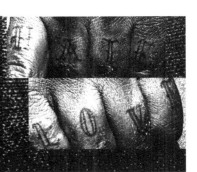

CHAPTER OBJECTIVES

- Examine the definitions of gangs.

- Examine civil gang injunctions and how they are used to combat gangs.

- Explore anti-gang laws and legislative acts.

- Explore the use of juvenile gang courts.

SENATE PASSES BILL TO CRACK DOWN ON THE RISE OF GANG VIOLENCE IN NEW YORK CITY (2018)

The New York State Senate passed two pieces of legislation that focus primarily on reducing gang activity. These legislations were established with the hope to protect children and teens from gang activity and enhance safety and security measures throughout the state of New York.

Bill S2410A establishes the Criminal Street Gang Enforcement and Prevention Act. This act was put into place to stop gang activity and recruitment through proactive community outreach. Specifically, Bill S2410A will enable the state to create anti-crime programs, expand education, intervention, and model curriculums, establish an ongoing system of tracking gang activity, and strengthen the legal options available to prosecute street gangs.

Bill S6211 establishes a Class D felony charge for gang members who seek to recruit new members on school grounds. This legislation was developed to "prevent gang activity in and around schools by making it a crime to coerce, solicit, recruit, or induce another person to join or remain a member of a criminal street gang."

Source: The New York State Senate. Retrieved from https://www.nysenate.gov/newsroom/press-releases/senate-passes-bills-crack-down-rise-gang-violence-new-york

Introduction

Like the police, the judicial and legislative components of the criminal justice system are alternate ways to combat street gangs. In an attempt to arrest and prosecute gangs, local, state, and federal officials have turned to laws and legislative acts to address the growing problem of street gangs when the methods of suppression, prevention, and intervention are less than successful. In the United States, specific anti-gang laws have been initiated at the state and federal levels, civil gang injunctions (CGIs) have been imposed by state and local district attorneys, and politicians have implemented legislative acts to help combat, prevent, and intervene in the growth of street gangs.

While many of these anti-gang measures have proven to be effective in combating street gangs, many of these laws, injunctions, and acts have been challenged on the basis of violating constitutional rights or so because the laws written were vague (i.e., "void for vagueness"). One particular concern with anti-gang laws and legislative acts is the use of the word "gang." The ambiguous nature of the term "gang" has left many legal scholars, researchers, and law enforcement officials challenging the validity of how one should define a gang. The definition is critical to how law enforcement deals with the gang problem and how to determine who is a gang member and what groups are gangs.

Definitions of (Street) Gangs

The biggest challenge lawmakers face when enacting laws, proposing legislative acts, or implementing gang injunctions is how to define a gang. Unfortunately, the definition of a street gang is a contentious one. Researchers, law enforcement officials, politicians, and academic professionals have long debated the appropriateness in trying to find an applicable definition but have failed to agree on a universal definition. In fact, defining a gang is largely dependent on who is asking the question, "What is a gang?"

One of the earliest attempts to define the term *gang* and *gangster* was found in New Jersey's criminal state statutes in 1939. In an effort to crack down on criminal gangs, the State of New Jersey established the following:

> Any person not engaged in any lawful occupation, known to be a member of any *gang* consisting of two or more persons, who has been convicted at least three times of being a disorderly person, or who has been convicted of any crime in this or in any other State, is declared to be a *gangster*.... (*Lanzetta et al. v. New Jersey,* 1939)

Originally upheld by the New Jersey State Supreme Court, Lanzetta and others were convicted under this law and declared to be *gangsters*. However, the U.S. Supreme Court overturned their convictions because New Jersey had failed to define the concept of *gang* and the term *gangster* in their criminal statue. In fact, the courts cited multiple dictionary definitions of a *gang* and *gangster* and other sources as the reasons for the "void for vagueness" and lack of consistency in defining *gang* and *gangster* in the New Jersey Criminal Statutes.

In 1960, the U.S. Supreme Court again addressed the issue of defining a gang and gang member this time by raising the question that belonging to a gang or criminal organization would be sufficient enough for criminal prosecution (*Abel v United States*, 1960). In this case, John Abel and two other associates were convicted of robbing a bank. They were also linked to the Aryan Brotherhood, a prison gang. The U.S. Supreme Court ruled that a person cannot be convicted for solely belonging to a criminal organization that advocates illegal activity. In 1999, the U.S. Supreme Court again specified the need to clarify the definition of a "gang" in *City of Chicago v. Morales* (1999). The case was the result of Chicago's Gang Congregation Ordinance Act which prohibited "criminal street gang members" from loitering in public places. If the police observe a person whom he/she reasonably believes to be a gang member loitering in a public place then the police can order them to disperse or be arrested. Morales was arrested for violating this ordinance. Morales challenged it and the USSC stated that the law was too vague and needed a clear definition of what is a gang.

The problems in defining a gang are not restricted to the courts or law enforcement. In fact, there is considerable debate in the academic literature (Ball & Curry, 1995; Bursik & Grasmick, 2006; Esbensen, Winfree, He, & Taylor, 2001; Horowitz, 1990; Klein, 2007; Wood & Alleyne, 2010). While gang researchers have been critical to the definitional shortcomings of what constitutes a gang (Esbensen et al., 2001), this lack of consensus creates problems for researchers when trying to measure, operationalize, make comparative analyses, and replicate studies. By having a universal and precise definition of what is a gang, the nature and extent of the gang problem in the United States could be better understood. Furthermore, by employing a precise definition of a gang, researchers could provide more reliable statistics and make better statistical comparisons between cities and states (Decker & Kempf-Leonard, 1991). A precise definition would also enable researchers, public officials, legal scholars, and community officials to have a clear understanding of what is and is not a gang and remove any ambiguity when creating laws, injunctions, or legislative acts that target gangs (Klein, 2007; Klein, Kerner, Maxson, & Weitekamp, 2001).

On the other hand, academic researchers argue that flexibility in defining a gang is more important than a precise or universal definition. Sociologist Ruth Horowitz (1990) pointed out that keeping definitions unrestricted would foster a debate and articulate variations in assessing gangs and gang behavior. Other gang researchers have criticized the search for the "correct" definition because law enforcement, social scientists, policymakers, and even gang members themselves define gangs to suit themselves (Greenan, Britz, Rush, & Barker, 2000; Petersen, 2004). Petersen (2004) argued that a universal definition is not necessary, while Zatz (1985) contended that a universal definition will create problems, such as labeling a gang and its members inappropriately.

Group vs. Legal Definitions

There are two perspectives that offer the definition of a gang: the academic/group perspective and the legal/crime perspective. From the academic/group perspective, gangs are observed as a group phenomenon. The emphasis on the group perspective is the social dynamics of how the group (i.e., gang) functions, operates, and interacts. From the crime/legal perspective, gangs are made of individuals belonging to groups who commit crimes and are often identified by their unique characteristics (e.g., colors, symbols, and graffiti).

The academic/group perspective on defining a gang has primarily been predicated by theories of group dynamics, without requiring the element of criminal behavior (e.g., Ball & Curry, 1995; Hagedorn, 1988; Moore, 1991; Sanchez-Jankowski, 1991; Thrasher, 1927). For those who follow the academic/group perspective, it is critical to understand the group's behavior when defining a gang. Those early analyses of the "group phenomena" have become the foundation for the definitions of gangs and subsequent research based on these definitions.

One of the earliest contributions to gang research was the work of gang scholar Frederick Thrasher, who followed Chicago's Polish and Jewish gangs in the late 1920s. In his works, he described juvenile gangs as "spontaneous playgroups" that evolved into adolescent groups that were in conflict with each other, as:

> an interstitial group originally formed spontaneously, and then integrated through conflict. It is characterized by the following types of behavior: meeting face to face, milling, movement through space as a unit, conflict, and planning. The result of this collective behavior is the development of tradition, unreflective internal structure, esprit de corps, morale, group awareness, and attachment to a local territory (Thrasher, 1927, p. 46).

Thrasher's (1927) description introduced a number of key points. Foremost is that a gang is a group. Thrasher emphasized that the social dynamics of the group (i.e., "play group") often lead to cohesion and then to the development of the gang. Second, the group's activities are both negative (i.e., involving conflict) and positive (i.e., having a sense of pride and support for one another). Interestingly, Thrasher did not mention delinquent or criminal activities in his identification of a gang, other than to say that not all gangs are delinquent/criminal. Finally, the gangs Thrasher observed came from deteriorating sections of the city. Thrasher used the term "interstitial" to describe those sections of the city where gang members often reside. According to Thrasher, gang members were poor, immigrant youths residing in Chicago's inner city.

Unfortunately, the perception of groups and how they are defined are often determined within their social and cultural context. For example, the term "gang" is often applied to youths in lower socioeconomic groups that typically reflect the minority population (Bloch & Niederhoffer, 1958; Cohen, 1955; Miller, 1958). As Bloch and Niederhoffer (1958) suggested, most of the sociological literature rarely refers to middle/upper-class youths as gangs, but rather focuses on the lower class. Today, those observations made by Bloch and Niederhoffer generally hold true, as seen in more recent gang studies (Brownfield, Sorenson, & Thompson, 2001; Moran, 2015), but there have been a few studies that explore the gang phenomenon in middle- to upper-class youths (Lowney, 1984).

Defining gangs from the group perspective was a primary focus for gang researchers prior to the 1970s. However, gang expert and researcher Malcolm Klein (1971) suggested a definition that moved away from the group phenomenon and emphasized the criminal activities of the group. Known as the "legal/crime" perspective, it suggested a descriptive list, or characterization, of what is included in defining a gang. By providing a list of characteristics, this approach effectively helps identify who is in a gang and the illegal activities associated with gangs. A descriptive list also provides the public with information as to how to identify a gang and who are the gang's members. For example, gang colors, organizational structure, gang name, monikers, and tattoos are unique identifiers to gangs. Also critical to the definition of a gang, from the legal perspective, is to include delinquent or criminal activities.

Based on his research on Los Angeles street gangs, Klein (1971) introduced the delinquent/criminal element as a critical component to the definition of a gang. Klein's definition is also one of the most cited definitions in the gang literature:

> a juvenile gang is any denotable adolescent group of youngsters who (a) are generally perceived as a distinct aggregation by others in their neighborhood, (b) recognize themselves as a denotable group (almost invariably with a group name), and (c) have been involved in a sufficient number of delinquent incidents to call forth a consistent negative response from neighborhood residents and/or law enforcement agencies (Klein, 1971, p. 13).

Malcom Klein's definition made a significant impact on gang research and public policy. In 1988, California passed the Street Terrorism Enforcement and Prevention (STEP) Act, which Klein was instrumental in helping shape. This act was one of the nation's first attempts to legally define a street gang for the purpose of criminal prosecution. This anti-gang legislation became the model for many other states to follow and specified the definition by using the expression "criminal street gang." Most gang statutes define a criminal street gang as "criminal groups of three or more, formal or informal, with names and signs, where members have committed such acts as murder, attempted murder, assault, drive-by shootings, robbery, arson, and witness intimidation" (Klein, 2007, p. 73). Twenty-five years later, Klein revised his definition, which further emphasized the term "street gang" and provided a more expansive list of descriptors such as age, gender, ethnicity, territory, and criminal patterns to define the gang. In all of his definitions, Klein excluded some groups, such as terrorists, football hooligans, motorcycle gangs, and prison gangs, so as to not create confusion about which type of group he was attempting to identify. Though definitions and the characteristics of a gang have been suggested by previous gang researchers (e.g., Cohen, 1955; Cloward & Ohlin, 1960; Thrasher,

1927; Whyte, 1943; Yablonsky, 1962), it was Klein who paved the way for a working definition of a gang.

Researchers that prefer this approach to find their definitions often utilized by law enforcement officials and policymakers, and these definitions are often implemented in state criminal codes. For example, the Department of Justice (NGIC, 2013, 2015) defines gangs as:

(1) an association of three or more individuals;

(2) whose members collectively identify themselves by adopting a group identity that they use to create an atmosphere of fear or intimidation frequently by employing one or more of the following: a common name, slogan, identifying sign, symbol, tattoo or other physical marking, style or color of clothing, hairstyle, hand sign, or graffiti;

(3) the association's purpose, in part, is to engage in criminal activity and the association uses violence or intimidation to further its criminal objectives;

(4) its members engage in criminal activity or acts of juvenile delinquency that if committed by an adult would be crimes;

(5) with the intent to enhance or preserve the association's power, reputation, or economic resources;

(6) the association may also possess some of the following characteristics: (a) the members employ rules for joining and operating within the association; (b) the members meet on a recurring basis; (c) the association provides physical protection of its members from other criminals and gangs; (d) the association seeks to exercise control over a particular location or region, or it may simply defend its perceived interests against rivals; or (e) the association has an identifiable structure; and

(7) this definition is not intended to include traditional organized crime groups such as La Cosa Nostra, groups that fall within the Department's definition of "international organized crime," drug-trafficking organizations or terrorist organizations (p. 7).

Despite the emphasis on criminal/delinquent activities in the definition of a gang, researchers also combine the use of demographics (e.g., race, age, gender, and social class), common descriptors of the group (e.g., identifiable leader, structure, permanence, territory, colors, and tattoos), and the criminal element to define a gang. Identifying the group as a "gang" and listing their unique characteristics separates gangs from non-gangs, such as the local Boys Scouts or a high school/college sports team. Thus, with the inclusion of a criminal element in the definition, the public is better able to understand what a gang is (Curry & Decker, 2003; Esbensen, 2000; Leet, Rush, & Smith, 2000; Tobin, 2008). Currently, federal law defines the term *criminal street gang* as:

an ongoing group, club, organization, or association of five or more persons—(A) that has as one of its primary purposes the commission of one or more of the criminal offenses described in subsection (c); (B) the members of which engage, or have engaged within the past five years, in a continuing series of offenses described in subsection (c); and (C) the activities of which affect interstate or foreign commerce *(Criminal Street Gangs Statute, 18 USC § 521)*.

Other Types of Gang Definitions

Terms such as street gangs, youth gangs, teenage gangs, juvenile gangs, and criminal gangs are often used interchangeably to mean the same thing. The interchangeability of these terms often creates confusion when trying to establish a precise definition of a particular type of gang. In some instances, the definition of the gang is to serve the interests of those dealing with gangs. For example, some state criminal statutes define a gang as having three or more individuals giving law enforcement officials scope when stopping and detaining suspected gang members (e.g., criminal statues in Alaska, Alabama, California, Colorado, and Florida; Gilbertson & Malinski, 2005; National Gang Center, 2019). But not all types of gangs have definitional problems, some gangs have unique qualities that separate them from other types of gangs that make them easy to distinguish from other gangs such as the use of a motorcycle or confinement in a prison.

Transnational gangs are a type of criminal street gang that has become a significant threat to the safety and security of the public. Transnational gangs are no longer considered street gangs because they are known to operate beyond the local neighborhoods and regional territories but rather across the borders (Sullivan, 2008). Transnational street gangs also have significant numbers of foreign-born members and are frequently involved in human and contraband smuggling, immigration violations, and other crimes with a connection to the border (U.S. Immigration and Customs Enforcement, 2015).

Outlaw motorcycle gangs (OMGs) are a type of gang whose members use their motorcycles and the clubs they belong to as conduits for criminal enterprises. OMGs are highly structured criminal organizations whose members engage in criminal activities such as violent crime, weapons trafficking, and drug trafficking (NGIC, 2013).

Domestic extremists (DE) are another type of gang that aligns more with White supremacist ideology. Domestic extremists are those who engage in activities known as domestic terrorism, which involve acts dangerous to human life that are a violation of the criminal laws of the United States or of any state (NGIC, 2013).

Gang Injunctions/Anti-Gang Loitering Laws

Since the late 1980s, one strategy to combat gang violence and gang membership has been the use of civil gang injunctions (CGI). The communities in Southern California were some of the first to use gang injunctions and have done so with moderate success resulting in the reduction of gang-related crimes (O'Deane & Morreale, 2012). A gang injunction is a restraining order issued by the court prohibiting gang members from engaging in certain activities in public places. A gang injunction can cover a one block neighborhood or several miles of a gang-inflicted area (O'Deane & Morreale, 2012). In theory, a CGI is an extension of the traditional public nuisance laws designed to protect the public from undue harm (Young, 2009). For example, shooting off fireworks, keeping diseased animals, playing loud music, or obstructing a highway are actions that warrant a public nuisance violation. Since gangs engage in a variety of criminal activities that warrant the need to arrest and prosecute them, a gang injunction targets gang members who also engage in noncriminal activities that can still interfere with the public's safety and security. Examples of these behaviors include standing with a group of other gang members on a street corner, putting up graffiti on the walls that are gang specific, wearing gang colors, and congregating as a group in a park or other public area. While it is possible that these noncriminal activities can include criminal conduct, the emphasis of a gang injunction is to punish those behaviors so the gang-related criminal conduct does not occur. Since gang injunctions are civil orders, the standard of proof is lowered to the clear and convincing standard and not beyond a reasonable doubt (Los Angeles City Attorney's Office, 2019b).

The first gang injunction was implemented in Cadillac-Corning (the West Side of Los Angeles). This 18-square-block community consists of Black and Latino working-class people. In 1987, a civil suit, known as *People v. Playboy Gangster Crips (PBGC)*, sought to prevent members of PBGC to wear gang colors and congregate in parks and street corners. Interestingly, at that time in the late 1980s, Cadillac-Corning was not plagued with gang-related violence such as drive-by shooting, murder, drug trafficking, and other gang-related crimes. In fact, according to Ana Muniz with the *Youth Justice Coalition Center*, the rationale for enacting this gang injunction in Cadillac-Corning was because of its close proximity to more affluent, predominantly white middle- to upper-class neighborhood, and the general fear of blacks. Muniz (2014) pointed out that "the injunction was meticulously designed to control the movement of black youth by criminalizing activities and behavior that is unremarkable and legal in other jurisdictions" (p. 217). Despite the lack of gang activity in the Cadillac-Corning area, prosecutors were concerned that gang violence would seep into this and other surrounding communities.

The suit against the Playboy Gangster Crips was initially successful and resulted in a 30% decline of gang-related crimes, an 18% drop in felonies, and the residents noticed a positive change in their community ("Westside Gang Crime Off," 1988). Since then, from 1992 to 1994, seven more CGIs were implemented and challenged in court: *People ex. rel. Fletcher v. Acosta; People v. Blythe Street Gang; People ex. rel. City Attorney vs. Acuna; People ex. rel. Jones v. Amaya; People ex. rel. City Attorney v. Avalos; People v. "B" Street Boys;* and *the City of Norwalk v. Orange Street Locos.* In all these cases, the courts upheld most of the provisions articulated in the injunction but reduced the scope of the order. In the case against the *"B" Street Boys* and *Amaya*, the CGIs were found to be in violation of the 1st and 14th Amendments of the U.S. Constitution and with California's constitutional right to privacy (Yoo, 1994). Since these challenges in the early 1990s, lawmakers and policymakers are more conscientious of keeping gang injunctions up-to-date (O'Deane & Morreale, 2012) and conscientious of maintaining constitutional standards (Hennigan & Sloane, 2013). To date, here are some of the common restrictions and prohibition of a court-ordered CGI:

- Do not associate with other gang members.
- Do not use gang hand signs and/or wear gang colors and attire.
- Do not use, possess, sell, or transport illegal drugs.
- Do not drink or possess alcohol.
- Do not own, use, or possess any dangerous or deadly weapons.
- Do not commit graffiti/vandalism and/or possess graffiti/vandalism tools.
- Do not intimidate, threaten, or harass people.
- Do not recruit someone to join a gang.
- Do not make hand signals associated with gang membership, also known as "throwing" gang signs (Hynes & Osgood, 2011; Los Angeles City Attorney's Office, 2019a).

In 2019 in the City of Los Angeles, there were 45 CGIs covering 72 street gangs (LAPD, 2019). In 2013 there were over 150 CGIs across the United States (National Gang Center, 2013). As of January 2020, there are currently eight states that use CGIs: California, Texas, New York, Florida, Tennessee, Minnesota, Utah, and Illinois.

The use of gang injunctions is not without critics (Bickel, 2012; Roberts, 1999; Stewart, 1998). Legal scholars, particularly the American Civil Liberties Union (ACLU), argue that CGIs are partially or completely unconstitutional (Crawford, 2009). In fact, the U.S. Supreme Court struck down an anti-gang loitering law in 1999 claiming that it was unconstitutional (*City of Chicago v. Morales*, 1999). The *Morales* case stemmed from a 1992 Gang Congregation Ordinance Act that the City of Chicago passed to combat the growing gang problem in their city. The ordinance prohibited street gang members from loitering in any public place and gave police officers the ability to disperse a suspected individual who was a gang member "with no apparent purpose." From 1992 to 1995, the Chicago Police Department issued more than 89,000 dispersal orders and made more than 42,000 arrests under the ordinance (Strosnider, 2002).

Another challenge to anti-gang loitering laws and CGIs are the potential violations to the 4th Amendment. Police have a tremendous amount of discretion on whether or not to serve an injunction, thus leaving the potential for abuse (Caldwell, 2010). In addition, because of the broad nature of public nuisance orders, prosecutors are able to list hundreds of "John Doe's" only to be later identified as a potential gang member (Myers, 2009). Myers (2009) also noted that using CGIs for gang suppression tactics leads to gang cohesion and police community tension. Finally, since the suit is a civil one and not a criminal one, gang members cannot ask for a public defender if they choose to appeal the charges unless they are on probation or parole for a previous crime (Muniz, 2014).

Aside from constitutional issues, Muniz (2014) argued that CGIs are racially biased (Rosenthal, 2001). Since CGIs were simply a response to the panic of youth violence and the war on gangs in the 1980s and 1990s. CGIs also led to an increase in youth incarceration. In other studies that examined the effectiveness of CGIs, the results are mixed. Grogger (2002) and Klein (1998) found that CGIs showed only a short-term reduction in crime rates and a reduction in gang presence. Other studies have shown that CGIs are ineffective and have little, if any, positive effect (Maxson & Allen, 1997). In areas with low gang activity, CGIs actually contributed to the rise of a gang presence, disorder, and greater victimization, thus creating an "us vs. them" mentality (Maxson, Hennigan, & Sloane, 2005).

However, some reports do show the positive results of using CGIs (Hoover & Reddell, 2007; National Crime Prevention Council, 2014; Siegel, 1997). Other media reports (Henderson, 2015) along with city and law enforcement officials have also reported a success in reducing gang violence by using CGIs (Cassidy, 1993; Solis, 2015). CGIs are also more effective in reducing gang violence with gangs that have been in place for an extended period of time in the neighborhood and that have "deep rooter gang cohesion" (McGloin, 2005). In a more recent study, O'Deane (2011) found that violent crimes decreased by 11.6% as a result of gang injunctions.

Anti-Gang Legislation (State and Federal)

In addition to the use of CGIs, legislative actions are another tool used by policymakers to deal with street gangs. Legislation examples against street gangs by local, state, and federal entities include: enhanced sentences for gang members, civil remedies for victims of gang violence, criminalization of gang recruitment, collaboration with schools to reduce truancy, gang prevention programs, graffiti awareness, and address violent crimes (Fearn, Decker, & Curry, 2001; Maxson et al., 2005). Table 7.1 is an overview of gang-related legislation in the United States. For a complete list of a compilation of gang-related legislation, see National Gang Center (2019) and https://www.nationalgangcenter.gov/Legislation.

At the local level, ordinances passed such as prohibiting individuals from wearing gang-related clothing, displaying graffiti, and/or promoting the symbols of the gang are ways to combat the gang problem in communities. At the state level, most legislative acts focus on increasing the penalties for gang members for when they serve jail/prison time, known as enhanced penalties. State legislators have also created penalties for recruiting minors into gangs, implemented prevention and education programs, and utilized gang databases for identification purposes (as discussed in Chapter 4).

Table 7.1:   Highlights of Gang-Related Legislation

All 50 states and the District of Columbia (DC) have enacted some form of legislation relating to gangs or gang-related activity.

- All 50 states, the District of Columbia (DC), and the United States (U.S.) have enacted legislation that can be leveraged to investigate gang-related criminal activity, apprehend and prosecute criminals, reduce gang involvement, and protect citizens.
- 43 states, DC, and the U.S. have laws that define "gang."
- 14 states and the U.S. provide statutory definitions for "gang member."
- 32 states and the U.S. have laws that define "gang crime," "criminal gang activity," "predicate gang crime," etc.
- 37 states, DC, and the U.S. have passed laws that may be used to prevent gang violence, reduce gang involvement, and suppress gang-related crime.
- 38 states and the U.S. have laws that prohibit racketeering, money laundering, criminal enterprise, or criminal profiteering.
- 49 states, DC, and the U.S. have laws that provide for penalties (including enhanced penalties), fines, or damages for gang-related criminal acts.
- 15 states, DC, and the U.S. have laws that prohibit and penalize carjacking.
- 31 states and DC have laws that prohibit graffiti.
- 31 states, DC, and the U.S. have laws on gangs and schools.
- 14 states and the U.S. have enacted laws that authorize the operation and use of gang-related databases.
- 39 states, DC, and the U.S. provide for some form of data reporting or sharing related to criminal gangs or gang-related activity.
- 35 states, DC, and the U.S. have some form of forfeiture laws.
- 21 states, DC, and the U.S. have laws that authorize, fund, or require training or technical assistance related to gang prevention, intervention, or suppression.

Source: National Gang Center. (2019). Compilation of gang-related legislation. Retrieved from https://www.nationalgangcenter.gov/Legislation.

Probably, the most important piece of anti-gang legislation that helped pave the way for other states to follow in dealing with the growing gang problem is California's Street Terrorism and Prevention (STEP) Act (1988). The STEP Act was established to create harsher penalties for gang-related activities. Many states have modeled their gang definitions and guidelines after California's anti-gang law. The STEP Act defines a criminal street gang as "any ongoing organization, association, or group of three or more people, whether formal or informal, having as one of its primary activities the commission of criminal acts" (California Penal Code, Section 186.22). In addition, the STEP Act criminalizes a "person who actively participates in any criminal street gang with knowledge that its members engage in or have engaged in a pattern of criminal activity, and who willfully promotes, furthers, or assists any felonious criminal conduct by members of that gang" (California Penal Code, Section, 186.22). In 2007, California passed a law requiring gang members who were arrested to attend violence prevention classes (Hammond, 2008).

In the State of Washington, a comprehensive Anti-Gang Act was passed to fund prevention, intervention, and suppression programs. Many other states have also focused legislative efforts to combat gang graffiti. For example, in Arizona and Hawaii, lawmakers created graffiti penalties. In Texas, gang members who deface property are required to make restitution to the owner and parents are responsible financially for the damage caused by gang graffiti in Tennessee (Hammond, 2008).

At the federal level, some of the early legislative acts were not directed at street gangs but rather at organized crimed groups. In 1970, the Organized Crime Control Act was passed in an effort to combat organized crime. Despite the focus on mafia and other criminal syndicates, the Organized Crime Control Act is also used to protect those who witness a gang-related crime and fear retaliation by the gang or a gang member. This act offers witness protection and increases the penalties and punishments for offenders. An extension of the Organized Crime Control Act is the Title IX, the Racketeer Influenced & Corrupt Organizations Act (RICO) statute. The statute is broad enough that it gives the federal law enforcement agencies enough resources to create specialized teams to focus on combating organized crime groups or criminal street gangs. The RICO statute could be used to prosecute gang members under federal laws and impose more severe sanctions.

In 1995, one of the first RICO statutes was used in California against the Mexican Mafia (La Eme). The case involved the shooting death of Ana Lizarraga, a gang counselor who worked with numerous California street gangs. Lizarraga, because of her gang knowledge, was a technical advisor for the 1992 film *American Me*. The film depicted various members of the Mexican Mafia including one of its founders raped in prison. This scene enraged the Mexican Mafia and contract hits were put on some of the cast and crew of the film, including Lizarraga. Sadly, Lizzaraga was gunned down by Jose "Joke" Gonzales, who was brought to justice along with other gang members under RICO (Valdemar, 2008).

In a more recent case, 45 members of the Los Angeles' Pueblo Bishop Bloods (PBB) street gang were indicted under the RICO Act (U.S. Attorney's Office, 2013). Evidence against some of the leaders of the PBBs included gang leaders passionately advocating to younger gang members that they needed to retaliate against rival gangs and force Hispanic residents out of the projects. Prosecutors were also able to show that the members of the PBB were a criminal enterprise that engaged in drug dealing, firearms trafficking, murder, witness intimidation, and armed robbery as part of the gang's efforts to control and terrorize the housing projects (U.S. Attorney's Office, 2013).

In November 2019, four members of the Detroit-based gang "Seven Miles Bloods" who terrorized Detroit's east-side neighborhoods for several years and engaged in public shoot-outs with rival gangs were convicted of RICO statutes: racketeering conspiracy, attempted murder in aid of racketeering, and possession of firearms in furtherance of a violent crime. Their prison sentences ranged from 18 years to two life sentences (Baldas, 2019).

Other early legislative acts that did not focus entirely on gangs but were still an integral part in addressing gang issues were the Omnibus Crime Control and Safe Streets Act of 1968 and the Anti-Drug Abuse Act of 1988. The Omnibus Crime Control and Safe Street Act was designed to create a partnership with schools and law enforcement officials where school resource officers are utilized to combat school-related crime and gang activity (Public Law 105-302, 1998). The Anti-Drug Abuse Act was established to allot more money for the prevention and education programs aimed at deterring youth from joining gangs and using drugs (Public Law 102-132, 1991).

In 1994, the Violent Crime Control and Law Enforcement Act was passed. It is considered one of the most important legislative acts that Congress enacted because it provided 100,000 new police officers, provided billions of dollars for funding crime prevention programs, and emphasized the need to combat street gangs by increasing penalties for gang members.

Often legislation (i.e., proposed bills) that includes gangs is not about combating street gangs but rather crime in general. Anti-gang legislation is not always positively received by members of Congress and the Senate. For example, the Gang Deterrence & Community Protection Act of 2005, better known as "The Gangbusters Bill," was proposed to increase federal funding for law enforcement officials to combat violent street gangs and give prosecutors more resources to punish street gang activities. While the Act was passed in the House, it failed in the Senate.

Another bill proposed by the Senate to combat street gang violence was the Gang Abatement and Prevention Act of 2009. This bill authorized over $1 billion in funds for federal, state, and local law enforcement agencies to identify, target, and eliminate violent gangs. Additional monies were to be used to enhance the witness protection program and gang prevention services. As a prosecutorial tool, this act also suggested increased penalties for violent street gang offenders, creating additional punishments for gangs who recruit minors or recruit from inside the prison. Like the "Gangbusters Bill," the Gang Abatement Act was not passed.

In 2007 and again in 2009, the Gang Prevention, Intervention, and Suppression Act was proposed, but it also failed to gain support as a congressional bill. The act would give law enforcement agencies and prosecutors more money and resources to help combat criminal street gangs. The act would also fund a new National Gang Research Evaluation and Policy Institute where crime prevention programs would be developed to deter future gang participation. In addition, grants and social service programs would be offered to gang members so they can reintegrate back into society.

In 2001, Project Safe Neighborhoods (PSN) program was initiated by the Justice Department and supported by the then-President George W. Bush, focused on reducing gun violence and criminal gang activity. The Project Safe Neighborhoods program was deemed successful because it provided block grants toward local, state, and community-level programs aimed at combating the street gang problem. According to a 2013 Michigan State University study funded by the Department of Justice, the cities that saw a high rate of participation in the Safe Neighborhoods program experienced a 13.1% decrease in violent crime. Those cities also saw a double-digit reduction in gun crimes and homicides (Bernstein, 2018). Unfortunately, funds dried up by 2012 and fewer cities received grants to combat the growing gang problem. As a result of no funding available for cities to combat their street gangs, there was a 20% increase in homicides in major gang-ridden cities and gang membership rose in nearly half of the U.S. jurisdictions surveyed from 2014 to 2016. Recognizing the need to address this problem and using the original language from PSN, Congress enacted and current-President Donald Trump signed into law the Project Safe Neighborhoods Grant Program Authorization Act of 2018. This law authorized $50 million in grant funds for areas in need of money to fight the gang problem. The new bill is aimed at funding regional gang task forces, and law enforcement entities that coordinate anti-gang measures across state lines.

While these legislative acts are meant to assist law enforcement officials and give prosecutors the necessary tools to eradicate the gang problem, these Acts are not without criticism. Some suggest that anti-gang legislation is the result of political frustration (Bjerregaard, 2003), while others argue that it fails to consider one's basic constitutional rights (Geis, 2002). Additional criticisms are concerned with the cost of imprisonment vs. prevention and rehabilitation efforts, mandatory minimums for gang members (Franco, 2008), and how imprisonment can actually strengthen gang membership (Arana, 2005). Other critics such as Sheldon, Tracy, and Brown (2013) point out that new legislative acts are creative sanctions that fail to adequately address the heart of the gang problem whereas more emphasis on social programs would be more effective. also put this sentence at the end of your paragraph on critics.. after (Bailey, 2008). just leave the manual by itself at the end.. or put it somewhere else. More recently, the concern for passing legislation that aims to combat the gang problem must do so by removing the identifying component of race and ethnicity when defining a gang member (Bailey, 2018).

In 2018, the Department of Justice (DOJ) announced a new and updated U.S. Attorneys' Manual to help U.S. and State attorney's prosecute criminal cases. Formerly the Criminal Resource Manual, the new manual is called the *Justice Manual* (Sollers, Sale, Kung, & Gulite, 2019; see https://www.justice.gov/jm/justice-manual for complete manual description). The purpose of the manual is to continue to provide federal assistance to states in need of prosecuting gangs and gang members.

Juvenile Gang Courts

As complex as the American criminal justice system is, there are innovative ways of dealing with different types of crimes that warrant special judicial attention. For example, there are Drug Courts, Family Courts, Domestic Violence Courts, Teen or Youth Courts, and Juvenile Justice Courts. However, in Yakima County, Washington (located in south central Washington) and Harris County, Texas (located outside of Houston), these counties have developed a court system that deals specifically with youth street gangs. Both courts began in 2011 and primarily focus on rehabilitating those individuals caught in the gang lifestyle.

The mission of the Yakima County Gang Court is "to create an environment of accountability and safety so kids who want to get out of gangs can, and kids who don't will engage in less violent, lethal and destructive behavior" (Yakima County, 2012). According to the Washington State Legislature (n.d.), the "juvenile gang court" is defined as:

> a court that has special calendars or dockets designed to achieve a reduction in gang-related offenses among juvenile offenders by increasing their likelihood for successful rehabilitation through early, continuous, and judicially supervised and integrated evidence-based services proven to reduce juvenile recidivism and gang involvement or through the use of research-based or promising practices identified by the Washington state partnership council on juvenile justice.

For a gang member to be eligible for the Gang Court and receive a deferred disposition, the gang member must not pose a risk to the community and the judge and prosecutor must agree. Once accepted into the program, a gang member completes a risk assessment form and meets with a probation officer, counselors, teachers, and other social service agencies to redirect youth behavior from negative actions to positive ones. The program is broken down into four levels. The first level is "evaluation" to determine the best course of action. The second is the "implementation" where treatment and behavioral specialist work with the youth. The third is the "stabilization" level where the youth settles into the program and begin to stabilize their behaviors. The fourth and final level is called "maintenance." This level is planning the exit strategy to ensure that the youth will not revert to the gang lifestyle. If for any reason the youth fails to complete the program, the judge may impose sanctions and remove them from the program (Yakima County, 2012).

Unfortunately, the promising solution to the gang problem in Yakima County failed. In 2017, the $300,000 grant was not renewed and finding willing and qualified participants was very difficult. The demands for the program were too great for youth gang members and their families to follow (Ferolito, 2017).

In Harris County, Texas, the presiding District Judge in cooperation with the Gang Recidivism Intervention Program (GRIP) has been working to reduce gang members in the county since 2011. Similar to the Yakima County Juvenile Gang Court, the goal has been "to reduce recidivism of youth by holding gang involved youth accountable while redirecting them toward healthy alternatives to gang activity" (Harris County, 2015). Youth receive intensive supervision on probation, mentoring, educational assistance, and local support from faith-based agencies in an effort to redirect the youth's gang lifestyle.

Concluding Thoughts

Anti-gang laws, gang legislation, gang injunctions, and gang courts are all tools used by law enforcement officials, prosecutors, and community leaders to help combat the growing gang problem in the United States. However, the greatest legal challenge seems to be finding an appropriate and applicable definition of a gang. Though most states define a gang in their criminal statues, very few define a gang member. While the debate continues over finding a useful definition, law enforcement and prosecutors have been successful in applying their definitions for the purpose of arresting and prosecuting gang members.

When a gang member commits a crime, it is easy to apply the appropriate criminal statutes to charge and punish the offender. However, law enforcement officials and prosecutors view gang-related crimes as more serious than crimes committed by non-gang members. Thus, the act of committing gang-related crimes often leads to enhanced forms of punishment (i.e., longer prison sentences). Local, state, and federal agencies are responding to this problem by using anti-gang laws and other legislative means in their pursuit to arrest and prosecute gang members.

One method that is regarded as a successful tool in disrupting gang activities, but also has been scrutinized, is CGIs. Though the basic premise of a CGI is to disrupt gang-related activities and noncriminal activities, the success of using CGIs is dependent on who you ask. Prosecutors, community leaders, and residents are in typically in favor of these injunctions because it is a way to reduce the gang presence and violence in neighborhoods. Prosecutors are particularly in favor of using CGIs because it gives law enforcement broader arrest powers. Since CGIs are basically public nuisance ordnances under civil law, the legal standards are much lower than those found in criminal law and this gives prosecutors more latitude to prohibit activities such as displaying gang colors or symbols, or associating in public with other gang members. As gang injunctions provide critical advantages for law enforcement officials and prosecutors, CGIs have been shown to decrease gang visibility, gang presence, gang intimidation, and reduce the fear residents have in their own neighborhoods (Maxson et al., 2005). But not all are quick to conclude that gang injunctions are the solution to reducing gang violence. There is mixed evidence about the effectiveness of CGIs. While some studies and police testimonials have shown promise in using CGIs (National Crime Prevention

Council, 2014; National Gang Center, 2013), others lack the extensive research necessary to truly provide a valid answer to its effectiveness (Curry, Decker, & Pyrooz, 2014) or is seen as an act of "symbolic politics" (Miethe & McCorkle, 2002). Maxson et al. (2005) likens CGIs to their short-term success as a more common outcome than any long-term success in reducing gang violence.

Politicians play a vital role in determining the amount of resources law enforcement can incur to combat the gang problem. As seen in 2007 and again in 2009, the Gang Prevention, Intervention, and Suppression Act and the Abatement and Prevention Act failed to provide any funding to combat the gang problem. However, the current political climate has shown support for addressing the gang problem in the United States with the recent enactment of the Safe Project Safe Neighborhoods Grant Program Authorization Act of 2018. While all 50 states have some type of gang legislation, most of the legislation is designed around prevention and intervention mandates. The gang legislation supports prevention programs in schools, provides gang awareness training, and assists communities in helping them develop appropriate responses to their gang problem.

While some laws and legislations are perceived as helpful, others are deemed unconstitutional, or too vague, to appropriately use to convict gang members. Though some anti-gang laws are found to be unconstitutional (*City of Chicago v. Morales*, 1999), this does not belittle the efforts by law enforcement and policymakers to stop gang violence and gang membership. In fact, questioning the anti-gang laws and having proponents go back and revive the laws helps maintain the integrity of the criminal justice system. Regardless, many of the anti-gang measures outlined in the federal and state criminal codes are helping to stop the proliferation of gangs, reduce the gang-initiated crimes, and protect communities.

As lawmakers push for legislation to strengthen the powers of the criminal justice system to reduce gang violence, gang courts are an alternate and innovative way to deal with the gang problem. Unfortunately, while the idea of a gang court is creative and can divert youth from gang life, money, time, and resources. Responding to the gang problem is an important endeavor and giving law enforcement officials, prosecutors, and policymakers the appropriate legal tools to reduce gang violence in their communities is necessary.

Discussion Points and Questions

1. If being a gang member creates problems for the police and communities, why not just make it illegal to be associated with a gang member? How could you create a law or legislative act that would virtually make it illegal to be in a gang?

2. What are some other legal maneuvers that can be done to eradicate gangs in the community?

3. What are the benefits of CGIs? Can you find recent examples of how the police and lawmakers were able to use them to tackle their gang problem? What are some of the legal concerns by implementing a CGI against a gang?

4. How effective would a gang court be in your community? What other incentives and programs can you establish within the gang court?

Web Links

Office of Juvenile Justice and Delinquency Prevention:
www.ojjdp.gov

National Gang Center (NGC): is a project jointly funded by the U.S. Department of Justice's (DOJ) Office of Juvenile Justice and Delinquency Prevention (OJJDP) and the Bureau of Justice Assistance (BJA). The NGC program works to further the mission of DOJ by providing national leadership, information, training, and technical assistance targeting gangs and street gang members of all ages. By serving researchers, policymakers, and practitioners nationally, NGC activities contribute to reductions in gang-related crime and violence and gang activity by juveniles and adults.
www.nationalgangcenter.gov

Youth Justice Coalition: is a nonprofit organization that works with youth and family who are victims of violence, corruption, and other related crime and justice issues.
www.youth4justice.org/

REFERENCES

Abel v. United States (1960), 362 U.S. 217, 80 S.Ct. 683.

Arana, A. (2005). How the street gangs took Central America. *Foreign Affairs, 84*(3), 98.

Bailey, P. (2018, April 13). Gang bill critics say targets black men and children passes Kentucky legislature. *Louisville Courier Journal*. Retrieved from https://www.courier-journal.com/story/news/politics/ky-legislature/2018/04/13/kentucky-senate-moves-gang-bill-forward-rejects-racial-impact-study/515293002/

Baldas, T. (2019, November 20). Seven Mile Bloods gangster gets 40 years prison, no parole. *Detroit Free Press*. Retrieved from https://www.freep.com/story/news/local/michigan/detroit/2019/11/20/seven-mile-bloods-gangster-sentencing/4250709002/

Ball, R. A., & Curry, G. D. (1995). The logic of definition in criminology: Purposes and methods for defining gangs. *Criminology, 33*, 225–245.

Bernstein, L. (2018, June 18). Trump signs bill giving cities, states $50M to combat gang activity. *WJLA.com*. Retrieved from https://wjla.com/news/nation-world/trump-signs-bill-giving-cities-states-50m-to-combat-gang-activity

Bickel, C. (2012, March 25). *Form Black codes to gang injunctions: Apartheid in the United States*. Paper presented at the Pacific Sociological Association Conference, San Diego, CA.

Bjerregaard, B. (2003). Antigang legislation and its potential impact: The promises and the pitfalls. *Criminal Justice Policy Review, 14*, 171–192.

Bloch, H., & Niederhoffer, A. (1958). *The gang: A study of adolescent behavior.* New York, NY: Philosophical Library.

Brownfield, D., Sorenson, A., & Thompson, K. (2001). Gang membership, race, and social class: A test of the group hazard and master status hypotheses. *Deviant Behavior, 22*(1), 73–89.

Bursik, R. J., & Grasmick, H. G. (2006). Defining and researching gangs. In A. Egley, C. Maxson, J. Miller, & M. Klein (Eds.), *The modern gang reader* (pp. 2–13). Los Angeles, CA: Roxbury.

Caldwell, B. (2010). Criminalizing day-to-day life: A socio-legal critique of gang injunctions. *American Journal of Criminal Law, 37*(3), 241–290.

California Penal Code, Section 186.20–27.

Cassidy, M. (1993, September 15). S. J. neighborhood on the rebound: Crackdown on gangs in Rocksprings gets credit for drop in crime. *San Jose Mercury*, p. 1B.

City of Chicago v. Morales. (1999). 527 U.S. 41, 119 S.Ct. 1849, 144 L. Ed. 2d 67.

City of Chicago v. Morales, 527 U.S. 41 (1999).

Cloward, R., & Ohlin, L. (1960). *Delinquency and opportunity*. Glencoe, IL: Free Press.

Cohen, A. (1955). *Delinquent boys*. Glencoe, IL: Free Press.

Crawford, L. (2009). No way out: An analysis of exit processes for gang injunctions. *California Law Review, 97*(1), 161–193.

Criminal Street Gangs Statute, 18 USC § 521.

Curry, G. D., & Decker, S. H. (2003). *Confronting gangs: Crime and community* (2nd ed.). Los Angeles, CA: Roxbury.

Curry, G. D., Decker, S. H., & Pyrooz, D. C. (2014). *Confronting gangs: Crime and community* (3rd ed.). New York, NY: Oxford University Press.

Decker, S. H., & Kempf-Leonard, K. (1991). Constructing gangs: The social definition of youth activities. *Criminal Justice Policy Review, 5*(4), 271–291.

Esbensen, F. A. (2000). *Preventing adolescent gang involvement. Office of Juvenile Justice and Delinquency Prevention, Juvenile Justice Bulletin.* Washington, DC: U.S. Department of Justice.

Esbensen, F. A., Winfree, L. T., He, N., & Taylor, T. (2001). Youth gangs and definitional issues: When is a gang a gang, and why does it matter? *Crime and Delinquency, 47*(1), 105–130.

Fearn, N. E., Decker, S. H., & Curry, G. D. (2001). Public policy responses to gangs: Evaluating the outcomes. In A. Egley, C. L. Maxson, J. Miller, & M. W. Klein (Eds.), *The modern gang reader* (pp. 312–324). Los Angeles, CA: Roxbury.

Ferolito, P. (2017, January 28). Yakima County gang court fizzles after little success. *Yakima Herald.* Retrieved from https://www.yakimaherald.com/news/crime_and_courts/yakima-county-gang-court-fizzles-after-little-success/article_2557e7ba-e5f4-11e6-84be-233249dfe537.html

Franco, C. (2008, January 30). *The MS-13 and 18th Street gangs: Emerging transnational gang threats?* (CRS Report RL34233). Washington, DC: Congressional Research Service, Library of Congress.

Geis, G. (2002). Gangs up on gangs: Anti-loitering and public nuisance laws. In C. R. Huff (Ed.), *Gangs in America III* (pp. 257–270). Thousand Oaks, CA: SAGE.

Gilbertson, D. L., & Malinski, S. J. (2005). Gangs in the law: A content analysis of statutory definitions for the term gang. *Journal of Gang Research, 13*(1), 1–16.

Greenan, S., Britz, M. T., Rush, J., & Barker, T. (2000). *Gangs: An international approach.* Upper Saddle River, NJ: Prentice Hall.

Grogger, J. (2002). The effects of the Los Angeles County gang injunctions on reported crime. *Journal of Law and Economics, 45,* 69–90.

Hagedorn, J. M. (1988). *People and folks: Gangs, crime and the underclass in a rustbelt city.* Chicago, IL: Lakeview Press.

Hammond, S. (2008). *Gang busters: States respond to rising gang violence.* Denver, CO: National Conference of State Legislators. Retrieved from https://www.ncsl.org/research/civil-and-criminal-justice/state-legislatures-magazine-gang-busters-june-20.aspx

Harris County. (2015). *313th District court, gang court—Gang recidivism intervention program (GRIP).* Retrieved from https://hcjpd.harriscountytx.gov/Published%20Reports/Annual%20Report%202017.pdf

Henderson, C. (2015, March 5). Officers train to enforce Surenos-13 gang injunction. Retrieved from https://tarrant.tx.networkofcare.org/ps/news-article-detail.aspx?id=59129

Hennigan, K. M., & Sloane, D. (2013). Improving civil gang injunctions: How implementation can affect gang dynamics, crime, and violence. *Criminology & Public Policy, 12*(1), 7–41.

Hoover, B., & Reddell, S. (2007). Battling gang violence. *The Prosecutor, 3*(5), 1–2.

Horowitz, R. (1990). Sociological perspectives on gangs: Conflicting definitions and concepts. In C. Huff (Ed.), *Gangs in America* (pp. 37–54). Newbury Park, CA: SAGE.

Hynes, T., & Osgood, J. (2011, December). Civil gang injunctions: What can they do for your city? *Western City*. Retrieved from http://www.westerncity.com/Western-City/December-2011/Civil-Gang-Injunctions-What-Can-They-Do-for-Your-City/

Klein, M. W. (1971). *Street gangs and street workers*. Englewood Cliffs, NJ: Prentice Hall.

Klein, M. W. (1998). The problem of street gangs and problem-oriented policing. In T. O'Connor Shelley & A. Grant (Eds.), *Problem-oriented policing: Crime-specific problems, critical issues, and making POP work* (pp. 57–86). Washington, DC: Police Executive Research Forum.

Klein, M. W. (2007). *Chasing after street gangs: A forty-year journey*. Upper Saddle, NJ: Pearson.

Klein, M. W., Kerner, H. J., Maxson, C. L., & Weitekamp, E. G. (2001). *The Eurogang paradox: Street gangs and youth groups in the U.S. and Europe*. Boston, MA: Kluwer Academic.

Lanzetta et al. v. New Jersey, 306 U.S. 451 (1939).

LAPD. (2019). About gang injunctions. *Los Angeles Police Department*. Retrieved from http://www.lapdonline.org/gang_injunctions/content_basic_view/23424

Leet, D. A., Rush, G. E., & Smith, A. M. (2000). *Gangs, graffiti, and violence: A realistic guide to the scope and nature of gangs in America* (2nd ed.). Incline Village, NV: Cooperhouse.

Los Angeles City Attorney's Office. (2019). *Important facts to know about gang injunctions*. Los Angeles, CA: Author. Retrieved from https://filedn.com/lOJqn8isbUNJvUBnJTlV5OS/GANG%20INJUNCTIONS%20EN.pdf

Los Angeles City Attorney's Office. (2019). *Gang division*. Retrieved from https://www.lacityattorney.org/gang-division

Lowney, J. (1984). The wall gang: A study of interpersonal process and deviance among twenty-three middle-class youths. *Adolescence, 19*(75), 527–538.

Maxson, C. L., & Allen, T. L. (1997). *An evaluation of the city of Inglewood's youth firearms violence initiative*. Los Angeles, CA: Social Science Research Institute, University of Southern California.

Maxson, C. L., Hennigan, K., & Sloane, D. (2005). It's getting crazy out there: Can a civil gang injunction change a community? *Criminology & Public Policy, 4*(3), 501–530.

McGloin, J. M. (2005). Policy and intervention considerations of a network analysis of street gangs. *Criminology and Public Policy, 4,* 607–649.

Miethe, T. D., & McCorkle, R. C. (2002). *Panic: The social construction of the street gang problem*. Upper Saddle River, NJ: Prentice Hall.

Miller, W. B. (1958). Lower class culture as a generating milieu of gang delinquency. *Journal of Social Issues, 14*(3), 5–19.

Moore, J. W. (1991). *Going down to the barrio: Homeboys and homegirls in change*. Philadelphia, PA: Temple University Press.

Moran, K. (2015). Social structure and bonhomie: Emotions in the youth street gang. *British Journal of Criminology, 55*(3), 556–577.

Muniz, A. (2014). Maintaining racial boundaries: Criminalization, neighborhood context, and the origins of gang injunctions. *Social Problems, 61*(2), 216–236.

Myers, T. A. (2009). The unconstitutionality, ineffectiveness, and alternatives of gang injunctions. *Michigan Journal of Race & Law, 14*(2), 285–306.

National Crime Prevention Council. (2014). *Protecting communities with anti-gang injunctions.* Washington, DC: Bureau of Justice Assistance, U.S. Department of Justice.

National Gang Center. (2013). Civil gang injunctions. *NGC Newsletter, 1,* 1–3. Washington, DC: Office of Juvenile Justice & Delinquency Prevention. Retrieved from https://www.nationalgangcenter.gov/Content/Newsletters/NGC-Newsletter-2013-Winter.pdf

National Gang Center. (2019). *Compilation of gang-related legislation.* Retrieved from https://www.nationalgangcenter.gov/Legislation

National Gang Intelligence Center. (2013). *2013 National Gang Report.* Washington, DC: Federal Bureau of Investigation, Department of Justice.

National Gang Intelligence Center. (2015). *2015 National Gang Report.* Washington, DC: Federal Bureau of Investigation, Department of Justice.

O'Deane, M. (2011). *Gang injunctions and abatement: Using civil remedies to curb gang-related crimes.* Boca Raton, FL: CRC Press Taylor and Francis.

O'Deane, M. D., & Morreale, S. A. (2012). Gang injunctions: A tool to control gang activity. *Law Enforcement Executive Forum, 12*(1), 86–96.

Petersen, R. D. (2004). *Understanding contemporary gangs in America: An interdisciplinary approach.* Upper Saddle River, NJ: Pearson Education.

Public Law 102-132. (1991). *Amendment to Anti-Drug Abuse Act of 1988,* Title III, Sections 3501–3505, 42 U.S.C. 11801–11805.

Public Law 105-302. (1998). *Amendment to Omnibus Crime Control and Safe Streets Act of 1968,* SEC 1, 42 U.S.C. 2796dd.

Roberts, D. E. (1999). Race, vagueness, and the social meaning of order maintenance policing. *Journal of Criminal Law and Criminology, 89*(3), 775–836.

Rosenthal, L. (2001). Gang loitering and race. *Journal of Criminal Law and Criminology, 91*(1), 99–160.

Sanchez-Jankowski, M. (1991). *Islands in the street: Gangs and American urban society.* Berkeley: University of California Press.

Sheldon, R. G., Tracy, S. K., & Brown, W. B. (2013). *Youth gangs in American society* (4th ed.). Belmont, CA: Wadsworth Cengage Learning.

Siegel, N. (1997). Ganging up on civil liberties. *The Progressive, 61,* 10.

Solis, N. (2015, May 14). *Highland Park's gang injunctions up for debate.* Retrieved from http://www.theeastsiderla.com/2015/05/highland-parks-gang-injunctions-up-for-debate/

Solis, N. (2015, May 14). *Highland Park's gang injunctions up for debate.* Retrieved from https://www.theeastsiderla.com/news/crime/highland-park-s-gang-injunctions-up-for-debate/article_e868c163-3ec0-5998-bf54-1220a634d97c.html

Sollers, W., Sale, D., Kung, C., & Gulite, K. (2019, February 5). DOJ issues updated U.S. Attorneys' manual. *American Bar Association.* Retrieved from https://www.americanbar.org/groups/litigation/committees/criminal/practice/2019/doj-issues-updated-us-attorneys-manual/

Stewart, G. (1998). Black codes and broken windows: The legacy of racial hegemony in anti-gang civil injunctions. *The Yale Law Journal, 107*(7), 2249–2279.

Strosnider, K. (2002). Anti-gang ordinances after *City of Chicago v. Morales*: The intersection of race, vagueness doctrine, and equal protection in the criminal law. *American Criminal Law Review, 39*, 101–146.

Sullivan, J. P. (2008, January 1). Transnational gangs: The impact of third generation gangs in Central America. *Air & Space Power Journal, Segundo Trimestre* (Spanish edition). Retrieved from https://www.academia.edu/927368/Transnational_gangs_The_impact_of_third_generation_gangs_in_Central_America?auto=download

Thrasher, F. M. (1927). *The gang: A study of 1,313 gangs in Chicago.* Chicago, IL: The University of Chicago Press.

Tobin, K. (2008). *Gangs: An individual and group perspective.* Upper Saddle, NJ: Pearson Prentice Hall.

U.S. Attorney's Office (2013, March 25). *Pueblo Bishops Bloods gang member sentenced to 40 years in federal prison for role in ambush killing of young father.* Central District of California. Retrieved from http://www.justice.gov/usao/cac/Pressroom/2013/042.html

U.S. Immigration and Customs Enforcement. (2015). *National Gang Unit.* Retrieved from http://www.ice.gov/national-gang-unit

Valdemar, R. (2008). How to make a RICO case against gangs. *Police Magazine.* Retrieved from http://www.policemag.com/blog/gangs/story/2008/11/how-to-make-a-rico-case-against-gangs.aspx

Washington State Legislature. (n.d.). RCW, Title 13, Chapter 40, Section 700, Juvenile gang Courts. Olympia: Author.

Westside gang crime off. (1988, June 2). *Los Angeles Times.* Retrieved from https://www.latimes.com/archives/la-xpm-1988-06-02-me-5750-story.html

Whyte, W. F. (1943). *Street corner society: The social structure of an Italian slum.* Chicago, IL: University of Chicago.

Wood, J., & Alleyne, E. (2010). Street gang theory and research: Where are we now and where do we go from here? *Aggression and Violent Behavior, 15*(2), 100–111.

Yablonsky, L. (1962). *The violent gang.* New York, NY: Macmillan.

Yakima County. (2012). *Gang court Yakima summary report.* Retrieved from http://164.116.19.35/safetycenter/Gangs/pubdocs/2012June/GangCourtYakimaCountySummaryReport.pdf

Yoo, C. S. (1994). The constitutionality of enjoining criminal street gangs as public nuisances. *Northwestern University Law Review, 89*(1), 212–267.

Young, R. (2009). Sharpen the blade: Void of vagueness and service of process concerns in civil gang injunctions. *McGeorge Law Review, 40*(4), 1001–1038.

Zatz, M. S. (1985). Los cholos: Legal processing of Chicano gang members. *Social Problems, 33*(1), 13–30.

Chapter 8

Corrections: Prison Gangs and STGs

CHAPTER OBJECTIVES

- Provide a history of prison gangs.

- Describe prison gang violence, misconduct, and inmate classification.

- Explain present prison gang estimates.

- Describe the most prominent prison gangs.

- Describe female and juvenile prison gangs.

- Explain the effects of prison gangs on other entities.

History of Prison Gangs

According to gang scholars, the most well-known and well-documented early American prison gang was the Mexican Mafia (La Eme), which emerged from California's prison system in the 1950s (Fleisher & Decker, 2001). In the mid-1980s, a thorough survey of the U.S. prison gang climate was conducted by Camp and Camp (1985). Their research included a brief reference to the Gypsy Jokers as the first U.S. prison gang, in the Washington State Penitentiary (WSP), in 1950. Since then, a handful of scholars have recited the same information, sometimes identifying the 1985 work and other times identifying tertiary sources (e.g., Orlando-Morningstar, 1997; Stastny & Tyrnauer, 1983). Although Stastny and Tyrnauer's (1983) work had an extensive analysis of the WSP (including the 1953 prison unrest), these authors made no mention of the Gypsy Jokes organization. Orlando-Morningstar (1997) documented no source for their information, but it was suspected they obtained the information from Camp and Camp (1985).

The Gypsy Jokers are and have been a motorcycle gang and are considered an Outlaw Motorcycle Gang (OMG) by law enforcement. Contact with several OMG investigators revealed no information that substantiated the allegation that they were ever a prison gang and even provided some evidence to the contrary. The Gypsy Jokers have consistently identified their origin beginning in 1956 in San Francisco, CA. If the Gypsy Jokers had a history in Washington State prior to the mid-1960s, specifically as the first documented prison gang, it was likely that the Gypsy Jokers organization would have made such a claim. They have not. In addition, the founder did not arrive in Washington State until after 1965. The Gypsy Jokers are not, nor have they ever claimed to be, a prison gang, and their first presence in Washington State was in the 1960s.

As the prison population has significantly increased over the past 50 years (see Figure 8.1 for state and federal population trends), so have the number of gangs in prisons and jails. According to the most recent National Gang Report (FBI, 2013), prison gangs comprise of 9.5% of all U.S. gang members. Today, prison gangs exist in nearly all prisons and jails across the United States, but California, Texas, and Illinois have the distinction of housing some of the country's most notorious prison gangs. According to the FBI (2013), prison gangs are:

> Criminal organizations that originated within the penal system that have continued to operate within correctional facilities throughout the United States. Prison gangs are also self-perpetuating criminal entities that can continue their operations outside the confines of the penal system. Typically, a prison gang consists of a select group of inmates who have an organized hierarchy and who are governed by an established code of conduct. Prison gangs vary in both organization and composition, from highly structured gangs . . . to gangs with a less formalized structure . . . (p. 7).

Figure 6.1: State and Federal Prison Population, 1925–2013.

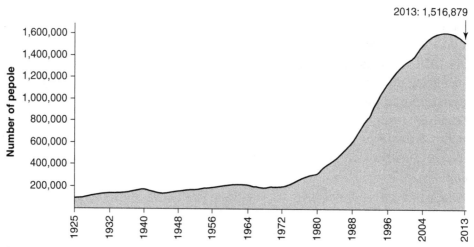

Source: Bureau of Justice Statistics. (2015). Prisoner series—The sentencing project. Retrieved from http://sentencingproject.org/doc/publications/inc_Trends_in_Corrections_Fact_sheet.pdf

> ## NEWS CLIP 8-1: LOCAL PRISON GANG INDICTED FOR RACKETEERING
>
> Honolulu, HI—Halawa prison in Hawaii was the headquarters for the gang members now accused of tax fraud, bribery, drug trafficking, and violence. At least twelve gang members of the USO Family were accused of running a crime ring from behind bars. The USO Family dealt crystal meth among other drugs and stole thousands of dollars from the IRS to fund their operation.

Source: KHON2 News. (2014, January 22)). Local prison gang indicted for racketeering. *Retrieved from https://www. youtube.com/watch?v=j_AbmGZAtoo*

As prison gangs have become more prevalent, correctional facilities are dealing with gang violence and the growth of illicit activities beyond the walls. While most prison gangs are usually structured along racial or ethnic lines, the distribution of drugs tends to overshadow those traditional boundaries. Today's prison gangs pose a greater threat to law enforcement because of their link to Drug Trafficking Organizations (DTO), street gangs, and OMGs (see News Clip 8.1).

Prison gangs are typically more powerful within state correctional facilities than federal prisons (FBI, 2013). The concern for the power that prison gangs have within correctional facilities and in the community is staggering (Winterdyk & Ruddell, 2010). Gangs occupy the street and the prisons. Table 8.1 provides a list of gangs who make frequent contact with incarcerated gang members in prison and jails across the United States.

Researchers have also reported that the borders between gangs in prison and gangs on the streets are becoming increasingly blurred (Curry & Decker, 2014). One reason is that these gangs are becoming more sophisticated in their threats toward institutional security and the public (Skarbek, 2014; Wilkinson & Delgado, 2006). As law enforcement officials continue to arrest gang members and prosecutors use gang laws to incarcerate gang members, the growth of gang membership in prisons and jails continues to grow (Decker, 2001; Hill, 2009; Ruddell, Decker, & Egley, 2006; Wells, Minor, Angel, Carter, & Cox, 2002).

From Prison Gangs to Security Threat Groups

Security Threat Groups (STGs) are defined as a formal and/or an informal group of inmates in a secure correctional facility. STGs are basically prison gangs. Typically, correctional officials use the expression "Security Threat Group" instead of "prison gang" in order remove any recognition or validation for being classified as a prison gang. According to William Sturgeon (2009a, 2009b), a security manager operations specialist for sheriffs' offices and correctional agencies, it was Gang Intelligence Units within the prison/jail system that coined the term

"Security Threat Groups." Sturgeon explained that Gang Intelligence Units were noticing that traditional prison gangs were not the only ones threatening the security of the institution as other groups were also deemed a threat. Thus, by moving away from the common identifying expression of "prison gangs" to STGs, this allows correctional officials to address all threatening groups within the penal system. STGs now include white supremacy groups who are religious and racist, members of organized crime groups, common street gangs, OMGs, and terrorists (foreign and domestic).

Table 8.1:   Community Gang Contact With Incarcerated Gang Members

18th Street	MS-13
415 Kumi	Nazi Low Riders
Mexican Mafia	Ñetas
Aryan Brotherhood	Norteños
Aryan Circle	Northern Riders
Bandidos	Northern Structure
Barrio Azteca	Outlaws
Black Guerilla Family	Paisas
Black Gangster Disciples	Raza Unida
Black P-Stone Nation	Simon City Royals
Bloods	Skinheads
Crips	Sureños
Dead Man Inc.	Syndicato De Nuevo Mexico
Dirty White Boys	Texas Chicano Brotherhood
Gangster Disciples	Texas Mexican Mafia
Grupo 25 (G-25)	(Mexikanemi-EMI)
Grupo 27 (G-27)	Texas Syndicate
Hells Angels	United Blood Nation
Hermanos de Pistoleros Latinos	Valluco
La Nuestra Familia	Tango Blast
Latin Kings	Vice Lords
Los Carnales	West Texas Tangos

Source: Federal Bureau of Investigation. (2011). National gang threat assessment—Emerging trends. National Gang Intelligence Center. Washington, DC: U.S. Department of Justice. Retrieved from http://www.fbi.gov/stats-services/publications/2011-national-gang-threat-assessment/2011-national-gang-threat-assessment-emerging-trends

STGs are basically criminal organizations within the U.S. correctional facilities. However, definitions of STGs may vary from state to state. According to the New Jersey Department of Corrections, "STGs" are defined as

> a group of inmates, designated by the Commissioner, who may gather together regularly and informally. The gang members possess common characteristics, interests and goals distinguishing them from other inmate groups or other inmates. And the group as a discrete entity poses a threat to the safety of the prison staff, other inmates, and the community. They also interrupt the safe, secure and orderly operation of the correctional facilities (*Fraise v. Terhune*, 2002).

Correctional facilities have categorized STGs depending on the characteristics of the group. These parameters include factors such as the gang's history, purpose, involvement in illegal activities, propensity for violence, organizational structure, and racial/ethnic composition. Like the formation of early prison gangs, STGs protect their members and are often involved in illegal activities such as assault, murder, drug trafficking, and extortion. STGs also have control and influence over street gangs outside the prison boundaries. One of the most famous and successful prison gangs operating inside the prison walls is the Aryan Brotherhood. (See News Clip 8.2.)

NEWS CLIP 8-2: FEARING THE ARYAN BROTHERHOOD—SO SHOULD YOU

The Brotherhood, also known as The Brand, AB, and One-Two, was formed during the 1960s by a group of white convicts serving time at San Quentin. They allegedly were fed up with white prisoners being victimized by the two predominant gangs—the Black Guerilla Family (BGF) and the Mexican Mafia—and decided to form a gang of their own for self-protection. While initially closely associated with Nazism ideologically, many adherents belong to the group for the identity and purpose it provides. The ironclad rule for entrée into the Brotherhood is simple: kill a black or a Hispanic prisoner. The other rule, which is just as ironclad, gave rise to their motto: "Blood In/Blood Out." Quitting isn't an option. There's only death.

Source: The Daily Beast.com. (2013, April 1). Why I fear the Aryan Brotherhood—And you should, too. Retrieved from http://www.thedailybeast.com/articles/2013/04/01/why-i-fear-the-aryan-brotherhood-and-you-should-too.html

---

George Knox, Executive Director of the National Gang Crime Research Center (NGCRC), details the significance of studying prison gangs, commonly referred to as STGs, which are identifiable collections of inmates whose misconduct poses various hazards to prison order because the gang members may merge into prison gangs or remain relatively disorganized (DeLisi, Berg, & Hochstetler, 2004). Knox (2005) indicated that the importance of studying STGs is to examine the effect upon the safety and security of correctional institutions and the emerging problems related to gangs. Besides the violence occurring in prison, the problems that directly affect the safety and security of prison staff and the operation of the prison include acts such as the abuse of religious freedom, the spreading of hate, and the ongoing racial conflict behind bars.

Conversely, Lyman (1989) defined a prison gang as "an organization which operates within the prison system as a self-perpetuating criminally oriented entity, consisting of a select group of inmates who have established an organized chain of command and are governed by an established code of conduct" (p. 48). Today, these identifying characteristics of prison gangs and STGs are used interchangeably.

Prison Violence and Misconduct

Unfortunately, prisons and violence are synonymous with one another. Gibbons and Katzenbach (2006) reported a chilling reality of prison life:

> There is disturbing evidence of individual assaults and patterns of violence in some U.S. prisons and jails. Corrections officers told the Commission about a near-constant fear of being assaulted. Former prisoners recounted gang violence, rape, [and] beatings by officers (p. 399).

> Prison gangs have been known to disrupt the everyday life of incarceration centers by engaging in violence toward other inmates and prison officials, trafficking contraband and narcotics, and provoking correctional officers to take part in their activities (Fleisher & Decker, 2001; Skarbek, 2014; Wood, Moir, & James, 2009). Members engage in these actions in order to fulfill their criminal goals of gaining money, power, and prestige.

NEWS CLIP 8-3: CORRECTIONS OFFICERS CHARGED IN CORRUPTION

Baltimore, MD—Fourteen current or former Maryland corrections officers were arrested in 2013, accused of aiding members of a violent prison gang. Charges include racketeering and drug- and money-laundering conspiracies. According to the grand jury indictment, the COs allegedly smuggled cellphones inside of sub sandwiches and Percocet (Oxycodone and Acetaminophen) pills in their underwear. One CO estimated making as much as $15,000 in one week.

Source: Marimow, A. E., & Hermann, P. (2013). How the Black Guerrilla Family gang took root in Maryland's prisons. The Washington Post. Retrieved from http://www.washingtonpost.com/local/how-the-black-guerrilla-family-gang-took-root-in-marylands-prisons/2013/07/15/cc4a9d92-cee7-11e2-9f1a-1a7cdee20287_story.html?wprss=rss_homepage

Research suggested that there is a substantive debate on the nature and extent of prison violence and disorder (Byrne & Hummer, 2007), as well as the accuracy and the risk reduction effects of current inmate classification systems (Austin, 2003; Austin & McGinnis, 2004). Prison systems classify gang affiliation and/or STG membership of incoming inmates based on the notion that violence and disorder is directly linked to STG involvement. Conversely, research has reported that the influence that gangs have on the community and the institutional violence and disorder in prisons is overstated (Byrne & Hummer, 2007). Despite this shortfall, an inmate identified as an STG member may potentially be placed in an administrative segregation housing unit or in a high-security facility (maximum security or super-max prison).

However, a significant impact on prison violence and misconduct is what the inmates bring in with them to the prison/jail. The importation (importation model) of the offender's characteristics (e.g., gang member status, type of crime, personality, attitudes, and coping mechanisms) are critical to the rate of prison violence and misconduct (DeLisi et al., 2004). Advocates of the importation model contend that gangs are primarily responsible for a disproportionate amount of community and prison violence and disorder (DeLisi et al., 2004). Thus, the importation model emphasizes that inmate behavior and conduct are predominantly an extension of the various antisocial behaviors that criminal offenders develop in the community. In other words, those involved in gangs are viewed as at-risk for prison misconduct.

According to DeLisi et al. (2004), penologists (those who study prison management and criminal rehabilitation) have long identified gang membership as an important determinant of prison misconduct. Prison violence, misconduct, and maladjustment usually take the form of one of two explanations: (1) street gang members usually bring their criminal lifestyles into the facility, thus complicating matters (Cao, Zhao, & Van Dine, 1997; Irwin & Cressey, 1962; Thomas & Foster, 1973) and (2) prison gang involvement is adaptive because of the structural conditions of the prison itself or the situational dynamics of prison life (Jiang & Fisher-Giorlando, 2002; Sykes, 1958; Thomas, 1977).

The deprivation model looks to explain prison violence and misconduct as the result of individual structural forces, specifically the pains of imprisonment (e.g., depression, isolation) as the primary cause of inmate behavior (Hochstetler & DeLisi, 2005; Sykes, 1958). Roth and Skarbek (2014) contended that inmates join gangs in order to promote cooperation and trust, which further facilitates illegal activities within the institution. One former inmate explained how the structure of gangs keeps order:

> The boys inside, they follow the rules and that means you work with your own boys and do what they say. Look, there is a lot of problems caused by the gangs, no doubt. The thing is, they solve problems too. You want a structure and you want someone to organize the businesses so the gangs have their rules. You don't run up a drug debt, you don't start a fight in the yard and stuff. Gangs are a problem but we took care of business. There is a code of silence, you don't

talk about all the stuff with others, the cops split up gangs if there's a big problem so we keep to ourselves and mind our own business (Trammell, 2009).

Regardless of the suggested models in which prison violence and misconduct develop among inmates within prison (i.e., importation or deprivation), researchers have found that gang-affiliated inmates disproportionately engage in acts of prison violence and other forms of misconduct (see, for example, Allender & Marcell, 2003; DeLisi, 2003; Gaes, Wallace, Gilman, Klein-Saffran, & Suppa, 2002). Other explanations for prison violence and misconduct integrate importation, deprivation, and situational effects. Byrne and Hummer (2007) addressed the importation versus deprivation debate in the following way:

> If this view is correct then the initial determination of gang membership is a critical step in the initial inmate classification and prison control process. Once gang membership is determined, it will likely affect both external (i.e., security level) and internal (i.e. location and movement within a particular prison) classification decisions. Of course, if gang membership is not associated with prison violence and disorder, we would be wasting valuable time and resources on a problem we don't need to solve. This general caveat about gang affiliation can be applied to other inmate characteristics as well. (p. 8)

Prison gang/STG members do cause a disproportionate number of prison-related issues for correctional administration (Camp, Gaes, Langan, & Saylor, 2003; Griffin & Hepburn, 2006). For example, in 1988, the FBI, in cooperation with local California authorities, conducted a three-year investigation known as "Operation Black Widow". The goal of "Operation Black Widow" was to flush out and prosecute the most violent members of the infamous La Nuestra Familia prison gang. To this day, "Operation Black Widow" remains the most expensive investigation into a U.S. prison gang at an estimated cost of $5 million. To their success, the operation uncovered a complex paramilitary hierarchy within the La Nuestra Familia. This included insight into the recruitment and membership activities, discipline structure, communication structure, and member tracking for the gang (Trulson, Marquart, & Kawucha, 2006).

Prisons and jails must maintain a safe and secure environment in order to protect their inmates, staff, visitors, and, ultimately, the community (Hutchinson, Keller, & Reid, 2009). Research with prison-based practitioners has often considered the design and condition of prisons and jails, and the staff's ability to physically defend themselves as a primary concern to achieve safety and security. However, the experiences of correctional officers have shown that prison/jails cannot rely on these measures alone. In order to have a safe and secure facility, prison/jail staff must actively supervise and manage inmate behavior. Furthermore, inmate classification is critical to the safety and security of the facility. It is one of the most beneficial tools for managing prison populations and identifying potential threats (see, for example, Clements, 1996; Hummer, 2009; Hutchinson et al., 2009).

Gang Classification in Prisons/Jails

Prior to the 1980s, a majority of the nation's prisons and jails used subjective classification. Prisons/jails relied heavily upon the judgment of prison officials to determine where a prisoner was housed and the type of supervision and security imposed on that inmate (Austin, 2003). Since then, prison systems have shifted to a more objective classification. These standardized and automated classification criteria "place greater emphasis on fairness, consistency, and openness in the decision making process" (National Institute of Corrections, 1992, p. 3). In the past 10 years, inmate classification has become a more critical aspect of the prison culture as U.S. prisons and jails are no longer able to segregate inmates—based on their racial and/or ethnic background alone—for extended periods of time within the institution (Hummer, 2009). In fact, it was *Johnson v. California* (2005) that challenged the unofficial policy of segregating inmates based on race/ethnicity by the California Department of Corrections (CDC). The CDC segregated inmates and "asserted that the rationale behind pairing inmates in cells by race or ethnicity during the risk assessment and classification period was to offset potential violence caused by racial gangs existing within the state's correctional system" (Hummer, 2009, p. 414). Ultimately, the U.S. Supreme Court rejected the CDCs claim. According to the Commission on Safety and Abuse in America's Prisons,

> Reducing violence among prisoners depends on the decisions corrections administrators make about where to house prisoners and how to supervise them. Perhaps most important are the classification decisions managers make to ensure that housing units do not contain incompatible individuals or groups of people: informants and those they informed about, repeat and violent offenders and vulnerable potential victims, and others who might clash with violent consequences. And these classifications should not be made on the basis of race or ethnicity, or their proxies (Gibbons & Katzenbach, 2006, p. 428).

As gang members are arrested and incarcerated, they often have to develop quick loyalties to prison gangs in order to defend themselves against their enemies (Hagedorn, 1990), and those loyalties fall in line with one's own race and ethnicity. Byrne and Hummer (2007) hypothesized that gang involvement and violence in prisons are more likely to mirror the patterns of gang involvement and violence in the community.

Gang-affiliated inmates continue to present problems within prisons/jails and for correctional staffers. The disruption of prison operations has led many state prison administrators to develop anti-gang programs, training, and implementation policies (DeLisi, 2003). Some local and state prisons have moved or transferred gang members in order to distance the gang member from the supporting and/or rival gangs. Other methods of relocating gang members identified as a threat is to completely transfer them to other institutions in the state, region, or nationally or to the Bureau of Prison (Trulson et al., 2006). Knox (2005) reported that about 63% of the prisons surveyed felt that gang members have significantly affected the correctional environment.

Research has reported that STG members commit a variety of illegal acts while incarcerated, and inmates who are affiliated with an STG are more frequently involved in violent prison misconduct than those that are not affiliated with an STG (see, for example, Cunningham & Sorensen, 2007; Fleisher & Decker, 2001; Griffin & Hepburn, 2006; Jones, Roper, Stys, & Wilson, 2004). MacDonald (1999) also found that former gang members are nearly 30% more likely to engage in violence in prison than inmates with no prior gang history, DeLisi et al. (2004) reported that prison gang members were 74% more likely than nongang inmates to commit serious disciplinary violations. Additionally, prisoners with prior incarceration history and substantial criminal records are reported to be more aggressive and are more likely to commit numerous prison infractions. Prison gang members or STGs are also more likely to assault prison staff compared with non-gang members (DeLisi et al., 2004). Other factors that contribute to violent institutional misconduct are the age of the inmate (the younger the more violent), the type of sentence, the alliance to a prison gang, a prior record of prison violence, and the type of crime committed. Finally, the risk of violence in prison is significantly increased by a history of assaultive misconduct in prison (Cunningham, Sorensen, Vigen, & Woods, 2011).

Prison gangs are so troublesome that they can cripple an entire state prison system under certain conditions. For example, Ralph and Marquart (1991) found that a loosening of social control in Texas prisons unleashed a gang problem that produced a 10% increase in the rate of murders, weapon assaults, and sexual assaults. In a two-year span, prison gang members committed more homicides than in the previous 20 years.

Jacobs (1977) argued that prison gangs are typically an extension of street gangs but prison gang behavior, often dictated by one's race/ethnicity, reflects a response to the structural order of the penitentiary. In this sense, it is unclear whether street gang members or prison gang members are the most difficult-to-manage inmates. Moreover, it is unclear whether inmates who are involved in prison gangs are the same individuals who are also involved in street gangs. But the National Gang Intelligence Center (NGIC) reports that there are connections between prison and street gangs, as well as prison–family connections:

> Many incarcerated gang members continue to engage in gang activities following incarceration and use their connections inside prison to commit crime in the community. Prison gang members' influence and control gang activity on the street, and exploit street gangs for money and other resources. [Additionally,] a gang member's incarceration often prompts his or her family to move closer to the correctional facility where the gang member is being housed. In some cases, family members assist or facilitate gang criminal activity and recruiting. Family members of gangs operate as outside facilitators, serving as messengers, drug couriers, or in any capacity benefiting the gang. Outside facilitators are provided instructions by the incarcerated gang member, often during a social or legal visit, and in turn pass this information to gang members on the streets. Family members have also been used to assist prison escapes and smuggle

contraband into correctional facilities, allowing incarcerated gang members to continue their operations inside prison (NGIC, 2011, p. 30).

Violence and misconduct among prison inmates does not always entail assaults with weapons (i.e., shanks) or other contraband activities. According to Steward (2014), cell phones are one of the most sought after, and smuggled, items in prisons (para. 1). According to the Bureau of Prisons (BOP) and the National Gang Report (FBI, 2013), cell phones smuggled into correctional facilities pose the greatest threat to institution safety. In a recent survey of prison officials, mobile phones were listed as one of the top identified issues in state and local prisons (see Figure 8.2).

The FBI (2013) has also reported that incarcerated gang members often rely on family, friends, corrections personnel, and other criminal justice professionals to transmit their messages to gang members on the street. Smuggled cell phones are a continuing problem for prison administrators in correctional facilities throughout the country. In 2010, it was reported that more than 10,000 illegal cell phones were confiscated from prisoners in California (Valdemar, 2013). In March of 2011, the California State Senate approved legislation criminalizing prison cell phones for both inmates and smugglers. Smuggled cell phones and smart phones provide incarcerated gang members the ability to influence and control street gangs through unrestricted access and unmonitored conversations via voice calling, Internet access, text messaging, email, and social networking websites, as well as directing or planning criminal activities (e.g., drug distribution, assault, and murder; NGIC, 2013). In 2014, a North Carolina inmate described as a high-ranking member of the Bloods street gang used a

Figure 8.2: Top identified issues in state and local prisons.

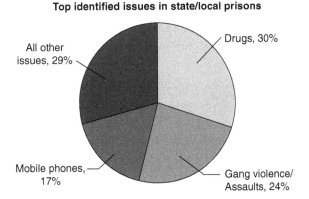

Top identified issues in state/local prisons

Drugs, 30%

All other issues, 29%

Mobile phones, 17%

Gang violence/ Assaults, 24%

Source: Federal Bureau of Investigation. (2013). 2013 National gang report. Washington, DC: U.S. Department of Justice, National Gang Intelligence Center.

smuggled mobile phone to help orchestrate the abduction of a prosecutor's father. The case highlights the problem of inmate access to smart phones.

Prison Gang Estimates

In the early 1990s, prison gang disturbances soared. Some estimates to the extent of the gang presence during this period in American correctional institutions are between 9% and 25% (Knox, 2000). In 2005, Knox reported, based on correctional institutional surveys, that about 94% of inmates were not affiliated with street gangs but joined a prison gang or were recruited by one after being incarcerated. Other studies in correctional settings reported smaller proportions of gang-involved prisoners. For example, Pyrooz, Decker, and Fleisher (2011) reported that gang membership comprises as much as 13% of jail populations, 12% to 17% of state prison populations, and 9% of the federal prison population (see also Gaes et al., 2002; Griffin & Hepburn, 2006; Krienert & Fleisher, 2001; Ruddell et al., 2006; Wells et al., 2002). The American Correctional Association reported averages of 11.7% of STG members in 2003 and 13.8% in 2008 (Hill, 2009). Variations in reporting STG membership between local, state, and federal correctional facilities are some of the reasons for limited factual knowledge on the actual prison gang population. Furthermore, some state correctional facilities do not collect or report on the gang affiliation of inmates.

According to the US Department of Justice, the National Drug Threat Survey (NDTS), and law enforcement data, in the year 2008, it was estimated that 780,000 street gang members currently reside within communities across the country and 230,000 were incarcerated in state correctional facilities. A similar statistic by West and Sabol (2009) was 200,000 inmates in the entire US prison population were gang related.

According to the Office of Special Investigations for the Minnesota Department of Corrections (MNDOC) in 2013, it was reported that of the 9,200 incarcerated males throughout the state of Minnesota, 30% (3,000+) were classified at some level of STG affiliation (active, suspected, inactive, inactive suspected). Ten percent were validated active members, 6% were inactive members (no reported activity last 3 years), 8% were suspected members (based on last 3 years of information), and 8% were inactive suspected (MNDOC, 2015). The Ohio Department of Rehabilitation and Correction (ODRC) identified approximately 14% of the total inmate population in 2006 were members of an STG (Wilkinson & Delgado, 2006). According to Gang Investigators Association for the Florida Department of Corrections, in 2001, the prison population in states such as Illinois may be comprised by as much as 60% of inmates belonging to gangs (Danitz, 2001). As regards the 143,000 inmates housed in Texas prisons, somewhere around 5,000 inmates have been classified as gang members, with another 10,000 are currently under suspicion (Danitz, 2001). In Texas in 2001, of the approximately 143,000 inmates, it was estimated that about 5,000 were gang members and 10,000 were suspected gang members (Danitz, 2001). According to an October 2013 report by the California Department of Corrections and Rehabilitation (CDCR), approximately 2,200 gang members and associates are housed in Security Housing Units (SHUs) and approximately 2,900 inmates throughout the CDCR are validated STG members and associates (CDCR, 2013). Nearly 21% of all CDCR inmates serving an indeterminate SHU term are validated STG members. These members are reported to have an ongoing, high level of influence over compliant street gangs and other incarcerated individuals within the prison population. The remaining 79% are validated STG associates. These validated associates are under the direction of gang members and assist in continued illegal actions (CDCR, 2013).

Results from a 2004 Prison Gang Survey conducted by the National Gang Crime Research Center (NGCRC), a national survey which sampled all U.S. states but Rhode Island, projected that approximately 30% of males and 6% of females were already street gang members upon entering prison (Knox, 2005). The survey also found that approximately 12% of the males first joined a gang or an STG while incarcerated, compared to 4% for the female inmates. This means that 1 out of 10 male prison inmates in America first joined a gang while they were in prison. This statistic sheds light on the importance of counter-recruitment efforts to prevent gangs from developing within the prison walls.

Prominent Prison Gangs/STGs

As of 2020 research by the U.S. Department of Justice's *Organized Crime and Gang Section* (see https://www.justice.gov/criminal-ocgs/gallery/prison-gangs) lists the following prison gangs/ STG as the most dangerous gangs within U.S. prisons (alphabetical order): Aryan Brotherhood (AB); Barrio Azteca; Black Guerrilla Family; Dead Man Incorporated (DMI); Four Horsemen, Tangos, and Tango Blast; Hermanos de Pistoleros Latinos (HPL); Mexican Mafia (La Eme); Mexikanemi; Nazi Low Riders (NLRs); Ñeta; La Nuestra Familia; Public Enemy Number One (PEN1); and the Texas Syndicate (TS) (see http://www.justice.gov/criminal/ ocgs/gangs/prison.html). Although there are numerous website articles and other various sources that summarize each of the prison gangs listed above (for more information, see Holthouse, 2005; Kelley, 2014; Marimow & Hermann, 2013), the Department of Justice provides an excellent and succinct summary of each gang's relationship to prison (Lyman, 2011). The following descriptions are taken directly from the DOJ organized crime page.

Aryan Brotherhood

At roughly 20,000 members, the Aryan Brotherhood, also known as AB, was originally ruled by consensus among inmates but is now a highly structured entity with two factions, one located within the CDC and the other within the Federal Bureau of Prisons (BOP). The majority of the members of the AB are Caucasian males, and the gang is primarily active in the Southwestern and Pacific regions of the United States. The main source of income for AB is derived from the distribution of cocaine, heroin, marijuana, and methamphetamine within the prison systems as well as on the street. Some AB members have established business relationships with Mexican Drug Trafficking Organizations that smuggle illegal drugs into California for distribution by the AB. The AB is notoriously violent and is frequently involved in murder for hire. Although historically linked to the California-based Hispanic prison gang the Mexican Mafia (La Eme), tension between the AB and La Eme is becoming increasingly evident as demonstrated by recent fights between Caucasians and Hispanics within the CDC.

Barrio Azteca

Comprising about 2,000 members, the Barrio Azteca is one of the most violent prison and highly structured gangs operating within the United States. Most members of the Barrio Azteca are either Mexican nationals or Mexican-American males. Barrio Azteca is most active in the Southwestern region of the United States, primarily in federal, state, and local correctional facilities in Texas, as well as on the outside in communities located in Southwestern Texas and Southeastern New Mexico. Barrio Azteca's main source of income is derived from the smuggling of heroin, powdered cocaine, and marijuana from Mexico into the United States for distribution both inside and outside the prison systems. Barrio Azteca members are also involved in crimes such as alien smuggling, arson, assault, auto theft, burglary, extortion, intimidation, kidnapping, robbery, and weapons violations.

Black Guerrilla Family

The Black Guerrilla Family (also called the Black Family or Black Vanguard), identified as BGF, emerged in San Quentin in 1966. The BGF is a highly organized paramilitary prison gang with a supreme leader and a central committee. BGF members operate primarily in the states of California and Maryland with about 1,000 identified gang members plus associates. Members are typically African-American males. BGF members obtain drugs primarily from La Nuestra Familia and Norteño members or from local Mexican drug traffickers. BGF members are also involved in other criminal activities including auto theft, burglary, drive-by shooting, and homicide.

Dead Man, Incorporated

DMI is a violent prison gang that was started in the 1980s by three prison inmates. DMI operates primarily within the Maryland Division of Corrections, where gang membership in 2006 was estimated to be more than 370 members and consists of predominantly white males. In 2006, leadership within Maryland's DOC gave the go-ahead to a DMI member to begin recruiting in Virginia. The DMI member assaulted a law enforcement official to ensure his incarceration and ability to begin recruiting DMI membership in the Virginia prison system. The main source of income for DMI gang members is committing murder for hire, acts of intimidation and violence, and drug distribution.

Four Horsemen, Tangos, and Tango Blast

Texas prison officials first noted the presence of a gang known as the Four Horseman in 1998. Some Hispanic gang members entering the Texas Department of Criminal Justice (TDCJ) from the cities of Austin, Dallas, Fort Worth, and Houston were not interested in joining an established prison gang and established the Four Horseman to protect one another and to engage in illegal activities, particularly drug trafficking, to make money. The Four Horseman became known as the Tangos, because its members wore tattoos that reflected the town (or tango) in which they resided prior to their incarceration. As interest in the Tangos grew among Hispanic gang members entering the TDCJ from other areas of Texas, only inmates from West Texas, the Rio Grande Valley, San Antonio, and El Paso were allowed into the gang. Of the eight groups now recognized as Tangos, six are part of what is now known as Tango Blast or Puro Tango Blast. Tango Blast includes Tangos from the four original cities as well as the West Texas and Rio Grande Valley areas. Tango Blast differs from the Tangos in that separate Tango Blast members sometimes band together to help one another. The rapid growth of the Tango Blast poses a significant new security threat within the TDCJ and elements of the Tango Blast appear to be challenging the Texas Syndicate for control of illegal prison activities. Upon release from prison, Tango members appear to return to their local street gangs, rather than continue their prison-based gang affiliations.

Hermanos de Pistoleros Latinos

The Hermanos de Pistoleros Latinos (HPL) is a Hispanic prison gang formed in the TDCJ in the late 1980s. HPL operates in most prisons and on the streets in many communities in Texas, particularly Laredo. HPL is also active in several cities in Mexico, and its largest contingent in that country is located in Nuevo Laredo. HPL is structured and estimated to have 1,000 members. HPL members maintain close ties with Mexican Drug Trafficking Organizations and are involved in the trafficking of large quantities of cocaine and marijuana from Mexico into the United States for distribution.

Mexican Mafia (La Eme)

The Mexican Mafia prison gang, also known as La Eme (Spanish for the letter M), was formed in the late 1950s within the CDC. La Eme is a loosely structured criminal organization with strict rules that must be followed by roughly 400 members and 1000 associates. Most members of La Eme are comprised of Mexican-American males who previously belonged to a Southern California street gang. La Eme is primarily active in the Southwestern and Pacific regions of the United States; however, its power base remains in California. The Mexican Mafia's main source of income is extorting drug distributors outside prison and distributing methamphetamine, cocaine, heroin, and marijuana within the prison systems and on the outside streets. Some members of La Eme have direct links to Mexican Drug Trafficking Organizations and broker deals for both themselves and their associates. La Eme is also involved in other criminal activities including controlling gambling and prostitution within the prison systems.

Mexikanemi

The Mexikanemi prison gang, also known as the Texas Mexican Mafia (La Eme) or Emi, was formed in the early 1980s within the TDCJ. The Mexikanemi is highly structured and is estimated to have 2,000 members, most of whom are Mexican nationals or Mexican-American males living in Texas at the time of their incarceration. Mexikanemi poses a significant drug-trafficking threat to communities in the Southwestern United States, particularly in Texas. Mexikanemi gang members reportedly traffic multikilogram quantities of powdered cocaine, heroin, and methamphetamine; multiton quantities of marijuana; and thousand-tablet quantities of ecstasy from Mexico into the United States for distribution both inside and outside prison. Mexikanemi gang members obtain narcotics from associates or members of the Jaime Herrera-Herrera, Osiel Cardenas-Guillen, and/or the Vicente Carrillo-Fuentes Mexican Drug Trafficking Organizations (DTOs). In addition, Mexikanemi members maintain a relationship with Los Zetas, a Mexican paramilitary/criminal organization employed by the Cardenas-Guillen Drug Trafficking Organizations as its personal security force.

Nazi Low Riders

The Nazi Low Riders (NLRs) are a violent California-based prison gang that subscribes to a white supremacist philosophy. The NLRs have approximately 800 to 1,000 members, most of whom are Caucasian males with a history of street gang activity and drug abuse. The NLRs operate in correctional facilities and communities, primarily in the Pacific and Southwestern regions of the United States. The NLRs' primary sources of income are derived from the distribution of multiounce to multipound quantities of methamphetamine, the retail-level distribution of heroin and marijuana, and the extortion of independent Caucasian drug dealers and members of other white power gangs. The NLRs also engage in violent criminal activity such as armed robbery, assault, assault with deadly weapons, murder, and attempted murder; in addition, they commit identity fraud, money laundering, witness intimidation, and witness retaliation.

Ñeta

Ñeta is a prison gang that began in Puerto Rico and spread to the United States. Ñeta is one of the largest and most violent prison gangs, with approximately 7,000 members in Puerto Rico and about 5,000 members in the United States. Ñeta chapters in Puerto Rico exist exclusively inside prisons; once members are released from prison, they no longer are considered to be part of the gang. In the United States, Ñeta chapters exist both inside and outside prisons in 36 cities and within nine states, primarily in the Northeastern region. Ñeta's main source of income is derived from the retail distribution of powdered and crack cocaine, heroin, and marijuana and, to a lesser extent, lysergic acid diethylamide, ecstasy, methamphetamine, and phencyclidine. Ñeta gang members also commit crimes including assault, auto theft, burglary, drive-by shooting, extortion, home invasion, money laundering, robbery, weapons and explosives trafficking, and witness intimidation.

La Nuestra Familia

La Nuestra Familia and its subordinate organization Norteños are highly structured and extremely violent prison gangs. Originating within the California penal system, La Nuestra Familia has an estimated 250 members, while Norteños membership is estimated to be over 1,000 persons, consisting primarily of Mexican-American males who formerly belonged to street gangs in Central and Northern California. La Nuestra Familia and Norteños are active primarily in state and federal prisons and in communities of the Pacific region of the United States. The main sources of income for La Nuestra Familia and Norteños are derived from distributing cocaine, heroin, marijuana, and methamphetamine within prison systems as well as in outside communities and by extorting drug distributors on the streets. La Nuestra Familia is also involved in other criminal activities including homicide and robbery.

Public Enemy Number One

Public Enemy Number One (PEN1) is the fastest-growing Caucasian prison gang in the U.S. with an estimated membership of between 400 and 500 persons. PEN1 operates in the prison systems and communities of California, and, to a lesser extent, in locations throughout the Northeastern, Pacific, Southwestern, and Southeastern and West Central regions of the United States. PEN1 members espouse a white supremacist philosophy and pose a criminal threat both inside and outside prison due to an alliance with the AB and the NLRs. PEN1 members derive their income from distributing mid-level and retail-level quantities of methamphetamine. In addition, PEN1 members engage in violent criminal activities such as assault, attempted murder, homicide, auto theft, burglary, identity theft, and property crimes.

Texas Syndicate

The Texas Syndicate (TS) is one of the largest and most violent prison gangs active on both sides of the United States–Mexico border and poses a significant drug-trafficking threat to communities located in the Southwestern United States. The TS is highly structured and is estimated to have 1,300 members, most of whom are Mexican-American males between the ages of 20 to 40 years. Members of the TS smuggle multikilogram quantities of powdered cocaine, heroin, and methamphetamine and multiton quantities of marijuana from Mexico into the United States for distribution both inside and outside of prison. TS gang members have a direct working relationship with associates and/or members of the Osiel Cardenas-Guillen Mexican Drug Trafficking Organizations. In addition, TS gang members maintain a relationship with Los Zetas, the paramilitary/criminal organization employed by the Cadenas-Guillen Drug Trafficking Organizations.

Women Prison Gangs

For many years, researchers largely neglected to study female gang members, especially in prisons. Most of the early studies on female gang membership focused on how women were used as sex objects, or provided support for the gang such as hiding weapons, drugs or other gang members from the police (Moore & Hagedorn, 2001; Sutton, 2017). While most female gang members are on the fringes of gang life, Brown's (1977) discussion of African American female gang members, and Quicker (1983) and Mendoza-Denton (2014) observations of Mexican American/Latina gangs explores the importance of female involvement in the gang. These female gangs are not just on the peripheral; they are heavily involved in the gang life.

According to Knox (2000), 8% of all females in correctional institutions in the United States were gang members. However, it is unknown whether those individuals joined a gang while in prison or continued their street affiliations after being incarcerated. One theory regarding the formation of female prison gangs explains that females engage in criminal activity in order to receive attention from prison officials and rebel against a male-dominated prison culture (Moore & Hagedorn, 2001). Nevertheless, females have still been found to join gangs in prison for some of the same reasons as males. Lauderdale and Burman (2009) uncovered that women join prison gangs to feel a sense of belonging and a familial connection. Once in the gang, the behaviors that female gang inmates engage in differ moderately from those typically associated with male prison gang inmates. Although female gang inmates have also been found to commit criminal offenses while in prison, they tend to engage in more verbal, rather than physical, disputes, and their crimes are more isolated, personal, and idiosyncratic in nature (Lauderdale & Burman, 2009). Generally, female prison gangs have typically not been recognized as STGs because they do not pose a high enough threat to prison officials and other inmates or severely interrupt the welfare of correctional institutions.

Juvenile Prison Gangs

While not studied as frequently as adult prison gangs, juvenile gangs have also been found to exist within correctional institutions. In a 1990 study, it was found that 52% of the 155 juvenile detention centers surveyed reported 10% or higher gang affiliation among their inmates (Knox, 2000). However, as with female gang inmates, it is unknown whether these individuals became involved in a gang while incarcerated or sustained the relationships they had with their respective street gangs prior to being detained. Compared with their adult counterparts, juveniles have been found to join prison gangs for much of the same reasons. Furthermore, the social theories regarding prison gang formation have also been found to apply to them. Some predictors of juvenile gang membership include being involved in group crime on the streets, experiencing higher levels of threat, placing a high value on one's social status, having a longer sentence, possessing strong anti-authority attitudes, and having higher levels of social dominance orientation (Wood, Alleyne, Mozova, & James, 2014).

While having a longer sentence has been found to increase the likelihood of joining a juvenile prison gang, it has the opposite effect on engaging in violent and aggressive acts. Scott (2014) found that juvenile gang members possessed stronger violent and aggressive attitudes than non-gang members during the first two years of being in an institutional gang; however, those tendencies decreased the longer that the individual stayed in the gang. Likewise, Gaes et al. (2002) unveiled that prison misconduct and violence among adult prison gang inmates decreased as the amount of time those individuals spent incarcerated increased. Thus, similar results have been found between juvenile and adult prison gang inmates. One reason this pattern may occur is that, as individuals remain in the gang and increase in status, they shift to giving orders, rather than executing those orders. Nonetheless, juvenile gangs still pose serious problems to correctional institutions. Juvenile gang inmates are violent and aggressive individuals who attempt to seduce and intimidate correctional staff, murder rival gang inmates, and transport contraband (see, for example, Abrams, Anderson-Nathe, & Aguilar, 2008; MacDonald, 1999). Thus, while they are not studied as often as adult prison gangs, juvenile gang inmates engage in much of the same criminal activities as their adult counterparts.

Prison Gang Exodus

Myth: Gang membership is a lifelong commitment. The reality is that that gang membership is *normally* a temporary status of 1 to 2 years. However, this status can be much longer for some (see, for example, Melde & Esbensen, 2014; Pyrooz, 2014). Briefly returning to the previous discussion on juvenile gang membership, Pyrooz and Sweeten (2015) found that roughly 2% of youth in the U.S. are gang members and youth aged 14 represent 5% of all youth gang members. Additionally, the authors found that gangs have turnover rates of about 36%, with about 400,000 youth joining gangs and another 400,000 youth leaving gangs every year. In other words, gangs have to constantly recruit new members to their groups. Therefore, the reintegration of prison gang inmates into society may be challenging for public safety professionals (see, for example, Hyatt & Barnes, 2017; Petersilia, 2001).

In fact, the personal barriers gang members (current or reformed) face may be greater than simply public fear, lack of education and employment opportunities, unstable housing, and negative support systems (see, for example, Morenoff & Harding, 2014; Petersilia, 2000). In addition to these barriers, prison gang inmates in particular are faced with the possibility of being assaulted or killed if they defect from their gangs upon release due to the strict "blood in, blood out" oath. However, previous research suggests that this oath is not always followed through. In 1995, Fong, Vogel, and Buentello surveyed 85 former prison gang members who were in protective custody and reported that 14% refused to carry out a *hit* on a fellow gang member. Because of these constraints, prison gang inmates have been found to have higher levels of recidivism than general prison inmates. As reported by Dooley, Seals, and Skarbek (2014):

> The same factors that are responsible for enhancing the chances of post-release rearrest or recommitment appear in greater proportions of gang members than non-affiliated inmates (p. 268).

Moreover gang members had a more criminally involved past. Research has found gang members reported an earlier age of arrest, less education, less commitment to legal employment, more drug use, and more prior arrests than nongang members (see, for example, Griffin, 2007; Krienert & Fleisher, 2001; Shelden, 1991). Gang members also have a similar number of prior convictions when compared with non-gang members despite their being younger overall. This is why the best developed body of research on the gang membership recidivism association has been generated from surveys of formerly institutionalized juveniles, although the results are split between those finding no consequence (i.e., a null effect) and those that find statistical significance between gang and non-gang members (see, for example, Lattimore, Visher, & Linster, 1995; Miethe & McCorkle, 1997; Tapia, 2010).

While some individuals may use their release from prison as a mechanism for separating from their prison gangs, other individuals may attempt to sever their relationships with their respective gangs while still incarcerated (Fong et al., 1995). Nevertheless, defecting from prison gangs remains an arduous task for inmates. In order to help individuals renounce their affiliations with prison gangs, some states have developed programs to help ease the transition from STG member to non-gang member. The most notable of these initiatives is the Gang Renouncement and Dissociation (GRAD) program implemented by the Texas Department of

Criminal Justice throughout its prisons. During the early program phase, inmates are exposed to programming and group recreation. Later, inmates graduate to stages that involve double-celled occupancy with other inmates (sometimes rival gang members). The Texas GRAD program relies heavily on cognitive interventions and is delivered over nine months (Pyrooz & Mitchell, 2018).

Although separating from a prison gang is a difficult, and often dangerous, action to undertake, there have been several incidences over the years in which high-ranking prison gang members dissociated from their gangs and ultimately aided law enforcement in infiltrating them. One of the most acclaimed stories of desertion, infiltration, and redemption regards Mexican Mafia member Rene "Boxer" Enriquez. In 2002, Enriquez, who had committed murder, assaults, armed robberies, and drug offenses, decided to dissociate from the Mexican Mafia and cooperate with law enforcement officials. Since then, he has testified against fellow prison gang inmates, provided information to law enforcement officials regarding the Mexican Mafia, helped uncover murder conspiracies, co-wrote a book, and spoke at conferences regarding prison gangs (Mather & Kim, 2015). In addition to Enriquez, another Mexican Mafia member and former hit-man, Ramon "Mundo" Mendoza, has also severed ties from his gang and cooperated with law enforcement officials. After being released from prison two separate times due to indeterminate sentencing laws and technicalities, Mendoza decided to abandon his prison gang and, instead, provide significant information about the Mexican Mafia to law enforcement. When Mendoza was asked his motivation for writing *Mexican Mafia: The Gang of Gang*, he stated:

> … motivation for writing is to get the book into the hands of gang members and inmates in the hope that it might prevent them from following in his footsteps
> (Valdemar, 2011, https://www.policemag.com).

Concluding Thoughts

Since the first erected prison in the United States, gangs have been a part of prison life. Prison gangs/STGs continue to plague U.S. prisons and jails. It is also likely that the prison gang/STG problem may be responsible for a majority of threats and assaults that occur within the prison walls. These threats and assaults have also been reported to stretch beyond the prison bars well into the community. As the correctional officials tackle this growing problem, there has been significant effort to establish standards and policies regarding prison gang control strategies.

Although data and precise figures regarding actual gang membership numbers, gang violence, and other forms of misconduct within prisons cannot be documented, the problem exists. Prison policy and structure are greatly impacted by the immediate threat prison gangs/

STGs impose on prisons and jails. Furthermore, there is evidence that family members, friends, and even prison personnel are responsible for contraband brought into prison facilities.

Gang recognition and suppression in correctional settings are important tools. Although reform and gang denouncement are a reality, prison gangs can and will be expected to expand in numbers, not only within institutions but into communities.

Discussion Points and Questions

1. Do you think that prison holds as much fear as a deterrent today for gang offenders as it did historically?
2. What impact do you think the importation or deprivation models have on the likelihood of an inmate joining a gang?
3. If in use today, do you think that the earlier prison models could prevent the formation of prison gangs? If so, how? If not, why?
4. If you were incarcerated, what would be your biggest fear? Would you join a gang for security or another reason?
5. Do you think that the denouncement examples provided are possible for all gang members or simply the exception?

Web Links

U.S. Department of Justice, Prison Gangs—overview of prison gangs in the U.S.
http://www.justice.gov/criminal-ocgs/gallery/prison-gangs

Prison Offenders—is a web-based prison research project that features penitentiary-related topics, a chronology of prison events, and detailed prison gang profiles.
www.prisonoffenders.com/prison_gangs.html

Gorilla Convict—is the home of recognized prison journalist and gangster chronicler, Seth "Soul Man" Ferranti, the Gorilla Convict Blog, and Gorilla Convict Publications
www.gorillaconvict.com/category/prison-gangs/

Florida Department of Corrections—overview of gangs and Security Threat Groups
https://web.archive.org/web/20170325005915/http://www.dc.state.fl.us/pub/gangs/index.html

National Geographic Channel—Hard Time, Prison Gangs
http://channel.nationalgeographic.com/hard-time/episodes/prison-gangs/

The Texas Department of Criminal Justice (Gang Renouncement and Disassociation (GRAD)
Process) https://www.tdcj.texas.gov/divisions/cid/stgmo_GRAD.html

REFERENCES

Allender, D. M., & Marcell, F. (2003). Career criminals, security threat groups, and prison gangs: An interrelated threat. *FBI Law Enforcement Bulletin, 72*(6), 8–12.

Austin, J. (2003). *Findings in prison classification and risk assessment.* Washington, DC: Department of Justice, National Institute of Corrections.

Austin, J., & McGinnis, K. (2004). *Classification of high-risk and special management prisoners: A national assessment of current practices.* Washington, DC: U.S. Department of Justice, National Institute of Corrections.

Biesecker, M. (2014). NC inmate charged with using cell phone to help orchestrate kidnapping of prosecutor's father. *Star Tribune.* Retrieved from http://www.startribune.com/nc-inmate-charged-in-kidnapping-of-da-s-father/254677581/#K8LBKzd4L2fSd5b3.97

Brown, W. K. (1977). Black female gangs in Philadelphia. *International Journal of Offender Therapy and Comparative Criminology, 21*(3), 221–228.

Bureau of Justice Statistics. (2015). *Prisoner series—The sentencing project.* Retrieved from http://sentencingproject.org/doc/publications/inc_Trends_in_Corrections_Fact_sheet.pdf

Byrne, J. M., & Hummer, D. (2007). In search of the "Tossed Salad Man" (and others involved in prison violence): New strategies for predicting and controlling violence in prison. *Aggression and Violent Behavior, 12*(5), 531–541.

California Department of Corrections and Rehabilitation. (2013, October). Security housing units: Fact sheet. Retrieved from https://www.cdcr.ca.gov/

Camp, G. M., & Camp, C. G. (1985). *Prison gangs: Their extent, nature, and impact on prisons.* South Salem, NY: Criminal Justice Institute.

Camp, S. D., Gaes, G. G., Langan, N. P., & Saylor, W. G. (2003). The influence of prisons on inmate misconduct: A multilevel investigation. *Justice Quarterly, 20*(3), 501–533.

Cao, L., Zhao, J., & Van Dine, S. (1997). Prison disciplinary tickets: A test of the deprivation and importation models. *Journal of Criminal Justice, 25*(2), 103–113.

Carlson, P. M. (2001). Prison interventions: Evolving strategies to control security threat groups. *Corrections Management Quarterly, 5*(1), 10–22.

Clements, C. B. (1996). Offender classification two decades of progress. *Criminal Justice and Behavior, 23*(1), 121–143.

Cunningham, M. D., & Sorensen, J. R. (2007). Predictive factors for violent misconduct in close custody. *The Prison Journal, 87*(2), 241–253.

Cunningham, M. D., Sorensen, J. R., Vigen, M. P., & Woods, S. O. (2011). Correlates and actuarial models of assaultive prison misconduct among violence-predicted capital offenders. *Criminal Justice and Behavior, 38*(1), 5–25.

Curry, G. D., & Decker, S. H. (2014). *Confronting gangs: Crime and community* (3rd ed.). Los Angeles, CA: Roxbury.

Danitz, T. (2001). *The gangs behind bars-prison gangs.* Washington, DC: National Criminal Justice Reference Service, Office of Justice Programs.

Decker, S. H. (2001). *From the street to the prison: Understanding and responding to gangs.* Indianapolis, IN: National Major Gang Task Force.

DeLisi, M. (2003). Criminal careers behind bars. *Behavioral Sciences & the Law, 21*(5), 653–669.

DeLisi, M., Berg, M. T., & Hochstetler, A. (2004). Gang members, career criminals and prison violence: Further specification of the importation model of inmate behavior. *Criminal Justice Studies, 17*(4), 369–383.

Dooley, B. D., Seals, A., & Skarbek, D. (2014). The effect of prison gang membership on recidivism. *Journal of Criminal Justice, 42*(3), 267–275.

Fleisher, M. S., & Decker, S. H. (2001). An overview of the challenge of prison gangs. *Corrections Management Quarterly, 5*(1), 1–9.

Fong, R. S., Vogel, R. E., & Buentello, S. (1995). Blood-in, blood-out: The rationale behind defecting from prison gangs. *Journal of Gang Research, 2*(4), 45–51.

Fraise v. Terhune, 283 F.3d 506, 509–510 (3d Cir. 2002).

Gaes, G. G., Wallace, S., Gilman, E., Klein-Saffran, J., & Suppa, S. (2002). The influence of prison gang affiliation on violence and other prison misconduct. *The Prison Journal, 82*(3), 359–385.

Gibbons, J. J., & Katzenbach, N. D. B. (2006). Confronting confinement: A report of the commission on safety and abuse in America's prisons. *Washington University Journal of Law & Policy, 22,* 385–562.

Griffin, M. (2007). Prison gang policy and recidivism: Short-term management benefits, long-term consequences. *Criminology & Public Policy, 6*(2), 223–230.

Griffin, M. L., & Hepburn, J. R. (2006). The effect of gang affiliation on violent misconduct among inmates during the early years of confinement. *Criminal Justice and Behavior, 33*(4), 419–466.

Hagedorn, J. M. (1990). Back in the field again: Gang research in the nineties. In C. R. Huff (Ed.), *Gangs in America* (pp. 240–259). Newbury Park, CA: SAGE.

Hill, C. (2009). Gangs/security threat groups. *Corrections Compendium, 34*(1), 23–37.

Hochstetler, A., & DeLisi, M. (2005). Importation, deprivation, and varieties of serving time: An integrated-lifestyle-exposure model of prison offending. *Journal of Criminal Justice, 33,* 257–266.

Holthouse, D. (2005). Intelligence report, leaders of racist prison gang Aryan Brotherhood face federal indictment. *Southern Poverty Law Center, 119.* Retrieved from http://

www.splcenter.org/get-informed/intelligence-report/browse-all-issues/2005/fall/smashing-the-shamrock

Hummer, D. (2009). Johnson v. California. In H. Greene & S. Gabbidon (Eds.), *Encyclopedia of race and crime* (pp. 414–416). Thousand Oaks, CA: SAGE.

Hutchinson, V. A., Keller, K. D., & Reid, T. (2009). *Inmate behavior management: The key to a safe and secure jail.* Washington, DC: U.S. Department of Justice, National Institute of Corrections.

Hyatt, J. M., & Barnes, G. C. (2017). An experimental evaluation of the impact of intensive supervision on the recidivism of high-risk probationers. *Crime & Delinquency, 63*(1), 3–38.

Irwin, J., & Cressey, D. R. (1962). Thieves, convicts and the inmate culture. *Social Problems, 10*(2), 142–155.

Jacobs, J. B. (1977). *Stateville: The penitentiary in mass society.* Chicago, IL: University of Chicago Press.

Jiang, S., & Fisher-Giorlando, M. (2002). Inmate misconduct: A test of the deprivation, importation, and situational models. *The Prison Journal, 82*(3), 335–358.

Johnson v. California. (2005), *543 U.S. 499.*

Jones, D., Roper, V., Stys, Y., & Wilson, C. (2004). *Street gangs: A review of theory, interventions, and implications for corrections.* Ottawa, Ontario: Research Branch Correctional Service Canada.

Kelley, M. B. (2014). America's 11 most powerful prison gangs. *Business Insider.* Retrieved from http://www.businessinsider.com/most-dangerous-prison-gangs-in-the-us-2014-2?op=1

Knox, G. W. (2000). A national assessment of gangs and security threat groups (STGs) in adult correctional institutions: Results of the 1999 adult corrections survey. *Journal of Gang Research, 7*, 1–45.

Knox, G. W. (2005). *The problem of gangs and security threat groups (STG's) in American prisons today: Recent research findings from the 2004 prison gang survey.* National Gang Crime Research Center. Retrieved from http://www.ngcrc.com/corr2006.html

Krienert, J. L., & Fleisher, M. S. (2001). Gang membership as a proxy for social deficiencies: A study of Nebraska inmates. *Corrections Management Quarterly, 3*(1), 47–58.

Lattimore, P. K., Visher, C. A., & Linster, R. L. (1995). Predicting rearrest for violence among serious youthful offenders. *Journal of Research in Crime and Delinquency, 32*(1), 54–83.

Lauderdale, M., & Burman, M. (2009). Contemporary patterns of female gangs in correctional settings. *Journal of Human Behavior in the Social Environment, 19*(3), 258–280.

Lyman, M. D. (1989). *Gangland: Drug trafficking by organized criminals.* Springfield, IL: Thomas.

Lyman, M. D. (2011). *Drugs in society: Causes, concepts and control.* Waltham, MA: Anderson Publishing, Elsevier.

MacDonald, J. M. (1999). Violence and drug use in juvenile institutions. *Journal of Criminal Justice, 27*, 33–44.

Marimow, A. E., & Hermann, P. (2013). How the Black Guerrilla Family gang took root in

Maryland's prisons. *The Washington Post.* Retrieved from http://www.washingtonpost.com/local/how-the-black-guerrilla-family-gang-took-root-in-marylands-prisons/2013/07/15/cc4a9d92-cee7-11e2-9f1a-1a7cdee20287_story.html?wprss=rss_homepage

Mather, K., & Kim, V. (2015). How a Mexican Mafia killer became a law enforcement darling. *LA Times.* Retrieved from http://www.latimes.com/local/crime/la-me-mexican-mafia-killer-20150215-story.html

Melde, C., & Esbensen, F. A. (2014). The relative impact of gang status transitions: Identifying the mechanisms of change in delinquency. *Journal of Research in Crime and Delinquency, 51*(3), 349–376.

Mendoza-Denton, N. (2014). *Homegirls: Language and cultural practice among Latina youth gangs.* New York, NY: John Wiley.

Miethe, T. D., & McCorkle, R. C. (1997). Gang membership and criminal processing: A test of the "master status" concept. *Justice Quarterly, 14*(3), 407–427.

Minnesota Department of Corrections. (2015). Retrieved from http://www.doc.state.mn.us/PAGES/

Moore, J. W., & Hagedorn, J. (2001). *Female gangs: A focus on research.* Washington, DC: US Department of Justice, Office of Justice Programs, Office of Juvenile Justice and Delinquency Prevention.

Morenoff, J. D., & Harding, D. J. (2014). Incarceration, prisoner reentry, and communities. *Annual Review of Sociology, 40*, 411–429.

National Gang Intelligence Center. (2011). *2011 national gang threat assessment report.* Washington, DC: Department of Justice.

National Gang Intelligence Center. (2013). *National gang report, 2013.* Washington, DC: Author.

National Institute of Corrections. (1992). *Jail classification system development: A review of the literature.* Washington, DC: U.S. Department of Justice. Retrieved from http://www.nicic.org/Library/010681

Orlando-Morningstar, D. (1997, October). Prison gangs. *Special Needs Offender Bulletin, 2,* 1–13.

Petersilia, J. (2000). When prisoners return to communities: Political, economic, and social consequences. *Federal Probation, 65*(3), 1–8.

Petersilia, J. (2001). Prisoner reentry: Public safety and reintegration challenges. *The Prison Journal, 81*(3), 360–375.

Pyrooz, D. C. (2014). "From your first cigarette to your last dyin' day": The patterning of gang membership in the life-course. *Journal of Quantitative Criminology, 30*(2), 349–372.

Pyrooz, D. C., & Mitchell, M. M. (2018). The hardest times: Gang members in total institutions. In N. Frost & B. Huebner (Eds.), *Handbook on the Consequences of Sentencing and Punishment Decisions.* American Society of Criminology (pp. 361-378). New York, NY: Routledge.

Pyrooz, D. C., & Sweeten, G. (2015). Gang membership between ages 5 and 17 years in the United States. *Journal of Adolescent Health, 56*(4), 414–419.

Pyrooz, D., Decker, S., & Fleisher, M. (2011). From the street to the prison, from the prison to the street: Understanding and responding to prison gangs. *Journal of Aggression, Conflict and Peace Research, 3*(1), 12–24.

Quicker, J. C. (1983). *Homegirls: Characterizing Chicana gangs.* Madison, CT: International Universities Press.

Ralph, P. H., & Marquart, J. W. (1991). Gang violence in Texas prisons. *The Prison Journal, 71*(2), 38–49.

Roth, M. G., & Skarbek, D. (2014). Prison gangs and the community responsibility system. *Review of Behavioral Economics, 1*(3), 223–243.

Ruddell, R., Decker, S. H., & Egley, A. (2006). Gang interventions in jails: A national analysis. *Criminal Justice Review, 31*(1), 33–46.

Shelden, R. G. (1991). A comparison of gang members and non-gang members in a prison setting. *The Prison Journal, 71*(2), 50–60.

Skarbek, D. (2014). *The social order of the underworld: How prison gangs govern the American penal system.* New York, NY: Oxford University Press.

Stastny, C., & Tyrnauer, G. (1983). *Who rules the joint? The changing political culture of maximum-security prisons in America.* New York, NY: Lexington Books.

Steward, T. (2014). Feds order cell phone access for cons in halfway houses. *Watchdog.* Retrieved from https://www.sayanythingblog.com/entry/feds-order-cell-phone-access-for-cons-in-halfway-houses/

Sturgeon, W. (2009a, April 27). *The evolution of "Security Threat Groups" into the twenty-first century—Part I.* Retrieved from http://www.corrections.com/articles/21102-the-evolution-of-security-threat-groups-into-the-twenty-first-century-part-i

Sturgeon, W. (2009b, August 31). *The evolution of "Security Threat Groups" into the twenty-first century—Part II.* Retrieved from http://www.corrections.com/news/article/22129

Sutton, T. E. (2017). The lives of female gang members: A review of the literature. *Aggression and Violent Behavior, 37,* 142–152.

Sykes, G. M. (1958). *The society of captives: A study of a maximum security prison.* Princeton, NJ: Princeton University Press.

Tapia, M. (2010). Untangling race and class effects on juvenile arrests. *Journal of Criminal Justice, 38*(3), 255–265.

Thomas, C. W. (1977). Theoretical perspectives on prisonization: A comparison of the importation and deprivation models. *Journal of Criminal Law & Criminology, 68*(1), 135–145.

Thomas, C. W., & Foster, S. C. (1973). The importation model perspective on inmate social roles: An empirical test. *The Sociological Quarterly, 14*(2), 226–234.

Trammell, R. (2009). Values, rules, and keeping the peace: How men describe order and the inmate code in California prisons. *Deviant Behavior, 30*(8), 746–771.

Trulson, C. R., Marquart, J. W., & Kawucha, S. K. (2006). Gang suppression and institutional control. *Corrections Today, 68*(2), 26–28, 30–31.

U.S. Department of Justice. (2008, April). National Drug Intelligence Center. Attorney General's Report to Congress on the Growth of Violent Street Gangs in Suburban Areas. Retrieved from http://www.justice.gov/archive/ndic/pubs27/27612/estimate.htm

Valdemar, R. (2011). The best argument against the death penalty. *Police Magazine.* Retrieved from https://www.policemag.com/373868/the-best-argument-against-the-death-penalty

Valdemar, R. (2013). How one gang corrupted 13 Baltimore COs. A federal indictment reveals how a gang corrupts corrections officers. *Police: The Law Enforcement Magazine.* Retrieved from http://www.policemag.com/blog/gangs/story/2013/05/prison-gangs-run-the-prison-system.aspx

Wells, J. B., Minor, K. I., Angel, E., Carter, L., & Cox, M. (2002). *A study of gangs and security threat groups in America's adult prisons and jails.* Indianapolis, IN: National Major Gang Task Force.

West, H. C., & Sabol, W. J. (2009). Prison inmates at midyear 2008—Statistical tables. *Bureau of Justice Statistics.* Washington, DC: U.S. Department of Justice.

Wilkinson, R. A., & Delgado, A. (2006). Prison gang and drug investigations: An Ohio approach. *Corrections Today, 68*(2), 36.

Winterdyk, J., & Ruddell, R. (2010). Managing prison gangs: Results from a survey of US prison systems. *Journal of Criminal Justice, 38*(4), 730–736.

Wood, J., Moir, A., & James, M. (2009). Prisoners' gang-related activity: The importance of bullying and moral disengagement. *Psychology, Crime & Law, 15*(6), 569–581.

Wood, J. L., Alleyne, E., Mozova, K., & James, M. (2014). Predicting involvement in prison gang activity: Street gang membership, social and psychological factors. *Law & Human Behavior, 38*(3), 203-11. doi:10.1037/lhb0000053.

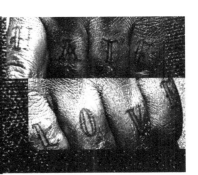

Chapter 9

Entrepreneurship, Finances, and Gangs

CHAPTER OBJECTIVES

- Describe the various income sources of gangs

- Associate types of "business" activities with specific gangs

- Examine examples of criminal business involvement

- Explore money laundering

In September 2017, "Operation Lights Out" led to the Jersey Shore arrest of 29 alleged gang members of G-Shine, a Long Branch-based faction of the Bloods street gang. Weekly, G-Shine members reportedly distributed about 150 to 200 grams of powder and crack cocaine—with an estimated street value of $225,000—and about 250 packets of heroin—with an estimated street value of $22,500.

In March 2017, nine members of the Trinitarios, a notorious Dominican street gang, were indicted for operating a major drug operation in Paterson, New Jersey leading to the seizure of cocaine with a street value of $300,000, suspected drug proceeds of $76,000, three handguns, heroin, and 82 pills containing fentanyl.

Source: Drug Enforcement Administration. National Drug Threat Assessment, 2018, p.108

Introduction

It is relatively straightforward to evaluate the financial results of a public company and determine profitability. Businesses use accounting rules that govern the presentation of financial statements, and financial statements are readily available for examination. In contrast, scholars only learn about the "business" side of gangs based on information gleaned from arrest records (see above narratives) and court proceedings. It is a difficult process comprised of estimations. What we know for sure is that gangs make their money through several nefarious activities including drug trafficking, human trafficking, extortion, financial crime, cybercrime, and various other profit-making activities that may come their way.

Gangs vary in their organizational structure. While some gangs are well organized with a leader and governing board at the top, others are comprised of subunits that function independently. In some situations, a percentage of cash earned through illegal business activities is transferred to the leadership, while in other cases the cash is pocketed by gang members.

In the business world, companies often merge or combine for the purpose of increasing profits. Likewise, gangs permanently or temporarily join efforts and become what Quijas (2015) refers to as "super gangs". Quijas (2015) notes that "MS-13, Hezbollah, Latin American cartels, the Mafia, outlaw motorcycle gangs, and even the IRA are all groups with varied and divergent interests and philosophies, yet they are clearly willing to work together with other criminal gangs to capitalize on—and profit from—each other's particular skills and assets."

Money Laundering

Money laundering is in itself a crime and involves taking money obtained from criminal activities and running it through numerous financial transactions to make the money appear to be from a legitimate business activity. In other words, "dirty" money is made to appear "clean."

Avoidance strategies are uncomplicated methods used by gangs to launder money. Because businesses are legally required to report any cash transactions greater than or equal to $10,000 to the Internal Revenue Service, gang members may fly under the radar by engaging in cash transactions valued under this threshold (Camacho, 2018). For example, if a gang member uses up to $9,999 in dirty cash to purchase a car from a used car dealer, the dealer does not have to report the cash transaction to the Internal Revenue Service. Similarly, a gang member may use dirty money to pay for his daily living expenses.

In contrast, sophisticated gangs use more complicated methods to money launder. For example, Puerta (2018) cites several methods used by MS-13 to launder money in El Salvador:

- The gang may steal an automobile, typically from the United States, Mexico, or Honduras, and then resell it. Cash acquired from the sale appears legitimate.
- Sometimes MS-13 uses companies to launder money. The gang would assert that a portion of the gang's illegal earnings was legally earned by a legitimate business and is therefore legitimate.
- Extorted businesses may be used to money launder. The gang may "acquire" product which would be sold through the extorted business. The gang would then demand a

portion of profit, sometimes reaching up to 70% of the total profit made. The intention is for this share of profit to appear legitimate.

- The gang may launder money by purchasing property. When they resell the property, the resale is meant to seem legitimate.

- Loan sharking is also used by the MS-13 to launder money. Interest charged on loans would appear to be legitimately earned.

- Finally, the gang sometimes launders by depositing small amounts of cash into a bank, demanding that victims electronically transfer money, or through Western Union.

Drug Trafficking

So, how do drugs enter the United States in the first place? According to the Drug Enforcement Administration's 2018 National Drug Threat Assessment report, it states that Transnational Criminal Organizations (TCOs) are typically responsible for the smuggling of drugs into the United States. Mexican TCOs, including the Sinaloa Cartel and Jalisco New Generation Cartel, have the greatest drug trafficking impact in the United States, bringing "significant quantities of heroin, cocaine, methamphetamine, marijuana, and fentanyl into the United States annually" (DEA, 2018, p. 97).

However, Mexican TCOs are not the only parties involved. Columbian TCOs supply Mexican TCOs with cocaine, which in turn enters the United States. Dominican TCOs act as the dominant middle-man for the Northeastern U.S., receiving shipments of cocaine and heroin, from Mexico, Colombia, Venezuela, and the Dominican Republic. Asian TCOs traffic MDMA from Canada into the United States. Once the drugs are in the United States, national and neighborhood-based street gangs as well as prison gangs act as retailers distributing the drugs. The gangs are profit oriented; they typically will work with whichever cartel offers them the best deal (DEA, 2018).

In the past, various MS-13 cliques have attempted to expand their business into the international drug trafficking market. Although these past attempts proved to be on a small scale, it is possible that some small cliques of MS-13 gang members are currently associated or work with international traffickers. Will MS-13 be a critical force in the international drug trafficking market anytime soon? It is important to consider that MS-13 consists of local cells respecting their local leadership. There is no single leader who commands the entire MS-13. "…the same organizational qualities that make the gang a formidable criminal structure — independent cells that respond as much or more to their local leadership, and that can quickly reproduce — are what inhibit it from developing into a sophisticated criminal organization capable of creating a vertically integrated drug trafficking organization" (Dudley & Ávalos, 2018). Consequently, MS-13 is far from transforming into a drug cartel.

Street-level drug trafficking is the business venture of choice for gangs. Neighborhood-based gangs conduct "business" in their respective neighborhood. Although they often fight over lucrative geographic areas, neighborhood-based gangs sometimes collaborate and form "hybrid" gangs. National-level gangs are more structured and operate in multiple areas of the country, often cooperating with one another to maximize profit for the entire gang. For example, the Latin Kings based in Texas will work with their counterparts based in Chicago (DEA, 2018).

In Chicago, several street gangs are involved in drug trafficking including Gangster Disciples, Black Disciples, Black P Stone Nation, Vice Lords, and Latin Kings. The street gangs typically are active in the "primary mid-level" and "retail-level" phase of the drug distribution process (U.S. Drug Enforcement Administration, 2017). The case below provides information related to the drug activities of the Traveling Vice Lords (TVL):

> On June 24, 2015, agents from DEA Chicago—with assistance from the Federal Bureau of Investigation (FBI), the Bureau of Alcohol, Tobacco, and Firearms, the Internal Revenue Service, and CPD—arrested 47 individuals associated with the TVL gang. The TVL controls heroin and cocaine sales at several locations on the West Side of Chicago; one of which is believed to be the largest open-air heroin market in the city, which intelligence indicates generates $2.5 million USC per year in revenue on its own. This particular distribution cell of the gang has been linked to individuals in Reynosa, Mexico, who are affiliated with members of the Gulf Cartel. In Chicago, the TVL has been involved in several shootings at and near corners controlled by the gang. These shootings are believed to be related to the fight between gangs for control of the heroin sales. Overall, this 11-month investigation resulted in the arrest of 47 individuals and the seizure of 3 kilograms of heroin, 850 grams of cocaine, $193,153 USC, 5 firearms (including 3 assault rifles), 2 luxury vehicles, and jewelry valued at $119,000. (U.S. Drug Enforcement Administration, 2017, p. 8)

Prison gangs operate in public and private correctional facilities. From prison, gang members orchestrate outside drug deals and the smuggling of drugs into prison. They also engage in the lucrative business of distributing drugs in prison (National Drug Threat Assessment, 2018). Drugs are the number one contraband item found in prisons including marijuana, synthetic cannabinoids, Suboxone, heroin, and methanphetamines. Accordingly, drugs are the number one source of income for prison gangs (Federal Bureau of Investigation [FBI], 2015). Below is an example of street and prison gang collaboration:

> In February 2018, prison gang leaders—including two inmates already serving time at Pelican Bay State Prison in California—and members of Varrio Bosque Norteño, a Norteño-affiliated street gang ... were indicted for participation in a massive street and prison-gang conspiracy that distributed methamphetamine, cocaine, and heroin using social media. The prison gang leaders used cell phones smuggled into the prisons to coordinate their activities, and

the subjects used multiple popular social media platforms to sell the drugs. The conspiracy involved suspects located in Northern California, Pennsylvania, and Oregon. Items seized in the investigation included 34 weapons, more than $71,000 in USC, several hundred pounds of marijuana, and 52 empty bottles of codeine syrup. (DEA, 2018, p. 110)

Outlaw motorcycle gangs (OMG) are violent, sophisticated, and territorial, and are also involved in the drug trade. Below is a narrative depicting the "work" of the Mongols OMG.

In January 2018, 12 members and associates of the Clarksville Chapter of the Mongols OMG were indicted in Tennessee on criminal charges including murder, attempted murder, assault, kidnapping, robbery, extortion, witness tampering, money laundering, interstate travel in aid of racketeering, and large-scale drug trafficking. The subjects traveled to California and transported an aggregate total of at least 50 pounds of methamphetamine back for distribution in Tennessee and Kentucky and delivered approximately $300,000 in USC to a member of the Mongols California Harbor Chapter. In March 2018, 19 members of the Clarksville Mongols were charged in a second, superseding indictment. (DEA, 2018, p. 111)

Prescription drug abuse has become a major health and criminal justice problem in the United States. Specifically, the misuse of opioids, CNS depressants (sedatives, tranquilizers, and hypnotics), and stimulants are devastating lives. According to the 2017 National Survey on Drug Use and Health, 18 million people from the United States have misused prescription drugs once or more in the past year. Furthermore, the survey found that "2 million Americans misused prescription pain relievers for the first time within the past year, which averages to approximately 5,480 initiates per day. Additionally, more than one million misused prescription stimulants, 1.5 million misused tranquilizers, and 271,000 misused sedatives for the first time" (National Institute on Drug Abuse, 2018).

Cognizant of the demand for opioids and other prescription drugs, gangs are attempting to help satisfy demand by robbing or burglarizing pharmacies. The increased demand for these pharmaceuticals has resulted in higher street prices, thereby making it lucrative to steal the drugs and resell (2018 National Drug Threat Assessment). The narrative below describes the burglary of a pharmacy located in Indiana:

In June 2017, a member of the 5th Ward Circle gang was charged with burglary and conspiracy to deal in oxycodone after burglarizing a Walgreens in Indiana. The gang member later attempted to mail 240 stolen tablets of 80 milligram oxycodone and pay for the shipment with counterfeit currency. The 5th Ward Circle gang was previously implicated in pharmacy burglaries in states throughout the country including Texas, Kansas, Virginia, Ohio, and Minnesota. One of the three subjects arrested along with the 5th Ward Circle member was a Black Disciples gang member. (DEA, 2018, p. 114)

Aside from robbing pharmacies to acquire prescription drugs, gangs have become involved with "pill mills". Pill mills are criminal undertakings involving a doctor, clinic, and/or pharmacy that dispenses or prescribes prescription drugs for nonmedical reasons. Conspirators are interested in profits as opposed to patient health. In the case below, the Pagans realized the potential profits associated with a pill mill:

> On July 14, 2015, a grand jury in Philadelphia charged Mitchell, along with William O'Brien, a former doctor of osteopathic medicine, and eight codefendants with conspiring to distribute controlled substances. Mitchell was a member of the Pagans Motorcycle Club ("Pagans"), an outlaw biker gang known for violence and drug dealing. O'Brien worked together with Pagans, and their associates, to operate a "pill mill" out of his medical offices. O'Brien wrote fraudulent prescriptions for oxycodone and other drugs, while the Pagans and their associates recruited "pseudo-patients" to buy the fraudulent prescriptions. O'Brien charged $250 cash for the first appointment to obtain prescriptions for controlled substances and $200 cash for each subsequent visit. Oxycodone (30 mg) was in high demand by drug dealers who could sell each pill on the street for $25 to $30. O'Brien sold prescriptions for these dangerous and addictive drugs to hundreds of "pseudo-patients." After filling the prescriptions, the Pagans and their associates resold the pills on the street. The investigation showed that from March 2012 to January 2015, more than 700,000 pills containing oxycodone and other Schedule II controlled substances were distributed by members of the conspiracy. (U.S. Department of Justice, 2016)

Human Trafficking

The U.S. Government defines human trafficking as:

- Sex trafficking in which a commercial sex act is induced by force, fraud, or coercion, or in which the person induced to perform such act has not attained 18 years of age
- The recruitment, harboring, transportation, provision, or obtaining of a person for labor or services, through the use of force, fraud, or coercion for the purpose of subjection to involuntary servitude, peonage, debt bondage, or slavery (National Institute of Justice, 2019).

According to the 2015 National Gang Report (FBI, 2015), 15% of respondent jurisdictions reported gangs engaged in human trafficking. This estimate may very well be somewhat higher given that oftentimes the crime is unreported by fearful and/or shameful victims. In addition, what constitutes sex trafficking may have been mistakenly reported as prostitution. (When victims are under eighteen, prostitution legally constitutes sex trafficking.) In addition, the 2015 National Gang Report states that "gangs in approximately one-third of jurisdictions have moderate-to-high involvement in prostitution" (p. 38). The Report also indicates that gangs involved with human trafficking and prostitution are collaborating in victim exchange and relocation efforts. These efforts increase profits as they result in a changing variety of victims to sexually exploit, thereby keeping customers happy. In addition, gangs are collaborating to increase operational efficiency. For example, in San Diego, the BMS gang was formed:

> According to the federal grand jury indictment, the primary business of the gang was sex trafficking in 46 cities across 23 states. The organization was known as "BMS," which is a combination of "Black MOB" and "Skanless" gangs, and these members are also allegedly aligned with other streets gangs, including Neighborhood Crips, Lincoln Park, and West Coast Crips, among others.
>
> The BMS gang was formed as a result of cooperation between these gangs, and the members took on different responsibilities within the criminal enterprise, according to the indictment. Some managed the prostitutes and transported them all over the country; some forcefully coerced these women into prostitution and maintained their obedience and loyalty through acts of violence; some handled the money; some placed advertisements to generate business or booked motel rooms in which acts of prostitution took place; and others distributed drugs. (FBI, 2014)

Women gang members may also victimize other women. In 2019, a Pennsylvania woman, Jordan Capone, pled guilty to sex trafficking charges:

> The United States Attorney's Office for the Middle District of Pennsylvania announced that Jordan Capone, age 24, of Mt. Pocono, pleaded guilty before U.S. District Court Judge Malachy E. Mannion, to participating in a sex trafficking conspiracy that involved using threats and coercion to force women to engage in prostitution in the Monroe County area between 2011 and 2014. Capone also pleaded guilty to possession with intent to distribute the drug "molly," a form of MDMA. (U.S. Attorney's Office Middle District of Pennsylvania, 2019).

According to United States Attorney David J. Freed, Capone admitted to being a member of the Black P-Stones, a street gang that engaged in sex trafficking and drug trafficking in the Stroudsburg area and the state of Maine. Members of the conspiracy advertised prostitutes on websites, transported the prostitutes, and rented hotel and motel rooms for the purpose of having the women engage in commercial sex acts with customers:

> The prostitutes were threatened, physically assaulted, and provided drugs, including heroin, by members of the conspiracy to persuade them to engage or continue to engage in prostitution. Virtually all of the money earned by the prostitutes was turned over to the gang leaders, and the prostitutes were compensated with illegal drugs. (U.S. Department of Justice, 2019)

A groundbreaking study was conducted by Carpenter & Gates (2016) that focused on gangs and sex trafficking in San Diego. The study concluded that over 110 gangs are involved in the sex trade in San Diego. In addition, gang members comprised approximately 85% of sex-trafficking facilitators. It was estimated that facilitators of the sex trade make an average of $670,625 annually, assuming the facilitator nets 75% of total revenue. The study describes different relationships between gangs and facilitators:

> Relationships range from individuals selling sex on the side (with no involvement from – or profit to – their gang), small cliques of members (in some cases collaborating with other groups or individuals outside of gang), to significant proportion of members involved & the group or at least group leaders profit. In some cases, individuals not involved in gangs reported that they have working relationships with gangs or gang members (p. 12).

Carpenter and Gates (2016) broke the facilitator/gang relationships into two categories: **directed** ("individual activities dictated by, and directly profiting, a gang") and **undirected** ("individual activities not dictated by, and directly profiting, a gang"). The study found that in San Diego pimping, "was almost evenly split between directed and undirected facilitation." (p. 12).

Extortion

Extortion is obtaining money, property, or services from a victim as a result of force or a threat. Extortion is MS-13's main source of income (Puerta, 2017). MS-13 uses violence as their basis for extortion. In the U.S., they extort money from the families of prostitution victims and also from residents for the protection of specific neighborhoods (Fox Business, 2017). In Los Angeles, the gang extorts illegal immigrants involved in dealing drugs and running underground nightclubs, while on the less lucrative East Coast, MS-13 targets illegal immigrants owning small stores and restaurants (InsightCrime, 2018). In addition, MS-13 also conducts extortion activities in U.S. jails. As an example, at the Prince George Jail in Virginia, MS-13 controls the Hispanic population, forcing them to pay "rent." Prisoners at the Fairfax County Jail are also extorted by MS-13 and another gang—the 43 Mob (Miller, 2018).

In California, Mexican Mafia members and their street gang associates were arrested for extorting prisoners in Los Angeles jails as well as extorting other Latino street gangs. Known as Operation Dirty Thirds by the FBI, the case involved:

> Gang members smuggling drugs into the jails, controlling and taxing the sales of methamphetamine, heroin, cocaine and cannibis, extorting inmates and laundering their profits.

> One-third of all drugs smuggled into the jails had to be turned over to a Mexican Mafia member or his shot-caller in each facility and if the gang member decided to sell his "thirds," all other inmates hold to hold off their sales.

> All Latino inmates had to give the gang a percentage of what they spent on food and hygiene items in the canteen. The gang then sold this "kitty" to inmates for additional income.

> The Mexican Mafia also used assault and fines to discipline inmates that violated its rules" (Meers, 2018).

At least four local gangs participated in the Mexican Mafia's "drug smuggling and assault network" including: the 12th Street Sharkies, Cherryville, Ghetto Family, and Pomona Sur. Furthermore, an attorney representing the Mexican Mafia, under the guise of attorney-client privilege, allegedly served as a messenger between prisoners and gang members on the outside. The attorney was charged with facilitating a scheme to extort $100,000 from the Mongols OMG (Cain, 2018).

Another example of this kind of behavior is in El Salvador where MS-13 runs extortion rackets throughout the country. The government looks the other way and in some instances even asks MS-13's permission to hold a community event. Barrio 18, a rival gang, also depends on extortion to make cash. It is estimated that gangs in El Salvador extort about $20 million annually. In addition, gangs have seized control of legitimate businesses thereby making money from the business (Whelan, 2018). Life in El Salvador can be terrifying:

> José Gualberto Claro Iglesias, a 48-year-old trucker from Suchitoto, a former Spanish colonial town in central El Salvador, sent his wife and four children to Los Angeles in 2015, after the family narrowly survived an attack by MS-13 members. The gang set fire to his pickup truck while Mr. Claro and his family were inside because he had refused to make extortion payments. (Whelan, 2018)

Financial Crimes

The 2015 National Gang Report indicates that street gangs continue to commit financial crimes including "identity theft, credit card fraud, prescription drug fraud, counterfeiting, check fraud, fencing stolen goods, money laundering, mortgage fraud, social security fraud, and tax fraud" (FBI, 2015). The aforementioned crimes represent a relatively easy method of making money. Also, contributing to the appeal of financial crimes is that if the perpetrator is caught, sentencing guidelines seem to be lenient compared to crimes associated with traditional gang activity.

New York officials have noticed that gangs are becoming increasingly involved with financial crimes. In 2012, officials started spotting the occasional gang member possessing a counterfeit credit card. By 2014, gang members involved in credit card schemes and other financial crimes became more prevalent. Although financial crimes are not typically violent, gangs may use the proceeds of financial crime to purchase guns and finance violent activities (Ramey & West, 2017).

Here are some examples of gangs involved in financial crimes:

- In California, over 30 street gang members and associates of the BullyBoys and the CoCo Boys were charged with over $1 million in credit card fraud. Gang members allegedly stole credit card terminals from medical and dental offices and used the terminals to process fake returns which were downloaded to debit cards. Gang members would then spend the funds on the debit card (Wu, 2018).

- In New York, members and associates of the Van Dyke Money Gang were indicted for a bank fraud scheme involving over 350 customer accounts and costing banks over $1.5 million. Allegedly, gang members obtained blank Postal Money Orders and Western Union Money Orders and printed dollar amounts on the money orders. They recruited bank account holders and deposited the money orders into the recruit's accounts. Finally, a gang member or associate would withdraw the money from the account (U.S. Department of Justice, 2015).

- Also in New York, 30 gang members (mostly from the Bloods) were indicted for a $1 million counterfeit check scam. Gang members recruited bank employees to take pictures of customer's checks. The gang used the information from the photographed checks to print counterfeit checks. College and high school students were recruited via social media to deposit the counterfeit checks into their bank account and the students were promised a share of the cash. Gang members withdrew money before the counterfeit check had a chance to be rejected by the bank. The account holders were instructed by the gang to report that their bank information was stolen (Kanno-Youngs, 2017).

- In Detroit, 8 members and associates of the Free Band Gang were indicted on 23 counts including "conspiracy to commit wire fraud, conspiracy to commit money laundering, and aggravated identity theft." The fraud ring obtained stolen credit card numbers from the internet and other sources. Gang members would create new credit cards using the stolen account numbers and use the fraudulent cards to purchase $500 Walmart gift cards. Allegedly, the gang often purchased over $100,000 in gift cards in a single day (U.S. Department of Justice, 2018b).

- Also in Detroit, Million-Dollar Man, Charles Mason, and his gang, stole over 3,000 personal credit card accounts. The gang made a boatload of money and started to boast about this on social media, which incited the wrath of rival gangs. Consequently, violence, including gunfire, broke out (Dietz, 2018).

- The FBI is currently investigating an organized burglary and identity theft ring known as the "Felony Lane Gang." The gang targets vehicles parked in "gyms, fitness centers, daycare facilities, and recreation areas where women would be more likely to leave their purses in their vehicles." Gang members break into a car and steal a victim's purses and then utilize the contents to steal a victim's identity. Typically, female drug addicts and prostitutes are recruited to impersonate victims and make large withdrawals from victim's accounts. They do so from the outer drive-thru lane of a bank. This lane is referred to as the "felony lane"—as in "Felony Lane Gang" (FBI, 2018).

- Reports of possible Felony Lane Gang activity have been reported in Chester County, Pennsylvania (WPVI, 2018). In addition, Indiana State Police arrested three women members of the Felony Street Gang because of several outstanding felony warrants issued in Georgia. Troopers stopped and searched the vehicle, and found a substantial number of stolen credit cards, check books, social security cards and identification cards. Allegedly, the suspects taunted police via social media saying 'do ya job (expletive)' (Fedschun, 2019).

Cybercrime

The internet facilitates knowledge and communication on a global scale, providing an excellent tool employed by students, professors, businesses, law enforcement, and more. Unfortunately, the internet is also utilized by criminals for the perpetration of crime. Cybercrime is crime committed using a computer and the internet.

The Dark Overlord is a cybercrime gang that hacks into databases, steals information, and then threatens to leak the information if a ransom is not paid. The group claimed to have hacked several insurance companies and legal firms and threatens to leak sensitive documents related to the 9/11 attacks. Victim insurance companies and legal firms must pay the Dark Overload if they do not want their organization's documents released (O'Flaherty, 2019).

One way for the Dark Overlord gang to recruit members is to post help wanted ads on the dark web.

> "Do YOU want to get Rich? Come work for us!," The Dark Overlord wrote in a November 14, 2018, thread on KickAss Forum, a cybercriminal marketplace on the dark web that charges for entry. Job requirements included experience with Windows, Linux as well as expertise in Unix-based design and network management and penetration testing. New employees would be paid 50,000 pounds ($63,500) monthly, plus add-ons and a likely pay bump up to 70,000 pounds ($89,000) monthly after two years. (Stone, 2019)

To the right people, that salary could look very enticing. Also, note that the salary mentioned in the above ad is monthly. Annually, the salary would be $762,000 plus.

Another cybercrime gang, Cobolt, also known as the Carbanak gang, has conducted over 100 hacking operations in 40 different countries. It is estimated that Cobalt made in excess of $1.24 billion and that individual attacks bring in as much as $12.4 million. The gang developed its own malware to attack victim computers: Anunak, Carbanak, and custom malware. Operations start with an email that is sent from what appears to be a "friendly" sender to victim organizations. The recipient of the email is asked to click on a link that contains malware that infiltrates the victim's computers. Once in, hackers steal money in one of three ways:

- Programming ATM's to release cash on a particular date and at a specific time—money mules would be sent to the ATM's for the cash pick-up.
- Transferring cash from legitimate accounts to accounts that Cobalt controls—money mules would drain accounts in next to no time.
- Inflating Cobalt-controlled accounts—money mules would drain accounts in next to no time (Cimpanu, 2018a).

Even though the gang leader was arrested in 2018, it appears that Cobalt is continuing "business" and has begun a new venture targeting financial organizations in Russia and other former Soviet states (Cimpanu, 2018b).

Retired Sgt. Richard Valdemar from the Los Angeles County Sheriff's Department with over 33 years of experience combating the gang problem, said it best when discussing the business of gangs:

> Gangs can be very enterprising. They will find a product or service that people want. Then some intelligent gang member will figure out a way to provide that product or service, no matter what law he must break to provide it. And a new enterprise will be born. Other competing gangs will imitate this system. They will war with each other, and the strongest and smartest gang will become dominant in the area. The organization will then seek to expand. They will follow the path of least resistance and establish outposts in the frontier area. And the cycle will repeat itself (Valdemar, 2007).

Concluding Thoughts

Gangs can be very enterprising. While they are destructive for communities, they also find products or services that people want such as drugs, weapons or women. With some ingenuity and cleverness, a street gang is able to make money off their venture and thus the enterprise is flourishes. Some gangs will compete and imitate the business, but only those with the best resources and wit can dominate the enterprise. As an organization seeks to expand, gangs will typically follow the path of least resistance, establish necessary contacts, and expand the business.

Like any legitimate company, gangs must identify a demand for a product or service, and then find a cost-effective way to satisfy that demand. Whereas most businesses operate within the law, gang business is nefarious. The dominant product for street and prison gangs are illegal drugs. There is a demand for drugs, and the trade is profitable. As a result, drug abuse is a serious problem plaguing our country as it devastates families and challenges the very core of our healthcare and criminal justice systems.

Like businesses, gangs compete for lucrative positioning and eventual expansion. Unlike in business, when gangs compete for positioning, it is often violent. Gang members and innocent bystanders are injured, or worst yet killed. Neighborhood families live in fear and are afraid to leave their homes.

Although we do not know the exact amount of money that gangs make, we can formulate estimates based on arrest and court records. We know that gangs get their money through drug trafficking, human trafficking, extortion, financial crime, cybercrime, and more. The internet is thriving with accounts of a gang's profit-making activities. Gangs are profit driven. Rival gangs will even work together for the sake of maximizing profits.

What does the future hold for the profit-making activities of gangs? Perhaps more gangs will succumb to the appeal of financial crimes—high payout and less risk. Rather than sell drugs, they will opt to steal identities. In fact, gangs may move away from the high risk commodities that attract law enforcement officials and instead have diversified their portfolio by engaging in legal economies. Currently, the Mexican drug cartels are in the market for avocados and other agricultural goods, including the wood and timber industry. These are valuable commodities because of all the money that is made on importing avocados to the U.S. and the rest of the world and the best part is it is legal (O'Dowd & Hagan, 2020).

Technology has also created many new money-making opportunities. The Dark Web provides criminals the opportunity to sell drugs, sex, guns, exotic animals, art, antiquities, and other collectables. The Tor Project, a 501(c)(3) US nonprofit organization, markets a browser advertised on their website to allow customers to:

- Browse privately.
- Explore freely.
- Defend yourself against tracking and surveillance.
- Circumvent censorship. (see https://www.torproject.org/)

Thus, the Tor browser allows criminals to transact anonymously, further complicating the efforts of law enforcement. According to former Tor executive director Andrew Lewman, "the criminal use of Tor has become overwhelming. I think 95 percent of what we see on the onion sites and other dark net sites is just criminal activity. It varies in severity from copyright piracy to drug markets to horrendous trafficking of humans and exploitation of women and children" (O'Neill, 2017). The expansion of the internet, specifically the Dark Web, has taken some gangs off the streets and into cyberspace where the money is lucrative and anonymity is critical to their success.

Discussion Points and Questions

1. Which money making activity of gangs concerns you the most? Why?
2. Define money laundering. Describe different methods of money laundering.
3. Why does making money via the commission of financial crime appeal to some gangs?
4. What is the impact of the internet on gangs and how they make money?
5. How can gangs prosper in legal economies such as avocados, but still wreak havoc on an industry (or the farmers)?

Web Links

2019 National Drug Threat Assessment Report:
https://www.dea.gov/sites/default/files/2020-01/2019-NDTA-final-01-14-2020_Low_Web-DIR-007-20_2019.pdf

Federal Trade Commission—federal agency that provides information that will protect you from being a victim of identity theft and other consumer scams.
https://www.consumer.ftc.gov/

National Institute on Drug Abuse:
https://www.drugabuse.gov/

REFERENCES

Cain, J. (2018, May 24). Dozens of Los Angeles-area gang members arrested in major FBI raid targeting Mexican Mafia. *Daily News*. Retrieved from https://www.dailynews.com/2018/05/23/fbi-raids-target-mexican-mafia-gang-in-los-angeles-county/

Camacho, P. (2018). *Whales, sharks and flounders: Conceptualizing real-world money laundering.* Retrieved from https://www.acamstoday.org/whales-sharks-and-flounders-conceptualizing-real-world-money-laundering/

Carpenter, A. C., & Gates, J. (2016). *The nature and extent of gang involvement in sex trafficking in San Diego County.* Retrieved from https://www.ncjrs.gov/pdffiles1/nij/grants/249857.pdf

Cimpanu, C. (2018a, March 26). *Leader of Carbanak (Cobalt) hacker group who stole over €1bil arrested in Spain.* Retrieved from https://www.bleepingcomputer.com/news/security/leader-of-carbanak-cobalt-hacker-group-who-stole-over-1bil-arrested-in-spain/

Cimpanu, C. (2018b, May 28). *Cobalt hacking group still active despite leader's arrest.* Retrieved from https://www.bleepingcomputer.com/news/security/cobalt-hacking-group-still-active-despite-leaders-arrest/

Dietz, K. (2018). *Feds cracking down as identity theft triggers violence between gangs in Metro Detroit.* (D. Hutchinson, Rep.). Retrieved from https://www.clickondetroit.com/news/defenders/feds-cracking-down-as-identity-theft-triggers-violence-between-gangs-in-metro-detroit

Drug Enforcement Administration [DEA]. (2018). *2018 national drug threat assessment.* U.S. Department of Justice. Washington, DC. Retrieved from https://www.dea.gov/sites/default/files/2018-11/DIR-032-18%202018%20NDTA%20final%20low%20resolution.pdf

Dudley, S., & Ávalos, H. (2018). *MS13 and international drug trafficking: Gang project vs. entrepreneurism.* Retrieved from https://www.insightcrime.org/investigations/ms13-drug-trafficking-project-entrepreneurism/

Federal Bureau of Investigation [FBI]. (2014). *North Park Gang members indicted in racketeering conspiracy.* Retrieved from https://archives.fbi.gov/archives/sandiego/press-releases/2014/north-park-gang-members-indicted-in-racketeering-conspiracy

Federal Bureau of Investigation [FBI]. (2015). 2015 N*ational Gang Report.* Retrieved from https://www.fbi.gov/file-repository/stats-services-publications-national-gang-report-2015.pdf/view

Federal Bureau of Investigation [FBI]. (2018). *Felony Lane Gang organized burglary and identity theft rings.* Retrieved from https://www.fbi.gov/wanted/seeking-info/felony-lane-gang

Fedschun, T. (2019). Women in "Felony Lane Gang" who taunted cops saying "do ya job (expletive)" arrested in Indiana. *Fox News.* Retrieved from https://www.foxnews.com/us/women-in-felony-lane-gang-who-taunted-cops-saying-do-ya-job-expletive-arrested-in-indiana

Fox Business. (2017, April 20). How the murderous MS-13 gang makes its money. *New York Post.* Retrieved from https://nypost.com/2017/04/20/how-the-murderous-ms-13-gang-makes-its-money/

Kanno-Youngs, Z. (2017, May 3). Gang members, others accused of running counterfeit-check ring. *Wall Street Journal.* Retrieved from https://www.wsj.com/articles/gang-members-others-accused-of-running-counterfeit-check-ring-1493849438

Meers, J. (2018). *FBI arrests dozens of Mexican Mafia members controlling US jails and street gangs.* Retrieved from https://www.occrp.org/en/27-ccwatch/cc-watch-briefs/8124-fbi-arrests-dozens-of-mexican-mafia-members-controlling-us-jails-and-street-gangs

Miller, M. (2018, February 4). "Vying for control": How MS-13 uses violence and extortion in America's jails. *Washington Post.* Retrieved from https://www.washingtonpost.com/local/vying-for-control-how-ms-13-uses-violence-and-extortion-in-americas-jails/2018/02/04/c8b8ab92-06c8-11e8-8777-2a059f168dd2_story.html?noredirect=on&utm_term=.160adc8e07ba

InsightCrime. (2018). *MS13 in the Americas. How the world's most notorious gang defies logic, resists destruction.* Retrieved from https://www.insightcrime.org/wp-content/uploads/2018/02/MS13-in-the-Americas-InSight-Crime-English.pdf

National Institute on Drug Abuse. (2018, December 13). *Misuse of prescription drugs.* Retrieved from https://www.drugabuse.gov/publications/research-reports/misuse-prescription-drugs/what-scope-prescription-drug-misuse

National Institute of Justice. (2019, February 25). *Overview of human trafficking and NIJ's role.* U.S. Department of Justice. Retrieved from https://nij.ojp.gov/topics/articles/overview-human-trafficking-and-nijs-role

O'Dowd, P. & Hagan, A. (2020, February 7). Why avocados attract interest of Mexican drug cartels. *WBUR.org.* Retrieved from https://www.wbur.org/hereandnow/2020/02/07/avocados-mexican-drug-cartels

O'Flaherty, K. (2019, January 3). Who is the Dark Overlord threatening to leak sensitive 9/11 documents? Retrieved from https://www.forbes.com/sites/kateoflahertyuk/2019/01/02/hacking-group-the-dark-overlord-threatens-to-leak-sensitive-911-documents/#6e1307844313

O'Neill, P H. (2017, May 22). *Tor's ex-director: 'The criminal use of Tor has become overwhelming'.* Retrieved from https://www.cyberscoop.com/tor-dark-web-andrew-lewman-securedrop/

Puerta, F. H. (2017, November 2). *Symbiosis: Gangs and municipal power in Apopa, El Salvador.* Retrieved from InSight Crime: http://www.insightcrime.org/investigations/symbiosis-gangs-municipal-power-apopa-el-salvador

Puerta, F. (2018). *5 Ways the MS13 launders money.* Retrieved from https://www.insightcrime.org/news/analysis/5-ways-ms13-launders-money/

Quijas, L. F. (2015, June 30). Countering super gangs with crime analytics. *Police Magazine.* Retrieved from https://www.policemag.com/341851/countering-super-gangs-with-crime-analytics

Ramey, C., & West, M. G. (2017). New York City gangs turn to white-collar crimes. *Wall Street Journal.* Retrieved from https://www.wsj.com/articles/new-york-city-gangs-turn-to-white-collar-crimes-1487631525

Stone, J. (2019, January 9). The Dark Overlord was recruiting employees and looking for attention before 9/11 data dump. *Cyberscoop.* Retrieved from https://www.cyberscoop.com/dark-overlord-recruiting-employees-looking-attention-911-data-dump/

Tor Project. (n.d.). Retrieved from https://www.torproject.org/

U.S. Attorney's Office Middle District of Pennsylvania. (2019, August 28). *Monroe County woman sentenced to seven years' imprisonment for sex trafficking and drug trafficking.* Retrieved from https://www.justice.gov/usao-mdpa/pr/monroe-county-woman-sentenced-seven-years-imprisonment-sex-trafficking-and-drug

U.S. Department of Justice. (2015). *Twelve members and associates of Brooklyn Gang indicted for committing bank fraud involving more than 350 bank accounts and more than $1.5 million in loss.* Retrieved from https://www.justice.gov/usao-sdny/pr/twelve-members-and-associates-brooklyn-gang-indicted-committing-bank-fraud-involving

U.S. Department of Justice. (2016). *Member of the Pagans outlaw motorcycle club sentenced to 9 years in prison for role in prescription pill mill.* Retrieved from https://www.justice.gov/usao-edpa/pr/member-pagans-outlaw-motorcycle-club-sentenced-9-years-prison-role-prescription-pill

U.S. Department of Justice. (2018a). *Three members of notorious international cybercrime group "Fin7" in custody for role in attacking over 100 U.S. companies.* Retrieved from https://www.justice.gov/opa/pr/three-members-notorious-international-cybercrime-group-fin7-custody-role-attacking-over-100

U.S. Department of Justice. (2018b). *Eight members of organized fraud ring in Detroit indicted.* Retrieved from https://www.justice.gov/usao-edmi/pr/eight-members-organized-fraud-ring-detroit-indicted-members-targeted-walmart-stores

U.S. Department of Justice. (2019). *Woman guilty of participating in sex trafficking conspiracy and drug trafficking.* Retrieved from https://www.justice.gov/usao-mdpa/pr/monroe-county-woman-guilty-participating-sex-trafficking-conspiracy-and-drug

U.S. Drug Enforcement Administration. (2017). *Cartels and gangs in Chicago.* Retrieved from https://www.dea.gov/sites/default/files/2018-07/DIR-013-17%20Cartel%20and%20Gangs%20in%20Chicago%20-%20Unclassified.pdf

Valdemar, R. (2007, June 1). The business of gangs. Retrieved from https://www.policemag.com/372952/the-business-of-gangs

Whelan, R. (2018, November 2). Why are people fleeing Central America? A new breed of gangs is taking over. *Wall Street Journal.* Retrieved from https://www.wsj.com/articles/pay-or-die-extortion-economy-drives-latin-americas-murder-crisis-1541167619?ns=prod/accounts-wsj

WPVI. (2018, December 11). *String of Chester County thefts possibly linked to Felony Lane Gang.* Retrieved from https://6abc.com/string-of-chester-co-thefts-possibly-linked-to-felony-lane-gang-/4874036/

Wu, G. (2018, September 11). 32 East Bay street gang members arrested in million-dollar fraud scheme. *San Francisco Chronicle.* Retrieved from https://www.sfchronicle.com/crime/article/32-East-Bay-street-gang-members-arrested-in-13218991.php?src=hp_totn

Chapter 10

Gangs in the U.S. Military

CHAPTER OBJECTIVES

- Outline the history of gang members in the military.

- Evaluate the presence of military-trained gang members and street gangs, outlaw motorcycle gangs, and domestic extremist groups.

- Examine the current trends of gangs in the military and gang-related crimes.

Introduction

The Military Criminal Investigative Organizations (MCIO) which include the Army Criminal Investigation Command (Army CID), the Air Force Office of Special Investigations (AFOSI), and the Naval Criminal Investigative Service (NCIS) are responsible for identifying military personnel with gang membership or gang affiliation in every branch of the United States Armed Forces. Although the military prohibits active membership in such groups, there are many examples of current and former service members who have enlisted in the military and came from street gangs, outlaw motorcycle gangs (OMGs), domestic extremist (DE) groups, and prison gangs or Security Threat Groups (STGs) (See *https://globalguerrillas.typepad.com/globalguerrillas/2011/10/journal-us-military-gangs.html*). Individuals have also joined street gangs after joining the military. Regardless, both types present a security challenge for military commanders and the civilian communities where the gang members live.

As military officials returned from deployment to Iraq and Afghanistan, investigators from the various branches of military and the FBI's National Gang Intelligence Center (NGIC) reported there were gang members in the military. However, a larger concern that many investigators now realize is that these gang members with military experience are bringing their training back to communities. This is presenting local law enforcement officials with a new kind of problem, and the need to find adequate ways to respond is becoming of utmost importance.

A military-trained gang member (MTGM) is defined as a gang member with military training or experience. MTGMs typically come from street gangs, domestic extremists groups, security threat groups/prison gangs, and OMGs. While in the past examining gangs in the military was largely ignored, today the focus is not only on gangs in the military but how to confront a gang member who has acquired military training.

Gang members and associates who enlist in the military often join in order to get away from the gang lifestyle and the criminal temptations associated with it. However, gang members also join to acquire military training, gain access to weapons, and obtain sensitive information for the benefit of the gang (NGIC, 2013). Regardless of their intent, the gang mindset that MTGMs bring with them can increase the risk for violent behavior in a community.

History of Gang Members in the Military

One of the oldest motorcycle clubs, formed in 1935 in McCook, Illinois, were The Outlaws. After World War II (WWII), motorcycle clubs grew because ex-servicemen returning from war found their civilian lives to be boring and monotonous (Valdemar, 2007). In San Bernardino, California, the "Pissed Off Bastards of Bloomington" (POBOBs) were formed by WWII veterans and later became famously known as the Hells Angels Motorcycle Club. Other gangs formed by WWII veterans included the first Los Angeles African American gang called the Purple Hearts. Among the founders was famous boxer and Army veteran Don Jordan, also known in the boxing ring as the "Geronimo Kid" (Valdemar, 2007).

During the Vietnam War, some of the elite fighters were also gang members from Chicago, New York, and Los Angeles. One group, comprised primarily of African American soldiers, was called the Head Hunters. Even the Viet Cong were afraid of them and placed bounties on their lives (Valdemar, 2007).

The presence of gang members in the military community became especially noticeable in the early 1990s. Military investigators and CID special agents began noticing indicators that groups of people were committing crimes such as burglaries, thefts, and breaking into cars (Smith, 2011). Other indicators included tattoos supporting their gang, pictures of soldiers flashing gang signs, and gang graffiti in foreign countries where U.S. gangs did not exist. Military investigators also found that there were juvenile family members of active duty service members claiming to be gang members.

One significant case that involved the military and a street gang resulted in the death of four people and the arrest of three Army soldiers. In December 1992, Allen King, Sr. and his three children, all military dependents of Sgt. Lisa King, the wife and mother, "were hacked and stabbed to death" in what is believed to be the first recorded gang-related homicide in the military (Egan, 1993, para. 1). The King family were killed by members of a Los Angeles street gang who were also Army soldiers at Fort Lewis in Washington, the largest Army post on the West Coast. The deaths prompted officials at Fort Lewis to take a closer look at gang ties to the base. Previously, officials stated that there was no organized gang activity on the installation, but the murders proved that gang violence did exist (Egan, 1993).

By the mid-1990s, there were more service members who were claiming gang membership within the military branches. Military investigators and special agents, as well as local police, discovered that they were seeing many of the same gang indicators in the military as on the street (Smith, 2011). It was evident that sharing information about gang activity in the military and near military bases was needed in order to combat the growing problem.

The following news excerpts are examples of military personnel engaging in a variety of crimes while having ties to street gangs, OMGs, and domestic extremists groups:

- In 1986, active duty military personnel provided guerrilla training and stolen military weapons to the White Patriot Party, a paramilitary Klan offshoot set up in 1980 by Frazier Glenn Miller, a Green Beret, and Stephen Samuel Miller. One Marine admitted selling the group 13 anti-tank rockets, 10 Claymore mines, and almost 200 pounds of C-4 explosives. A government investigation identified 32,000 rounds of ammunition, 1,500 grenades, and 3,600 pounds of explosives missing (Southern Poverty Law Center, n.d.).

- In 1990, five military policemen at Carswell Air Force Base in Texas were discharged for participating in Klan activity. One of them, Sgt. Timothy Hall, was identified as the KKK's chief recruiter in Texas. Hall was subsequently fired from his part-time job as a Tarrant County deputy sheriff, along with two fellow deputies he had recruited (Southern Poverty Law Center, n.d.).

- In 1991, Army Sgt. Michael Tubbs, a Green Beret demolitions expert was arrested along with another soldier on charges that they stole a vast arsenal of military weapons and explosives for Tubbs' Knights of the New Order. Tubbs had a list of black and Jewish targets. In 2004, Tubbs was active in the Sons of Confederate Veterans and the League of the South (Southern Poverty Law Center, n.d.).

- In 1991, Green Beret Sgt. Steven Barry formed the Special Forces Underground, a white supremacist organization for active duty and veteran Special Forces soldiers. He published a magazine, *The Register*, at Ft. Bragg in North Carolina. Barry was later reprimanded and left the military without further sanctions. He briefly joined the neo-Nazi National Alliance in the late 1990s (Southern Poverty Law Center, n.d.).

- In 1994, Lance Corporals Mark D. Jimenez, Kenneth E. Ruiz, and Michael R. Stelling were charged with killing Sgt. Michael A. Allen of Pittsburg, California, who was found floating in a ditch. The three killed Allen because they thought he was giving investigators information about the Hispanic gang *La Nuestra Familia*. All four of the Marines were members of the gang (Associated Press, 1994).

- In 1994, five soldiers at Ft. Benning, GA, stole machine guns, hand grenades, military explosives, and booby trap components. Their intent was to provide the weapons and explosives to the Aryan National Front, a white supremacist group based in Alabama and the *Confederate Hammerskins*. The *Hammerskins* were the Georgia-based chapter of a national neo-Nazi skinhead organization (Southern Poverty Law Center, n.d.).

- In 1995, Army veteran Timothy McVeigh, ignited a bomb in Oklahoma City, destroying the Alfred P. Murrah federal Building, and leaving 168 people dead. Also convicted in the attack was fellow veteran Terry Nichols, who McVeigh met at Fort Benning, GA. While in the Army, McVeigh encouraged fellow soldiers to read *The Turner Diaries*, a neo-Nazi novel that served as a blueprint for the bombing (Southern Poverty Law Center, n.d.).

- In 1995, three white soldiers from Fort Bragg drove around Fayetteville, North Carolina, in search of black people to kill. Coming upon a couple walking down the street, two soldiers got out of their car and confronted the couple with a 9-mm pistol. One forced the couple to kneel and fired several shots into their heads. When police searched the principal shooter's room, they found swastika flags, white supremacist pamphlets, and bomb-making equipment (Smith, 2011).

- In 1996, Eric Rudolph, a former member of the U.S. Army who had briefly trained at Fort Campbell in Kentucky, set off a bomb at the Atlanta Summer Olympics, killing one person and wounding 111. Rudolph later bombed a lesbian nightclub and two abortion clinics, killing a police officer, before leading authorities on a five-year manhunt ending in 2003 (Southern Poverty Law Center, n.d.).

- In 1997, Army Specialist Jacqueline Billings, from Fort Hood, Texas, ordered three gang members to kill Basel Maaz, the manager of a nightclub in Killeen, Texas, near Fort Hood. Billings was the "governor" of a 40-member faction of the Gangster Disciples—many of whom were soldiers. Instead of killing Maaz, the gang members shot Dorian Castillo and Robert Davidson, who were driving Maaz's car from the nightclub to his home. Billings' gang also committed an armed robbery at the management office of the Monaghan Apartments, stealing approximately $2,500 in cash and a gold watch, valued $18,500. Billings claimed her hangout was like a social club, similar to the Elks or Moose Lodge, and she called it "Growth & Development" (Associated Press, 1999).

- In 2003, Jerome A. Smith, a Gangster Disciple from Fort Hood, was among many gang members charged with robbery at a residence in Harker Heights and an armed robbery of a convenience store. Smith reportedly motivated his gang members by placing a plastic bag over the head of one of them and ordering him to explain how he was going to get money before the air ran out (Guffey, 2005).

- In 2005, Andres Raya, a 19-year-old Marine, was scheduled to return to Camp Pendleton in Modesto, California, for redeployment to Iraq. Instead, Raya chose to stop in the city of Ceres near San Jose. Wearing a poncho and carrying an SKS assault rifle, he fired several rounds from his rifle to presumably to attract the attention of local police. There he waited to ambush the police. Raya shot and injured Officer Sam Ryno and killed Sergeant Howard Stevenson. Raya then ran into a nearby residential area to hide. Raya was shot and killed approximately three hours later during a second shootout (Valdemar, 2007).

- In 2005, three soldiers stationed at Fort Wainwright, Alaska Army base, got involved in a dispute with civilian gang members off-post. After an exchange of gunfire, one civilian was killed. The three soldiers were indicted in the gang-related shooting death of a Crip member at a local nightclub off-post near Fairbanks, Alaska. They were later acquitted. The incident occurred just days before being deployed to Iraq (Friedenaur, 2006, as cited by NGIC, 2007).

- In 2005, Army Staff Sergeant Juwan Johnson was beaten in Kaiserslautern, Georgia, by nine Gangster Disciples in similar fashion to an initiation or disciplinary violation. After six minutes and more than 200 blows, Johnson was taken to the local hospital where he died from his injuries (Mraz, 2007).

- In 2015, the *Air Force Times* reported that Captain Leon Brown, leader of a violent street gang that ran a prostitution ring with underage girls, distributed marijuana and psilocybin and gave alcohol to teenagers. Brown was also convicted of sexual assault of a child younger than 16 years, the use of psilocybin, willful dereliction of duty, conduct unbecoming of an officer and a gentleman, pandering, unlawful entry, and four specifications of communicating threats (Davis, 2015).

Gangs and Gang-Related Crimes in the Military

MTGMs are routinely involved in criminal offenses such as drug distribution and possession, physical and sexual assaults, weapon smuggling, murder, intimidation, burglaries and robberies, fencing stolen goods, and vandalism (NGIC, 2009; Sazonov, 2011; U.S. Army CID, 2006, 2011, 2012, 2013). Since 2005, the U.S. Army CID has assessed the extent of the gang problem by investigating numerous gang activities. Annual surveys have shown increases in the total number of gang-related criminal investigations. Since 2003, the U.S. Army CID's reports on gang and extremist activity have reported an increase in gang activity and a twofold increase in felonies since 2006. Only in 2010 did the Army CID report a 68% decrease in gang activity (Unfortunately, there is no explanation for the decrease). Unfortunately, the number of felony reports of investigations (ROIs) have increased 600% (from 7 cases in 2002 to 49 in 2012). The number of non-felony investigations has also increased by 450% (from 22 cases in 2002 to 121 in 2012). Only in 2010 there was a decrease in the number of ROIs and non-felony investigations (U.S. Army Criminal Investigations Command [U.S. Army CID] (2006, 2011, 2012, 2013).

The U.S. Navy, and its investigative branch NCIS, also conducted a review of gang-related offenses within the Navy. The Navy concluded that a number of reports identifying gang activity largely stayed the same from 2009 to 2011 and that gang activity did not appear to pose a significant threat to the operational readiness of the U.S. Navy or U.S. Marine Corps. However, the report did address threats to civilian communities suggesting that gang members purposely entered the military to gain skills so they could teach fellow gang members not enlisted in the military. Similar to the Army's report, the Navy experienced increases in gang-related investigations only from 2008 to 2011(U.S. Navy, 2012).

As for the United States Air Force, they also had identifiable gang assessment results similar to the Army and Navy. The U.S. Air Force Office of Special Investigations (AFOSI) collected data as to the extent that U.S. Air Force personnel or resources were adversely affected by gang activity. The AFOSI found that gang members who joined the military were a problem compared with the previous decade. The AFOSI also found that gang members were becoming increasingly more sophisticated in their recruitment of young people, including military dependents by using popular culture (i.e., hip hop music, websites, and chat rooms) to influence new members. Gang members would also seek to join the military for weapons training and learn combat tactics such as the evasive skill of cover and concealment to use against law enforcement officials (U.S. AFOSI, 2007).

Street Gangs and the Military Connection

In a recent Army CID Assessment Report (U.S. Army CID, 2017), there were 26 investigative criminal reports involving members of street gangs. However, only four investigations involved gang-motivated crimes. The remaining 22 reports involved crimes for which the gang member was the subject, offender, or victim but with no apparent gang-related motivation. Most of the crimes committed were murder, drug distribution, and assaults. The majority (69%) of the street gang members were active-duty, African American soldiers, junior enlisted, and between 20 and 24 years of age.

According to the U.S. Department of Justice (2015a), while street gangs pose a serious domestic threat to communities in the United States, street gangs are expected to increase their role in trafficking drugs because of their military connections. By using military experiences, gang members are able to increase their relationships with international criminal organizations and drug-trafficking organizations as a means of obtaining access to the global illicit drug market. In a recent survey, MTGMs involved in street gangs were mostly comprised of single black males between the ages of 20 and 24 years, and most MTGMs come from the following street gangs: the *Bloods*, the *Crips*, the *Gangster Disciples*, the *Vice Lords*, and *Mara Salvatrucha* (Smith & Choo, 2014).

The *Bloods* are structured and unstructured gangs that have adopted a single gang culture. *Blood* gangs are active in 123 cities and in 33 U.S. states. The main source of income for the *Bloods* is derived from the street-level distribution of cocaine and marijuana, methamphetamine, heroin, and, to a lesser extent, phencyclidine (PCP) (U.S. DOJ, 2015a).

The *Crips* are another group of structured and unstructured gangs that have adopted a common gang culture. *Crips* gangs operate in 221 cities and 41 states. The main source of income for *Crips* gangs is derived from the street-level distribution of powdered cocaine, crack cocaine, marijuana, and PCP (U.S. DOJ, 2015a).

The *Gangster Disciples* gang was formed in Chicago, Illinois, in the mid-1960s. The *Gangster Disciples*, most of whom are African American males from the Chicago metropolitan area, are structured like a corporation and are led by a Chairman of the Board. The *Gangster Disciples* are active in 110 cities and 31 states, and their main source of income comes from street-level distribution of cocaine, marijuana, and heroin (U.S. DOJ, 2015a).

The *Vice Lord Nation*, also based in Chicago, is a collection of structured criminal street gangs operating in 74 cities and in 28 states. Led by a national board, the *Vice Lord Nation* consists primarily of African American males. The main source of income for the *Vice Lord Nation* comes from street-level distribution of cocaine, heroin, and marijuana (U.S. DOJ, 2015a).

Mara Salvatrucha, also known as MS-13, is involved in the smuggling of illicit drugs into the United States, primarily powdered cocaine and marijuana, and the transportation and distribution of drugs throughout the United States (U.S. DOJ, 2015a).

NEWS CLIP 10-1: STREET GANG ACTIVITY IN THE MILITARY IS INCREASING

A recent internal report from the U.S. Army shows that street and outlaw motorcycle gang activity are increasing, while incidents of domestic extremism remain roughly constant. Though criminal investigations about gang involvement are less than 1%, the report shows that gangs in the military continue to be problematic for base commanders and other service leaders. In 2018, the Gang and Domestic Extremist Activity Threat Assessment from Army Criminal Investigation Command (CID) found 83 law enforcement reports across the military with known or suspected gang or domestic extremist member involvement, a 66% increase from the previous year, "the highest percentage increase thus far" according to the report. Street gang activity shows a 68% year-over-year increase, from 38 to 64 incidents, while outlaw motorcycle gangs had a 60% increase, from 10 to 16 incidents. Domestic extremist events remained few, increasing from 2 to 3 year over year.

Source: Seck, H. (2020, August 17). Army street gang activity is increasing, internal report shows. Retrieved from https://www.military.com/daily-news/2020/08/17/army-street-gang-activity-increasing-internal-report-shows.html.

Outlaw Motorcycle Gangs and the Military Connection

The U.S. Department of Justice (U.S. DOJ, 2015b) reported that OMGs are organizations (type of gang) whose members use their motorcycle clubs as conduits for criminal enterprises. There are more than 300 active OMGs within the United States, ranging from single chapters (with less than 10 members) to large chapters (hundreds to thousands of members) with ties to national and international clubs worldwide. OMG members engage in a multitude of criminal activities but violent crime, weapons trafficking, smuggling, and drug trafficking are the most common (U.S. DOJ, 2015b).

OMGs, and their support clubs, purposefully recruit active-duty military personnel for their knowledge, reliable income, tactical skills, and dedication to a cause. According to the U.S. Bureau of Alcohol, Tobacco, and Firearms, a large number of support clubs recruit active-duty military personnel and contractors and employees from the U.S. Department of Defense. OMG members continue to represent their gang by flying (wearing) their colors even while serving in the military regardless of where they are deployed (ATF, 2010).

The ATF has published numerous reports on OMG MTGMs over the past several years. Information in those reports includes the following:

- OMG support clubs are recruiting a large number of active-duty military personnel;
- Outside Ft. Bragg and Eglin Air Force Bases, explosives have turned up in residences of U.S. Army Special Forces operators;
- Violence between OMGs has increased; and
- OMG members, especially those affiliated with the *Hells Angels*, *Bandidos Warlocks*, and *Mongols*, continue to fly their colors while serving in Iraq, Afghanistan, and other destinations across the globe (ATF, 2010).

In a recent report by the U.S. Army CID (2017), there were 10 felony investigations involving OMG members. However, only two investigations involved gang-motivated crimes. The remaining eight reports involved crimes for which the gang member was the subject, offender, or victim but with no apparent gang-related motivation. Most of the crimes committed were robbery, thefts, and drug distribution cases. The majority (60%) of the street gang members were active-duty, white, non-commissioned officers (middle management).

In a recent survey, the most common MTGMs that had ties to OMGs included *the Outlaws* (88%), the *Hells Angels* (20%), and the *Black Pistons* (16%; Smith & Choo, 2014). The *Outlaws* Motorcycle Club has more than 86 chapters in 20 states. The Outlaws are involved in the production, transportation, and distribution of methamphetamine and the transportation and distribution of cocaine, marijuana, and, to a lesser extent, ecstasy (U.S. DOJ, 2015b).

The *Hells Angels* Motorcycle Club is an OMG that poses a criminal threat on six continents with more than 92 chapters in 27 states. The Hells Angels are involved in the production, transportation, and distribution of marijuana and methamphetamine and the transportation and distribution of cocaine, hashish, heroin, lysergic acid diethylamide (LSD), ecstasy, PCP, and diverted pharmaceuticals (U.S. DOJ, 2015b).

The *Black Pistons* Motorcycle Club is the official support club for the *Outlaws*. The *Black Pistons* have an estimated 70 domestic chapters in 20 states and an unknown number of foreign chapters in Belgium, Canada, Germany, Great Britain, Norway, and Poland. The Black Pistons transport and distribute a variety of drugs and engage in assault, extortion, fraud, intimidation, and theft (U.S. DOJ, 2015b).

Domestic Extremists and the Military Connection

According to the U.S. Department of Homeland Security (U.S. DHS, 2011), *domestic terrorists* engage in unlawful acts of violence to intimidate civilian populations or attempt to influence domestic policy without direction or influence from a foreign actor. Domestic terrorism defines those actions that appear to intimidate or coerce a civilian population, to influence through intimidation or coercion the policy of a government, or to affect the conduct of a government by mass destruction, assassination, or kidnapping. The U.S. Departments of Defense, Homeland Security, and Justice typically use the terms extremist and terrorist interchangeably. According to the FBI (2010), the use of the term "extremism" suggests that individuals follow a particular ideology and use criminal activities to advance their beliefs. However, using the term "extremist" allows prosecutors, policymakers, and investigators to discuss terrorist-like activities without having to actually label the activity as terrorism (Bjelopera, 2013). Because of the multiple and potentially confusing uses of the terms terrorist and extremists, unless inappropriate based on definition or context, we will use the term Domestic Terrorist Extremist (DTE) to identify such groups and their members. DTEs are those individuals who engage in activities known as domestic terrorism, which involve acts dangerous to human life that are a violation of the criminal laws of the United States or of any State. DTEs appear to intimidate or coerce the civilian population, influence the policy of a government by intimidation or coercion, or affect the function of a government by mass destruction, assassination, or kidnapping, and this occurs primarily within the territorial jurisdiction of the United States (see Title 18, U.S. Code, Section 2331[5]). In a recent survey (Smith & Choo, 2014), MTGMs involved with DTE organizations included White Supremacists, Sovereign Citizens, Racist Skinheads, and Black Supremacists.

White Supremacist Extremists (WSEs) and Racist Skinhead Extremists (RSEs) believe that Caucasians are intellectually and morally superior to other races and that Jewish people control the government. Sovereign Citizen Extremists (SCE) believe that the legitimacy of U.S. citizenship should be rejected and all forms of established government, authority, and institutions are illegitimate. SCEs believe that they are immune from federal, state, and local laws. Black Supremacist Extremists (BSE) claim to oppose racial integration and/or the efforts to eliminate non-black people and Jewish people (U.S. Department of Homeland Security, 2011).

One DTE group that has received attention from the military criminal investigators is called FEAR (Forever Enduring Always Ready), a militia group. In July 2011, investigations discovered that the group members planned to destroy a dam and poison several apple orchards in Washington State, set off explosives in a park in Georgia, and try to assassinate the U.S. President Barack Obama (Labi, 2014). The group leader had purchased 90 acres of property in Washington State and had stockpiled nearly $90,000 worth of military-grade weapons. In addition, the group leader was investigated for killing his wife and purchasing property and weapons with the insurance money he received after her death (Labi, 2014).

In 2016, there were two investigative criminal reports involving members of DTE groups, and both involved DTE-motivated crimes. One of the crimes involved drug possession while attempting to unlawfully enter a military installation and the other involved domestic terrorism for posting terroristic threats on social media. One of the suspects was a white civilian with no military affiliation, and the other was an African American non-commissioned officer in his 40s (U.S. Army CID, 2017).

Enlisting, Training, and Prohibiting Gang Members

The U.S. Department of Defense (2009) stated that military personnel must reject active participation in criminal gangs and other organizations that advocate supremacist, extremist, or criminal gang doctrine, ideology, or causes, especially those that advocate racial, gender, or ethnic hatred or intolerance. Furthermore, if the actions adversely affect the good order and discipline of the military and impact the ability of the unit to work together regardless of background, the individual is removed or rejected from the military (Smith, 2011). The regulation also prohibits active participation in public demonstrations, meetings, fundraising, recruiting, leadership roles, or distributing literature for groups that espouse extremist views, and the recruitment of others. While membership to these types of organizations is not forbidden, the actions and behaviors listed above including wearing colors, identifiable clothing, having tattoos, or going to meetings in uniform is considered active participation.

The increase in gang presence in the U.S. armed forces in recent years is not surprising. With the economic downturn in the early part of the 21st century, this may have inspired some to seek better employment opportunities. However, the military has also been struggling to meet its recruitment goals since 9/11. With the demand for troop increases for operations Iraqi Freedom and Enduring Freedom in Afghanistan, the military needed to lower its recruiting standards, grant waivers, or simply overlook many disqualifying factors for those interested in joining the military (Sazonov, 2011). While the average gang members' criminal record and associations would typically preclude them from joining the military, gang members managed to still find a way into all branches of the military.

In today's society, most young people aged 17 to 24 years are fully qualified and capable to join the Army. As long as the potential enlistee has a high-school diploma, meets the aptitude test scoring requirements, and passes the fitness standards, they could join (Alvarez, 2007). However, granting fitness waivers has lowered the physical standards of recruits, and moral waivers have allowed soldiers with criminal histories to enlist without further restriction. The U.S. Army reported a 65% increase in the use of moral waivers from 2003 (4,913 waivers) to 2006 (8,129 waivers). The Marine Corps issued a total of 20,750 moral waivers in 2006 (Alvarez, 2007). Individuals who would not otherwise have qualified were also able to enlist, including felons, gang members, and other delinquents (Sazonov, 2011). Sadly, more than 10% of recruits in the U.S. Army had criminal histories in 2006 (Alvarez, 2007).

Moral waivers were also granted using a holistic concept approach during the review of the recruitment and enlistment stage (Eyler, 2009). Those reviews consider the severity of the offense(s), the applicant's capacity for reform, and the degree to which the applicant meets other U.S. Army standards (Eyler, 2009). Army policies directed recruiters to balance competing interests, share information, and give discretion to the individuals most familiar with the applicant when determining whether or not the applicant should enlist.

Gang members who enlist in the military or have connections with military personnel receive their training either directly while serving or indirectly from someone who is or has served in the military. In order to differentiate gang members that have a military background or some type of training against those that do not, MTGMs use military tactics, know how to handle weapons and equipment, and use distinctive military skills such tactical assault and organizational leadership strategies (NGIC, 2009, 2013). The knowledge a gang member receives from military training can make all the difference when committing a crime or when confronted by a non-military trained police officer. For example, a home invasion robbery might be treated as a typical robbery but when gang members with military experience forcefully enter a home armed with weapons and control the actions of the occupants, this is a very different kind of crime (McGoey, 2014). The actions of MTGMs invading a home are more similar to the military tactic of breaching and clearing a dwelling as part of close-quarters combat tactics than a street gang member searching for quick cash (U.S. Army, 1993).

In a recent survey conducted by a retired Army CID Special Agent (Smith & Choo, 2014), 44% of survey respondents reported that MTGMs received some form of direct military training while serving as a member of the U.S. Military. Other survey respondents indicated that only 10% of MTGMs received indirect military training from another member or former members of the U.S. Military, while only 1% reported that MTGMs identified received training from another branch in the military besides the Army.

Perhaps the most dangerous aspect of MTGMs is their potential to escalate gang violence in the community. As indicated above, gang members with military training are familiar with military-type weapons, equipment, and tactics and may be able to use all three in their furtherance of their gang's activities. Gang mentality and military training is a deadly combination that cannot be ignored.

Concluding Thoughts

It should come as no surprise that there are gang members in the military. Since the end of WWII, members of the various branches in the military found solace with various motorcycle clubs. Unfortunately, some of these motorcycle clubs were actually OMGs. But history has shown us that members of street gangs, OMGs, and domestic extremists have served in the U.S. Military, and as many as 10% of a community's street gang members have military training.

Some gang members enter the military because of the lowered recruiting standards and the process of granting waivers or because the background of a potential enlistee is simply overlooked despite many disqualifying factors. While there has been increased awareness and examination into the presence of gang members in the military, it is important to limit the effect on the military. However, civilian communities have also seen an increase in recent years regarding gang members using military-type weapons and equipment and using their skills to commit home invasions and armed robberies. As more communities continue to report gang members currently in the military, law enforcement officials in those communities need to learn the indicators of MTGMs and be prepared to counter the negative influence that these types of gang members have on the community.

Despite efforts to prevent gang members from joining the armed forces, gang members still find ways to enlist and get trained. The proliferation of gang activity in communities adjacent to military installations has also made it impossible to totally shield the military community. For service members requiring a security clearance, past gang affiliation should be prohibited—even passive or associate membership—unless accompanied by a complete, public renunciation of the gang and follow-up evaluation by representatives of the appropriate law enforcement, psychological, medical, or other military-affiliated authority. Nonetheless, in an effort to combat the gang problem in the military, military leadership should continuously examine the activities of all suspected military gang members to determine active gang affiliation for retention purposes while evaluating any gang affiliation for security clearances. Current guidelines established by the U.S. Department of Defense prohibit active gang membership in the service, but the only indicator to determine gang membership is a criminal record. Unfortunately, not all gang members are identified and caught by law enforcement officials. Therefore, alternative ways to determine gang membership need to be explored.

In the 2016 Criminal Investigation Division gang assessment (U.S. Army CID, 2017) report, it was suggested that commanders should continue to enforce the U.S. Department of Defense instructions, rejecting those who actively participation in criminal gangs and other organizations that advocate supremacist, extremist, or criminal gang doctrine, ideology, or causes. Thus, the presence of gang members in the military should be aggressively examined, questioned, and reported. Instead of accepting the existence of gang members in the military community, the goal should be to limit opportunities to join and be retained and subsequently released to the civilian community (Smith & Choo, 2014).

Although the MCIOs do well to identify the gang-related crimes committed in their ranks, the larger problem is not the presence of gangs in the military but the more significant one of gang members with military training going back to their local communities. With many more former military than active military, the number of MTGMs who are no longer on active duty is clearly the larger problem. Their ability to increase the dangerousness of the organized criminal element and avoid detection by law enforcement because of their skills must be addressed.

Discussion Points and Questions

1. Should the military change their admissions process when it comes to those who have ties to gangs?

2. What are some of the challenges that having gang members with military training in the community present to law enforcement officials? How could those challenges be addressed? Who is responsible for addressing the challenges?

3. Which type of MTGMs concerns you the most: Street Gangs, OMGs, or Domestic Extremists? Why?

4. What would you propose to assist communities with countering the negative effects of MTGM s?

Web Links

Gangs in the Military—a website that provides information about gangs in the military. Provides those interested access to the latest research, investigations, and media coverage of all things concerning gangs in the military and MTGMs members in the community. (http://www.gangsinthemilitary.com/)

Academia.edu—Articles about MTGMs http://www.academia.edu/Documents/in/Military-Trained_Gang_Members

Gang in the Military—presentation at the Northwest Gang Investigators Association https://www.youtube.com/watch?v=_8ZF_MLDPPs

Gangland—Basic Training, Season 1, Episode 12—Television series produced by the History Channel, https://www.youtube.com/watch?v=RHDhoCyden8

REFERENCES

Alcohol, Tobacco, Firearms, and Explosives [ATF]. (2010). *ATF outlaw motorcycle gangs (OMGs) and the Military 2010 report.* Washington, DC: Department of Justice, Office of Strategic Intelligence and Information.

Alvarez, L. (2007, February 14). Army giving more waivers in recruiting. *The New York Times.* Retrieved from http://www.nytimes.com/2007/02/14/us/14military.html

Associated Press. (1994, September 12). *US Marine sentenced in stabbing of fellow Marine.* Retrieved from http://www.apnewsarchive.com/1994/US-Marine-Sentenced-in-Stabbing-of-Fellow-Marine/id-b11a2b845749ef1efbbb4c34ad4b4ec5

Associated Press. (1999, January 11). *Soldier accused of ordering murders.* Retrieved from http://amarillo.com/stories/011199/tex_LD0639.001.shtml

Bjelopera, J. P. (2013, January 17). The domestic terrorist threat: Background and issues for Congress (R42536). *Congressional Research Service,* 7-5700. Retrieved from www.crs.gov.

Davis, K. (2015, February 3). AF: Missileer who ran "violent street gang" gets 25 years. *Air Force Times* [online edition]. Retrieved from http://www.airforcetimes.com/story/military/crime/2015/02/02/minot-air-force-base-missileer-leon-brown-sentenced-25-years/22753751/

Egan, T. (1993, February 3). Military base jarred by specter of gang killings. *New York Times.* Retrieved from http://www.nytimes.com/1993/02/03/us/military-base-jarred-by-specter-of-gang-killings.html

Eyler, G. (2009). Gangs in the military. *The Yale Law Journal, 118,* 696–742.

Federal Bureau of Investigation. (2010). *Domestic terrorism: Anarchist extremism, a primer.* Retrieved from http://www.fbi.gov/news/stories/2010/november/anarchist_111610/anarchist_111610

Friedenaur, M. (2006, March 22). Jury acquits three soldiers of shooting. *Anchorage Daily News.*

Guffey, M. (2005, January 25). Hood soldier guilty in gang-related trial. *Killeen Daily Herald.* Retrieved from http://kdhnews.com/news/hood-soldier-guilty-in-gang-related-trial/article_89d6c512-b905-5ff8-a00a-8b6a3b4ee9b4.html

Labi, N. (2014, May 26). Rogue element. *The New Yorker [online].* Retrieved from http://www.newyorker.com/reporting/2014/05/26/140526fa_fact_labi

McGoey, C. E. (2014). *Home invasion robbery: Protect your family with a security plan.* Retrieved from https://alfred.camera/forum/t/home-invasion-robbery-protect-your-family-with-a-security-plan/9686

Mraz, S. (2007, May 13). Sgt. Juwan Johnson: His death and what it's meant for a gang. *Stars and stripes.* Retrieved from http://www.stripes.com/article.asp?section=104&article=36663

National Gang Intelligence Center. (2007). *Intelligence assessment: Gang-related activity in the US armed forces increasing.* Crystal City, VA: Author.

National Gang Intelligence Center. (2009). *National gang threat assessment, 2009.* Washington, DC: Author.

National Gang Intelligence Center. (2013). *National gang report, 2013.* Washington, DC: Author.

Sazonov, S. A. (2011). *American soldier: Gangs in the military, a preliminary look at active gang members in the U.S. Armed Forces* (Unpublished master's thesis). John Jay College of Criminal Justice, City University of New York, New York.

Smith, C. F. (2011). View from the field: The early days of military gang investigating. *Journal of Gang Research, 18*(4), 46–52.

Smith, C. F., & Choo, T. (2014, March). Military-trained gang members in the Volunteer State: Four year follow-up with the gang investigators. Paper submitted to the Academy of Criminal Justice Sciences Conference proceedings, Orlando, FL.

Southern Poverty Law Center. (n.d.). Retrieved from http://www.splcenter.org/

U.S. Air Force Office of Special Investigations. (2007). *AFOSI criminal analysis assessment: The threat of street gangs on/near USAF installations.* Washington, DC: U.S. Department of Defense.

U.S. Army. (1993). Close quarters combat techniques. Appendix K, *Field Manual (FM) 19-10.* (Change 1, 1995). Retrieved from http://www.globalsecurity.org/military/library/policy/army/fm/90-10/90-10apg.htm

U.S. Army Criminal Investigations Command. (2006). *Summary report gang activity threat assessment fiscal year 2004–2005: A review of gang activity affecting the Army.* Washington, DC: U.S. Department of Defense.

U.S. Army Criminal Investigations Command. (2011). *Summary report gang and extremist activity threat assessment fiscal year 2010: A review of gang and extremist activity affecting the Army.* Washington, DC: U.S. Department of Defense.

U.S. Army Criminal Investigations Command. (2012). *Summary report gang and extremist activity threat assessment fiscal year 2011: A review of gang and extremist activity affecting the Army.* Washington, DC: U.S. Department of Defense.

U.S. Army Criminal Investigations Command. (2013). *US Army Criminal Investigation Command's Fiscal Year 2012 (FY12) Gang and domestic extremist activity threat assessment* (GDEATA). Washington, DC: U.S. Department of Defense.

U.S. Army Criminal Investigations Command. (2017). *US Army Criminal Investigation Command's Fiscal Year 2016 (FY16) Gang and domestic extremist activity threat assessment* (GDEATA). Washington, DC: U.S. Department of Defense.

U.S. Department of Defense. (2009). Enlistment/reenlistment document. *Armed Forces of the United States: DDForm4/1.* Retrieved from http://www.dtic.mil/whs/directives/corres/pdf/132506p.pdf

U.S. Department of Homeland Security. (2011). *Domestic terrorism and homegrown violent extremism lexicon. Washington, DC:* Office of Intelligence and Analysis, Homeland Counterterrorism Division, Homegrown Violent Extremism Branch.

U.S. Department of Justice. (2015a). *Street gangs.* Retrieved from https://www.justice.gov/criminal-ocgs/gallery/criminal-street-gangs

U.S. Department of Justice. (2015b). *Outlaw motorcycle gangs.* Retrieved from https://www.justice.gov/criminal-ocgs/gallery/outlaw-motorcycle-gangs-omgs

U.S. Navy (2012). *Gang threat assessment 2011—Criminal intelligence brief.* Naval Criminal Investigative Service Multiple Threat Alert Center. Washington, DC: U.S. Department of Defense.

Valdemar, R. (2007). Criminal gangs in the military: Although the military may deny it, gang members do infiltrate the ranks—and bring newly acquired tactical skills back to our streets. *Police: The Law Enforcement Magazine.* Retrieved from http://www.policemag.com/blog/gangs/story/2007/10/criminal-gangs-in-the-military.aspx

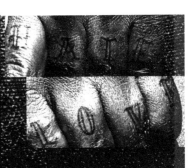

Chapter 11

The World of Sports, Athletes, and Gangs

Introduction

One of America's favorite extracurricular activities is to play sports. Whether it is a team sport like football, basketball, or soccer or an individual sport like tennis, golf, or swimming, sports provide individuals a chance to improve their physical and mental health by staying active. Sports give youth an opportunity to learn sportsmanship as well as potential job careers. In areas where life is difficult because of economic hardship or the influence of gang life, sports often provide an outlet for troubled youth. In some instances, an athlete who excels in their given sport is able to make a living playing such sports. For others, playing a sport keeps them from joining gangs or being influenced into a life of crime and violence. By playing a sport, the hope is for a better life. However, there are also times when the athlete excels in their given sport professionally but they continue to maintain their association with the criminal underworld or street gangs. Today, most professional sports leagues have some athletes that were once a member of a street gang or still maintain their ties to the gangs.

One of the earliest known athletes who was a gang member was Mel Sheppard. The former United States Olympian was known to run with the "Grays Ferry Roaders" gang from South Philadelphia at the turn of the 20th century. Sheppard, a south Jersey native won four

Olympic gold medals (1908 London and 1912 Stockhom), an Olympic silver medal (1912 Stockholm), and seven AAU titles as well as three world records as a middle-distance runner. Known as "Peerless Mel," Sheppard clashed with rival gangs such as the Ramcats, Pine Streeters, and Race Streeters (Anastasia, 2008).

Sports teams and the media often do not report on individual athletes and their possible connection to street gangs. Most athletes do not participate in the gang world even if they came from areas where gang activity had a strong presence. However, despite earning multi-million dollar salaries, there are some professional athletes with gang ties. In the U.S., there are former and current gang members in the NFL, NBA, NHL, Major League Soccer (MLS), Major League Baseball (MLB), and others sports. Teams that hire athletes with gang ties could risk negative consequences. On the other hand, these athletes can be great role models for overcoming challenges to achieve success.

The sports teams are not the only ones impacted by their association to individual gang members. Large sportswear companies such as Adidas, Nike, and Reebok and others have found themselves unwittingly tied to the gang world. The gangs often use the name or logo of the sportswear company to represent the gang in the neighborhood. When Michael Jordan, the famous Chicago Bulls basketball player started his own clothing line, he was well aware of the influence sportswear had on the gang culture, particularly colors (e .g., red and blue) (see ESPN video: https://www.youtube.com/watch?v=LWc0QOmteXQ).

The Connection between Gangs and Sports

Researching gangs in sports is a very difficult endeavor. One of the first problems in trying to collect data about gang membership and sports is the individual admitting gang affiliation. If a sports star is successful and wealthy, admitting past gang membership or even perceived gang affiliation might prove to be detrimental to his/her career. For example, Desean Jackson, a player for the Philadelphia Eagles 2008-2013, was allegedly connected to a gang and flashed gang signs during NFL games and on social media. While Jackson has maintained that he is not in a gang, he has admitted to associating with gang members. Jackson was released from the Eagles in March 2013 after the news broke out about his gang affiliation (he returned to the Eagles in 2019). The NFL and the Eagles said his dismissal was not related to the alleged gang membership (Breech, 2014) but football-related matters. Regardless, many leagues are taking notice when players display gang signs after scoring a touchdown, basket, goal, and winning an important match or celebrating because of a great play.

Most reporting about the relationship between gangs and sports involve journalistic reports (anecdotal evidence) of a pro/college athlete from a gang-infested neighborhood that has/ had ties to local street gangs. They are often regarded as feel-good stories of young kids getting out of gang life by playing sports. Those types of reporting do not address the magnitude of the problem that gangs might have on an individual and their sport. It is not so much that the gang is trying to capitalize on the athlete's success but rather the crime and violence associated with a gang is not what the league or team wants in the public eye.

Jeff Benedict, legal expert, author, and former director of research at the Center for Study of Sports and Society at Northeastern University, wrote several articles exploring the relationship between gangs and sports. What Benedict found was neighborhoods filled with gang violence and sports being used as an outlet to leave the crime-ridden, gang-infested neighborhoods, but the athletes are not exempt to the violence that comes with living in the gang world.

One study that examined the prevalence and extent of gang-involved student-athletes in college sports was conducted by Alpert, Rojek, Shannon, and Decker (2011). The study, funded by the Justice Department, found 19% of campus Police Chiefs reported knowledge of student-athletes with gang memberships compared with only 4% of athletic directors and coaches. Many of the directors and coaches canvassed in the survey believed that their student-athletes who were former gang members prior to college had ceased their membership when arriving on campus. While some would argue that the sample size of the study was too small to make a generalization about the impact on gangs in college sports (Przemieniecki, 2016), Scott Decker, a criminology professor from Arizona State University and one of the key authors of the study stated that "the kinds of crimes that gang members are most likely to be involved in are the kind of crimes that ought to concern athletic directors, police chiefs, university presidents and coaches"(Keteyian, 2011). Decker further stated that "gang membership in Division One athletics is a significant problem" (Keteyian, 2011). The study also indicated that the most problematic male and female student-athletes play football, basketball, baseball, and track-n-field.

While the NCAA has acknowledged the concern about gangs and college sports and that some schools are more prone to this than others, further research needs to be done. Since 2011, there has not been a major study examining the impact of gang membership on NCAA sports. An update is needed in this regard. The authors of this book are currently involved in a nationwide study of gangs in college sports.

Gangs and Sports Logos

Historically street gangs proclaimed their identity though names, colors, and graffiti. Since the 1980s, gangs began using sportswear companies and team logos to establish who they are and where they come from. In fact, the popularity of sportswear for general consumers has made it more difficult for law enforcement to separate those in a gang and those supporting their favorite sports team.

It is easy to do a Google search for the most common sports team's logos that represent a street gang. These sites are often created by journalists. One example is a story by ESPN on the relationship between gangs and sports. The story included interviews with George Knox, Executive Director of the National Gang Research Center in Chicago, and Steve Nawojczyk, gang expert and former Little Rock, Arkansas coroner, who was featured in Mac Levin's 1994 HBO special Gang War: Bangin' in Little Rock. (See https://www.youtube.com/watch?v-LWc0QOmteXQ&t=68s).

Whether it is wearing a team cap, shoes, or jersey with a number, the sports attire can link an individual to a particular gang. For example, the University of Michigan's letter "M" which is found on hats, shirts, and sweatshirts is also used to identify with the Mexican Mafia. The Philadelphia Phillies' letter "P" logo is used to represent the Piru Bloods.

According to Block (2013), "the hat is one of the most essential pieces of style." When you put on the hat you are representing that team, and that team only. However, for gang members, the hat they display typically represents their set (i.e., their gang). It dictates what gang they are affiliated with and how significant the gang is. Whether it's a team logo or a color scheme, street gangs all over the United States have claimed a sports team to identify with a gang.

Below is a list of popular hats that gang members wear to represent their gang (as of this writing, in 2020). They are not necessarily fans of the teams.

BASEBALL
Seattle Mariners
Adopted by: The Crips (specifically L.A.'s Rollin' 60's)
Why: The Rollin' 60's Crip set prefers the Mariners shade of blue, as well as the "S" (for sixty) logo.

Oakland A's
Adopted by: Almighty Ambrose Nation (Chicago), Orchestra Albany (Chicago), Spanish Cobras (Chicago)
Why: The Athletics' "A" represents Ambrose and Albany, while the team's green matches the Spanish Cobras' colors.

Pittsburgh Pirates
Adopted by: Latin Kings (Chicago, New York), Piru Bloods (L.A.)
Why: Black and gold Yankee hats used to be a staple among the Latin Kings, but recently the Pittsburgh Pirate fitted hat has become more prominent. The "P" logo makes an obvious match for L.A.'s Piru Bloods.

Minnesota Twins
Adopted by: Maniac Latin Disciples (Chicago), Crenshaw Mafia Gangsters (L.A.)
Why: The "M" logo stands for "Maniac" and "Mafia" for these two gangs.

Houston Astros
Adopted by: People Nation (Chicago), Folk Nation (Chicago), The Bloods (L.A.), Hoover Criminals (L.A.), Puro Tango Blast (Houston)
Why: People Nation adopted the Astros because of the team's five-star pointed logo—a star which also symbolizes the gang. Rival Folk Nation (their main symbol is the Star of David, which has six points) also takes to the Astros' logo, because the star is broken, which is a dig at People Nation. Thankfully for these gangs, New Era makes different colorways of the hat—Folk Nation takes to the blue hued iterations, eschewing any confusion over who's who. The Hoover Criminals have adopted the retro version of the hat, which features a distinctive and Hoover-worthy "H" in Old Western typeface. Puro Tango Blast naturally takes to the hat because of the home-town Houston affiliation, and the modern scarlet-colored Astros hat plays into the Bloods' red colors.

Cincinnati Reds
Adopted by: The Bloods (specifically L.A.'s Cedar Block Piru)
Why: Despite popular thinking, the Bloods' usage of the Reds hat isn't that wide-spread. Popularized by Lil Wayne and his Bloods' sympathies (he raps "I'm a grown ass Blood, stop playin with me" on the song "It's Good," and also The Game (who's from L.A.), the hat became a universal identifier of the Bloods, but this was not nec-essarily the case in practice. In reality, the Reds hat and the "C" logo is limited to the L.A.'s Cedar Block Piru set of Bloods.

Los Angeles Dodgers
Adopted by: The Crips (L.A.), Sureños (Southern California), Latin Aspects (nation-wide), Gangster Disciples (Chicago)
Why: The Crips and Sureños are all about Dodger blue. The interlocking "LA" makes the hat the perfect choice for Latin Aspects, and the Dodger "D" emblazoned version of the hat makes it a Gangster Disicples selection.

COLLEGE
Georgetown Hoyas

Adopted by: Folk Nation (Chicago), Gangster Disciples (Chicago), Black Disciples (Chicago)

Why: "Hoyas," acting as an acronym for "Hoover's On Your Ass," pays homage to Gangster Disciples founder Larry Hoover. Hoover also organized the all-encompassing Folk Nation, which includes the Black Disciples, among other Chicago-area gangs.

NFL
San Francisco 49ers

Adopted by: Norteños (Northern California), Stoned Freaks (Chicago)

Why: The 49ers' red and gold is representative of northern California's Norteños. The interlocking "SF" logo is supposed to disrespect rival southern gangs, as the Norteños commonly refer to them as "scraps" or "sewer rats." The "SF" also stands for Chicago's "Stoned Freaks."

NBA
Chicago Bulls

Adopted by: The Bloods (nationwide), Black Peace Stone Nation (Chicago), Vice Lords (Chicago), People Nation (Chicago), Mickey Cobras (Chicago)

Why: Peace Stone Nation and the Bloods got creative with their acronym game here, with "Bulls" standing for "Boy U Look Like Stone," and "Bloods Usually Live Life Strong/Smart." Mickey Cobras, People Nation, and the Vice Lords all endorse the red and black color scheme of the Bulls.

Source: Block, J. (2013, August 2). The 10 most gang-affiliated hats in sports today. Complex.com. Retrieved from https://www.complex.com/sports/2013/08/most-gang-affiliated-hats-sports-today/

The most in-depth and complete resource guide for explaining the meaning behind a sports' team/sportswear logo and how a street gang uses it for its own identity is provided by the Gang Enforcement Company (see https://www.gangenforcement.com/uploads/2/9/4/1/29411337/gang_enforcement_-_gangs_and_sport_team_clothing.pdf).

NFL and Gangs

One of the primary professional sports organizations in the U.S. that has had a number of former and current gang members playing in their league is the NFL. The challenge in reporting which professional football player is in a gang or rumored to be in a gang is driven by media reports and police arrests. While some gang members in the NFL are verified through multiple sources (more than one media story, police reports, social media, photographs), others admit their involvement with the gang.

One of the most serious actions of gang violence resulted in the death of Darrent Williams, cornerback for the Denver Broncos. Williams was not involved with gangs but was killed by a Crip gang member in drive-by shooting, after an altercation in a night club (Wyatt, 2010). The death of Williams promoted the NFL to take steps to ensure that gangs, specifically gang hand signs, were not infiltrating the NFL. The NFL hired gang experts to review games and identify any hand signals of street gangs (see News Clip 11.1).

NEWS CLIP 11-1: NFL STEPS UP MONITORING OF PLAYERS FOR GANG SIGNS

NFL – As an NFL player does a celebratory dance after a touchdown or a significant tackle, NFL officials are taking notice of hand gestures that might be related to street gangs. The NFL has hired gang experts to review game tapes and identify any hand signals that belong to street gangs. What prompted NFL officials to keep an watchful eye on players was the recent shooting death of Denver Broncos cornerback Darrent Williams involving known gang members, and Paul Pierce of the NBA's Boston Celtics who made a "menacing gesture" which appeared to be the gang hand sign the Bloods use.

Source: NFL. (2008, July 16). NFL steps up monitoring of players for gang signs. Retrieved from http://www.nfl.com/news/story/09000d5d80955352/article/nfl-steps-up-monitoring-of-players-for-gang-signs

---

One player who was an active gang member as a teenager but eventually turned away from a life of crime and violence is Jason Avant, the former Philadelphia Eagle/Carolina Panther/Kansas City Chief football player. Avant belonged to Chicago's "Gangsters Disciples." He sold and took drugs and alcohol, and lived a life of dodging bullets and running from the police. Avant denounced the gang lifestyles and became a successful professional football player (Maadi, 2012).

One of the most notorious gang members who played in the NFL was Aaron Hernandez of the New England Patriots. According to the Chicago Tribune Associated Press (Lavoie, 2017), Hernandez was a member of the Bristol Bloods, a street gang from Connecticut. He was convicted of murder in 2013, serving a life sentence when, in April 2017, he committed suicide in prison. Throughout his prison stay, Hernandez was disciplined for having gang paraphernalia and was considered a member of the Bloods in prison. TMZ also posted pictures of Hernandez flashing gang signs as a teenager and noted tattoos referring to the Bloods (NESN.com, 2013)

Another former Blood gang member was Charles Jordan, who spent 8 seasons in the NFL with Miami, Green Bay, Los Angeles, and Seattle, and one season with Memphis in the XFL. Jordan was a member of a Blood gang, the LA Swans, and was known as "Lucky" by his fellow gang members. He spent six months in an L.A. County jail for murder but the charges were eventually dismissed. Jordan was known to pay tribute to his gang back home with a hand sign after scoring a touchdown (Cole, 1996).

NBA and Gangs

The National Basketball Association (NBA) is also known to have employed former and current gang members on their teams. While much of the gang connections in the NBA are driven by social media allegations and often unfounded, the NBA still has a significant amount of verified basketball players with ties to gangs, more than all the other professional sports (NFL, MLB, NHL, and MLS) combined. While speculations are plentiful, the point where the NBA finally admitted that some players might have gang ties was in April 2008 during a game between the Boston Celtics and the Atlanta Hawks. Toward the end of a playoff game, Celtic Paul Pierce made a gesture to the Atlanta bench that resembled the gang sign of the Piru Bloods, a street gang from the Compton area of Los Angeles. While this was also the same place where Peirce grew up, the media and professional sports organizations took great notice of this as a potential problem damming the image of their sport. The NBA called the gang sign a "menacing gesture" and fined Pierce $25,000. Pierce denies it was a gang sign and, in fact, denounces gang activity altogether. But, that incident created a media firestorm and brought the issue of gangs to the NBA as a serious problem that needed to be addressed.

Here are some of the more storied NBA players with ties to street gangs before and during their careers.

- J.R. Smith, formerly of New Orleans, New York, Denver, and Cleveland, was often seen flashing blood signs during games. In Fact, on Twitter, Smith would tweet and replace the letter "c" with the letter "k"- a common practice that gang members do when they want to show their allegiance to the Blood gang and disrespect their rivals, the Crips. Once the media caught wind of this, he closed his Twitter account (Complex, 2009).

- Zach Randolph, who played for 20 seasons (Portland, New York, Los Angeles, Memphis, and Sacramento), was known to be a gang member with the Hoop Family while he was in Portland. Randolph was no stranger to trouble and has been arrested for robbery, battery, and other activities before becoming an NBA star (Dawkins, 2011).

- DeMar DeRozan is another NBA star from Compton, California, the birthplace of the Crips. Growing up in Compton, DeRozan was a member of the Poccet Hood Compton Crips and lived a hard life of death, destruction, and chaos as a youngster. Basketball was his way out (Kriegel, 2018).

- Carmello Anthony is currently (2019–2020 season) with the Portland Trail Blazers. Anthony grew up in Baltimore surrounded by drugs/alcohol, crime, gangs, and violence. While there are no direct ties to Anthony's involvement with gangs, Anthony was featured in a DVD (possibly unknowingly) called "Stop Snitchin," which was part of a campaign going on in Maryland at the time to convince people to stop providing information to police when it comes to gang crime (Stefani, 2015).

- Stephen Jackson, now retired, after 14 years (played with New Jersey, San Antonio, Atlanta, Indiana, Golden State, Charlotte, Milwaukee, and the Los Angeles Clippers), was one of the few athletes to openly admit his affiliation with the Bloods. However, Jackson made it clear that while he had ties to the Bloods and often wore red, he made it very clear that he is not involved in the gang (Stafani, 2015).

- Current NBA player James Harden, Houston Rockets, often throws a Blood sign after scoring baskets that only generates concern among NBA officials. Harden may not be in a gang, but his relationship with Lil Wayne, a self-promoted Blood gang member, who refers to Harden as "5"- a reference to the Blood's 5-pointed star, worries officials. Harden also associates with other rappers and gang members, which lends to the complicated perception that Harden lives a gangster lifestyle (Stefani, 2015).

- The one player that joined gangs after becoming an NBA star was Javaris Crittenton. Crittenton joined the Mansfield Gangster Crips once he signed with the Los Angeles Lakers before ending his career with the Wizards. In 2011, Crittenton pulled a gun on his teammate and was promptly removed from the team shortly after that incident. His career ended when he was convicted of killing a mother of four. Crittenton was also indicted on other gang-related charges. He is currently serving a 23-year prison sentence (Barr & Armante, 2014). .

Other Sports Stars

The NFL and the NBA are not the only sports associations that have had former and current gang members playing in their leagues. Before embarking on a successful Major League Baseball career, Tony Tarasco was a member of the Santa Monica Graveyard Crips at the age of 13, but thanks to his baseball talent, the gang never allowed him to do things that would jeopardize his future with baseball. Tarasco is quoted as saying that "A lot of what I was doing in the early part of the '80s was no different from what you would see in West Side Story, a lot of street gangs and fighting and stuff. As I got into high school, it started to get a little rougher. It was a lot more violent. There was more shooting and stuff" (Wood, 2001).

In 2012, tennis star Serena Williams celebrated her Olympic gold-medal winning by performing the C-walk. The C-walk, also known as the Crip walk, is a dance that originated with Crip gang members from South Central Los Angeles and was popularized by rap artists. Williams was criticized for performing the victory dance after her match, with media outlets slamming her for glamorizing street gangs (Sieczkowski, 2012). In fact, in the 1980s and early 1990s, MTV (the Music Television show) banned music videos featuring the C-walk in their music videos because of its gang association (Fiorillo, 2012). However, others found humor and downplayed the dance (Yates, 2012). What complicated matters is the fact that Serena Williams is from Compton, CA, the birthplace of the Crip walk, and her half-sister Yetunda Price was gunned down by Southside Compton Crips gang members. While the murder was ruled an accident, it nonetheless was gang-related (Poole, 2003). It was Serena's connection to the gang world, no matter the circumstances, that brought her C-walk victory dance to the center of media frenzy.

Other Sports Impacted by Gangs

While the NBA and NFL have most current and former gang members in their respective leagues, other sports such as soccer (Major League Soccer) and hockey (National Hockey League) are also confronting their own gang problems, but in a much different way. With respect to soccer, also known as football, hooliganism is most often associated with soccer teams around the world. Hooliganism is a problem that many European, South/Central American, and Asian leagues face. Hooligans are essentially gang members but are tied to a local professional club. In the 1970s and 1980s, Hooliganism was a significant problem in England, and while it has been curtailed since then, the problem still exists around the world, especially in Turkey. In the United States, Major League Soccer has not experienced the same level of Hooliganism as those countries abroad, but tensions between fans of rival teams is growing. As the sport of soccer continues to grow in popularity, the support for attending games has increased. What was once a low-attendance sport has now turned into a cult-following for fans of their favorite teams, and this means fans are starting to clash. For example, in 2016, fans of NY Red Bulls and NYCFC clashed at Yankee Stadium, resulting in multiple arrests (Block, 2016). While it was not gang-related, it was problematic for the police. The question remains if soccer in the in the U.S. will ever resemble the Hooligan problem of the 1970/1980s English Premier League Football or will it be small scuffles between fans. While it is too early to make the connection, fan violence at soccer stadiums does occur (Bondy, 2016; Goff, 2019).

In a more recent controversy, the Chicago Fire, a Major League Soccer team, changed their original logo from the Florian Cross, a symbol for firefighters which represented the Great Chicago Fire of 1871, to what now resembles a three-pointed gold crown (or triangles) facing up and a three-pointed red crown (or triangle) facing down. The bottom triangles are red and represent the Great Chicago Fire, and the top three are gold and represent the modern-day city and its people. While it is not uncommon for professional sports teams to modify and change their logos, many associated the new logo with the famed Latin Kings because of the 3-pointed crown (Sandalow, 2019). It will remain to be seen if this sports logo will be used by the Latin Kings.

In the National Hockey League, one of the most popular of all NHL logos is the Los Angeles Kings. The logo is supported by Latin King gang members. For obvious reasons the name 'Kings' is appealing for the Latino gang as is the use of the crown. Interestingly, from the late 1960s to the late 1980s, the Los Angeles Kings' primarily colors were Gold and Purple. In 1988, the Kings changed their colors to black and silver to better associate their image with toughness and winning like the Oakland Raiders were experiencing. In the early 2000s, the Kings adopted the crown as the new logo, and this further appealed to Latin King gang members despite not actually necessarily supporting the LA Kings NHL team (GangEnforcement.com, 2019).

Using Sports to Stop Gang Involvement

One way to encourage youth to stop engaging in gang violence is to play sports. While it doesn't guarantee results, research has shown that sports can redirect youth behavior. Some of the most common places to find the promotion of sport activities to reduce gang violence are Police Athletic Leagues (PAL), the YMCA, Community Youth Centers, and after-school programs. There are many sports that are used to help redirect youth behavior away from gangs. Examples include football, basketball, boxing, soccer, baseball, rowing, karate, swimming, surfing, bowling, horseback riding, tennis, golf, adventure camps, canoeing, ropes courses, rock climbing, scouting, softball, dancing, volleyball, and weight-lifting.

As reviewed in Chapter 7, prevention and intervention programs often have utilized sports to reduced gang activity. As early as the 1920s, Frederick Thrasher (1927) noted that the best approach to secure the initial interest of gang members away from gang violence is through athletics and sports. There is plenty of research supporting the use of a sports program to reduce delinquency (Donaldson & Ronan, 2006; Landers & Landers, 1978; Purdy & Richard, 1983) and reduce the use of drugs and alcohol (Raithel, 2004). However, there are also studies showing that jock identity was associated with more incidents of minor delinquency (Miller, Melnick, Barnes, Sabo, & Farrell, 2007), individual sports are more positive than team sports (Raithel, 2006), unsupervised sports activities results in higher levels of delinquency (Yin & Katims, 1999), and the positive correlation between participation in sports and involvement in aggressive behavior (Burton & Marshall, 2005). With respect to gang involvement, adolescents who do not have adult supervision (while playing sports) at least 3 days/week are two times (2×) as likely to hang out with gang members and three times (3×) as likely to be engaged in criminal behavior (Donaldson et al., 2006). Sociologist J. B. Nolan (1955) said it best that "a sports program is a tool but it is not in itself an answer to reducing juvenile delinquency" (p. 265) or gang behavior.

As with every program designed to address delinquency and gangs, there are positives and negatives in adopting a sports program aimed at reducing gang involvement. Table 11.1 outlines the "pros" and "cons" of promoting sports activities in order to reduce gang involvement.

Table 11.1: PROS and CONS of Promoting Sports Activities

PROs:	CONs:
• Teaches sportsmanship	• Negative influence from delinquent peers
• Emphasis on teamwork	• Many delinquent peers together
• Builds trust	• Share gang experiences
• Improves motor and cognitive skills	• Potential recruitment
• Improves physical fitness	• Rival gangs competing with and against each other
• Role models (esp. male)	
• Individual attention	
• Relieves stress, anger, aggression	
• Learn to respect authority	

Examples of Sports Programs Aimed at Reducing Gang Involvement

In soccer, from 2012 to 2014, the former MLS Club Deportivo Chivas USA collaborated with Orange County, CA Gang Reduction & Intervention Partnership program. The program was designed to prevent juveniles from being victims of or participants in gang crimes by identifying at-risk youth, increasing school attendance, and decreasing gang activity. As an incentive for positive behavior and staying out of gangs, the students earned tickets to upcoming games and would meet the players.

In Southern California, a softball and a football league was started to help reduce the gang violence that was plaguing the neighborhoods. In 2000, Duade Sherrills, a Grape Street Crip member and founder of the the Grass Roots Confederate Crips and Bloods Sports League, was awarded a $100,000 grant to initiate a league to curb gang violence. There were 16 participating neighborhoods, which included L.A. County Watts, South Central, Venice, Compton, and Long Beach. This was considered "gladiator football"—there were no pads. While there was no violence associated with the league, renting out high school stadiums and utilizing parks still proved to be too much for residents and law enforcement. The league only last one year (*The Source*, 2000).

Another program in South Central Los Angeles that was created to combat gang violence was a softball league. In 2016, six different neighborhoods associated with Crips gangs each created a softball team and formed a league. While the hatred between Crips and Bloods is ingrained in popular culture, a less well-known fact is that Crips on Crips gang violence is just as deadly. In 2017, the Rollin' 30s Harlems and the Rollin' 40s, mortal enemies, reached the softball championships. The Bloods have also started their own softball league, and there is a chance that one day the Bloods and Crips will meet for the Ultimate Softball Championship (Chang, 2017). As of this writing, no Blood vs. Crip softball game has taken place.

Other programs that focused on reducing gang involvement include golf, basketball, surfing, and horseback riding. In 2008, the World Golf Foundation received a $500,000 grant from the Department of Justice to engage youth in positive youth development. The World Golf Foundation focused on high-risk kids, especially those influenced by gangs, and gave them golf clubs to learn a life sport skill, encourage school attendance or participation, and teach prosocial skills. Another golf program that also focuses on gang prevention is State University of New York-Stony Brook University's Par Fore program. Par Fore targets group and individual life skills activities including anger management, anti-bullying, time management, academic preparation, self-esteem building, and, most importantly, gang prevention and intervention (see parfore.org). The group activities are held on a golf course or driving range.

In Chicago, former Detroit Pistons Isaiah Thomas helped start the Peace League Basketball Tournament hosted by St. Sabina Church, in the city's Gresham neighborhood. The tournament aims to promote peace over gun violence and has since garnered the attention of other NBA players, celebrities, and music artists. Initially, the idea was to get gang members off the street for a weekend of basketball (Saint Sabina, 2019). Today, there are two 12-week leagues and one six-week league that run throughout the year. In 2018, the league expanded so Chicago's West Side could compete against South Side teams (Edwards, 2018)

Another program that originated in California was the Turf to Surf Program. Conceived in 2001, founders Manny "Fozzy" Raya and J.J. Ortiz, bitter Mexican-American gang rivals had an unknowing common bond—a love for surfing. After years of arrests and court appearances, Raya and Ortiz were given one last chance to change their ways. The former gang members teamed up and created Turf 2 Surf, a gang intervention program designed to focus on Santa Barbara's toughest gang members. It was a summer two-week course that met Monday–Friday from 9 a.m. to 5 p.m. Each summer, the camp took 8 to 12 gang members and Raya and Ortiz taught the youth how to surf, but they also focused on changing their behavior. The program featured activities that promoted discipline, developed a respect for nature, was fun, and focused on establishing a truce among Mexican gang members (ESPN, 2008).

One program that would seem outside the norm of a typical team or individual sport-based gang prevention/intervention program is horseback riding. Horse Sense: Running with the Mustangs is a North Carolina Department of Juvenile Justice and Delinquency Prevention program that targets gang-identified and high-risk youth. Horse Sense is also an equine-assisted therapy program for personal growth, life skills, and empowerment (North Carolina Department of Crime Control and Public Safety, 2009). Some of the youth that attend this program are court-ordered by the North Carolina Department of Crime Control and Public Safety. According to Shannon Knapp, the founder and director of Horse Sense, it was observed that "horses give unbiased feedback to a client (i.e., gang member), so they are a very useful in therapy sessions" (Przemieniecki, 2018). Since gang members are typically distrusting individuals, putting them with a large animal and trying to gain the animals' trust changes their demeanor. This program still exists today and is now called Horse Sense of the Carolinas, Inc. (for more information see, https://www.horsesenseotc.com/).

Conclusions

Playing sports or cheering for your favorite sports team can be rewarding, but for some fans, it can be dangerous. Street gangs use logos of sports teams and sportswear companies to "fit" the needs to promote the gang. Logos are used to give a street gang an identity. Sadly, if an unassuming outsider is supporting a sports team logo on a hat that represents a rival gang, the consequences could be deadly.

It is important to note that most athletes are NOT in a gang or do not come from a gang lifestyle, but some do. Some athletes continue to associate with gang members from their hometown, while others continue to represent the colors of the gang. The power, influence, and visibility of these athletes with what the wear, who they associate with, and the gestures they make have caused the NFL, NBA, and other professional sports organization to take note of when behaviors might be seen as inappropriate or deemed to promote the gang culture. This is something these sports organizations do not advocate for and work very hard to encourage their athletes to be positive role-models.

Sports can also be used as a conduit to reduce gang involvement. Programs across the United States utilize sports to reduce gang involvement, redirect negative youth behavior, and aim to stop gang violence in the community. While some programs are deemed successful and are funded through grants and supported by the community, other programs do not last, not for lack of trying but instead because such programs lose their volunteers or do not have enough qualified staff, there is a lack of funding, or the community loses interest in supporting the sports initiative. Regardless, running a successful gang prevention/intervention program that emphasizes a sport aimed at reducing gang activity is a labor of love.

Websites

https://www.youtube.com/watch?time_continue=260&v=FuTrqiZEGuQ&feature=emb_title (Story of the Rollin 30s and Rollin 40s now playing softball)

http://www.parfore.org/Gangs.html (playing golf instead of gang bangin')

https://www.youtube.com/watch?v=Z0XutqGb7Q8 (story of former Mexican gang members Turf to Surf program)

http://static1.1.sqspcdn.com/static/f/797780/14824701/1319641737727/RWM+Sample_2011.pdf?token=UN6vzaWGMfQCZsEtrFujpymYQ4k%3D (program of Horse Sense: Running with the Mustangs).

REFERENCES

Alpert, G., Rojek, J., Hansen, J. A., Shannon, R. L., Decker, S. H. (2011). *Examining the prevalence and impact of gangs in college athletic programs using multiple sources. Final report.* Washington, DC: Bureau of Justice Assistance. Retrieved from https://www.cbsnews.com/htdocs/pdf/NCAA_Report_June_13.pdf

Anastasia, P. (2008, July 14). A century ago, Mel Sheppard set the standard. *Philadelphia Inquirer.* Retrieved from https://www.inquirer.com/philly/hp/sports/20080714_A_century_ago__Mel_Sheppard_set_the_standard.html

Barr, J. & Amante, G. (2014, April 5). Crittenton gang ties questioned. *ESPN.com.* Retrieved from https://www.espn.com/espn/otl/story/_/id/10732937/ex-nba-player-javaris-crittenton-gang-ties-questioned-suspected-gang-member

Block, J. (2013, August 2). The 10 most gang-affiliated hats in sports today. *Complex.com.* Retrieved from https://www.complex.com/sports/2013/08/most-gang-affiliated-hats-sports-today/

Block, J. (2016, May 23). Wannabe MLS Hooligans are adopting the worst of soccer culture. *HuffPost.com.* Retrieved from https://www.huffpost.com/entry/wannabe-mls-hooligans-are-adopting-the-worst-of-soccer-culture_n_5743285ce4b0613b512ad621

Bondy, S. (2016, May 22). Two arrested as fans clash outside Yankee Stadium before Red Bulls-NYCFC game. *New York Daily News.* Retrieved from https://www.nydailynews.com/sports/soccer/video-nycfc-red-bulls-fans-clash-yankee-stadium-article-1.2645178

Breech, J. (2014, June 28). Report: DeSean Jackson still associates with gang members. *CBS News.* Retrieved from https://www.cbssports.com/nfl/news/report-desean-jackson-still-associates-with-gang-members/

Burton, J. M. & Marshall, L. A. (2005). Protective factors for youth considered at risk of criminal behavior: Does participation in extracurricular activities help? *Criminal Behavior and Mental Health, 15*(1), 46-64.

Chang, C. (2017, December 31). Going to bat for peace; Wearing blue uniforms—what else?—Crips battle for primacy not on the streets but in a softball league. *Los Angeles Times,* p. A.1.

Cole, J. (1996, June 2). Overcoming the scars. *Sun-Sentinel.* Retrieved from https://www.sun-sentinel.com/news/fl-xpm-1996-06-02-9606010194-story.html

Complex. (2009, August 6). *Is the NBA gang related? A Complex investigation.* Retrieved from https://www.complex.com/sports/2009/08/is-the-nba-gang-related-a-complex-investigation

Dawkins, B. (2011, August 27). *The contradictory case of Zach Randolph.* Retrieved from https://bleacherreport.com/articles/823117-the-contradictory-case-of-zach-randolph

Donaldson, S. J. & Ronan, K. (2006). The effects of sports participation on young adolescents' emotional well-being. *Adolescence, 41,* 369-389

Edwards, L. (2018, August 31). Peace League tournament at St. Sabina puts rival gang members on the same court to find common ground. *BlockClubChicago.org.* Retrieved from https://blockclubchicago.org/2018/08/31/peace-league-tournament-at-st-sabina-puts-rival-gang-members-on-the-same-court-to-find-common-ground/

Esbensen, F. A. & Deschenes, E. P. (1998). A multi-site examination of gang membership: Does gender matter? *Criminology, 36*(4), 799–828.

ESPN. (2008, September 12). Surfing becomes new turf for gang bangers; program gets national spotlight. *Surfline.com.* Retrieved from https://www.surfline.com/surf-news/press-release/surfing-becomes-new-turf-for-gang-bangers-program-gets-national-spotlight-on-sept-16_18540/

Fiorillo, V. (2012, August 6). How to crip walk like Serena Williams. *PhillyMag.com.* Retrieved from https://www.phillymag.com/news/2012/08/06/how-to-crip-walk-video/

GangEnforcement.com. (2019). *Gangs and sport team clothing.* Retrieved from https://www.gangenforcement.com/uploads/2/9/4/1/29411337/gang_enforcement_-_gangs_and_sport_team_clothing.pdf

Goff, S. (2019, September 23). Police investigating alleged assault of Seattle Sounders fans near Audi Field. *WashingtonPost.com*. Retrieved from https://www.washingtonpost.com/sports/2019/09/23/dc-police-investigate-after-seattle-sounders-fans-say-they-were-assaulted-near-audi-field/

Grummert, D. (1993, October 22). WSU football taking the city of the man Cougar back Hicks abandons L.A. double life for starter's role. *Lewiston Morning Tribune*, p. B1.

Hill, K. J., Howell, J. C., Hawkins, J. D., & Battin-Pearson, S. R. (1999). Childhood risk factors for adolescent gang membership: Results from the Seattle Social Development Project. *Journal of Research in Crime and Delinquency, 36*, 300-322.

Hooper, E. (1997, December 5). Coach: Buffs recruited gangs. *St. Petersburg Times*, p. C2.

Keteyian, A. (2011, December 8). Violent gangs impact college sports. *CBS News*. Retrieved from https://www.cbsnews.com/news/violent-gangs-impact-college-sports/

Kriegel, M. (2018, February 16). The virtue of DeMar DeRozan. *ESPN*. Retrieved from https://www.espn.com/nba/story/_/id/22454605/the-virtue-demar-derozan

Landers, D. & Landers, D. (1978). Socialization via interscholastic athletics: Its effects on delinquency. *Sociology of Education, 51*(4), 299-303.

Lavoie, D. (2017, May 5). Records: Aaron Hernandez was member of Bloods street gang. *Chicago Tribune*. Retrieved from https://www.chicagotribune.com/sports/ct-records-aaron-hernandez-bloods-street-gang-20170505-story.html

LiCari, J. & Hall, A. (1994, December 1). Moss admits gang ties; drug use also detailed in interview with police. *Wisconsin State Journal*, p. A1.

Maadi, R. (2012, December 25). Avant goes from gang life to man of God. *Daily Local News*. Retrieved from https://www.dailylocal.com/avant-goes-from-gang-life to-man-of-god/article_92184ef6-2ae1-597c-87ab-f4d831a735d6.html

Miller, K.E., Melnick, M.J., Barnes, G.M., Sabo, D., & Farrell, M.P. (2007). Athletic involvement and adolescent delinquency. *Journal of Youth and Adolescence, 36*(5), 711-723.

NESN.COM. (2013, June 27). *Aaron Hernandez flashes alleged Bristol Bloods gang sign in photo taken in high school*. Retrieved from https://nesn.com/2013/06/aaron-hernandez-flashes-alleged-bristol-bloods-gang-sign-in-photo-taken-in-high-school-photo/

Nolan, J. B. (1955). Athletics and juvenile delinquency. *Journal of Educational Sociology, 28*, 263-265.

North Carolina Department of Crime Control and Public Safety. (2009). *Gangs in North Carolina: A 2009 Report to the General Assembly*. Retrieved from https://files.nc.gov/ncdps/documents/files/Gang%20Grant%20Rpt%20to%20Gen%20Assembly.pdf

Poole, O.(2003, September 15). Sister of Serena and Venus shot dead. *The Telegraph.com*. Retrieved from https://www.telegraph.co.uk/news/1441434/Sister-of-Serena-and-Venus-shot-dead.html

Przemieniecki, C. J. (2016, August). The Role of Sports in Gang Prevention/Intervention. Presented at the 19th Annual International Gang Training Specialist Conference hosted by the National Gang Crime Research Center (NGCRC), Chicago, IL.

Purdy, D. A. & Richard, S. F. (1983). Sport and juvenile delinquency: An examination and assessment of four major theories. *Journal of Sport Behavior, 6*(4), 179-193.

Raithel, J. (2004). Risk behavior among adolescents with different leisure time engagements: A comparison between art, music, and sport activities. *Musik-, Tanz- Und Kunsttherapie, 15*, 137-143.

Raithel, J. (2006). Health relevant behavior, delinquency, and sport participation during adolescence. Findings based on a comparison between sport activity and types of sports. *Kunsttherapie, 17*(4), 201-211.

Saint Sabina. (2019). *The Peacemakers basketball story*. Retrieved from https://saintsabina.org/peace-basketball-tournament.html

Sandalow, B. (2019, November 21). Fire unveil new logo, tweaked name. *ChicagoSunTimes.com*. Retrieved from https://chicago.suntimes.com/2019/11/21/20975330/chicago-fire-unveil-new-logo-tweaked-name-joe-mansueto-nelson-rodriguez-major-league-soccer

Schlabach, M. (2000, March 19). NFL image taking losses—With several players charged in recent high-profile criminal cases, pro football is seeking answers. *The Atlanta Journal Constitution*, p. E1.

Sieczkowski, C. (2012, August 6). Serena Williams' Crip Walk dance criticized as inappropriate (Video). *HuffingtonPost*. Retrieved from https://www.huffpost.com/entry/crip-walk-dance-serena-williams_n_1747593

Stefani, A. (2015, October 25). Top 20 athletes with alleged gang ties. *The Sportster*. Retrieved from https://www.thesportster.com/entertainment/top-20-athletes-with-alleged-gang-ties/

Thornberry, T. P., Krohn, M. D., Lizotte, A. J., Smith, C. A., & Tobin, K. (2003). *Gangs and delinquency in developmental perspective*. New York: Cambridge University Press.

Thrasher, F. M. (1927). The gang: A study of 1,313 gangs in Chicago. Chicago, IL: University of Chicago Press

Wood, N. (2001, July 5). A touch of Tarasco sauce. *Daily Press*. Retrieved from https://www.dailypress.com/news/dp-xpm-20010705-2001-07-05-0107050009-story.html

Wyatt, K. (2010, March 12). Man convicted in slaying of Broncos cornerback. *Enid News & Eagle*. Retrieved from https://www.enidnews.com/sports/local_sports/man-convicted-in-slaying-of-broncos-cornerback/article_e2c5fbda-c3be-57a1-8a76-c2de73425d7b.html

Yates, C. (2012, August 5). Serena Williams and the Crip Walk. *WashingtonPost*. Retrieved from https://www.washingtonpost.com/blogs/therootdc/post/serena-williams-and-the-crip-walk/2012/08/05/ade59954-df25-11e1-a19c-fcfa365396c8_blog.html

Yin, Z., & Katims, D.S. (1999). Participation in leisure activities and involvement in delinquency by Mexican American adolescents. *Hispanic Journal of Behavioral Sciences, 21*(2), 170-185.

Chapter 12

Gangs, the Internet, and Social Media

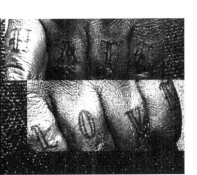

CHAPTER OBJECTIVES

- Examine the extent and prevalence of Internet usage by gang members.

- Describe the severity of online gang violence.

- Examine how gangs utilize the Internet and social media sites.

NEWS CLIP 11-1: DETROIT GANGS USING SOCIAL MEDIA TO POST HIT LISTS THAT LEAD TO MURDERS, INVESTIGATORS SAY: OFFICIALS RAMPING UP EFFORTS TO END GANG VIOLENCE IN DETROIT

Detroit, MI—The Detroit zip code 48205 is known by gangs as the "red zone," referring to the color of blood. It is this area that law enforcement is trying to put a stop to violence in one of the most dangerous neighborhoods in the country. However, the gang violence starts on social media where the notorious Seven Mile Bloods gang is waging a drug war with the 6 Mile Chedda Boys. The warring gangs are using social media to post pictures of rival gang members they want killed and this has caught the attention of federal investigators. There have been far too many shooting and incident bystanders and young gang members being killed.

After a recent post on Instagram, law enforcement and prosecutors are using social media to fight back. Fortunately for law enforcement, the gangs are leaving a digital trail to follow and more clues have been found on YouTube videos produced in the "red zone," providing evidence that has led to dozens of arrests from both gangs.

"We bring together the Detroit police, who have the best kind of street-level intelligence with ATF, which is the best with tracing guns, with DEA, who is the best at understanding drug-trafficking laws nationally and internationally, with FBI, which is the best with connecting the dots with all of their intelligence apparatus and the ability to exploit social media," U.S. Attorney Barbara McQuade said.

"But it also makes good evidence for us," McQuade said. "In our trials, we've shown pictures of gang members holding guns and drugs with their gang colors, schemes on shirts." Officials are charging drug-dealing gang members the way the mafia used to be charged, with racketeering. "These gangs are just as organized as organized crime families," McQuade said. "They have a hierarchy. They're organized, and they're involved in a whole multitude of things that constitute racketeering."

Source: WDIV. (2017, February 2). Detroit gangs using social media to post hit lists that lead to murders, investigators say. Retrieved from https://www.clickondetroit.com/news/2017/02/02/ detroit-gangs-using-social-media-to-post-hit-lists-that-lead-to-murders-investigators-say/

Introduction

While the entertainment medium gives consumers a unique look into the world of gangs from a safe distance, even those depictions of gangs in the media continue to present a problem for law enforcement and their communities. However, one place that gangs have now turned to is the Internet and various social media sites such as Facebook, YouTube, Instagram, and Twitter. These platforms have given gangs the ability to embrace, glamorize, showcase, and sometimes recruit individuals into the world of gangs without meeting face-to-face. This new form of communication has not only complicated things for law enforcement but in turn has given law enforcement new tools to combat the street gang problem in their communities.

In 1989, the World Wide Web was created by British scientist Tim Berners-Lee (CERN, 2019), and it did not take long for criminal gangs to utilize the web to promote their gang, sell their drugs, and recruit new members. However, in 1996, one of the earliest known documented gangs called Glock 3 from Detroit used the Internet to promote their group by creating a website, spreading stories about how the gang proliferated, and claimed to be a menace in the community, spreading fear and engaging in extortion, robbery, and other crimes. The brazenness of the gang was different from other gangs that started to use the web, and other media outlets began to report on this new Internet gang, and law enforcement took notice. In fact, on the gang's website, Glock 3 claimed to be "tha site of one of tha most famous street gangz in tha world today" (Weeks, O'Harrow, Pishvanov, & Light, 1996).

There was only one problem with the gang—it did not exist. It was a hoax. The Glock 3 gang was created by 16-year-old Nick Woomer, who used his knowledge from gangster movies and gangsta rap, to promote Glock 3 on the web. Though Glock 3 was not real, the *Washington*

Post reporters found other gangs using the internet promoting their gangs called the "Gangsta Net Crew" and "Internet Thugs" (Weeks et al., 1996).

While gangs began to utilize the internet, so too did the police. Jim Ledy, a former criminal intelligence analyst for the Arizona Department of Public Safety stated that, "the ones that are using the Internet most successfully are motorcycle gangs and organized crime. These groups use cyberspace to disseminate information to members quickly and anonymously" (Weeks et al., 1996).

The Internet, Social Media, and Gangs

Since the 1990s, the Internet and social media sites have provided a new venue for gangs to linger, influence adolescents, and potentially create havoc for law enforcement. As technology has changed, so has the gang culture. Today, gangs are able to recruit, conduct business, and engage in violent behavior all from the comfort of their homes. The streets are no longer made of concrete; but instead, the gang world is tangled up in a web of digital information.

In the 1970s and 1980s, pay phones and beepers were the technological tools that gangs used. Now, sites such as Facebook, Twitter, Instagram, Snapchat, YouTube, and other social media sites, including applications on cell phones and laptops, are the latest tools that gang members prefer to use when promoting their gang or communicating with each other. As home computers and laptops have become increasingly affordable, access to the Internet is more prevalent for gang members to utilize. A particularly helpful caveat is the anonymity in the online environment. This anonymity provides individuals, particularly gang members, the ability to hide from their normative and social constraints, further enabling them to engage in hostile, inappropriate, and illegal behavior (e.g., Moore, Nakano, Enomoto, & Suda, 2012; Pyrooz, Decker, & Moule, 2013). For law enforcement, the need to pay attention to the gang presence online is more important than ever. Online gang violence and online gang recruitment are new venues where law enforcement need to become more proficient in their efforts to combat street gangs.

Online Gang Presence

Ironically, gang members spend a significant amount of time surfing the Internet, predominantly social media sites (Pelfrey & Weber, 2013). Research reports that gang members often use Facebook, Twitter, MySpace, YouTube, and other social media outlets to spread inflammatory messages and encourage rival gangs to respond (Patton, Eschmann, & Butler, 2013).

A study by the National Assessment Center of Internet Safety Education (i-SAFE) examined the use of the Internet by gangs, and its impact on youth, by collecting data on more than 100,000 students and 137 gang associates from an urban population (King, Walpole, & Lamon, 2007). The authors found that 25% of gang members use the Internet four times per week and that 45% of gang members gain access to the Internet at community centers (e.g., YMCA, library). The most alarming data was that 70% of gang members reported that it was easier to make friends online than in the real world. Since i-SAFE's findings, there has been more research examining the relationship(s) between gangs and online activity. Criminologists Scott Decker and David Pyrooz (2012) conducted in-person interviews with gang members and non-gang members in Cleveland, Fresno, Los Angeles, Phoenix, and St. Louis to determine gang online presence. The authors conducted 585 interviews and classified interviewees as current gang members, former gang members, and non-gang members. Decker and Pyrooz found that 78% of current gang members, 79% of former gang members, and 81% of non-gang members use the Internet. What is most concerning about the study is the authors found that 43% of current gang members, 31% of former gang members, and 32% of non-gang members had committed an online offense in 6 months prior to their interview.[1]

As technology advances, the FBI has realized that understanding online gang behavior has become more important. The 2009 National Gang Threat Assessment reported that "many gangs actively use the Internet to recruit new members and to communicate with members in other areas of the United States and in foreign countries" (NGIC, 2009, p. iii). Additionally, the report went on to state that (1) Internet-based methods such as social networking sites, encrypted e-mail, Internet telephony, and instant messaging are commonly used by gang members to communicate with one another and with drug customers and (2) gang members use social networking Internet sites such as MySpace, YouTube, and Facebook as well as personal webpages to communicate and boast about their gang membership and related activities (NGIC, 2009, p. 10). Two common stories that are shared in the 2009 National Gang Threat Assessment report are:

(1) According to open source data and law enforcement reporting, members of Crips gangs in Hampton, Virginia, use the Internet to intimidate rival gang members and maintain websites to recruit new members. On October 23, 2007, a 15-year-old Crips gang member was arrested for shooting a rival gang member in the leg. Additionally, he was charged with the recruitment of persons for a criminal street gang through the use of the gang's social networking site.

---

1. Decker and Pyrooz qualified an online offense as one or several of the following: (1) illegally downloading movies, songs, or software; (2) selling stolen property online; (3) conducting drug sales via the Internet; (4) harassment; (5) coordinating assaults online; (6) searching online to find targets to rob or steal; (7) uploading deviant videos (typically of fights); (8) assaults that took place in the street that were motivated by an online communication (p. 2).

(2) Gangs in Oceanside, California, are recruiting new members and claiming new turf on the Internet. Gang members flash gang signs and wear gang colors in videos and photos displayed on Internet sites. Sometimes, rivals "spar" on Internet message boards. Oceanside Police Department officers who investigate the city's resident Crips and Bloods easily find well-produced, self-promoting songs, and videos featuring local gang members on Internet websites (p. 10).

So how prevalent is the relationship between gangs and online activity? Sela-Shayovitz (2012) found that the Internet does not play a role in gang formation or promote gang delinquency but instead influences the socialization of gangs online. Subsequently, Pyrooz et al. (2013) arrived at similar conclusions after analyzing data from current and former gang members across five cities. Pyrooz et al. noted that gang members use the Internet and social networking sites as equally, or more, than non-gang members, gang members have a greater propensity for online crime and deviance than former and non-gang members, and the Internet is rarely used to further the instrumental goals of gangs.

Online Gang Violence

No other social group has garnered more attention in the studies of criminological research than youth gangs have over the past 40 years. In fact, the disproportionate involvement in delinquency and violence by active youth gangs is "one of the most robust and consistent observations in criminological research" (Thornberry, 1998, p. 147). Although several studies report that youths who belong to a gang commit more crimes than those who do not (see, for example, Matsuda, Melde, Taylor, Freng, & Esbensen, 2013; Melde & Esbensen, 2013), the popular perception is that extreme hatred and violence occurs between rival gang members (Bolden, 2014). In examining gang violence, it is important to distinguish between criminal and noncriminal online activities because the motives might be different.

While the use of the Internet has become normative across many social groups in the United States and around the world, this is particularly true for gang members whose ages are consistent with the age of increased use of the Internet, especially social media sites. Additionally, it is essential to recognize whether or not the involvement in crime by gang members also occurs in their online behavior or if gang members pose a significant threat to those engaging in online activities (see, for example, Hanser, 2011; Morselli & Décary-Hétu, 2013). One could argue that Elijah Anderson's (1999) "code of the street" study is applicable to online gang violence:

> The rules prescribe both proper comportment and the proper way to respond if challenged. They regulate the use of violence and so supply a rationale allowing those who are inclined to aggression to precipitate violent encounters in an approved way (Anderson, 1999, p. 33).

In other words, those who prescribe to this street code would view a minor event like a person making direct eye contact with them as highly disrespectful. This level of disrespect would then require a violent response. This is similar to someone disrespecting a gang member through the comments section on a social media platform such as YouTube.

One example of gang violence that began on YouTube and spilled onto the streets was the death of Chicago rapper Joseph Coleman (also known as, Lil JoJo). In September of 2012, Chicago rapper Keith Cozart made a video that went viral with over 19 million hits with his song "I Don't Like." Cozart, better known as Chief Keef, allegedly has ties to the Chicago street gang Black Disciples. After signing a multimillion dollar label, rival Chicago rapper, Lil JoJo, also an alleged member of the rival street gang Gangster Disciples, responded with his own YouTube video called "3 Hunna K." In the video, Lil JoJo disrespects Chief Keef and makes numerous implied threats. In less than 36 hours, Lil JoJo was gunned down. Shortly after the shooting, a tweet mocking the death of Lil JoJo from Chief Keef's twitter account was posted. This prompted police to initially look at Chief Keef for his responsibility in the murder. Unfortunately, no one has been charged in connection to the shooting, but speculations continue. Many believe that Lil Jojo was killed due to his ongoing beef with Chief Keef, and the most likely scenario is that a member of the "Black Disciples" killed him due to the numerous disses against them in songs such as "BDK (3Hunna K)" and "I got dat sack." In many of his songs, Lil Jojo can be heard saying the "300k," "3hunnak," and "BDK"; 300, 3hunna, and BD are various names the Black Disciples go by, adding K after a gang's name means they are your enemy and you will kill them, thus BDK really stands for "Black Disciples Killer" (*TheDailyBeast.com*, 2012).

Social media has become a universal mode of communication for all youth (Skoric, 2011). The desire to stay connected even with delinquent peer networks on Facebook is important for many youth (Lim, Chan, Vadrevu, & Basnyat, 2013). Research examining Internet use, specifically Facebook, among marginalized youth (see Haynie, 2002; Moule, Pyrooz, & Decker, 2013; Rice & Barman-Adhikari, 2014) and gang members shows that often they are interested in trying to make a name for themselves (i.e., *street cred*) or are posturing. King et al. (2007) reported that 74% of gang members who frequent the Internet propose that these members are using social media websites to display or gain respect for themselves or their respective gang. These displays on social media sites often lead to bragging about criminal acts that may or may not have occurred. However, there are also individuals who promote themselves as a gang member even though they may not be associated with a gang (i.e., *wannabe*). A *wannabe* is defined as an individual who "does not genuinely possess ganger-banger-like abilities" and that "the typical hardcore wannabe acts hard for fashion's sake, and not for the sake of surviving the streets, he incites disrespect" (Dance, 2002, p. 61). It is important to note that recent research has expanded this *wannabe* definition to bullying in school settings (see Forber-Pratt, Aragon, & Espelage, 2014; Struyk, 2006). Regrettably, posts by these *wannabe* youth are often misinterpreted or perceived as a personal threat that may trigger a violent retaliation. This type of activity is known as trolling, or more commonly called *cyberbullying*, which is defined as an act of writing inciting posts meant to illicit responses from readers and hostile expression toward others (Lapidot-Lefler & Barak, 2012; Moore et al., 2012).

Today, social media outlets such as Twitter, Facebook, and YouTube are valuable sources for gang members to share information about their gang and gang exploits. For example, in 2012, the New York Police Department doubled the size of their gang unit to 300 detectives to combat teen violence driven by the dares and insults exchanged on social media sites (Hays, 2012, para. 1). In February of 2015, four friends uploaded selfie photos to Facebook and provided the address for a house party. Their actions resulted in three people being shot dead and a rival gang wounding five others after reading the Facebook post. Authorities suspected that the rival gangs retaliated to the group after a shooting that took place about a month prior (Skelton, 2015, para. 5). It is not uncommon for gang members to advertise their allegiance on Facebook profiles (Carmicino, Foucher, & Shadduck, 2014). In fact, King et al. (2007) indicated that with the introduction of smart phone technology, youth can now upload pictures and videos to social media sites very quickly, as events occur. Unfortunately, these pictures or videos typically display some type of gang initiation ("jumped-in" or "beat-in") or other acts of violence that are shared among gang members.

When gangs promote their actions and/or comments on social media sites, this is typically known as *Internet banging*, *netbanging*, or *cyber-banging*. Regardless of the term used to describe the online gang activity, several themes emerge from this type of behavior: (1) promotion of gang affiliation and/or communication of interest in gang activity, (2) achievement of status and notoriety by reporting participation in a violent act or communicating an impending threat, and (3) sharing information about rival gangs or networking with other gang members in different locations to incite dares, trade insults, or make threats of violence that may result in crime (Patton et al., 2013). Below are examples of individuals (most likely gang members) threatening others in the comment section of various YouTube videos:

> I like 2 meet other b-dogs freaky girls cuz u got 2 be very freaky 2 talk 2 me. some crabs so i can beat the c-monstas. but mainly other girls. and 2 talk 2 my freaks

> I'm a tru g nd u dont need ta kno da alphabets ta b - sabg!! wut do u tell a bitckh wit 2 black eyes........nuth n smug u already twicke!! 30k..ek aim trakkboiz

fucc you talkin a8out nigga, got a pro8 wit Mexicans you Lil dum8 ass hoe, I dare your ass to say that to my face, I roll on ya Lil punk ass an put you on that 187 ya feel me, 8est watch ya tongue, you don't wanna fucc wit the Crip Nation or you gonna get put 6 feet under nigga

Amor De Rey!!!! King love, Black & Gold NEVER fold!! 1418
5 crowning, 6 drowning all day…
cK gdK sK and rK all day!!
Fuck dah cKrabz and dah folkz
Amor De Rey 4 Lyfe Ya Digg??

Online Gang Recruitment

With gangs establishing themselves on the Internet, the use of social media sites acts as a magnet for future gang members to take an interest in potentially joining a gang. Through YouTube, Facebook, Instagram, and other social networking venues, gangs and gang members are *cyber-banging* online. *Cyber-banging* is the promotion of or participation in gang activity through the use of social media sites such as by posting videos; making comments in the comment section of a video post, or blog; the promotion of a gang's webpage; and the sending of hashtags out on Twitter. As early as 1996, news media outlets were quick to explore the link between gang recruitment and the use of social networking sites (see "Cops say gangs now recruiting on the 'Net'," 1996), Other examples of media reports about online gang recruitment include "Gangs using MySpace to recruit younger members" (TechRadar Staff, 2008), "Authorities nationwide watch gang Web sites for signs of crime, recruitment" (Frith, 2001), and "Oklahoma gangs turn to social media to boost recruiting" (McNutt, 2009). As the media continues to report the dangers of gangs recruiting online, law enforcement continues to monitor gangs and gang members in the cyberworld (see News Clips 11.2).

Though there is still no conclusive report that states gangs have made the permanent change from face-to-face to online recruiting, anecdotal evidence offered by gang officers clearly indicate that gangs have moved online. Current research argues that gang recruitment online is difficult to assess because most youth still join gangs the traditional way, mainly through living in a particular neighborhood, friends, in a school setting, and other social events (i.e., parties) (Krohn, Ward, Thornberry, Lizotte, & Chu, 2011). But gang members are no different than the average youth; they want to hang out with friends both face-to-face and online.

Although Facebook, Twitter, Instagram, and other similar web-based platforms offer a convenient forum that did not historically exist 25 years ago, these platforms allow youth to *see* in real time the information to which they can respond to quickly. Furthermore, most social media platforms feature "tagging" or GPS-type software displaying where an individual is at any particular time or place. These types of location services make an easy avenue for

---

NEWS CLIP 11-2: ONLINE TURF – UTAH GANGS USE SOCIAL MEDIA TO RECRUIT

Salt Lake City, UT (ABC4 News) – In North Salt Lake City, Utah is facing a new epidemic of gang violence. According to the director of the Salt Lake Area Gang Project, Lieutenant Mike Schoenfeld, "gang activity hasn't increased in the last 10 years but it has evolved." That evolution has taken on the form of gangs using social media to recruit younger, more aggressive and more active gang members.

The Gang Project monitors dozens of active street gangs online including 37 Hispanic Gangs, 11 Crip Gangs, 6 Blood Gangs, 6 Asian Gangs, 5 Midwest Influenced such as Chicago Gangs and 6 White Supremacist Gangs

"Recruiting is on the rise," Lt. Schoenfeld said. "They are getting smarter about their recruiting. They're recruiting on social media." Their turf is now Facebook, Twitter and Instagram where they boast of criminal activities and taunt rivals.

Source: ABC 4 News. North Salt Lake, UTor Aaron, R. (2019, January 16). Online turf: Utah gangs use social media to recruit. ABC4 News. Retrieved from https://www.abc4.com/news/local-news/online-turf-utah-gangs-use-social-media-to-recruit/

retaliation and increased opportunities for violent confrontations. Moreover, social media sites function as a tool through which gangs can become more organized and coordinated than ever before and provide an easy avenue for recruiting, planning, and sharing of intelligence on rivals (National Gang Intelligence Center, 2015).

Concluding Thoughts

As the gang culture continues to penetrate into the psyche of youth, the latest medium that has given gangs and gang members a more realistic platform to feature who they are, what they do, where they frequent, and, generally, how "cool" they are is the Internet. Gangs are now able to reach a wider audience and possibly attract more potential gang members. Using social media sites such as the former MySpace pages, Facebook, Hoodup, Instagram, YouTube, SnapChat, Twitter, and TikTok gives gang members a whole new approach in showcasing themselves and the gang world.

As the presence of gangs increase online, so too do the threats. Gang and gang members who give "shout-outs," brag about the gang and their exploits, or disrespect rival gangs with videos and pictures are at risk of creating a problem outside the boundaries of social media. It is in this digital world where the implied violence spills onto the concrete world (i.e., the streets). This is commonly referred to as "cyber-banging" or "netbanging." Search Facebook, YouTube, or Hoodup and one can easily find examples of videos and pictures where gang members are engaging in "cyber-banging." In addition to the violence that is generated online, the concern for many parents, school officials, and law enforcement personnel is the potential for recruitment of future gang members by using the Internet and the various social platforms. While much of the evidence is anecdotal (research in this area has just begun) and news stories claim that there is a connection between gangs online and recruitment of new gang members, most of this is speculation and there is no significant proof to back this claim.

Regardless of how gangs use the Internet, parents, school officials, and law enforcement officials need to recognize that social media sites, webpages, and other aspects of the Internet are a driving force behind perpetuating the gang culture into popular culture by showcasing gangs, gang members, and gang life. For law enforcement officials, it is not just about using social media to track gang members and their criminal activity but also the learning of how to gather evidence so it can be used to successfully prosecute gang members.

Discussion Points and Questions

1. What makes depicting various types of gangs in movies, video games, magazines, etc. in the mass media so appealing for consumers?
2. What other examples can you suggest where gangs are portrayed in the mass media that were not provided in this chapter? How successful were those portrayals?
3. Which type of medium (print, sound, visual, or interactive) that features the gang world has the most influence on youth behavior? Why?
4. What tools can law enforcement use to combat gangs online?
5. How are gangs successfully able to recruit young people into their organization via social media sites? Find examples online.

Web Links

Internet Education Safety
https://www.isafe.org/

Chi Town Gangs From Past To Present
https://www.facebook.com/Chi-Town-Gangs-From-Past-To-Present-820306751362791/

History of Chicago Gangs

https://chicagoganghistory.com/

History of South Central LA Gangs

http://www.southcentralhistory.com/gang-history.php

REFERENCES

Anderson, E. (1999). *Code of the street: Decency, violence and the moral life of the inner city.* New York, NY: W.W. Norton.

Bolden, C. L. (2014). Friendly foes: Hybrid gangs or social networking. *Group Processes & Intergroup Relations, 17*(6), 730–749.

Carmicino, P., Foucher, M., & Shadduck, L. (2014, January 21). *Chicago gang violence and social media team members.* Retrieved from https://wiki.digitalmethods.net/Dmi/Winter2014Project6

CERN. (2019). *Where the web was born.* Retrieved from https://home.cern/science/computing/where-web-was-born

Dance, L. J. (2002). *Tough fronts: The impact of street culture on schooling.* New York, NY: Routledge.

Decker, S. H., & Pyrooz, D. (2012). Gang offending and online behavior. *Justice Research and Statistics Association Forum, 30*(3), 1–5. Retrieved from http://www.jrsa.org/pubs/forum/sep2012_30-3/sep2012_30-3.pdf

Forber-Pratt, A. J., Aragon, S. R., & Espelage, D. L. (2014). The influence of gang presence on victimization in one middle school environment. *Psychology of Violence, 4*(1), 8–20.

Frith, S. (2001, September 5). *Authorities nationwide watch gang Web sites for signs of crime, recruitment.* Retrieved from www.lexisnexis.com/hottopics/lnacademic

Hanser, R. D. (2011). Gang-related cyber and computer crimes: Legal aspects and practical points of consideration in investigations. *International Review of Law, Computers & Technology, 25*(1–2), 47–55.

Haynie, D. L. (2002). Friendship networks and delinquency: The relative nature of peer delinquency. *Journal of Quantitative Criminology, 18*(2), 99–134.

Hays, T. (2012, October 2). Social media fueling gang violence in New York. *Associated Press.* Retrieved from http://www.komonews.com/news/national/Social-media-fueling-gang-violence-in-New-York-172282191.html

King, J. E., Walpole, C. E., & Lamon, K. (2007). Surf and turf wars online—Growing implications of internet gang violence. *Journal of Adolescent Health, 41*(6), S66–S68.

Krohn, M. D., Ward, J. T., Thornberry, T. P., Lizotte, A. J., & Chu, R. (2011). The cascading effects of adolescent gang involvement across the life course. *Criminology: An Interdisciplinary Journal, 49*(4), 991–1028.

Lapidot-Lefler, N., & Barak, A. (2012). Effects of anonymity, invisibility, and lack of eye-contact on toxic online disinhibition. *Computers in Human Behavior, 28*(2), 434–443.

Lim, S. S., Chan, Y., Vadrevu, S., & Basnyat, I. (2013). Managing peer relationships online-investing the use of Facebook by juvenile delinquent and youths-at-risk. *Computers in Human Behavior, 29*(1), 8–15.

Matsuda, K. N., Melde, C., Taylor, T. J., Freng, A., & Esbensen, F. A. (2013). Gang membership and adherence to the "code of the street." *Justice Quarterly, 30*(3), 440–468.

McNutt, M. (2009, November). *Oklahoma gangs turn to social media to boost recruiting.* Retrieved from http://newsok.com/oklahoma-gangs-turn-to-social-media-to-boost-recruiting/article/3421190

Melde, C., & Esbensen, F. A. (2013). Gangs and violence: Disentangling the impact of gang membership on the level and nature of offending. *Journal of Quantitative Criminology, 29*(2), 143–166.

Moore, M. J., Nakano, T., Enomoto, A., & Suda, T. (2012). Anonymity and roles associated with aggressive posts in an online forum. *Computers in Human Behavior, 28*(3), 861–867.

Morselli, C., & Décary-Hétu, D. (2013). Crime facilitation purposes of social networking sites: A review and analysis of the "cyberbanging" phenomenon. *Small Wars & Insurgencies, 24*(1), 152–170.

Moule, R. K., Pyrooz, D. C., & Decker, S. H. (2013). From "What the F#@% is a Facebook?" to "Who Doesn't Use Facebook?": The role of criminal lifestyles in the adoption and use of the Internet. *Social Science Research, 42*(6), 1411–1421.

National Gang Intelligence Center. (2009). *National gang threat assessment, 2009.* Washington, DC: Author.

National Gang Intelligence Center. (2015). *2015 national gang report.* U.S. Department of Justice. Retrieved from https://www.fbi.gov/file-repository/stats-services-publications-national-gang-report-2015.pdf/view

Patton, D. U., Eschmann, R. D., & Butler, D. A. (2013). Internet banging: New trends in social media, gang violence, masculinity and hip hop. *Computers in Human Behavior, 29*(5), A54–A59.

Pelfrey, W. V., Jr., & Weber, N. L. (2013). Keyboard gangsters: Analysis of incidence and correlates of cyberbullying in a large urban student population. *Deviant Behavior, 34*(1), 68–84.

Pyrooz, D. C., Decker, S. H., & Moule, R. K., Jr. (2013). Criminal and routine activities in online settings: Gangs, offenders, and the Internet. *Justice Quarterly* [online]. doi:10.1080/07418825.2013.778326.

Rice, E., & Barman-Adhikari, A. (2014). Internet and social media use as a resource among homeless youth. *Journal of Computer-Mediated Communication, 19*(2), 232–247.

Sela-Shayovitz, R. (2012). Gangs and the web gang members' online behavior. *Journal of Contemporary Criminal Justice, 28*(4), 389-405. doi: 10.1177/104398621245819.

Skelton, A. (2015, February 2). Gang violence fueled by clicks on social media. *World-Herald*. Retrieved from http://www.omaha.com/news/crime/gang-violence-fueled-by-clicks-on-social-media/article_b7da3145-b853-5ea3-9b52-6cda881a5c1a.html

Skoric, M. (2011). Introduction to the special issue: Online social capital and participation in Asia-Pacific. *Asian Journal of Communication, 21*(5), 427–429.

Struyk, R. (2006). Gangs in our schools: Identifying gang indicators in our school population. *The Clearing House: A Journal of Educational Strategies, Issues and Ideas, 80*(1), 11–13.

TechRadar Staff. (2008, February). *Gangs using MySpace to recruit younger members.* Retrieved from http://www.techradar.com/us/news/internet/gangs-using-myspace-to-recruit-younger-members-231701

TheDailyBeast.com. (2012, October 7). *Rapper Lil JoJo was slain after an Internet feud with rival Chief Keef.* Retrieved from http://www.thedailybeast.com/articles/2012/10/07/rapper-lil-jojo-was-slain-after-an-internet-feud-with-rival-chief-keef-videos.html

Thornberry, T. P. (1998). Membership in youth gangs and involvement in serious and violent offending. In R. Loeber & D. P. Farrington (Eds.), *Serious & violent juvenile offenders: Risk factors and successful interventions* (pp. 147–166). Thousand Oaks, CA: SAGE.

Weeks, L., O'Harrow, R., Jr., Pishvanov, N., & Light, C. (1996, December 5). The homey home page. *The Washington Post*. Retrieved from https://www.washingtonpost.com/archive/lifestyle/1996/12/05/the-homey-home-page/44e08e10-68da-4d36-97cb-6c142b3fca41/

Chapter 13
Gang Prevention, Intervention, Suppression, and Best Practices

---

CHAPTER OBJECTIVES

- Provide an overview of gang prevention, intervention, and suppression programming

- Explain and apply prevention, intervention, and suppression programming to gang dynamics

- Provide an overview of prevention, intervention, and suppression programming as applied to criminal justice and community entities

---

Introduction

One of the central questions with regard to gang prevention programs is *why youths choose to join gangs*. Research has argued that the act of choosing to join a gang can be described as numerous *pulls and pushes* on an individual. The *pull* refers to the attraction of gang membership to certain youths (Decker, Decker, & Van Winkle, 1996; Decker, Pyrooz, & Moule, 2014; Roman, Decker, & Pyrooz, 2017). On the one hand, studies have reported that gang membership can enhance prestige or status among friends and members of the opposite sex, provide excitement, and give the illusion of being lucrative through the selling of drugs (Baccaglini, 1993; Bowker & Klein, 1983; Howell, 1998; Hughes & Short, 2005; Levitt & Venkatesh, 2000). Then again, and as discussed previously, social, economic, and cultural forces push many young people into gangs. For example, Melde, Taylor, and Esbensen (2009) argue that protection from other gangs and general well-being are key factors in the decision to join or not join a gang. In addition, Rizzo (2003) and Alleyne and Wood (2014) contend that the underclass status of many minority youths can also *push* these youth into gang membership. Lastly, and as mentioned throughout previous chapters, gangs can provide a solution for social adjustment problems such as a need for *belonging*. (Although detailed in previous chapters, Table 12.1

Table 12.1:   Gang Risk Factors

Individual
Antisocial/delinquent beliefs
Life stressors
Low intelligence quotient
Victimization and exposure to violence
Violent victimization

Family
Abusive parents
Delinquent siblings
Having a teenage mother
High parental stress/maternal depression
Lack of orderly and structured activities within the family

School
Bullying
Low math achievement test scores (males)
Low school attachment/bonding/motivation/commitment to school
Poorly organized and functioning schools/inadequate school climate/negative labeling by teachers
Unsafe schools

Community
Availability and use of drugs in the neighborhood
Community disorganization
Economic deprivation/poverty/residence in a disadvantaged neighborhood
Exposure to violence and racial prejudice
High-crime neighborhood

Peer
Association with antisocial/aggressive/delinquent peers; high peer delinquency
Association with gang-involved peers/relatives
Gang membership

Source: Adapted from Best Practices to Address Community Gang Problems. (2008). Washington, DC: U.S. Department of Justice, Office of Justice Programs, Office of Juvenile Justice and Delinquency Prevention. Retrieved from http://www. ojjdp.gov/publications/PubAbstract.asp?pubi=253257

provides an extensive list of gang risk factors that may contribute to youth gang involvement.) We have discussed earlier that a substantial increase in the number of gangs has been seen in American society. Therefore, and as the gang problem becomes more severe, the need to find effective strategies to address this problem is essential.

Isolating quality evidence in relation to reducing or preventing gang crime is challenging. What is known, and presented throughout this textbook, is that the majority of available research available focuses on explanations of risk factors, gang definitions, and theoretical explanations of gang membership. However, these *theories* did not focus on the effectiveness of approaches or interventions that impact on gang violence. It is difficult to assess which strategy or combination of strategies is the most effective. The reason is that the research that has described strategies to be designed and implemented to prevent gang violence problems has been limited in its thoroughness (see, for example, Hodgkinson et al., 2009). For example, Klein (1968) identified a typology gang member and the need for interventions targeted at the specific needs of individuals in describing the Ladino Hills project. Many of these programs are designed to address the risk factors for gang membership by providing protective factors to strengthen a youth's resilience toward gang involvement. It cannot be understated that the greater the number of risk factors to which youths are exposed, the greater their risk of joining a gang (see, for example, Hill, Howell, Hawkins, & Battin-Pearson, 1999; Merrin, Hong, & Espelage, 2015). Once a youth enters a gang, the nature of gangs and their involvement in serious crime and violence produces many additional risk factors for that individual. For example, longitudinal studies (i.e., repeated observations of the same variables over short or long periods of time) of youths in multiple sites (e.g., Seattle, WA and Rochester, NY) have identified the causal risk factors for gang membership within each area (see Thornberry, Krohn, Lizotte, Smith, & Porter, 1998; Hill et al., 1999, respectively). We acknowledge that the list of gang prevention, intervention, and suppression programs is long and detailed. Therefore, the purpose of this chapter is to not provide an exhaustive analysis of each of these programs as there are many great publications that provide this service, rather we provide a brief and focused summary of several programs where the focus is on the *gang*.[1]

Gang prevention and intervention cannot be addressed without collectively addressing gang prevention and intervention. We are not being redundant. The reason for this is that gang programs can be grouped broadly into three categories:

(1) *prevention* (strategies that keep youths from joining gangs),

---

[1]. For a thorough, detailed evaluation of the Comprehensive Gang Model developed by the Office of Juvenile Justice and Delinquency Prevention (OJJDP), we encourage the reading of Best Practices to Address Community Gang Problems. (2008). Washington, DC: U.S. Department of Justice, Office of Justice Programs, Office of Juvenile Justice and Delinquency Prevention. Retrieved from http://www.ojjdp.gov/publications/PubAbstract.asp?pubi=253257

(2) *intervention* (psychological, contextual, and criminal justice–based strategies that seek to reduce the criminal activities of gangs by pulling youths away from gangs; see Goldstein & Huff, 1993), and

(3) *suppression* (a broad range of criminal justice activities in which criminal justice–related agencies focus their resources to deter the criminal gang activities, dissolve gangs, and remove individual gang members from gangs).

These strategies most often include community organization, school-based interventions, and afterschool programs and have been implemented with some degree of evaluation or follow-up report published, with a majority of prevention and intervention strategies directed toward youth.

A Brief: Gang Prevention and Intervention and Suppression

Gang-based prevention programs are proactive strategies. The objectives of these strategies is to discourage youths from joining gangs. These strategies may include early childhood development programs, programming for parents, community mobilization, programs which refer fringe members and their parents to youth services for counseling and guidance, vocational training, and providing preventative services for youths who are clearly at risk (see Fritsch, Caeti, & Taylor, 1999; Spergel et al., 1994). According to the National Data Intelligence Center (NDIC, 1994), prevention programs have been cited as the most cost-effective method of reducing gang-related crime. Although there is not a large amount of research regarding these types of programs, Goldstein and Huff (1993) and Bilchik (1999) suggested that comprehensive programs are most successful by arguing that the most effective strategies are likely to be comprehensive, multi-pronged approaches that incorporate prevention, intervention, and suppression activities. As an example, the Beethoven project in Chicago's Robert Taylor Homes, an early childhood developmental program addressing the preventing of delinquency and gang membership, was designed as a head start program for mothers and their preschool children. This program provided parental assistance in child care and family planning in one of Chicago's worst housing projects (Sampson, 1990).

Soriano (1993) reports that for any intervention to be successful, it must be culturally sensitive and relevant to the ethnic groups it seeks to target. In other words, a one-size-fits-all intervention approach that ignores collaborative, community-based programs is unlikely to succeed (see Wood et al., 1997). In one of the early studies of gang-related criminal activity in the United Kingdom (UK), Bullock and Tilley (2002) describe the nature of gang-related violence problem in Manchester, specifically South Manchester.[2] They outline a problem-

---

2. We acknowledge that numerous studies have addressed UK gang-related issues. Readers are encouraged to explore those additional studies for a greater foundation that covers UK gang-related problems beyond the scope of this chapter (see, e.g., Bennett, T., & Holloway, K. (2004). Gang membership, drugs and crime in the UK. *British Journal of Criminology, 44*(3), 305–323; Pitts, J. (2007). Reluctant gangsters: youth gangs in Waltham Forest. *Unpublished internal document*; Bullock, K., & Tilley, N. (2008). Understanding and tackling gang violence. *Crime Prevention and Community Safety, 10*(1), 36–47).

oriented approach to the issue by providing a detailed analysis of the problem to identify modifiable conditions for violent events to occur. The authors, based on their analysis, then propose a series of measures designed to address the problem. Their work draws heavily on the Boston Gun Project (aka Operation Ceasefire) (Braga, Kennedy, Waring, & Piehl, 2001), but distinguishes the differences and acknowledges that strict replicability is problematic. Bullock and Tilley also recognize significant data issues that may influence the validity of the findings.

Community Intervention Programs

Community intervention strategies attempt to mobilize the community affected by gang behavior to become actively involved in controlling it. One of the best-known programs that attempted to reduce juvenile delinquency by improving the conditions of neighborhood residents is the Chicago Area Project (CAP). Implemented in the 1930s by Clifford Shaw, CAP was focused in on three juvenile gang proliferation areas on South Chicago. Essentially, the approach was to rally the parents and to lessen the attraction of delinquency for gang youth. Families were encouraged to take leadership roles in the community committees. The result was that residents in neighborhoods with high rates of crime are able to implement strategies to address the problems of residential children (Kobrin, 1959).

Interventions focus on public education, enlisting the support and cooperation of community members in identifying gang members, building trust between community members and public agencies (such as citizens and police), involving parents in recognizing problems in children, and instructing them on the dangers of gang membership (Spergel, Chance, & Curry, 1991). Community interventions may also include crisis intervention or mediation of gang fights as well as targeting, arresting, and incarcerating gang leaders and repeat violent gang offenders. Certain community intervention strategies have been attempted repeatedly despite the fact that they have shown no positive effects. In fact, in some cases these programs have resulted in an increase in delinquency or crime.

The most commonly cited of the negative strategies is the *detached street workers* approach that arose in the late 1950s and appeared in Britain (Hughes, 2013). Historically, many of the early youth work pioneers were involved in making contact with young men and women on the streets. Maud Stanley's work around *The Five Dials*, which was one of the poorest and dirtiest parts of London, was a pioneering example of this work (Childs, 1992). In some cases, they had a club or institute which they encouraged young people to join. This intervention stemmed from the assumption that gang members would be more likely to respond to programs taken directly to them as opposed to those they have to seek out by their own initiative (Klein, 1965). The worker establishes him/herself on the streets where gangs meet and hang out. The worker then tries to work with the youth in order to transform the gang or to influence members to desist. A detached worker may take part in social activities with the youth, such as sporting activities, but would also provide various social services, including tutoring, employment counseling, advocacy work with the police and court, individual counseling, and family services (Lawrence & Hesse, 2009; Thompson & Jason, 1988). Research on the use of detached workers in gang intervention strategies has demonstrated that it is ineffective (see, for example, Andersson, 2013; Welsh & Hoshi, 2002). In fact, one national review indicated that none of the evaluations of detached worker programs found any evidence of reduced crime (Klein, 1971). In truth, Miller (1962) is credited with one of the most rigorous gang program evaluations on a detached worker program in Boston—The Midcity Project, with the objective to provide legitimate opportunities to youth, had a *negligible impact* on certain delinquent behaviors. Despite research that demonstrates the lack of effectiveness of such a strategy, detached workers continue to be used and remain a component of many gang-related initiatives today (Stinchcomb, 2002).

The Crisis Intervention Services Project (CRISP) operated in a gang-ridden area of Chicago for 10 months (Church, Springer, & Roberts, 2014). The project's purpose was to reduce gang violence through (1) crisis intervention and mediation with gangs of youths and young adults on the streets, (2) intensive work with individual gang youth aged 14 to 16 referred by the Youth Division of Chicago Police Department, (3) mobilization of local neighborhood groups to deal with the problem, and (4) development of local and city-wide advisory groups if the model proved successful. Spergel (1986) described the project as achieving modestly positive results. The rate at which more serious offenses were curbed improved significantly in the target area vis-à-vis the comparison areas. There was no evidence that the project was able to reduce the general level of delinquency of gang offenders.

The Little Village Project in Chicago is an exceptional example of a community-based intervention that has shown encouraging initial results. The project is an innovative approach in the control and prevention of serious gang problems based on interrelated strategies of community mobilization, social intervention, suppression, opportunities provision, organizational development, and targeting. Briefly, the Little Village Project is an interrelated, balanced, and community-based set of various strategies (suppression, social intervention, etc.) required by but not limited to police, youth agencies, schools, employers, probation, faith-based organizations, and neighborhood groups (Przemieniecki, 2018). In essence, if the gang members can receive educational and vocational skills then their chances of gaining access to legitimate opportunities, such as continued education or employment, will be improved and their gang involvement will decline (Yearwood & Hayes, 2000).

The strategy of the Little Village Project included outreach services from youth workers with ties to the local community, which included former gang members, referrals for service and supervision from police and probation officers, and gang violence suppression efforts conducted by the police (Spergel, Wa, Choi, Grossman, Jacob, Spergel, A., & Barrios, 2003). In addition, taking into account prior criminal history, the project had a significant effect in reducing violent criminal activity, particularly for those youths who were older when the project began. Those who were 19 years or older did better over time and had fewer arrests when they received project services and contacts compared to project cases who were younger. Moreover, all age categories reduced their levels of arrest for serious violent crimes. Again, those aged 19 years and older experienced the greatest reduction. Based on police arrest data, the project was effective in reducing total as well as serious violence all age levels. Finally, Little Village had the lowest increase in gang violence compared to six similar, mainly Hispanic, areas in Chicago with similar attributes and high levels of gang violence. It cannot be stressed enough that what is particularly promising about this project is the positive effect that was found for those gang members aged 19 and above (Spergel et al., 2003).

CASE IN POINT 7.1: A MODEL FOR GANG INTERVENTION

Racine, WI, developed the Community-University Model for Gang Intervention and Delinquency Prevention in Small Cities. This team model consists of six major steps that communities experiencing an emerging gang problem can take:

- A genuine commitment to youth. This can be demonstrated by working directly with youth, developing an understanding of their problems and concerns, building trust, and empowering them to solve problems.
- Gang problem assessment. The team will need to investigate, observe, and document the developing gang problem while learning from neighboring jurisdictions through the exchange of information. Meetings with community leaders and individuals must be organized.
- Initial networking. A task force should be formed to collaborate on possible solutions. Its work includes organizing community meetings and neighborhood hearings to identify solutions and develop a collaborative response to gangs.
- Local study of the gang situation. The task force should identify a local college, university, or other community resource that can study the local gang problem.
- Timeout. In this stage, the task force should publish and disseminate research findings, expand its network via conferences and other communication outlets, identify funding sources, establish political foundations for funding, and prepare grant/contract applications for the second set of awards.
- Development of new programs. The final stage is program development and implementation. The overall plan should include long-term goals and a master plan. New programs should be implemented through continued collaborative efforts. Research and program development would continue during the implementation of the program.

Source: Adapted from Office of Juvenile Justice and Delinquency Prevention. (2000). Youth gang programs and strategies: strategies using multiple techniques." OJJDP juvenile justice bulletin. Washington, DC: Office of Juvenile Justice and Delinquency Prevention. Retrieved from http://www.ncjrs.gov/html/ojjdp/summary_2000_8/strategies.html; Lawrence, R., & Hesse, M. (2009). Juvenile justice: The essentials. Sage Publications, pp. 93, 94).

School-Based Intervention Programs

Spergel et al. (1994) state that public schools, especially middle schools, are potentially the best community resource for the prevention of and early intervention into youth gang problems as the peak recruitment period for gang members is between 5th and 8th grade. Most schools, overwhelmed by other concerns, tend to ignore or deny the problem. In addition, job orientation, training, placements, and mentoring for older youth gang members are available. Lawrence and Hesse (2009) indicate that one suggested approach is the delivery of a flexible curriculum targeted to youth gang members who are not doing well in their classes. This position is supported by research that purports that the goal is to enhance the students' basic academic and work-related problem-solving skills (see Spergel et al., 1994). Additionally, experts have made several of the following recommendations for an effective gang control and suppression strategy by schools: (1) training programs should inform and prepare teachers and administrators to recognize and respond to gang problems in schools; (2) programs should make a clear distinction between gang- and non-gang-related activities so as not to exaggerate the scope of the problem; (3) clear guidelines and policies should be developed for responding to gang behavior; controlling intimidation, threats, and assaults among students; and strictly forbidding any weapons; (4) rules and regulations should be enforced through open communication and positive relationships between school personnel, students, and parents; and, (5) work closely with police and probation agencies, communicating regularly and sharing information for monitoring gang activity (see Arbreton & McClanahan, 2002; Lawrence & Hesse, 2009; Simon, Ritter, & Mahendra, 2013).

A school-related intervention program that has demonstrated positive preliminary results is the Bureau of Alcohol, Tobacco, and Firearm's Gang Resistance Education and Training (G.R.E.A.T.) program. The G.R.E.A.T. program is a nine-week curriculum program with sessions in victims' rights, cultural sensitivity/prejudice, conflict resolution, meeting basic needs, drugs and how they affect the neighborhood, responsibility, and goal setting (Lawrence & Hesse, 2009). Numerous evaluations of G.R.E.A.T have been conducted over the years (see, for example, Esbensen & Osgood, 1997, 1999; Esbensen, Freng, Taylor, Peterson, & Osgood, 2002). In 2011, an evaluation of this program by the National Gang Center (NGC) reported that results from a seven-city experimental evaluation of the revised G.R.E.A.T. Program (one-year post-treatment) are positive overall. According to the authors, the program appears to have short-term effects on the intended goals of reducing gang involvement (but not general delinquency) and improving youth–police relations (more positive attitude about police) as well as on interim risk or skills. Specifically, compared with non-G.R.E.A.T. students, the G.R.E.A.T. students were more likely to report more frequent use of refusal skills, greater resistance to peer pressure, less positive attitudes about gangs, and lower rates of gang membership (Esbensen et al., 2011).

In Montreal, Tremblay, Mâsse, Pagani, and Vitaro (1996) implemented a prevention program to address early childhood risk factors for delinquency, including gang involvement. This program was designed to identify and prevent antisocial/disruptive behavior of young boys from lower socioeconomic families who displayed behavior problems in kindergarten. The approach incorporated both risk and protective factors, demonstrating that parent training and childhood skills development may well deter the child from future delinquent/gang association. Training sessions were for both the parent (monitoring and giving positive reinforcement for prosocial behavior) and the boys (improving social skills, self-control). Sessions on coaching, role-playing, peer modeling, and reinforcement of positive behavior were utilized to build positive skills. As in Montreal, the teaching of social skill steps, modeling, and role-playing has been seen in other gang-based intervention programs (see, for example, Jolstead, Caldarella, Hansen, Korth, Williams, & Kamps, 2017). A longitudinal evaluation (10 years) of the Montreal program in both short- and long-term gains illustrated that boys who participated in the program were significantly less likely to engage in gang involvement. Howell (1998) indicates that Project Broader Urban Involvement and Leadership Development (BUILD) demonstrated significant gang prevention results. The BUILD prevention program was implemented in grade eight classes of lower and lower-middle-class areas prone to high levels of gang activity in Chicago. The prevention component of the program involved a 12-week classroom curriculum that focused on educating the students on gangs, gang activities, violence, substance abuse, methods of gang resistance, consequences of membership, and values clarification. In addition, youth that were identified as higher risk were asked to participate in an after-school program. In this component of the program, the focus was on both recreational activities as well as education and job skills assistance programs.

Arbreton and McClanahan (2002) researched two initiatives developed by the Boys and Girls Club of America (BGCA): (1) Gang Prevention Through Targeted Outreach (GPTTO), which is designed to help youth stay out of the gang lifestyle; and (2) Gang Intervention Through Targeted Outreach (GITTO), which is designed to help youth get away from their gang-associated behaviors and values. Focusing on gang members and targeted at-risk youth, a comprehensive intervention comprised of educational, enforcement, criminal justice, juvenile justice, diversion, community mobilization elements, and individualized case management elements. The authors report that prevention clubs drew in a significant number of new youth that were at high risk of gang involvement, and clubs kept a majority of youth engaged for a year. In addition, more frequent GPTTO Club attendance was associated with delayed onset of one gang behavior, less contact with the juvenile justice system, fewer delinquent behaviors, improved school outcomes, and more positive social relationships and productive use of out-of-school time (Arbreton & McClanahan, 2002). Finally, Arbreton and McClanahan note that an influx of new staff, staff turnover, and case management documentation were the main challenges faced by clubs implementing these programs, that is, the issues faced were of an administrative nature.

NEWS CLIP 12.1: G.R.E.A.T. PROGRAM TEACHES MIDDLE SCHOOLS STUDENTS CRIME PREVENTION, LIFE SKILLS

Officer Mark Bennett, as School Resource Officer from the Metro Nashville PD spoke to a Gang Resistance Education and Training (G.R.E.A.T.) class about the dangers of gangs but also about how to respect their classmates and community. The students at Creswell Middle School 5th grade class are learning simple lessons and life skills aimed at changing the mindset of the students.

The program includes role-playing, recognizing bullying and what to do, and building relationships with the police. The Metro Nashville PD has expanded their G.R.E.A.T. program into a summer camp for 2nd, 3rd and 4th graders. The G.R.E.A.T program encourages parental involvement. Students are sent home with letters to share with their parents, and they're encouraged to talk about the lessons they've learned.

Source: Wielgus, H. (2018, November 8). GREAT program teaches middle schools students crime prevention, life skills. Retrieved from https://www.wkrn.com/news/special-reports/great-program-teaches-middle-schools-students-crime-prevention-life-skills/1579781555

Gang Suppression Programs

Suppression, emerging in the 1970s and 1980s, is the application of a variety of informal and formal controls on the behavior of individual youths and the structure and process of their gangs (Spergel et al., 1994). According to these authors, suppression strategies are dominant because of a number of factors: (1) the decline of local community and youth outreach efforts with respect to the youth gang problem; (2) the insufficiency of opportunity provision approaches to target or modify gang structures; (3) the changing structure of a labor market that can no longer adequately absorb unskilled and poorly educated older youth gang members; and (4) and the consequent increased criminalization and sophistication of youth gangs (Spergel et al., 1994, pp. 7, 8). As a result, these factors have resulted in the reliance on law enforcement-dominated suppression approaches. The main reason for this is that juvenile gangs are mainly viewed by the public and presented in the media as dangerous and evil (Altheide, 1997). Therefore, community protection has become a key goal that includes vigorous law enforcement.

Organizational change and development consists of units of workers across key organizations that collaborate to develop a common set of objectives for reducing and preventing gang crime and mainstreaming gang youths or those at risk. Finally, targeting is done by a team of workers from different disciplines who target specific youths, gangs, and social contexts that in some way induce crime situations (Spergel & Grossman, 1997). This strategy shifts the focus from the causes of gang development to its most problematic characteristics: criminal behavior (Stedman & Weisel, 1998). In the U.S., there have been literally hundreds of specialized modifications in law enforcement, prosecution, adjudication, intelligence gathering, and laws themselves targeting gang-related crime. Since the 1980s suppression programs have expanded considerably as a result of several factors: (1) increase in gang-related violence and its relationship to the drug war, and (2) the perception that intervention has largely been unsuccessful having contributed to an increase in the use of suppression tactics. Research advocates intense evaluation and analysis of these tactics in order to completely understand their effectiveness to eliminate gangs and gang-related crime (see, for example, Klein, 1995).

Law Enforcement Gang Suppression Programs

Suppression tactics include tactical patrols by law enforcement, gathering and organizing intelligence information on youth gangs and their members, and prosecution by District Attorneys and intensive supervision by probation departments (Fritsch et al., 1999; Spergel et al., 1994). In general, it includes the arrest, prosecution, and incarceration of gang members. Suppression tactics have also taken the form of *crackdowns*, sharp increases in law enforcement resources applied to the previously underenforced laws, with a clear goal of enhancing general deterrence of the misconduct (Sherman, 1990). Although crackdowns at first appear to be effective, they are frequently followed by a return to preintervention levels of crime (Sherman, 1990). Not all gang suppression programs have taken the form of crackdowns. Some programs, such as the Operation Safe Streets program in Los Angeles, have adopted a technique in which only hard-core gang members are targeted (Fritsch et al., 1999). Others, such as the Tri-Agency Resource Gang Enforcement Team (TARGET) in Westminster, California, have focused on information sharing and intelligence gathering to identify, arrest, and successfully prosecute gang members (Vila & Meeker, 1999). Tita, Riley, and Greenwood (2003) replicated Boston's *Operation Ceasefire* in the Hollenbeck area of the Los Angeles Police Department. The Hollenbeck project predicted that the type of problem addressed, and the nature of the intervention might differ from that followed in Boston. The intervention was focused in the southern part of Hollenbeck, known as Boyle Heights. In Boyle Heights, gang crime decreased significantly compared with other regions of Hollenbeck during the suppression period of the intervention. Overall, the violent crime, gang crime, and gun crime decreased during prevention and intervention methods. However, the results generally suggest that gang intervention is most effective when resources are applied, during the suppression period. Unfortunately, there is less evidence that gang intervention succeeded in bringing about long-term changes in gang-related behaviors.

The effectiveness of suppression programs is unknown as they have not been rigorously evaluated to this point. However, most studies of areas where gang suppression tactics have been used have not found a decrease in gang problems (Klein, 1995). As stated by Shelden, Tracy, and Brown (2013), "[i]n the case of youth gang interdiction, this tactic is analogous to an attempt to put out a forest fire with a water bucket" (p. 269). While Spergel (1995) notes "[w]e have no systematic or reliable assessments of the effectiveness of a gang suppression strategy by criminal justice agencies, particularly law enforcement" (p. 198). One of the most unsuccessful examples of a police suppression program was Operation Hammer, based out of Los Angeles in 1988. In this program, approximately 1000 police officers took to the streets on a Friday night and again on Saturday, arresting likely gang members on a number of offences. In total, 1,454 arrests were made. However, 1,350 of those arrested were later released with no formal charges being filed (Fritsch et al., 1999). Almost half of those arrested were not gang members. In the end, only 60 felony arrests were made and charges were filed in only 32 instances (Spergel, 1995). Furthermore, following these sweeps it was noted that not only did hundreds of youths join gangs, but citizens actually began to sympathize with them (Stinchcomb, 2002).

Effectiveness of Gang Interventions

It would appear from the major reviews that gang intervention strategies have proliferated in the U.S. in the absence of sound theory behind the interventions evaluations of their outcomes (see, for example, Klein, 1995; Lafontaine, Ferguson, & Wormith, 2005; Stinchcomb, 2002). The result is that there is little evidence that gang intervention has any impact on either deterring gang membership or the growth of new gangs in the nation's urban centers (Howell, 2006; Howell & Griffiths, 2018). Most research concludes that efforts to intervene in gang formation have generally failed, and many are pessimistic about the future (Jones et al., 2004). However, gang intervention is far from futile and that the failure of gang suppression may have been the result of a misperception of the gang phenomenon (see Hu & Dittman, 2016).

In a review of a number of gang interventions, Spergel (1995) indicated that the strategy of targeting gangs and gang members only for suppression purposes is flawed and that community organization, as a primary strategy, was perceived to be more effective in *emerging* gang problem settings than in *chronic* settings, while opportunities provision programs were seen as more effective in settings where the gang problem was *chronic*. According to research, neither social intervention-type programs nor gang suppression was perceived as an effective primary strategy and most street gang outreach programs were evaluated as non-effective (see, for example, Jones et al., 2004; Spergel, 1995). These interventions appeared to sustain, rather than solve, gang problems (Klein, 1971). Finally, street gang suppression efforts may actually make the problem worse by calling attention to the gang and providing the very status and identity that drive youths to join gangs (Jones et al., 2004).

A retrospective reexamination of earlier gang interventions reveals that few programs were adequately evaluated and that many promising efforts were weakly implemented or were prematurely discontinued (Goldstein & Sorano, 1994). For example, where attention is focused on targeting criminogenic factors (anger, social skills, moral reasoning, family dysfunction) and ensuring program integrity, the outcome of gang intervention research may be very different (Jones et al., 2004). Goldstein's Aggression Replacement Training (ART), a 10-week, 30-hour cognitive behavioral program administered to groups of 8 to 12 adolescents, reported positive results when tested with gang-involved youth in Brooklyn, New York (Howell, 2010), specifically, a 13% re-arrest rate in a four-month post-treatment follow-up compared with a 52% re-arrest rate for a matched control group (Goldstein, 1994). It is important to note that Goldstein made no attempt in his program to discourage gang membership, and his intention was to simply target antisocial attitudes and behaviors and to reduce criminal behavior.

Finally, as previously mentioned, not all gang interventions have failed. Reviews of gang intervention research have suffered historically from methodological *tunnel vision*, which ignored or glossed over evidence of successful interventions in favor of a premature conclusion that nothing works (Cullen & Gendreau, 2001). According to research, a more thorough meta-analyses of gang intervention research may not only discredit premature conclusions but also determine appropriate criminogenic factors for effective intervention (see, for example, Wong, Gravel, Bouchard, Morselli, & Descormiers, 2012).

Gang Interventions in Correctional Settings

We have previously presented and discussed prison gang issues. In order to avoid redundancy, suffice it to say that even though the growth of the prison gang population over the years has increased, there has been very little empirical research conducted or reported in regard to methods of dealing with gangs within correctional settings. Again, and as mentioned earlier, and regardless of the size of these groups, their negative influences on the safety and security of correctional institutions are well known and documented. According to research, the threats are expressed in a manner of different forms, ranging from major incidents to the distribution of contraband, which contributes to higher rates of violence to racial, ethnic, or inter-group tensions within facilities (see, for example, Winterdyk & Ruddell, 2010). Each of these forms undermines the rehabilitative programming efforts within the correctional institution by supporting criminogenic values and contributing to failure in community reintegration if parolees return to gang activities upon release. Thus, the role of corrections in the gang problem is not primarily gang intervention or gang suppression, but rather gang management. Given the challenges that prison gangs pose, and the fact that gang management is an important component in maintaining their mission of community safety and rehabilitative services to inmates, it is important to develop strategies that can reduce the influence of such groups, as well as preventing recruitment. This section will outline some of the ways in which correctional institutions are managing their gang populations.[3]

Intelligence gathering and dissemination is a key priority for many prison systems. Studies have reported that over 75% of prisons had established gang management strategies that included monitoring inmate communication, collecting and compiling information from searches, and, in most cases, sharing of this information with local, state, and federal law enforcement agencies (see, for example, Mitchell, Fahmy, Pyrooz, & Decker, 2017; Ruddell, Decker, & Egley, 2006; Travis, Western, & Redburn, 2014; Wells, Minor, Angel, Carter, & Cox, 2002). These investigations may result in the development of profiles on individual gang members or gangs, aiding in solving crimes committed in the community via Geographic Information System Mapping (GIS) or other technologies (see, for example, Meeker, Parsons, & Vila, 2002; Ruddell et al., 2006; Sorensen, 1997). Correctional officials routinely share information seized from gang members with law enforcement, and these relationships result in increased prosecutions of gang members, benefiting both parties (Katz, 2003). A variety of investigative approaches have been used by law enforcement and corrections officials. For example, social network analyses to better recognize the structure and organization of gangs, data mining, or partnering with private sector vendors (Winterdyk & Ruddell, 2010). Pyrooz, Decker, and Fleisher (2011) report the need for better information gathering and sharing between law enforcement and corrections officers. The authors state that that law enforcement can provide corrections officials with background information on street conflicts among inmates entering facilities, while corrections officers can provide similar information for offenders returning to the community. Another strategy that correctional agencies have used to weaken prison gangs is by assigning members of different prison gang factions to the same work detail and living quarters. The presumption behind this strategy is that it would limit the numbers and power of one prison gang over another (Pyrooz et al., 2011). This was unsuccessfully tried in Illinois because the inmate prison gang population was too large to control effectively within a few locations.

In addition to information sharing, many jurisdictions used different forms of containment strategies to prevent the proliferation of STGs and to reduce the flow of new members into gangs (Gaston & Huebner, 2015). These strategies had taken the form of isolating leaders or validated members, and transferring leaders throughout the prison system to reduce their influence. In 1985, Camp and Camp reviewed 33 States reporting gang problems in their correctional institutions, and the authors reported that 13 techniques were used for dealing with these gangs: (1) the use of informers and prevention of incidents, (2) segregation of gang

---

3. We encourage the reading of Wood's Atlantic publication of gang life within prison (see, Wood, G. (2014). How gangs took over prisons. *Atlantic*, 46–54. Retrieved from https://www.theatlantic.com/magazine/archive/2014/10/how-gangs-took-over-prisons/379330/).

members, (3) locking up of leaders, (4) lockdown, (5) prosecution, (6) interception of communications, (7) ID and tracking, (8) dealing with situations on a case-by-case basis, (9) refusing to acknowledge the gang, (10) putting different gangs in particular institutions, (11) infiltration, (12) the coopting of inmates to control, and (13) bus therapy, a move or transfer. The last option, bus therapy, a move or transfer, was the most commonly used strategy and is a control strategy that sends key prison gang members out of state, in the hope of stopping or slowing a prison gang's activities. While no single gang suppression approach is used in all jurisdictions, many prison systems have developed a common set of strategies, such as staff training and intelligence sharing, while others have developed more specialized interventions based on research (e.g., Camp & Camp, 1985). It should be noted that gang containment approaches vary by jurisdiction. Research has reported that several states have experimented with isolating gang members in specific units or facilities to minimize their influence (see, for example, Hill, 2009). Other states had introduced gang-free prisons where STG-involved inmates are transferred to designated facilities that intended to reduce the likelihood of inmates being recruited because they were fearful of gang violence or drawn to gangs for better access to drugs or other contraband (see, for example, Olson, Dooley, & Kane, 2004; Rivera, Cowles, & Dorman, 2003).

The idea of gang recognition was used in an Illinois institution in the 1970s with dismal results (Jones et al., 2004). Knox, Gilbertson, Etter, and Smith (1994) reported that the administration met with the respective gangs at special times in hopes that the gang issues would be eased and levels of inter-gang conflict would be reduced. Unfortunately, these meetings aided the gangs to create violence, pressure inmates and staff, and assume authority over institutional officials. Bobrowski's (1988) study concluded that allowing gang members to meet as groups, recognizing them as groups, and officials negotiating with the gang leaders was a result of misdirected and misguided prison policy. Attempts to reduce gang-related violence by allowing meetings between gang leaders (and non-gang adjudicated youth) had the reverse effect of facilitating further organizational development, appearing to contribute to the rapid expansion of gangs, and ultimately the replacement of the prison's mission by the opposing and violent agendas of warring gangs (see, for example, Dmitrieva, Gibson, Steinberg, Piquero, & Fagan, 2014; Jones et al., 2004).

NEWS CLIP 12.2: NBP'S BIGGEST COMPOUND NOW GANG-FREE

Over 17,000 or more than 64% of the 26,930 inmates at New Bilibid Prison (NBP) have agreed to renounce their gang affiliations, a step that the Bureau of Corrections (BuCor) hopes will help dismantle the gang system that has thrived in the national penitentiary for decades. There's no family that is happy when its head joins a gang, and we are taking away their macho mentality here.

Source: www.newsinfo.inquirer.net

Best Practices

The strategies for dealing with prison gangs that have been discussed to this point have concerned methods for primarily managing adult prison gangs, and most of these gang management strategies are of a suppressionary nature. It goes without saying that several jurisdictions have used rehabilitative and other programing resources with the purpose of preventing gang recruitment or membership (see, for example, Melde, Gavazzi, McGarrell, & Bynum, 2011; Trulson, Marquart, & Kawucha, 2006). Di Placido, Simon, Witte, Gu, and Wong (2006) reported that a long-term treatment program for gang-involved offenders reduced recidivism. What has been established is that a number of differences exist between gang members and nongang members in correctional institutions (see, for example, Shelden, 1991). These differences may help in determining the target areas for programming in order to help gang members break ties with their gangs. In Winterdyk and Ruddell's (2010) study, the authors make the following conclusions regarding gang intervention in prisons:

> Inmate containment and sanctions were perceived to be very effective at managing gangs. These interventions isolated gang members, reduced their privileges and typically resulted in higher security levels. Not only do these approaches increase the deprivations of prison life, but they could also delay the prisoner's transition to the community on parole.

> Investigative strategies based on analysis of phone records and recordings, searches of incoming mail, as well as tracking STG associates were very effective in reducing gang involvement

Knox (2005) identified six potential solutions to make their institutions safer: (1) increased sanctions against gang members, (2) special housing for gang members (3) new restrictions on benefits for prison misconduct, (4) new services for prison gang members, (5) new policies to deal with prison gang members, and (6) increased staffing and resources.

Concluding Thoughts

There is no one-size-fits-all approach when addressing gang prevention, intervention, and suppression. What is vital is the understanding that youth gang membership is associated with significantly higher levels of delinquency and crime. There are several characteristics of gang structure, the social contexts in which gangs emerge, and strategic responses. As discussed and revisited in this and previous chapters, there are basic strategies that have emerged when addressing youth gangs (e.g., social and community intervention, gang suppression and incarceration, and an organizational development strategy).

A discussion of institutional responses that focuses on the police, prosecution, judiciary, probation/parole, corrections, schools, community organizations, and employment are effective tools for intervention and prevention. Gang prevention, intervention, and suppression policies, procedures, and approaches have shown to be effective to varying degrees.

Recognizing there is a gang problem and finding ways to reduce it for significant time periods, proactive leadership by representatives of significant criminal justice and community-based agencies, and a focus on community activities that contribute to positive development. Recognizing there is a gang problem and finding ways to reduce it can be successful in communities via proactive leadership of criminal justice and community-based agencies. In other words, proactive leadership of criminal justice and community-based agencies using best practice techniques customized for each community are important pillars in reducing the gang problem in America.

Discussion Points and Questions

1. How could gang prevention, intervention, or suppression programming work in your hometown?
2. Think about the theories discussed in Chapter 7. Which theories "work best" with gang prevention, intervention, and suppression programming?
3. How has recent legislative change or policy impacted gang prevention, intervention, and suppression programming?
4. Contact a local correctional facility and report on any gang prevention, intervention, and suppression programming that is utilized.

Web Sources

Anti-Gang Strategies
https://www.nij.gov/topics/crime/gangs/pages/anti-gang-strategies.aspx

Gang Prevention: An Overview of Research and Programs
https://youth.gov/feature-article/gang-prevention-overview-research-and-programs

The National Gang Center (NGC)
https://www.nationalgangcenter.gov/

The Office of Juvenile Justice and Delinquency Prevention (OJJDP)
http://www.ojjdp.ncjrs.org/

REFERENCES

Alleyne, E., & Wood, J. L. (2014). Gang involvement: Social and environmental factors. *Crime & Delinquency, 60*(4), 547–568.

Altheide, D. L. (1997). The news media, the problem frame, and the production of fear. *The Sociological Quarterly, 38*(4), 647–668.

Andersson, B. (2013). Finding ways to the hard to reach—considerations on the content and concept of outreach work. *European Journal of Social Work, 16*(2), 171–186.

Arbreton, A. J., & McClanahan, W. S. (2002). Targeted outreach: Boys & Girls Clubs of America's approach to gang prevention and intervention. New York, NY: Public/Private Ventures.

Baccaglini, W. F. (1993). *Project youth gang-drug prevention: A statewide research study.* Rensselaer, NY: New York State Division for Youth.

Bilchik S (1999) *Report to Congress on juvenile violence research.* Washington: US Department of Justice. Retrieved from https://www.ncjrs.gov/pdffiles1/176976.pdf

Bobrowski, L. J. (1988). *Collecting, organizing and reporting street gang crime.* Chicago, IL: Chicago Police Department.

Bowker, L. H., & Klein, M. W. (1983). The etiology of female juvenile delinquency and gang membership: A test of psychological and social structural explanations. *Adolescence, 18*(72), 739–751.

Braga, A. A., Kennedy, D. M., Waring, E. J., & Piehl, A. M. (2001). Problem-oriented policing, deterrence, and youth violence: An evaluation of Boston's Operation Ceasefire. *Journal of Research in Crime and Delinquency, 38*(3), 195–225.

Bullock, K., & Tilley, N. (2002). *Shootings, gangs and violent incidents in Manchester: Developing a crime reduction strategy.* London, England: Home Office.

Camp, G. M., & Camp, C. G. (1985). *Prison gangs: Their extent, nature, and impact on prisons*. Washington, DC: U.S. Department of Justice, Office of Legal Policy, Federal Justice Research Program.

Childs, M. J. (1992). *Labour's apprentices: working-class lads in late Victorian and Edwardian England*. Montreal, Quebec, Canada: McGill-Queen's University Press.

Church, W. T., Springer, D., & Roberts, A. R. (Eds.). (2014). *Juvenile justice sourcebook*. Oxford, England: Oxford University Press.

Cullen, F. T., & Gendreau, P. (2001). From nothing works to what works: Changing professional ideology in the 21st century. *The Prison Journal, 81*(3), 313–338.

Decker, S. H., Pyrooz, D. C., & Moule, R. K., Jr. (2014). Disengagement from gangs as role transitions. *Journal of Research on Adolescence, 24*(2), 268–283.

Decker, S., Decker, S. H., & Van Winkle, B. (1996). *Life in the gang: Family, friends, and violence*. Cambridge, England: Cambridge University Press.

Di Placido, C., Simon, T. L., Witte, T. D., Gu, D., & Wong, S. C. (2006). Treatment of gang members can reduce recidivism and institutional misconduct. *Law and Human Behavior, 30*(1), 93–114.

Dmitrieva, J., Gibson, L., Steinberg, L., Piquero, A., & Fagan, J. (2014). Predictors and consequences of gang membership: Comparing gang members, gang leaders, and non–gang-affiliated adjudicated youth. *Journal of Research on Adolescence, 24*(2), 220–234.

Esbensen, F. A., Peterson, D., Taylor, T. J., Freng, A., Osgood, D. W., Carson, D. C., & Matsuda, K. N. (2011). Evaluation and evolution of the Gang Resistance Education and Training (GREAT) program. *Journal of School Violence, 10*(1), 53–70.

Esbensen, F. A., & Osgood, D. W. (1997). *National evaluation of GREAT* (p. 15). Washington, DC: U.S. Department of Justice, Office of Justice Programs, National Institute of Justice.

Esbensen, F. A., & Osgood, D. W. (1999). Gang Resistance Education and Training (GREAT): Results from the national evaluation. *Journal of Research in Crime and Delinquency, 36*(2), 194–225.

Esbensen, F. A., Freng, A., Taylor, T. J., Peterson, D., & Osgood, D. W. (2002). National evaluation of the gang resistance education and training (GREAT) program. In W. L. Reed & S. H. Decker (Eds.), *Responding to gangs: Evaluation and research* (pp. 139–168). Washington, DC: U.S. Department of Justice, Office of Justice Programmes, National Institute of Justice.

Fritsch, E. J., Caeti, T. J., & Taylor, R. W. (1999). Gang suppression through saturation patrol, aggressive curfew, and truancy enforcement: A quasi-experimental test of the Dallas anti-gang initiative. *Crime & Delinquency, 45*(1), 122–139.

Gaston, S., & Huebner, B. M. (2015). Gangs in correctional institutions. In S. H. Decker & D. C. Pyrooz (Eds.), *The handbook of gangs* (pp. 328–344). Oxford, England: Wiley Blackwell.

Goldstein, A. P. (1994). *The prosocial gang: Implementing aggression replacement training*. Thousand Oaks, CA: SAGE.

Goldstein, A. P., & Huff, C. (1993). *The gang intervention handbook.* Champaign, IL: Research Press.

Goldstein, A. P. and Sorano, F. I. (1994). Juvenile gangs. In L. D. Eron, J. H. Gentry, & P. Schlegel (Eds.), *Reason to hope: A psychosocial perspective on violence and youth* (pp. 1-22.). Washington, DC: American Psychological Association.

Hill, C. (2009). Gangs/security threat groups. *Corrections Compendium, 34*(1), 23–37.

Hill, K. G., Howell, J. C., Hawkins, J. D., & Battin-Pearson, S. R. (1999). Childhood risk factors for adolescent gang membership: Results from the Seattle Social Development Project. *Journal of Research in Crime and Delinquency, 36*(3), 300–322.

Hodgkinson, J., Marshall, S., Berry, G., Reynolds, P., Burton, E., Dickson, K., . . . Newman, M. (2009). *Reducing gang related crime: A systematic review of "comprehensive" interventions* (Technical report). London, England: Institute of Education, University of London.

Howell, J. C., & Griffiths, E. (2018). *Gangs in America's communities.* Thousand Oaks, CA: SAGE.

Howell, J. C. (1998). *Youth gangs: An overview.* Washington, DC: U.S. Department of Justice, Office of Justice Programs, Office of Juvenile Justice and Delinquency Prevention.

Howell, J. C. (2006). *The impact of gangs on communities.* Washington, DC: U.S. Department of Justice, Office of Juvenile Justice and Delinquency Prevention.

Howell, J. C. (2010). Gang prevention: An overview of research and programs. *Juvenile Justice Bulletin.* Washington, DC: Office of Juvenile Justice and Delinquency Prevention.

Hu, X., & Dittman, L. (2016). Nothing works or something works? Gang-crimes and interventions in the print media. *Journal of Gang Research, 23*(4), 29–50.

Hughes, L. A. (2013). Group cohesiveness, gang member prestige, and delinquency and violence in Chicago, 1959–1962. *Criminology, 51*(4), 795–832.

Hughes, L. A., & Short, J. F., Jr. (2005). Disputes involving youth street gang members: Micro-social contexts. *Criminology, 43*(1), 43–76.

Jolstead, K. A., Caldarella, P., Hansen, B., Korth, B. B., Williams, L., & Kamps, D. (2017). Implementing positive behavior support in preschools: An exploratory study of CW-FIT Tier 1. *Journal of Positive Behavior Interventions, 19*(1), 48–60.

Katz, C. M. (2003). Issues in the production and dissemination of gang statistics: An ethnographic study of a large Midwestern police gang unit. *Crime & Delinquency, 49*(3), 485–516.

Klein, M. W. (1968). *The Ladino Hills Project* (Final report). Washington, DC: Office of Juvenile Delinquency and Youth Development.

Klein, M. W. (1971). *Street gangs and street workers.* Englewood Cliffs, NJ: Prentice-Hall.

Klein, M. W. (1995). *The American street gang: Its nature, prevalence, and control.* Oxford, England: Oxford University Press.

Knox, G. W. (2005). *The problem of gangs and security threat groups (STGs) in American prisons today: Recent research findings from the 2004 prison gang survey.* Peotone, IL: National Gang Crime Research Center.

Knox, G. W., Gilbertson, D. L., Etter, G., & Smith, C. F. (1994). *An introduction to gangs*. Bristol, IN: Wyndham Hall Press.

Kobrin, S. (1959). The Chicago area project—a 25-year assessment. *The Annals of the American Academy of Political and Social Science, 322*(1), 19–29.

Lafontaine, T., Ferguson, M., & Wormith, J. S. (2005). *Street gangs: A review of the empirical literature on community and corrections-based prevention, intervention and suppression strategies*. Saskatoon, Canada: Saskatchewan Corrections, Public Safety and Policing.

Lawrence, R., & Hesse, M. (2009). *Juvenile justice: The essentials*. Thousand Oaks, CA: SAGE.

Levitt, S. D., & Venkatesh, S. A. (2000). An economic analysis of a drug-selling gang's finances. *The Quarterly Journal of Economics, 115*(3), 755–789.

Meeker, J. W., Parsons, K. J., & Vila, B. J. (2002). Developing a GIS-based regional gang incident tracking system. In S. H. Decker & W. L. Reed (Eds.), *Responding to gangs: Evaluation and research* (pp. 289–329). Washington, DC: National Institute of Justice.

Melde, C., Gavazzi, S., McGarrell, E., & Bynum, T. (2011). On the efficacy of targeted gang interventions: Can we identify those most at risk? *Youth Violence and Juvenile Justice, 9*(4), 279–294.

Melde, C., Taylor, T. J., & Esbensen, F. A. (2009). "I got your back": An examination of the protective function of gang membership in adolescence. *Criminology, 47*(2), 565–594.

Merrin, G. J., Hong, J. S., & Espelage, D. L. (2015). Are the risk and protective factors similar for gang-involved, pressured-to-join, and non-gang-involved youth? A social-ecological analysis. *American Journal of Orthopsychiatry, 85*(6), 522–535.

Miller, W. B. (1962). The impact of a total-community delinquency control project. *Social Problems, 10*(2), 168–191.

Mitchell, M. M., Fahmy, C., Pyrooz, D. C., & Decker, S. H. (2017). Criminal crews, codes, and contexts: Differences and similarities across the code of the street, convict code, street gangs, and prison gangs. *Deviant Behavior, 38*(10), 1197–1222.

Olson, D. E., Dooley, B., & Kane, C. M. (2004). *The relationship between gang membership and inmate recidivism*. Chicago: Illinois Criminal Justice Information Authority.

Przemieniecki, C. J. (2018). The Little Village gang violence reduction program. *Encyclopedia of Juvenile Delinquency and Justice.* Scholar One Publications.

Pyrooz, D., Decker, S., & Fleisher, M. (2011). From the street to the prison, from the prison to the street: Understanding and responding to prison gangs. *Journal of Aggression, Conflict and Peace Research, 3*(1), 12–24.

Rivera, B. D., Cowles, E. L., & Dorman, L. G. (2003). An exploratory study of institutional change: Personal control and environmental satisfaction in a gang-free prison. *The Prison Journal, 83*(2), 149–170.

Rizzo, M. (2003). Why do children join gangs? *Journal of Gang Research, 11*(1), 65–75.

Roman, C. G., Decker, S. H., & Pyrooz, D. C. (2017). Leveraging the pushes and pulls of gang disengagement to improve gang intervention: findings from three multi-site studies and a review of relevant gang programs. *Journal of Crime and Justice, 40*(3), 316–336.

Ruddell, R., Decker, S. H., & Egley, A., Jr. (2006). Gang interventions in jails: A national analysis. *Criminal Justice Review, 31*(1), 33–46.

Sampson, R. J. (1990). The impact of housing policies on community social disorganization and crime. *Bulletin of the New York Academy of Medicine, 66*(5), 526–533.

Shelden, R. G. (1991). A comparison of gang members and non-gang members in a prison setting. *The Prison Journal, 71*(2), 50–60.

Shelden, R. G., Tracy, S. K., & Brown, W. B. (2013). *Youth gangs in American society* (4th ed.). Belmont, CA: Wadsworth.

Sherman, L. W. (1990). Police crackdowns: Initial and residual deterrence. *Crime and Justice, 12*, 1–48.

Simon, T. R., Ritter, N. M., & Mahendra, R. R. (2013). *Changing course: Preventing gang membership*. Washington, DC: U.S. Department of Justice.

Sorensen, S. L. (1997). SMART mapping for law enforcement settings: Integrating GIS and GPS for dynamic, near-real time applications and analysis. In D. Weisburd & J. T. McEwen (Eds.), *Crime mapping and crime prevention* (pp. 349–378). Monsey, NY: Criminal Justice Press.

Soriano, F. (1993). Cultural sensitivity and gang intervention. In A. Goldstein & C. Huff (Eds.), *The gang intervention handbook* (pp. 441–461). Champaign, IL: Research Press.

Spergel, I. A. (1986). The violent youth gang in Chicago, IL: A local community approach. *Social Service Review, 60*, 94–131.

Spergel, I. A. (1995). *The youth gang problem*. New York: Oxford University Press.

Spergel, I. A., Chance, R. L., & Curry, G. D. (1991). National youth gang suppression and intervention program. *NIJ Reports, 224*, 21–24.

Spergel, I. A., Wa, K. M., Choi, S. E., Grossman, S. F., Jacob, A., Spergel, A., & Barrios, E. M. (2003). *Evaluation of the gang violence reduction project in Little Village: Final report summary*. Chicago, IL: School of Social Service Administration, University of Chicago and Calgary Police Service.

Spergel, I. A., & Grossman, S. F. (1997). The Little Village Project: A community approach to the gang problem. *Social Work, 42*(5), 456–470.

Spergel, I., Curry, D., Chance, R., Kane, C., Ross, R., Alexander, A., & Oh, S. (1994). *Gang suppression and intervention: Problem and response: Research summary*. Washington, DC: Office of Juvenile Justice and Delinquency Prevention.

Stedman, J. & Weisel, D. L. (1998). *Addressing community gang problems: A model for problem-solving*. Washington, DC: Police Executive Research Forum (PERF). Retrieved from https://www.ncjrs.gov/pdffiles/164273.pdf

Stinchcomb, J. B. (2002). Promising (and not-so-promising) gang prevention and intervention strategies: A comprehensive literature review. *Journal of Gang Research, 10*(1), 27–46.

Thompson, D. W., & Jason, L. A. (1988). Street gangs and preventive interventions. *Criminal Justice and Behavior, 15*(3), 323–333.

Thornberry, T. P., Krohn, M. D., Lizotte, A. J., Smith, C. A., & Porter, P. K. (1998). *Taking stock: An overview of findings from the Rochester Youth Development Study.* Paper presented at the 54th Annual Meeting of the American Society of Criminology, Washington, DC.

Tita, G., Riley, K. J., & Greenwood, P. (2003). From Boston to Boyle Heights: The process and prospects of a "pulling levers" strategy in a Los Angeles barrio. In S. Decker (Ed.), *Policing gangs and youth violence* (pp. 102–130). Belmont, CA: Wadsworth.

Travis, J., Western, B., & Redburn, F. S. (2014). *The growth of incarceration in the United States: Exploring causes and consequences.* Washington, DC: National Academies Press.

Tremblay, R. E., Mâsse, L. C., Pagani, L., & Vitaro, F. (1996). From childhood physical aggression to adolescent maladjustment: The Montreal prevention experiment. In R. D. Peters & R. J. McMahon (Eds.), *Banff international behavioral science series, Vol. 3. Preventing childhood disorders, substance abuse, and delinquency* (pp. 268–298). Thousand Oaks, CA: SAGE.

Trulson, C. R., Marquart, J. W., & Kawucha, S. K. (2006). Gang suppression and institutional control. *Corrections Today, 68*(2), 26–28, 30, 31.

Vila, B., & Meeker, J. W. (1999). *Gang activity in Orange County, California: Final report to the National Institute of Justice.* Washington, DC: U.S. Department of Justice, National Institute of Justice.

Wells, J. B., Minor, K. I., Angel, E., Carter, L., & Cox, M. (2002). *A study of gangs and security threat groups in America's adult prisons and jails.* Indianapolis, IN: National Major Gang Task Force.

Welsh, B. C., & Hoshi, A. (2002). Communities and crime prevention. In L. W. Sherman, D. P. Farrington, B. C. Welsh, & D. L. MacKenzie (Eds.), *Evidence-based crime prevention* (pp. 165–197). London, England: Routledge.

Winterdyk, J., & Ruddell, R. (2010). Managing prison gangs: Results from a survey of US prison systems. *Journal of Criminal Justice, 38*(4), 730–736.

Wong, J., Gravel, J., Bouchard, M., Morselli, C., & Descormiers, K. (2012). *Effectiveness of street gang control strategies: A systematic review and meta-analysis of evaluation studies.* Report prepared for Research and National Coordination, Organized Crime Division. Public Safety Canada.

Wood, M., Furlong, M. J., Rosenblatt, J. A., Robertson, L. M., Scozzari, F., & Sosna, T. (1997). Understanding the psychosocial characteristics of gang-involved youths in a system of care: Individual family, and system correlates. *Education and Treatment of Children, 20*, 281–294.

Yearwood, D. L., & Hayes, R. A. (2000). *Perceptions of youth crime and youth gangs: A statewide systemic investigation.* Raleigh: North Carolina Criminal Justice Analysis Center, Governor's Crime Commission.

INDEX